Donated to
Augsburg College
by the Resource Center
of the Americas
November 2007

Honorable Lives

Pitt Latin American Series

Billie R. DeWalt, *General Editor*
G. Reid Andrews, Catherine Conaghan, and
Jorge I. Domínguez, *Associate Editors*

Honorable Lives

Lawyers, Family, and Politics in Colombia, 1780–1850

Victor M. Uribe-Uran

University of Pittsburgh Press

*To the memory of
Manuel J. Uribe Angel, my father,
and Carlos Horacio Uran, my uncle*

Published by the University of Pittsburgh Press,
Pittsburgh, Pa. 15261
Copyright © 2000, University of Pittsburgh Press

All rights reserved
Manufactured in the United States of America
Printed on acid-free paper

Frontis: "El Juzgado Parroquial," engraving
by Ramón Torres Méndez, c. 1850.
Design by Dariel Mayer

10 9 8 7 6 5 4 3 2 1

Library of Congress Cataloging-in-Publication Data

Uribe-Uran, Victor
   Honorable lives : lawyers, family, and politics in Colombia,
  1780–1850 / Victor M. Uribe-Uran
     p. cm. – (Pitt Latin American series)
   Includes bibliographical references and index.
     ISBN 0-8229-4125-2 (acid-free paper)
   1. Lawyers–Colombia–History 2. Sociological
jurisprudence–History. I. Title. II. Series.
KHH207 .U75 2000
340'.115'09–dc21   99-050964

Portions of Chapter 2 and Chapter 3 were originally published
as "The Lawyers and New Granada's Late Colonial State," in
Journal of Latin American Studies 27, 3 (October 1995): 517–49.
Copyright © 1995 Cambridge University Press. Reprinted by
permission of Cambridge University Press.

Portions of Chapter 4 and Chapter 5 were originally published
as "Kill All the Lawyers!" in *The Americas* 52, 2 (October 1995):
175–210. Reprinted by permission of *The Americas*.

Contents

Tables and Illustrations   vii

Acknowledgments   ix

Preface   xi

Introduction   1

Chapter 1.   State Service and Status-Honor   9

Chapter 2.   The Lawyers and the Late Colonial State   20

Chapter 3.   Family Networks and Colonial Stability   32

Chapter 4.   Independence: A "Revolution from Above"   45

Chapter 5.   Kill All the Lawyers!   60

Chapter 6.   Changing Generations and Regions in the 1820s   71

Chapter 7.   Politics and the "Public Sphere of Civil Society," 1820s–1830s   86

Chapter 8.   Legal Education: The Making of Bureaucrats and Citizens   103

Chapter 9.   The War of the *Supremos*   118

Chapter 10.   The "Liberal Revolution": A Friendly Affair   138

Conclusion   155

Chronological Outline   161

Appendix 1.   Background and Trajectory of Some of New Granada's Colonial Lawyers   163

Appendix 2.   Lawyers Who Died Shortly Before or After Independence   174

Appendix 3. "Transitional" Generation: Lawyers Trained during 1805–1820   **176**

Appendix 4. Background and Trajectory of the "Aristocratic" Lawyers of the 1820s and 1830s   **178**

Appendix 5. Background and Trajectory of the "Provincial" Lawyers of the 1820s and Beyond   **189**

Appendix 6. Key Provincial Lawyers and Law Students Active in Opposition Politics during the Late 1830s, by Region   **198**

Abbreviations Used in Note Citations   **201**

Notes   **203**

Glossary   **265**

Index   **269**

Tables and Illustrations

Tables

2.1	Elite Male Occupations in Late Colonial New Granada	25
2.2	New Granada Lawyers in the State Bureaucracy, 1806, by Rank	27
3.1	Lawyers and Law Students Charged with Subversion in 1795	41
4.1	Composition of the Junta Suprema of Bogotá, 1810	47
4.2	Ties Between the Junta Suprema of Bogotá and the Legal Profession	48
4.3	Lawyers in Other Juntas of the Viceroyalty	49
4.4	The Junta Suprema of Bogotá and the Colonial Bureaucracy	56
5.1	Lawyers and Other Elite Figures Who Helped to Link New Granada's Main *Cabildos* for Independence	64
5.2	Participation of Lawyers in Institutional Reforms, 1810–1815	67
5.3	Lawyers Executed during the Spanish Antirevolutionary "Terror"	69
6.1	New Granada Lawyers in High State Jobs, 1821	73
6.2	Regional Origin and Occupation of Delegates to the Congress of Cúcuta, 1821	74
6.3	Occupation of Delegates to Greater Colombia's Early Parliaments	75
6.4	Civilians and Military Personnel in High State Positions, 1821	76
6.5	Distribution of Colonial Bureaucratic Jobs by Town	81
7.1	Composition of the Ocaña Convention, 1828	91
7.2	Composition of the Constitutional Congress, 1830	92
7.3	Family Ties Between the Colonial Tribunal de Cuentas and Bolívar's and Urdaneta's Dictatorships, 1828, 1830	93
7.4	Regional Composition of Lawyers at the 1831 Constitutional Congress	94
7.5	Young Lawyers at the 1831 Constitutional Congress	95
8.1	Number of Law Graduates in New Granada, 1790–1850	115
9.1	Cauca Lawyers Who Supported the Government during the *Supremos* Civil War, 1840	129

9.2	Cartagena Lawyers within the *Ministerial* Group, 1840–1842	**130**
9.3	Examples of Provincial Lawyers Exiled Abroad or Expelled from Bogotá and other Cities following the War of the *Supremos*	**134**
10.1	Number of Lawyers and Evolution of Their Activities in the Late 1830s, Mid-1840s, Late 1840s	**141**
10.2	Sample List of Young Radical Law Students and Lawyers Active in the Revival of Provincial Political Projects in the Late 1840s and Early 1850s	**147**

Figures

3.1	The Alvarez Bureaucratic Dynasty (1730s–1810s)	**34**
3.2	The Vergara Bureaucratic Network (1740s–1810s)	**38**
9.1	The Montoya Sáenz Clan, a Network of Antioqueño Businessmen, Lawyers, and Bureaucrats (1820s–1850s)	**121**

Map

Colombia **8**

Acknowledgments

This book would have not been possible without the support of numerous persons and institutions through the years. Financial support from the Tinker Foundation; the Andrew Mellon Foundation; the Fundación para la Promoción de la Investigación, la Ciencia y la Tecnología of Colombia's Banco de la República; and Florida International University's Latin American and Caribbean Center and the Faculty of Arts and Sciences' Office of the Dean allowed me to complete different parts of the manuscript.

My thanks to individuals go, first, to Reid Andrews, who directed the doctoral dissertation from which this book sprang, generously putting up with and editing the clumsy English and writing of a novice Latin American historian. Peter Karsten, John Markoff, and Harold Sims, my professors at the University of Pittsburgh and readers of the dissertation, also contributed a great deal to its completion and refinement. I am also thankful to the members of the Department of History's staff, in particular the secretaries—Judy Lamonde, Faye Schneider, Gerry Tanack, and Grace Tomcho—who were always supportive, friendly, and patient. Eduardo Lozano deserves my and the academic community's recognition for having put together an excellent Latin American collection at the University of Pittsburgh's Hillman Library, where I did most of the secondary reading and even some research on primary materials. This library's collection was vital; moreover, the library staff, including Eduardo Lozano himself and Patricia Colbert, were generous with time, advice, and technical assistance. So too were the officials at the Biblioteca Nacional de Colombia's Sala de Investigadores Anselmo Pineda, particularly Mercedes Curcio de Borrero and Alfredo Convers. At a later stage, my colleagues at Florida International University, especially Noble David Cook, Eduardo Gamarra, and Mark Szuchman, helped me greatly in ways too numerous and diverse to cite here. Collegial support from other colleagues and friends, including Alan Kahan, Joseph Patrouch, Darden A. Pyron, and Erika Rappaport, is also much appreciated. Valuable and timely help with copyediting and also insightful criticism were kindly provided by Alisa Newman.

I acknowledge my colleagues from the Universidad Nacional de Colombia at Medellín, especially Dario Acevedo, Oscar Almario, Gloria Mercedes Arango, Fernando Botero, Rodrigo Campuzano, Roberto Luis Jaramillo, Blanca J. Melo, Luis Javier Ortíz, Luis Antonio Restrepo A., Catalina Reyes, María Claudia Saavedra, and the members of the Grupo de Ciencia Política. Teaching at this university with all of them was a true pleasure and a magnificent learning experience. I was also afforded the opportunity there to complete a significant part of my manuscript, for which I am most grateful. Finally, I am indebted to Professors David Bushnell, Howard Kaminsky, Jane Rausch, and Frank R. Safford for detailed comments and suggestions to correct factual errors, strengthen the book's overall arguments, and improve its structure.

I cannot provide the long list of other colleagues and friends from whom I received feedback on specific chapters or with whom I discussed parts of this manuscript at academic conferences and other gatherings. Certain excerpts published elsewhere cite their help individually, and here I thank them once more as a group.

Finally, I could not have finished this book without the love and support of my wife, Valerie, my mother, my siblings, my late grandfather, "Papatoño," and my late father, Manuel J. Uribe Angel. My little daughter Ana Luna, a last-minute cause of the book's postponement, was an even more significant and much-needed source of further inspiration and drive, as is my newborn baby, Antonia. All the book's shortcomings, and any mistakes I may have made despite the abundant support received, are of course mine alone.

Preface

I learned firsthand that lawyers occupy a special place in Latin American societies and politics when, as a young attorney, I spent several years working in low-income communities in the city of Bogotá and in some rural areas of Colombia. Not only were my colleagues and I treated with much decorum in the neighborhoods and communities whose legal interests we represented, but we were perceived as having a sort of mystical power to solve people's vital problems.

In spite of a conventional distrust toward lawyers, people saw us as valuable agents in addressing conflicts over housing, freedom, marital relations, property, and payment of salaries and other labor compensations, and even in mediating legal and familial conflicts resulting from frequent teenage pregnancy. They trusted our judgment and authority to arbitrate family disputes and also endowed us with larger-than-life ability to understand the world of institutional politics and regulations, and confront state agents, legislators, politicians, their opponents' lawyers, and their adversaries themselves. This was so often the case that we had difficulty teaching people to take care of numerous legal activities by themselves, thus avoiding dependence upon the expensive, frequently dishonest, or abusive services of other professional attorneys. Urban and rural dwellers seemed accustomed to trusting attorneys' skills and knowledge more than their own. To our dismay, as they opened their houses and communities to us with kindness and generosity, Bogotá's marginal urban dwellers also seemed ready to facilitate the entrance of traditionally unscrupulous lawyer-politicians from Colombia's Conservative party, Liberal party, or both. In exchange for electoral support, these politicians offered short-term solutions to the residents' multiple needs (e.g., title deeds, sewage, phone services, electricity, jobs), leaving them unsatisfied and abandoned once elections were over.

After an instructive but frustrating period of litigation and community work, I left legal practice and concentrated on the academic study of theories concerning the intriguing relations between law and social change, law and the state, and law and politics. Nevertheless, theories of law as a social relation of domination and control, legal and other professional knowledge as general sources of social and political power, and law as a grammar of social confrontation were insufficient for my purposes. They did not allow me to understand clearly the complexity and significance of lawyers' day-to-day intervention in society and politics. Instead, I saw myself gravitating toward historical research into the legal profession itself. Studying specific places and time periods, and a community or group of attorneys, seemed the more concrete, logical, and fruitful way to learn something about the law, lawyers, society, politics, and their mutual connections and interactions. Thus I chose to explore the history of Colombia's early modern (postcolonial) lawyers.

Although I wished to learn about the legal profession, I hoped at the same time to understand the origins of the political parties that still dominate Colombia. I later realized that attempts to elucidate the origins of the Conservative and Liberal parties have for too long been a kind of black hole, consuming recent generations of Colombian academics. For better or worse, I was sucked into this hole and began a project concerning Colombian lawyers' historical participation in state formation and politics during the three decades immediately following independence, when the Liberal and Conservative parties emerged. I soon realized that it would be a mistake to neglect the colonial bar and those lawyers who participated in the movement for independence. The project thus came to embrace a longer span of time and a larger group of attorneys.

Similarly, the original issues, questions, and historical processes under scrutiny were broadened and reshaped. I became interested in social stratification, political sociability, the independence revolution, and the emergence of a liberal project of state and society in the mid-nineteenth century. The social origins of mid-nineteenth century liberalism were particularly intriguing, given the neoliberal watershed that Latin America is currently experiencing—as controversial a trend as the one this region experienced a century and a half ago.

While tackling all of these issues and processes and answering some of my original and later queries, I was handicapped and perplexed by the lack of monograph-length historical research on the bars of other Latin American countries. Comparative literature on Europe and the United States was not terribly enlightening, motivated as it was by an overwhelming interest in explaining the historical emergence of law as a "profession," an issue I was not interested in studying. This literature also dealt with bars quantitatively and qualitatively different from the Latin American ones in my study. Finally, because of my initial training as an attorney I was overly attentive to institutional aspects, and this focus may have distracted attention from relevant social data. Nevertheless, I tried my best to provide as in-depth a social history of the group of attorneys in question as possible. In the process of writing this book I have learned a great deal. I hope my readers will in turn learn from it.

Introduction

The typical elite families of colonial and early postcolonial Latin America were large clans whose members strengthened the family's potential by entering diverse economic and political activities (the legal profession, the clergy, the bureaucracy, the military, landownership, mining, and eventually trade) and establishing marriage alliances with members of similar elite families. The characteristics and survival strategies of these groups have been demonstrated in a growing body of literature on gender roles and family life, and the economic, political, and social significance of elite trades and occupations. Much has been learned about the families and activities of landowners, miners, merchants, and priests.[1]

Among all these occupations, we know the least about the legal profession—despite the large number of men from elite families who embraced it.[2] It is surprising how obscure the history of lawyers and their families in Latin America is when compared to the historiography devoted to lawyers in Europe and North America. Studies of those regions have demonstrated that as part of their constant striving for honor, prestige, power, and wealth, lawyers played prominent public roles, enjoying an overwhelming presence in public office and revolutionary bodies.[3]

In Latin America, as in Europe and North America, the legal profession traditionally dominated bureaucracy and politics. Many official posts, particularly some of the highest public offices of the colonial period *(oidor* and *fiscal),* and many of the judicial jobs of the postcolonial period, required a law degree as a prerequisite. In addition, because of their upbringing and functions, numerous lawyers filled postcolonial parliaments, cabinet ministries, and executive offices. All of the profession's members, even those out of public office, were strategically located between the state and key segments of society, whether these included their own family groups or their diverse clienteles.[4] Lawyers thus provide valuable information related to state and family formation, as well as their evolution and interaction.

This book presents a portrait of New Granada's lawyers, filling some of the gaps in the current historical knowledge of this key group in Latin American society. It focuses on those qualified to practice law before the *Audiencia* and the republican courts. The study is comprehensive; it deals not only with practicing lawyers but also with individuals who were qualified to practice law but chose other occupations, particularly those in the bureaucracy and politics.

The sources for this study include genealogical information on several elite and nonelite clans and individuals, contemporary memoirs and newspapers, various collections of public and private documents, and notarial and government records.[5] These materials enable us to examine the social characteristics, family strategies, and bureaucratic careers of lawyers. As chief competitors for state jobs, lawyers complemented their clans' power in important ways. By providing a vital component of the elite's survival kit–bureaucratic power–lawyers increased their families' overall influence, honor, and social status. In doing so, they built true family-bureaucratic networks in the late colonial period that proved resistant to the pressure of the Bourbon reforms. Similarly, postcolonial lawyers fought to control powerful segments of the state. Within a republican context, however, the emergence of family networks inside the state bureaucracy gave way to the formation of regional cliques, political factions, and parties. This fragmentation caused intense electoral competition and at times resulted in open military confrontation.

Although this study also touches on family history, the history of education, and cultural history, its main contribution is to the social history of Latin American politics.[6] It answers such questions as: What were the social origins of late colonial lawyers? What does the makeup of the law profession teach us about the main features of colonial elites? How did they and their families relate to the colonial state? What was their attitude toward independence? How were their families, regional origins, and ideas affected by the social divisions, political factionalism, strife, instability, and chaos that characterized many Latin American countries in the early independence period? How did they and their families relate to the new state? What do their lives and careers teach us about the liberal-minded elites who managed to establish hegemony by the mid-nineteenth century? In sum, what were the key social and political changes and continuities experienced between 1780 and 1850 in the composition of Latin American societies, particularly their elites and state managers?

This book uses information on both the late colonial and early postcolonial *letrados* (lawyers) and bureaucrats of New Granada and their families to revisit the politics, state, and elite social stratification of this long period (ca. 1780–1850), social stratification being a topic that remains especially confusing and little studied.[7] It suggests considering the culture-driven concept of status–understood in the Weberian sense of social esteem or social prestige flowing from the honor attached to a particular life style–as a notion required to understand some of the colonial and postcolonial social hierarchies in Spanish America.[8] Status is supplementary or alternative to the economy-centered concept of social class, or the race-, ethnic- and color-centered ones of estate and caste, categories that by themselves cannot explain the character of Spanish America's late colonial and early postcolonial societies and political processes.

In addition, this study argues that one of the changes Latin American societies underwent as they progressed from the colonial to the national period was that the elites, and probably other social groups, ceased to be regarded (and to regard themselves) as socially diverse status factions. Instead, as market relations expanded, such groups (which had long been economically homogeneous) became more unified, letting economic factors ultimately dictate their social homogeneity, or lack thereof. In other words, one's social position was determined less by colonial-era concepts of status and more by the modern idea of one's economic identity.

Finally, the book also examines the links between social stratification and postcolonial political disputes. By understanding the transition from status to class among some elite segments, which paralleled the switch from colonial to national societies, we can make sense of postcolonial political conflicts. Such conflicts were not strictly class (i.e., economic) conflicts, although they did involve socially diverse groups. However, those groups' social differences stemmed mostly from cultural rather than material factors. That is, social and political conflicts occurred among more or less economically homogeneous groups that carried over status-honor (cultural) rivalries and differences from the colonial period. These considerations were relegated to a secondary or marginal place over time.

This study is also significant for the following reasons. Implicit academic assumptions concerning periodization, subjects of analysis, and social mobility have hindered the advancement in historical knowledge of one of the principal eras in the formation of Latin America's economy, society, and politics: the long period from 1780 to 1850. They have also obscured understanding of important segments of Latin America's elite, including lawyers, who were enmeshed in a critical web of intellectual, political, bureaucratic, business, and other economic activities. Three such assumptions are discernible in the historiography: an orthodox periodization separating colonial from modern issues; a predilection for economic and military actors; and skepticism as to the significance of upward mobility through intellectual and political (electoral) activities in this period.

The first tendency, the separate treatment of colonial and modern history, became a standard of the historical profession. Except for important works addressing diverse, especially economic, dimensions of the long-term "heritage" or "persistence" from colonial to national Latin America, studies on the late colonial and early modern eras like this one were rare and incongruous.[9] This separation deprived postcolonial political history of its essential colonial social roots, resulting in oversimplified or completely atomized historical analyses. Oversimplification consisted of forcing the data to fit clear but inadequate frameworks of analysis, especially class analysis—that is, analysis based on the belief that postcolonial politics followed the dynamics of contending economic interests and groups.[10] Noneconomic disputes, especially tensions over prestige or status carried over from the colonial period, were entirely neglected. Atomization, by contrast, was reflected in such strategies as the selection of allegedly representative individual actors as analytical subjects, especially distinguished and influential *caudillos,* who supposedly gave some direction and logic to the period's political and social life.[11] That life was depicted as a series of chaotic and messy personal feuds, punctuated by the periodic but futile exercise of holding elections and producing constitutions and laws that few obeyed.[12] Authority was not successfully embodied in Spanish America's political institutions, constitutions, and laws, such studies argued; it rested, instead, with a myriad of individual *caudillos* and local military chiefs. The biographies of these leaders therefore became worthy topics for research and were required reading to understand political alignments and succession, and to make sense of postcolonial politics.[13] Except for the false clarity provided by either of these strategies, the messy early postindependence period was otherwise regarded as a "long pause" or "long wait" between the stability of the colonial period and the stability brought about by the agrarian export boom that started around 1850.[14]

When historians did focus on social groups rather than individuals, they tended to take the second approach, giving priority to analyzing military or economic agents. Some works, hoping to find clues about the relative power of creoles vis-à-vis Europeans or the social discontinuities between the colonial and postcolonial states and their military establishments, studied the composition and transformation of late colonial and early postcolonial armies.[15] Other studies focused on economic groups, especially landowners, mineowners, and merchants.[16] Still others, particularly studies of Mexico, tried to discern the state's evolution and political conflicts by focusing on interactions between the state and the most powerful economic and ideological agent, the Catholic Church.[17] There have been relatively few studies of nonmilitary and noneconomically defined elite segments, such as individual state officials, professionals, or intellectuals.[18] Any attention given to groups of bureaucrats or other collective actors in nonmilitary or not purely economic settings was truly exceptional.[19]

The third approach, the study of upward mobility, was given even less respect. Except for the acknowledged rise of some ethnic minorities through the army, which conferred certain dynamism to the emerging nations, early postcolonial societies were considered to be as socially (in particular, ethnically) rigid as late colonial ones. Factors such as education or electoral politics allegedly served no significant progressive function until a later period. This bias reinforced the aforementioned view of postcolonial states and social life as stagnant environments where urban dwellers and professionals played subordinate roles and depended upon military bosses from the countryside, those rural bosses who were also planters and ranchers; that is, the so-called oligarchy.[20]

This study tries to bring together colonial and postcolonial history. It attempts to highlight the significance of nonmilitary and noneconomically defined actors, especially lawyers and bureaucrats, and to demonstrate that politics was a dynamic social force in the early postcolonial period, affording a mechanism for upward social mobility and constantly widening elite circles.[21]

The argument of this book is developed as follows: Chapter 1 revisits the colonial state, examines its nature, and discusses the general links between the state and elite social stratification in Latin America during the long Age of Revolution (ca. 1780–1850). Special attention is dedicated to colonial society's perception of the state as a source of status-honor and the changes in postcolonial elites' approaches to state service and state-building. This chapter introduces two ideal types used throughout the text (especially from Chapter 6 on) as analytical categories to distinguish an individual's presumed status-honor: *aristocrat* and *provincial*. By aristocrats I mean individuals whose claims to higher status-honor were based on the fact that their relatives were either linked to the high colonial state bureaucracy or ecclesiastical hierarchies, or possessed noble titles, and/or, to a lesser degree, had been awarded royal land or labor grants such as *encomiendas*. They generally came from Cartagena, Santa Fe de Bogotá, Tunja, and Popayán, regions with a high concentration of clerical and state bureaucracy, titled nobles, and *encomiendas*. This was not exclusively an aristocracy of titled nobles or gentry in the European sense, but one primarily of individuals and families (sometimes of relatively modest wealth) in high-ranking bureaucratic circles. Provincials generally lacked any of the above family traits and regional origins. To be sure, these two broad social categories, as do all of Weber's ideal types, reduce the complexity of the society under study. They are mere interpretative tools that arbitrarily highlight some salient common features, thereby aggregating individuals and family groups who ultimately, and strictly speaking, were one-of-a-kind. Furthermore, there were a few individual exceptions within each group (not everyone in the aristocratic group was aristocratic in *origin*, nor was everyone in the provincial group from the provinces) and, on occasion, individuals from either group were assimilated (mainly by marriage, business alliance, or patronage) into the other camp. These exceptions and relative fluidity should not alter group's general outlook or contradict the book's claim that there generally was a connection between social status-honor and political beliefs.

Chapter 2 examines the social history of colonial lawyers and their connections with the state. It argues that lawyers were a key asset for ambitious colonial families, who through them could gain a foothold, or a promotion, in the state bureaucracy. In this way, lawyers perpetuated their families' control over significant sources of individual and familial honor, status, patronage, economic well-being, and stability. This chapter suggests that the state had an overwhelming importance in the reproduction of elite status.

Chapter 3 examines evidence of the symbiotic relationship between the colonial state and the family/bureaucratic networks to which lawyers belonged. Late colonial lawyers' political activities illustrate their loyalist attitude during that period, not long before independence. Their experience underlines the significance of the colonial state as a strategic source of personal and familial status and livelihood. As the state collapsed, however, lawyers and their families did not remain idle.

Chapter 4 deals with the active participation of New Granada's lawyers and their families in the independence movement. It argues that their participation was not spurred primarily by lawyers' revolutionary inclination or their exclusion from office. Instead, it demonstrates that independence was a "revolution from above"; that is, an elite movement. This movement was caused mostly by external crises and pressures and by elite perceptions of the Spanish Crown's unwillingness to participate in political bargaining and coalition building.

By examining the mechanisms of collective action adopted by the legal elite, Chapter 5 further illustrates the unfolding of this revolution from above. It looks at the state's complex reaction to elite revolutionary projects, in particular the execution of one-quarter of the viceroyalty's lawyers during the 1810s. The chapter also examines the consequent transformation of the elite movement into a relatively massive and protracted revolutionary war.

Chapter 6 portrays the early postcolonial state as an unstable and ever-changing coalition of civilian and military sectors, fraught with serious ideological and social tensions. The chapter looks at the composition of the legal elite during the 1820s, taking into account generational, regional, and social changes among the legal and bureaucratic elites of the late colonial period. It emphasizes the upward mobility experienced during and after independence.

Chapter 7 shows the nature of the clashes between civilian and military factions that resulted in the failure of New Granada's first postcolonial state. These engagements were characterized by intense journalistic, electoral, legal, and constitutional disputes taking place in what appears to be an ever-expanding public sphere. The chapter also charts, through the example of some lawyers' social profiles and careers, the ascent and decline of a contradictory provincial-aristocratic coalition government in New Granada in the 1830s. The progression of New Granada's most economically powerful provincial elite, the upwardly mobile Antioqueños, is examined along with the ascent of provincial elites from the region of Neiva.

Chapter 8 discusses the intra-elite tensions reflected in the postindependence disputes over the reform of legal education. It confirms the continuing link between state formation and stability on the one hand and legal training on the other. The conflicting discourses surrounding legal education and training expressed different visions of state and society, the public and the private. Some of the conflicts were intimately connected to the first nationwide civil war of the colonial period. That war helped to shape subsequent battles for control of the state and education, which again reflected an increasing gap between aristocrats and provincials.

Chapter 9 focuses on Colombia's first nationwide civil war, tracing the regional and social bases of the confrontation. In examining Colombia's new generation of law graduates, this chapter highlights the provincial nature of an insurgent group of lawyers, intellectuals, and politicians. This group's heated struggles against the traditional colonial elites represented not so much class confrontations as status tensions within otherwise similar socioeconomic groups. Such tensions provide a means for reconsidering the class explanations of early postcolonial politics and addressing the elite perception of the state mainly as a source of status-honor.

Chapter 10 charts the emergence of a liberal coalition made up of traditional and provincial elites. This coalition was instrumental in promoting a secular, free-trade, economic revolution. The class (bourgeois) nature of this liberal revolution is highly debatable; the revolution seems to have been the result, instead, of an unstoppable trend supported by almost all elite sectors of society—merchants, mineowners, and landowners alike. Even its "Liberal" nature turns out to be questionable, given that members of the newly created Conservative party eventually also backed it.

Finally, much biographical information and other vital materials required to substantiate the book's general arguments and the claims made in specific chapters are contained in several appendices. For the reader's convenience, they include valuable capsule biographies of over 150 lawyers, drawn from the documentary evidence.

A good part of the recent historiography on Latin American states and societies has argued that the history of both politics and of the dominant elites has monopolized scholarly attention for too long. Critics argue that this focus has led to a distorted or slighted interpretation of social evolution and change. Scholars over the last two or three decades have turned to the study of economic, social, and cultural history, paying special attention to the oppressed: workers, peasants, women, Indians, and blacks. This shift has been refreshing and enlightening. It has made scholars and students aware that economic production and exchange, collective meaning, bargaining, and conflict at all levels underlie historical change. It has also made clear that history is shaped by all people and not just a few select individuals, and that it takes place on streets, in plantations and mines, and in factories and households—not merely in diplomatic conferences, parliaments, cabinet meetings, or state structures. Nevertheless, as this book will show, the state and the elites—the owners of the plantations and mines, the merchants and the military, the diplomats and bureaucrats, the clergy, the intellectuals, and others in positions of power—should be brought back into the discussion of history.[22]

Traditional political history may be overly formal and old-fashioned, and its revival may be undesirable. Yet the formation and evolution of elites and the state, and their actions and interactions over time, are essential components of history. In shaping and enforcing policies concerning, for example, military drafts, taxation, wages, landownership, and education, the state and the elites had a significant impact on the lives of ordinary people. Rather than neglecting these actors, therefore, historians must examine them in new ways. This book favors the development of a social history of high politics. In Latin America, this type of history is still in its infancy.

This is, in fact, the first monograph in the English language about the social history of lawyers and politics in any Latin American country. As this work will make clear, lawyers occupied a strategic intermediary position between society and the state, and were also central and active participants within each of these two spheres. Therefore, I expect that other scholars and students of state-society interactions will start to see them as a valuable avenue for further innovative research on Latin America's social and political history. Historians of the family, culture, education, and the professions may also gain much from adding lawyers to their list of analytical subjects.

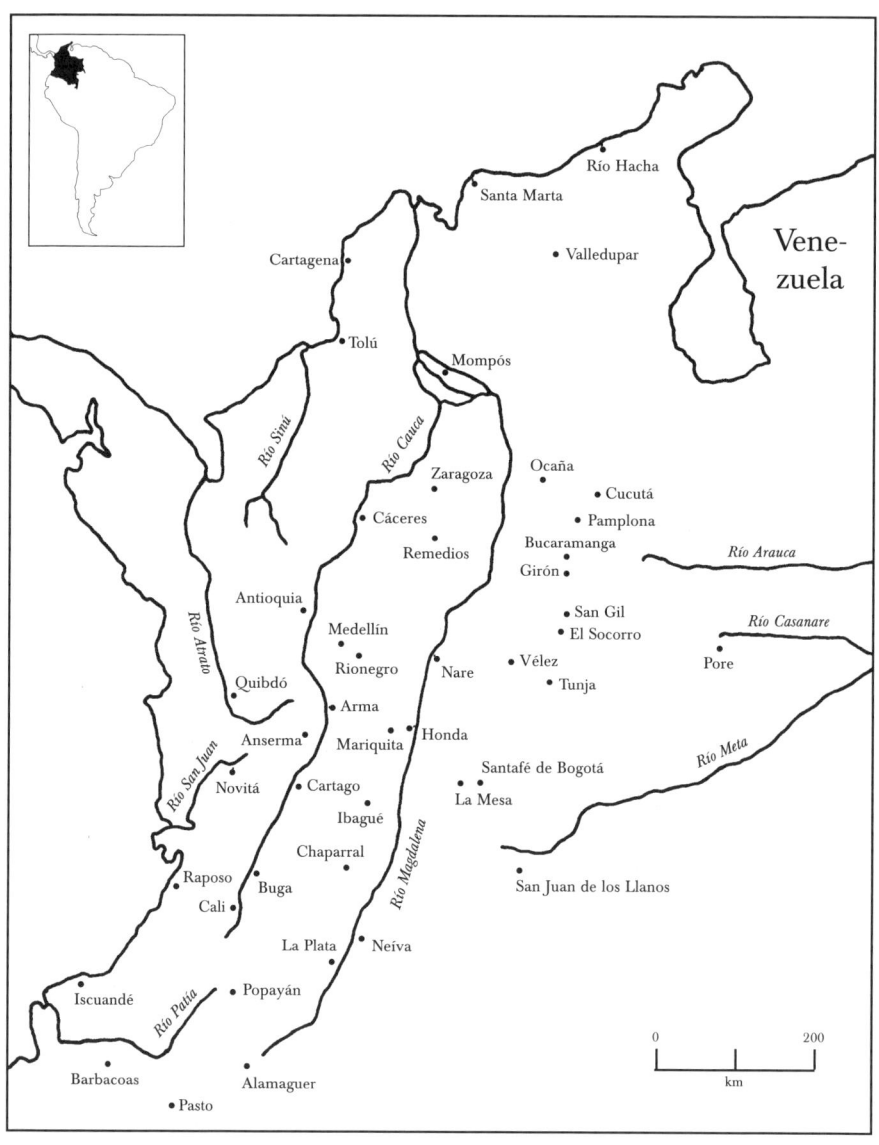

Colombia

Chapter 1
State Service and Status-Honor

The centrality of the state and its symbiotic relation with groups of civil society has been well documented for both the colonial[1] and the postcolonial eras.[2] Apart from general syntheses, however, until recently the specific manner in which state-society relations evolved throughout the entire period spanning the late colonial era, independence, and the next two or three decades has been less clearly shown.[3] We know little about the ways certain occupational groups and families, whose livelihood and prestige had depended upon service within the colonial state, continued to relate to both the state and other social groups during the crisis of the 1810s and beyond.[4] It is thus appropriate to revisit the colonial state, examine its nature, and discuss the general links between state and elite social stratification in Latin America during the long Age of Revolution (ca. 1780–1850).

Spanish America's Colonial State

For more than three centuries, the Spanish colonies in America were subject to a structure of government and administration that, following Weber, has been defined as both patrimonial and legal (bureaucratic).[5] This implied that the Spanish king—a patrimonial lord, source of authority and law, to whom all government offices belonged—governed his colonies not through free vassals (i.e., allies) but by means of a retinue of dependent functionaries. These functionaries were the king's personal servants, or what Weber would have called household officials.[6] In spite of forces pushing in the opposite direction, personal hereditary rights to rents and services (such as those enjoyed by the feudal nobility) were not granted to these officials. The benefits (tips, profit sharing, gifts, social recognition, opportunity for bribes) and administrative prerogatives that they received as a reward for their services strictly corresponded to the jobs themselves not, as in the feudal system, to the persons who held them. Finally, the ambiguous division of authority among the various officials made them mutually suspicious, which is typical in patrimonial systems.[7]

Such patrimonial prerogatives (temporarily granted or bought) were combined with more definitely modern legal (bureaucratic) forms. For instance, the Crown controlled the officials within critical institutions by means of free appointment, removal, and rotation. In particular, it controlled the institutions that centralized the fiscal administration *(Cajas Reales* and *Tribunales de Cuentas)* and two other vital areas of power: the *Audiencias,* which were key institutions for the administration of justice, and the army. Officials and members of these institutions were predominantly professional functionaries. To be sure, favoritism, political patronage, and even bribes occasionally played a role in their selection, rotation, and promotion, but qualifications and experience were important criteria as well. Instead of shares, fees, gifts, and tips, the holders of those positions were paid regular salaries by the state.[8]

In sum, the Crown's power thus distinguished itself from that of feudal kingdoms, in which military and key judicial activities were controlled by feudal vassals who were the ruler's allies and not his personal dependents. In addition, an almost modern royal bureaucracy became vital to policing colonial society.

The colonial state was society's main economic engine. It closely ensured the provision of labor, and participated in and regulated all sorts of economic activities. It appropriated a significant share of the surplus produced by slaves, Indians, and peasant workers toiling in mines, haciendas, plantations, ranches, textile workshops, independent agriculture, and crafts. It also ensured that another substantial share went to white merchants, mineowners, ranchers, hacendados, and plantation owners.[9] And yet, the state's interventionist role did not always favor the colonial elites. Ultimately, the colonial state was evenhanded in its restrictiveness. Its policies extended to all social sectors, sometimes negatively affecting the interests of the elites with whom it had such an inconsistent relationship.

In representing the interests of the Spanish monarchy and the somewhat contradictory forces of legal (bureaucratic) and patrimonial domination that it embodied, the colonial state had a contradictory relationship with the highest social strata of the different territories. On the one hand, it sought to regulate and limit them, and in so doing its bureaucrats represented themselves as acting in a technical and neutral fashion (at the service of and *por amor al Rey* [for love of the King]). This policy caused periodic clashes with local elites over Indian labor, tributes, economic restrictions, bureaucratic performance, the treatment and prerogatives of the Church, and so on.[10] On the other hand, state bureaucrats tended to favor those same elites by granting them, with relatively equal largesse, honors, prestige, power, and economic prerogatives, in exchange for political loyalty and economic support. The Crown expected to receive substantial tributes and backing from each of these groups and accorded them, in return, economic, social, political, and cultural privileges. Thus, despite periodic clashes, the state formed a tight alliance with the colonial elites by sanctioning of their exploitative economic relations with the masses and, more important, offering them privileges.

Among such privileges was the granting of access to intellectual professions, especially law and the priesthood. In addition, and often in conjunction with educational accomplishments, access to state service was another key state-granted prerogative reserved for the elites. It appears evident that both the professions and state service became a vital way—as vital as their respective trades or economic occupations—for the dominant social groups to maintain, reproduce, and increase their individual and familial prospects and social status.

The king's patrimonial servants and the professional functionaries in the colonial state performed activities highly valued by the Crown and society. As a result, even noble families coveted state service and were willing and eager to contribute their sons to the state ranks. Dedication to king and public service were grave endeavors. Over time, as they went about their official work, state servants and their families developed a certain aura of separateness from the rest of society. Career bureaucrats became an especially prominent social group, for they personified the king's power and justice. To better understand why these bureaucrats were so elevated, it is worth discussing how honor and status worked themselves out among some segments of the late colonial elite.

Social Stratification: How Honor, Status, and Class Apply in Colonial Historiography

The importance of honor to colonial Iberians and Latin Americans has been widely recognized in discussions of attitudes toward manual and mercantile activities, and the nature and evolution of gender roles.[11] Little has been said about education and state service as sources of honor and status. Yet honor was not solely linked to noblemen's concerns over the demeaning character of manual labor or trade. Nor was it chiefly a question of patriarchal preoccupations over keeping one's word, manliness, and female sexual virtue and purity. Honor was a motivating sentiment and code of conduct observed by individuals and families looking for ways to accumulate prestige, esteem, influence, and other opportunities to improve their social standing. This is why, for instance, there were so many legal battles over *hidalguía* and the use of deferential expressions such as *don* and *doña,* which were intended to ensure a good social standing or public recognition of whiteness *(limpieza de sangre)* and its associated privileges.[12] Such privileges included access to higher education, municipal government, and state jobs.

Access to and graduation from academic institutions confirmed honor and prestige. As they facilitated entrance into both the Church and the state ranks, these achievements also constituted an avenue to increase one's social prominence. Racial purity, an appropriate religious background, legitimacy of birth, and membership in a family headed by nonmanual workers were qualities presumed of all college students, and consequently of all graduates. In addition, students and graduates were identified by strict dress codes that visibly distinguished them from the rest of society. They also participated in pompous academic ceremonies and processions, which provided further public opportunities to be honored and to display, loudly if possible, their superior social status.[13]

Besides education and its associated privileges and rituals, membership in the state bureaucracy, although a little-investigated and not frequently acknowledged source of social preeminence, was another determinant of social superiority. Being a part of the state's higher ranks was not merely a source of material benefits such as a stable income, the security accruing from a lifetime position, and power. More important, it also afforded prestige, deference, and honor. Honor, in turn, entitled its possessors to a higher status, or "right to pride."[14] This right was not strictly individual, but was extended or passed on to kin. In other words, honor was both a personal and familial affair and trait.[15]

In sum, in addition to being concerned over their individual and familial *hidalguía,* families and individuals strove to get closer to the state (and the Church) to augment their social stature. They saw proximity and services to the Crown and Church as a convenient avenue to accumulate further honor and thereby increase their individual and familial standing and opportunities.

As anthropologists have argued, honor had an "intimate connection with the realm of the sacred" and was attached to the authority of the Church. Yet, it also emanated from the king. Indeed, honor was attached to the authority of the Crown, the state, and its functionaries; it was a result of the "power of rank."[16] The bestowing of honor upon state officials is characteristic of Anglo-Saxon and other cultures. Samuel Haber has argued in the case of England that as kings came to monopolize violence and civil affairs took precedence over military ones, honor was gradually bestowed more and more upon civil functionaries rather than warriors. "Honor, therefore, became the reward of closeness to and assistance to the sovereign," and the king and the royal household became coveted "fountains of honor."[17] This same phenomenon was also true of pre- and postrevolutionary France and Habsburg and Bourbon Spain, and, by extension, colonial Latin America.[18]

Bureaucratic activities were, therefore, sources of significant moral or cultural rewards. To be sure, royal service or government employment carried material benefits—in particular, job security and steady, sometimes high, salaries or other monetary returns (fees, gifts, bribes, and pensions)—let alone power and influence.[19] Yet, it also provided nonmaterial incentives, with prestige, honor, and status among them. Paraphrasing Weber, one could say that bureaucratic power was valued not just for its material benefits but also for its own sake, for the social honor it entailed.[20]

That bureaucratic careers were honorable positions is suggested by the fact that "service to the Crown in civil and military affairs could help one obtain noble status and the associated rewards."[21] Indeed, bureaucrats sought to acquire and were granted "aristocratic or semi-aristocratic symbols of status" in the form of noble titles and, more frequently, knighthood in the military-religious orders of Santiago, Calatrava, and Alcántara.[22] The honor springing from bureaucratic service was also implicit in late colonial complaints about the ostentatious objectives of many job seekers.[23] Bureaucrats in general made it a point to draft and update their résumés, indicating their academic credentials and, most important, summarizing their personal and familial *méritos* (i.e., virtues, dignity, worthiness). These *méritos* resulted essentially from a series of services ranging from nonremunerative employment in city councils *(cabildos)* to jobs in prestigious Audiencias. These services were rendered to the Crown or the Church by individuals and their kin. As the abundant colonial *relaciones de méritos* make clear, individuals and families alike frequently boasted of the honor derived from Church and state service, including the service of even their most distant relatives.[24] Furthermore, public rituals, celebrations, and parades were regular occasions for prestige, honor, and status to surface and become visible objects of display and ostentation on the part of bureaucrats and their rivals.[25]

The existence of diverging statuses across elite groups surfaced during some of these public rituals, when ceremonial display and deference were matters of great concern. In seventeenth-century Potosí, for instance, religious processions witnessed the parading of "the officers of law and justice" apart from artisans, tradesmen, and the members of the *cabildo*. The officials stayed close to the nobility and the wealthiest members of society—the plutocracy of quicksilver refiners. Like their counterparts in eighteenth-century Chihuahua or any other colonial city, these officials wore special attire and headgear distinctive of their office. Along with other royal and municipal officials, such as officers of the mint and treasury, they were afforded distinctive privileges, including preferential seats and personal meetings with the viceroy.[26] As a result of the key social value attributed to rituals, seating arrangements and dress codes caused frequent disputes over precedence. Such disputes pitted honor-conscious bureaucrats, particularly high-ranking ones, against honor-hungry members of the elite-staffed secular city councils or *cabildos*.[27]

Differences in status between bureaucrats and the rest of society, including wealthy segments of the elite, were also noted in the self-perceptions of contemporary actors. In his early-nineteenth-century genealogical remarks, a late colonial bureaucrat who was part of a colonial clan with a long bureaucratic history in the viceroyalty of New Granada referred to the "muy honorificos" (very honorific) bureaucratic services of his ancestors and boasted of the unspecified "honores" (honors) to which their bureaucratic appointments entitled them and himself. Furthermore, he indicated that his own father, a *contador* of the Royal treasury, was quite modest and tended not to "exaltar sus méritos" (emphasize his merits) but instead "procuraba rebajarlos o disimularlos para ponerse a nivel de todas las gentes" (play them down, or disguise them, so as to be at the same level as the rest of the people). The very fact that he pointed this out suggests that as a bureaucrat he was not at the same level as the rest of society.[28]

This distinction was also reflected in restrictions on bureaucrats' social intercourse. Marriages were confined to one's own status circle; that is, to relatives of other bureaucrats, nobles, or *gentes principales*.[29] These restrictions were in part self-imposed by the bureaucrats' perceptions that alliances with only certain families would further their careers. But some of the restrictions were also enforced and sanctioned by the Crown—partly to avoid conflicts of interest and corruption, but mostly because of a concern over state administrators' social prestige. Public perceptions of the honorable character of royal servants, as it turned out, required that a superior oversee the choice of marriage partners for high officials and, in general, officials of all ranks.[30]

Finally, there were other instances in which the higher honor and status of bureaucrats was expressed in material rather than cultural terms. It has been demonstrated that preferential treatment for appointment and promotion (and thereby honor and status) was accorded to the aspiring sons and relatives of former bureaucrats, who profited from the *servicios contrahidos* between the Crown and some of their ancestors and kin.[31] This practice ultimately determined the establishment of a sort of dynastic succession in office. Officials continued to build family-bureaucratic networks even during the second half of the eighteenth century, when the bureaucracy became increasingly professional.[32] This familial right to office denotes, but should not be confused with, the convertibility of honor and status into material advantages for family and self. These advantages included both the direct economic benefits of having a bureaucratic job and the perquisites that came with access to office (e.g., leverage for business deals, attractiveness for marriages into elite families, power to deliver patronage and receive allegiance in exchange).[33] Material benefits were undeniably linked to a superior status; however, more significant was the fact that this status had clear moral repercussions and created major cultural differences.

The honor implications of Church and bureaucratic service naturally differentiated insiders–and their respective families, to whom honor and status were extended–from outsiders and their families. Distinctions were made even within the circles of those insiders and outsiders who belonged to relatively similar ethnic, religious, and economic groups. Yet we cannot refer to such differences as class differences, for though they could have translated into economic advantages or disadvantages, they were not the result of economic factors, from whence class differences spring.[34]

In other words, if the concept of social class could, after all, be applied to groups in colonial settings where social stratification in reality responded to numerous noneconomic factors (e.g., religious antecedents, legitimacy and place of birth, ethnic origin, noble titles, nonmanual occupation, services to the Crown), certainly one could not claim significant class differences between elites within the state bureaucracy and their respective families, and elites outside of this network.[35] That is, it would be impossible to draw such distinctions between, on the one hand, certain bureaucrats and their landowning, mineowning, merchant, or professional relatives and, on the other hand, nonbureaucrats and their similarly wealthy or middling landowning, mineowning, merchant, or professional relatives. Still, as this work will demonstrate, noneconomic factors–especially state service and its associated status-honor–definitely determined social differences among such familial groups. Furthermore, like other economic, social, and political features of the colonial period, the series of status disparities between state and Church insiders and outsiders did not magically disappear after independence.[36] Their images were carried over to the postcolonial period, this time causing not mere petty disputes over access to symbols of honor and the appropriate etiquette, but unleashing regional rivalries, political factionalism, and even true military confrontations.

Affiliations with political factions and parties and postcolonial political conflicts over state-building had much to do with the continuities and changes in the composition of governing and administrative elites from the colonial period to the republican or modern period. These continuities and changes are one of the main concerns of this book, which adopts an unconventional periodization that bridges colonial and national history.[37] It is not possible to comprehend the nature or origin of party affiliations and the political conflicts of the first half of the nineteenth century, nor in general the difficulties involved in building new states, without first studying the identity of the colonial state's governing elites. Such a project necessarily involves understanding the ruptures and continuities that existed between this group and the elites of the postcolonial period. We can best understand the state-building projects and political inclinations of different groups and networks of individuals during the postcolonial period by considering the "status" that those individuals, and the regions in which they lived, had enjoyed during the colonial period.[38]

Despite the arguments of some early historians of Latin America and Colombia, postcolonial factions and parties were not clearly differentiated in terms of the social class of their membership,[39] although they *were* clearly differentiated regarding their members' status and social power. This status resulted from individuals' connections to the high colonial state bureaucracy or ecclesiastical hierarchies, noble titles, and, to a lesser degree, royal land or labor grants. These factors, in turn, were directly related to whether the regions where the members were located had a high concentration of clerical and state bureaucracy, titled nobles, and royal grants of land or labor.[40] Such factors allow us to construct some Weberian ideal types, which distinguish "aristocratic" groups later linked to the Conservative Party from "provincial" ones linked to the Liberal Party. The reciprocal conflicts among these ideal-typical groups are then explained as resulting from the clash between the material and ideological interests that corresponded to each status.[41]

Postcolonial Changes and the Advancement of Liberalism

As state offices, officials, and legitimacy were detached from the patriarchal and mythic figure of the king, a new kind of state was slowly established in postcolonial Latin America. Access to government was now determined by revolutionary, intellectual, or electoral merits. The state's legitimacy came to derive from impersonal constitutions and laws; the old patrimonial aspects of the state were being displaced by its expanding legal-bureaucratic features. In addition, along with a new kind of state, a new type of society also began to emerge during the first half of the nineteenth century: religious and ethnic background, noble titles, the manual character of one's occupation, and the place and even the legitimate or illegitimate nature of one's birth gradually ceased to fix one's social standing.[42] But it was not just that ethnicity, religion, and birth factors slowly lost weight in determining social hierarchies and perceptions. What also changed, and in the process caused significant transformations in social arrangements and stratification, was society's–particularly the elites'–relationship to the state. The social meaning and importance attributed to membership in the state's bureaucratic ranks suffered major transformations. All of these changes were slow to come and took place amidst much social tension.

The independence movement opened up numerous avenues of social mobility for provincial and racially mixed social sectors. Both the army and, later, the expanded state bureaucracy became available not just to traditional elite groups with a family tradition of bureaucratic service but to all who had revolutionary or intellectual merits, some connections, or electoral success. Along with the introduction of liberal ideas, the mere increase in the number of official positions to be filled as a result of independence and the adoption of a republican constitutional system made it vital for the state to select and hire new personnel. There were now three separate branches of government and Colombians were doing everything themselves, not relying on the Spanish monarchy to handle their foreign relations, settle judicial disputes, enact regulations and laws, and so on. This proliferation of jobs and political positions in itself generated upward mobility for individuals and family groups. Naturally, this liberal trend was resisted by those accustomed to monopolizing state service and the prestige accruing from it.

Soon after independence, what Costeloe calls "the opening of the world of politics" brought about an intense competition for public office.[43] All regions started to experience, to a greater or lesser extent, electoral disputes and other more informal struggles for control of the swollen local and regional bureaucracies and the national congress, not to mention the presidency itself. Some disputes were military; most, however, took on an electoral character and were fought through, and reflected in, the press and other new forms of political sociability emerging during the first half of the nineteenth century.[44]

Along with political and journalistic disputes in the growing "public sphere of civil society," regions throughout Colombia witnessed the migration of local individuals to the main provincial capitals and urban centers. There educational institutions provided professional training in both theology and the law. The latter was a favorite choice for those with political ambitions. Besides preparing for the legal profession and politics, individuals trained in the law also gained the skills needed for journalism and education.

Politics, journalism, and educational projects all contributed to polarize elite groups, who were clustered into two main sectors. Before the 1850s, one sector had a traditional vision of state and society similar in many respects to colonial times: a strong central state, active in regulating all kinds of economic activities, vigilant of unorthodox ideas, closely allied with the Catholic Church, not widely open to popular access through constant and noisy elections but controlled by a few prominent individuals and family groups and, if possible, run by a strong chief executive. The other sector had progressive inclinations; that is, it generally favored a decentralized government, a more open intellectual arena, secular education and a limited role for the Catholic Church in other realms, competition for state jobs through elections and on the basis of merit, access to education, the bureaucracy, and the army (or, still better, national guards) by all social sectors, and democratic government. The former, the conservative group, was led mostly by individuals whose ancestors had dominated the high-ranking colonial Church or state bureaucracy. The liberal faction was presided over predominantly by provincial elites with no colonial tradition of bureaucratic or ecclesiastical service. The two groups, however, were in many respects economically identical. Probably some conservatives were wealthier (and whiter) than many liberals. Yet, both sectors included affluent landowners, merchants, entrepreneurs, independent professionals, members of the clergy, and so forth. What tended to differentiate them was not any sort of economic heterogeneity but their connections (or lack thereof) to the colonial Church and state apparatus.

Controlling the postcolonial state was for the conservatives a matter of preserving their colonial heritage, especially the high status-honor they and their families were accustomed to deriving from public office. For the liberals, gaining access to the top state positions was a means to break out of the colonial mold and demonstrate that those with enough intellectual or revolutionary merits could enjoy the honor and prestige reserved in the recent past to just a select group of families. While preserving their alleged heritage or demonstrating the existence of equal opportunities for prestige and honor, each of the two groups was also intent on achieving and using power with other ends in mind. Beyond gaining personal and familial recognition, honor, and social prestige, a position within the state was instrumental for dispensing patronage[45] and introducing policies favorable to one's vision of both society and the state itself. But were such policies geared toward the economic benefit of certain social classes or class segments? Did conservative-liberal disputes over control of the postcolonial state hide class confrontations and class interests? In all societies and historical periods the state guarantees certain property relations and enforces the distribution of wealth; its control cannot be entirely separate from social or economic interests.[46] However, although New Granada's postcolonial state continued to sanction economic relations in favor of an elite group of landowners, mineowners, merchants, and financiers, it apparently did not act as the exclusive tool of any of these elite segments. In New Granada, political factionalism or intra-elite struggles over control of the state apparatus did not result from certain economic segments' need to promote and ensure particular policies favoring their own exclusive economic interests.

Unlike the situation in Peru or Mexico, where early postcolonial elites engaged in intense class-tainted disputes over free trade policy,[47] in other regions disputes over free trade, or the lack thereof, do not appear to have determined political affiliation. In New Granada, both the future conservative (aristocrats) and the liberal (provincial) elites, with a few exceptions, favored protectionism during the early postcolonial decades. They agreed on the need to maintain high tariffs and to preserve the state monopoly over certain economic activities (e.g., tobacco trade and cultivation) during the 1820s, 1830s, and part of the 1840s. Tariffs and monopolies were both needed to alleviate the chronic fiscal crisis of an emerging state whose main source of revenues were fees and custom duties. These protectionist policies and the maintenance of state monopolies were not the means to promote the interests of a specific economic group, but were primarily a way to guarantee the subsistence of the state itself. They were not, as has been well illustrated in the case of Colombia, industrial or mercantile policies, but mainly *fiscal* policies.[48] Later, by the mid-1840s, aristocrats and provincials began to advocate free trade reforms.[49] The two groups shared economic activities and interests and frequently entered into common business partnerships.[50] They were definitely not class adversaries.

Still, the conservative and liberal elites were true social antagonists due to cultural and social disparities centering on prestige, honor, and status. Access to and control of the state apparatus was a way to perpetuate or achieve desired cultural goods—namely, social recognition, dignity, and rights to deference. We are aware, of course, that the two political factions had major ideological disagreements over such issues as the role of the Church, the nature of education, the best means to preserve political order and guard against popular insurrection, and the most suitable policies concerning public administration at the local, regional, and national levels. However, all of these ideological disagreements were generally not why provincial elites clustered in the liberal camp, and aristocrats in the conservative. Except for a few visible leaders (i.e., F. de P. Santander, V. Azuero, M. Ospina) who articulated a political vision and a public program they wished to advance, those ideological differences resulted from the deeper status-honor tensions inherited from the colonial era. In brief, ideological disputes generally did not cause people to join one party or another, but they were the ultimate outcome of status-honor disputes.

Recent scholarship has established that political life in several parts of postcolonial Latin America was intense and dynamic. In Argentina, Brazil, or Chile, strong regimes under the tight control of dictatorial, monarchic or authoritarian civilian sectors restricted political activities. But in Mexico, Peru, or Colombia, nonhegemonic and unstable polities prevailed. Different segments of the upper classes constantly wrestled over control of the state apparatus. They were unable to establish a forceful, longlasting, and persuasive (i.e., hegemonic) economic and political project. The state apparatus thus switched hands frequently and abruptly. Though at times violent, confusing, and seemingly chaotic, those disputes were not senseless or random.

Quantitative and qualitative evidence uncovered in this and other recent works suggests that postindependence political conflicts had their roots in the colonial period's social structure.[51] Other works have demonstrated that most such conflicts tended to revolve around the search for employment and promotion in public sector jobs.[52] In Colombia, the social tensions inherited from the colonial epoch, the postcolonial absence of clear intra-elite economic disputes, and the avid search for state jobs in the postcolonial era all suggest that political factions were primarily a means of fighting to perpetuate or acquire status-honor via state service. Struggles among such factions reflected not class, but rather status antagonisms.

Over time, however, the elites' desire and rush to seek public office and its associated privileges backfired, providing incentives to revolt that perpetuated instability. More important, as the bureaucracy became overcrowded, the luster of state jobs gradually disappeared. For the first time, after the late 1830s, public sector job holders and seekers were perceived not as honorable characters, but, in Colombia and elsewhere, as society's mediocre and unproductive parasites, or *empleomanos*.[53] As this negative perception of state occupations gained ground, and as plentiful economic opportunities in commerce and agriculture opened up, former political rivals not surprisingly tended to converge. After all, the state was no longer a marker of social distinction; economic identity finally gained priority. The ruling elites ceased to be predominantly state-driven status-seekers and became primarily a group of profit-seeking entrepreneurial capitalists.

To this newly found socioeconomic identity was added another incentive for elite unity: the growing danger of popular insurrection.[54] Before the 1840s, the elites' common preoccupation with popular participation in politics and insurrection caused clashes over contradictory strategies for policing society and ensuring order. It also resulted in diverse approaches to suffrage rights. Upper-class political sectors attempted in diverse ways to coopt the masses and benefit from their political support. However, as the masses gained autonomy from both liberal and conservative groups, found allies among the top military officers, and began to threaten the established order, intra-elite political disputes gave way to the formation of an anti-insurgent common front.

Like other elites, New Granada's colonial and postcolonial lawyers tried to live what they understood to be "honorable lives." In doing so, they spent an inordinate amount of their time bickering over political sinecures. As an expanding agro-export economy came to offer other 'honorable' alternatives for making a living, the elites' cultural perceptions of both each other and the state changed. Subsequent intra-elite conflicts thus had a different, not primarily state-centered character. Expanding market forces were likely to cause conflicts of a different kind—over economic concerns. Until recently, historians have dedicated time and effort to demonstrating that Colombia's late-nineteenth-century civil wars were not primarily over public job-seeking, but rather hid contradictory economic interests.[55] The demons of the early postcolonial past seem to have cast their shadow onto late-nineteenth-century political disputes, making them look like conflicts over honorific *empleos,* which they no longer were. However, those same historians do not acknowledge that in an earlier period, conflicts over state-derived status-honor may indeed have mattered more than conflicts over material goods. Conflicts regarding what Weber termed the "means of administration" took precedence over conflicts concerning the "means of production." The lives and careers of New Granada's lawyers from 1780 to 1850 demonstrate as much.

Chapter 2
The Lawyers and
the Late Colonial State

Along with the priesthood and the military, law became one of the main careers for New Granada's colonial elites, as well as a steppingstone to more coveted bureaucratic positions. Although most lawyers belonged to the upper economic segments of society, not all had equal chances to climb the bureaucratic ladder, and many had to content themselves with middle-level positions, nonbureaucratic legal practice, or other pursuits. Nevertheless, local law graduates were eager to attempt the somewhat hazardous and uncertain bureaucratic path that traditionally symbolized a stable career, a family investment, and an opportunity to acquire steady income and wealth. More important, a state job was a significant source of power, honor, and prestige. This chapter traces the history of New Granada's colonial lawyers, looks at their social characteristics, and focuses on their professional activities and career paths, especially in the colonial state bureaucracy.

Reception and Evolution of Colonial Lawyers

Lawyers were present in New Granada and other Spanish colonies from the early sixteenth century.[1] Luis Martín Fernández de Enciso was one of the first lawyers to settle in New Granada. Arriving sometime between 1500 and 1510, he became *alcalde* of a village in the region of Darién, located in what is today Panama, although shortly thereafter he was removed by rival conquerors. Various sources mention at least ten more lawyers who had actively participated in the conquest of New Granada between 1500 and 1550.[2] One, Gonzalo Jiménez de Quezada, in addition to serving as chief magistrate of the Atlantic coast city of Santa Marta, set out to explore the headwaters of the Magdalena River, the area's Mississippi. He eventually sailed up the river itself and, after a long march, founded Bogotá in 1538, making it the capital of the newly conquered territory.[3] Since he converged on this place at the same time as other conquistadores, litigation followed to resolve their conflicting claims. Jiménez de Quezada also faced a legal suit posed by another lawyer, *Licenciado* Fernández Gallego, who claimed rights to the booty collected in Bogotá.[4] These were but a few of the many lawyer-inspired conflicts that flared very early in the Spanish colonies and prompted the king's concern.

In 1509, Charles V ordered the Spanish Casa de Contratación (Board of Trade) not to let any lawyers travel to the Indies without special license; the Crown feared that litigation would increase otherwise. In 1521, Charles restricted the number of lawyers in Cuba. Following numerous petitions from the viceroyalty of New Spain, in 1528 the king also ordered the local audiencia to regulate the legal profession and limit the number of practitioners.[5] The following year, 1529, the king banned all lawyers from the colony of Peru.[6] Nevertheless, probably because of their valuable skills in the rules of formal administration and government, by 1542 no fewer than nine lawyers were performing bureaucratic jobs in New Granada; despite the opposition, lawyers continued arriving in other colonies as well.[7]

Although lawyers were trained locally in New Granada by the late seventeenth century, the various royal prohibitions were probably effective at curbing the presence of lawyers in the Spanish American colonies. In the late 1600s, the Jesuits of the Colegio Mayor de San Bartolomé, one of Bogotá's two institutions of higher education, argued that the lack of lawyers left the courts "without direction" and litigants "without advice."[8] The Jesuits were disputing the Dominican University of San Tomás's monopoly on granting legal degrees in the viceroyalty, so their protest could have been just a rhetorical device. In 1694, however, a royal *cédula* requested the Audiencia of Bogotá to increase the number of courses in jurisprudence. The audiencia itself underlined the need to promote the study of law, as there was still a shortage of lawyers in Bogotá.[9] Most lawyers, it was alleged, "stay in the city of Cartagena";[10] although Bogotá was the capital of the then Presidencia of New Granada and therefore the colony's main administrative center, Cartagena was the major port through which other regions sent their surplus to the transatlantic market, receiving a broad variety of imports in return. Cartagena was thus the central commercial entrepôt for New Granada's economy, and this might have brought more business for the small number of practicing lawyers, who tended to cluster there.

Decades later the situation had substantially changed. Lawyers were reportedly numerous, and many could be found in Bogotá. New Granada had been elevated to the condition of viceroyalty in the late 1730s, thus expanding the bureaucratic opportunities available to all, even local, aspirants. By 1771, Francisco Antonio Moreno y Escandón–*fiscal,* or prosecutor, of the Royal Audiencia– demanded a reduction in the number of law graduates as part of his challenge to the Dominicans' degree-granting monopoly. Moreno y Escandón, a first-generation creole, was the son of a mid-level bureaucrat and mineowner who had settled in the Mariquita region northwest of Bogotá. Although he and his brothers Miguel and Santiago had graduated from one of Bogotá's law schools, thereby benefiting from local training and related bureaucratic fortunes, he did not hesitate to request that the Royal Audiencia limit the number of lawyers and subject them to a four-year apprenticeship before graduation.[11]

It is unclear to what extent the *fiscal's* claim as to the abundance of lawyers was true, although some historians have accepted it at face value.[12] It, too, could have been a rhetorical strategy, this time to advance some of the Bourbon policies aimed at curtailing the power of the Church. These policies were designed to increase the power of the civil authorities by secularizing the content of legal education and creating, as the *fiscal* requested, a state-controlled or public university.[13] The *fiscal,* in any case, argued that "the multitude of lawyers" in New Granada was a result of the Dominicans' failure to enforce the graduation requirements, particularly the possession of a *bachiller* degree and subsequent practical training. The *fiscal's* dispute with the Dominicans generated litigation that dragged on from 1768 until at least 1783. In the end, the religious order was allowed to continue its monopoly; the alleged lack of state funds, disturbing tax riots indicative of other priorities and needs, and most of all the Dominicans' legal maneuvers prevented the Crown from creating the public university Moreno y Escandón so wanted. Some changes in the duration of the practical training were introduced, however; it was extended from two years to four, and new courses were added to the curriculum.[14]

Nevertheless, contemporaries seemed to feel that these reforms did not reduce the number of lawyers. In a description of the viceroyalty of New Granada written in 1789, Francisco Silvestre, a career bureaucrat, former viceregal secretary, and governor of the province of Antioquia, was still demanding that the Crown "not allow the persistence of so many lawyers, establish the number of lawyers in proportion to the population of different regions, and pay with public funds the few that should be allowed to continue."[15] Silvestre's complaints reiterated the colonial authorities' earlier concerns. This time, however, the motivation was different from the preoccupations of the early sixteenth century. Excessive litigation and lawyer-inspired quarrels had not ceased to be a major problem, but lawyers' political demands and bureaucratic pretensions had turned out to be even greater ones, especially when we consider that lawyers belonged to the dominant social groups who expected preferential treatment from the Crown. Access to and graduation from academic institutions was for the elites a confirmation of honor and prestige, and, as it was expected to facilitate entrance into both the Church and state ranks, constituted an avenue to increase one's social prominence.

Social Characteristics of Late Colonial Lawyers

Regardless of the exact number of its members or the bureaucratic position they might attain, the legal profession was a rather exclusive circle. Research on the social origins of the applicants to Bogotá's Colegio Mayor del Rosario and other upper-level institutions shows that of 219 applicants in the period 1660 to 1800, 43 had fathers in the military; 24 and 21 were sons of officials in the Audiencia Real and the fiscal bureaucracy, respectively; 55 were sons of *alcaldes, alférez reales,* or *procuradores generales* of local *cabildos;* and 29 had fathers with unspecified *títulos honoríficos.* Only six belonged to families of workers–*escribanos* (clerks), *plateros* (silversmiths), *boticarios* (pharmacy owners)–or merchants.[16] Comprehensive biographical information on New Granada's colonial lawyers also indicates that, with but a few exceptions, they came from prominent social groups. By 1800, the profession comprised first- to fifth-generation white male creoles who belonged to families of mineowners, landowners, merchants, and incumbent or former military and bureaucrats. Finally, several of the profession's members were themselves sons of lawyers.[17]

The elitist character of the profession was guaranteed by the demanding standards needed for admission to one of the local *colegios mayores,* and thereby for a university degree. Access was restricted to white, male, old-family Catholic Americans or Spaniards, who did not come from families that practiced manual trades *(oficios viles).* Candidates had to prove their *pureza de sangre* and their legitimate birth *(legitimidad).* Indeed, before admission, the *colegios* carried out a short trial-like procedure, the *procesillo,* aimed at determining, though the testimony of various witnesses, the applicants' religious, ethnic, family, and economic background.[18]

Following the *procesillo,* the *colegios* could reject an applicant without explanation. This privileged secrecy lent itself to additional and, not rarely, capricious rejection of students. In 1808, for instance, Cartagena native Joaquín José Gori, a future lawyer and vice president of the republic, complained about the inexplicable reluctance of a *colegio* to admit him as a student. Gori feared the damage such unexplained rejection would cause to his "honor" and interests. Declaring his preoccupation with his bureaucratic future and his social status, he scorned "the offense caused to his family name, source of major obstacles to those who aspire to obtain honorific jobs or to marry into prominent families." His anger was aggravated by the fact that his *procesillo* had not even been completed when he was refused admission.[19]

During the early seventeenth century, the *procesillo* went back three generations to review an applicant's ancestors. By the middle of the eighteenth century, investigation was apparently restricted largely to the applicant's parents.[20] There is also evidence that by this same period the *colegios'* right to reject applicants arbitrarily was being curtailed.[21]

Some relaxation of racial standards was also taking place. In New Granada, Cristóbal Polo, a mulatto, earned a law degree as early as 1755, but only after much opposition from the Cartagena elites. This group repudiated permitting members of the "castes" to enter the legal profession, which they regarded as their exclusive domain.[22] Overcoming new restrictions introduced in the mid-1760s to the admission of mulatto lawyers, José Ponceano Ayarza finally received his law degree in 1798, after filing a petition in 1794 to be recognized as a lawyer by the audiencia.[23] The petition stated that he had been born in the northwestern region of Portovelo, his father's native city. Not exactly a typical mulatto, the father, Pedro Antonio Ayarza, was captain of Portovelo's *pardo* militia for twenty years and was in charge of the administration of the city's church funds. Owner of a major cacao plantation, he accumulated enough wealth to send three of his sons–Antonio, Pedro, and José Ponceano–to study at the faraway Bogotá *colegios.* He also donated his salary to the Crown to help pay for the war against England during the 1790s. After three years of litigation, his son José Ponceano was allowed to take his final law exams, although his admission to the local bar became effective only in 1803.[24] The Crown decided to "dar por extinguida la calidad de pardo del peticionario y dispensarle la gracia de admitirlo a grados," that is, to overlook the petitioner's *pardo* condition and allow him to graduate. This case symbolizes the changing attitudes toward mixed-race individuals, in that prominent members of the local society backed Ayarza's petition and provided him with letters of recommendation. His supporters included the Pey brothers–an attorney and an influential priest–and the lawyers Frutos Gutiérrez, Pedro Groot, and Joaquín Rivera. This was a period when economic fortunes, particularly those of merchants, were becoming as much a source of prestige and power as noble titles, landholdings, legitimacy, and whiteness had been in the past. A wealthy *pardo* could gain a foothold in the upper segments of society, and if they too were wealthy, even illegitimate sons could become prominent citizens.[25] Both Polo and Ayarza, moreover, gained their right to a degree thanks partly to their fathers' military service to the Crown. Still, both succeeded only after protracted litigation, and both cases were exceptional. Most lawyers were white.

As with race, exceptions were allowed for socioeconomic status. As noted above, the offspring of prominent colonial families of mineowners, landowners, merchants, lawyers, and incumbent or former military and bureaucrats dominated the legal profession in New Granada, New Spain, and possibly other colonial regions.[26] Yet, the Colegio del Rosario, for instance, had a few fellowships for poor applicants, making it possible for individuals of modest background to obtain law degrees. Reflecting the significance of bureaucratic service, preference was given to the sons of mid-level state officials. Antonio Martínez Recamán, son of an *escribano* in the fiscal bureaucracy, and Fortunato Gamba Valencia, son of an *oficial* in a provincial Caja Real, obtained law degrees in the 1780s and early 1810s, respectively. Such individuals, however, were unlikely to achieve economic prosperity through legal practice or to gain access to high state positions, the supreme aspiration of colonial lawyers.[27] Those positions presupposed elite background, economic resources, and good connections.

Professional Activities and Career Paths

Along with the priesthood, the military, the bureaucracy, and medicine, law was one of the most common occupations among colonial elites. In comparative terms, however, lawyers were outnumbered by all but high-ranking bureaucrats and physicians (see Table 2.1). Priests were more numerous than lawyers in the late eighteenth century and remained so during much of the nineteenth. Bogotá alone, a city of close to thirty thousand according to a 1793 census, had seven monasteries housing 452 monks, in addition to at least 76 secular priests.[28] An 1810 account refers to the existence of approximately 3,504 members of the secular and regular clergy in the whole viceroyalty.[29] Elite families supplied the Church with 48.5 percent of those members born in the period 1650–1700 and 30 percent of those born between 1700 and 1750.[30] This figure corresponded both to the society's strong Catholic culture and to the high status and economic well-being derived from the position of parish priest.[31]

In absolute terms, military men were as numerous as priests. The army had expanded by the end of the eighteenth century; in 1794, the regular army numbered 3,597 and the militia about 7,860.[32] However, the officer class in both forces was relatively small and quite select. In the 1760–1810 period the regular

Table 2.1. Elite Male Occupations in Late Colonial New Granada

Year	Occupation	Number of members
1810	Priests	3,504
1784	Regular army officers	485
1806	Lawyers	130 to 150
1806	Top bureaucrats	100
1768–1808	Medical doctors	27

Sources: "Padrón general de la población de esta capital," *La Bagatela,* Santafé de Bogotá, October 1, 1853, 79; José M. Restrepo, *Historia de la revolución de la república de Colombia,* 8 vols. (Bogotá, 1942), 1:xxxviii; Allan J. Kuethe, *Military Reform and Society in New Granada* (Gainesville, 1978), 204–05; Renán Silva, *Universidad y sociedad en el Nuevo Reino de Granada* (Bogota, 1992), 152; Antonio García de la Guardia, *Kalendario manual y guía de forasteros en Santafé de Bogotá capital del Nuevo Reino de Granada para el año de 1806* (Bogotá, 1988), 57–72; Juan Marchena Fernández, "The Social World of the Military in Perú and New Granada," in *Reform and Insurrection in Bourbon New Granada and Peru,* ed. Fisher, Kuethe, McFarlane (Baton Rouge, 1990), 84–87.

army of Cartagena and Bogotá, where the most important garrisons were located, had 363 and 121 officers, respectively, a third of whom were creoles or American-born Spaniards.[33] The creole army officers belonged to families of hacendados and merchants, most of them natives of the two cities. The militia officers, whose exact number is unknown, were also recruited from prominent local groups. Like the professional military, the militia officers enjoyed great social prestige, authority, and Crown-granted privileges. In both army and militia, a handful of *pardos,* or mestizos, came to integrate certain companies and, in the late colonial period, managed to reach high military ranks.[34]

In contrast to priests and military officers, there were few medical doctors. Medicine was not yet institutionalized as a professional career, despite some efforts during the late eighteenth century, and many of New Granada's doctors were foreigners. In 1796, Viceroy Ezpeleta alerted the Crown to "the Kingdom's general lack of physicians" and urged the king to send some physicians from Europe. In 1803, Viceroy Mendinueta also argued that "the lack of physicians and abundance of quacks calls for the promotion of the study of this [medical] science."[35] In 1802, only seven students were registered for the scattered medical classes offered in Bogotá; between 1768 and 1808, only 27 medical degrees had been granted.[36]

The shortage of physicians in the capital caused alarm in 1803, when a smallpox epidemic attacked the city. In smaller cities, such as Rionegro in the northwestern region of Antioquia, the situation was even worse; people died readily of minor diseases for lack of medical care.[37] At the same time, some locals seem to have practiced medicine without a degree. The profession was seen as an *oficio vil,* or ignoble manual occupation, and therefore was not highly regarded by local society. This low status might have fostered the acceptance of practitioners without formal training and permission for *zambos* (offspring of unions between blacks and Indians) and mulattos to practice in places like Cartagena—although, it should be noted, their presence made the whites of the city very unhappy.[38]

Finally, the number of bureaucrats in New Granada was close to one thousand in the early nineteenth century. Much like the army, the higher ranks of the state bureaucracy were smaller and select. They comprised over one hundred individuals, several of whom were members of the local elite and the legal profession.[39]

An almanac published in New Granada in 1806 lists roughly 130 *letrados,* as lawyers were also known, although the number could have been as high as 150.[40] Seventy-two of those listed, or more than half, were in Bogotá, and the rest were in other cities (19 in Cartagena; nine in the southern and southwestern regions of Neiva, Buga, Popayán, Cartago, and Chocó; 11 in the eastern regions of Socorro, Tunja, and San Gíl; and 23 scattered inside and outside of the viceroyalty). The total number of lawyers was small compared to the thousands of priests and hundreds of military officers, yet, as noted earlier, some contemporary observers seem to have considered it too large. Numerically, law was the third most important occupation in New Granada.[41] Because many lawyers developed into career bureaucrats, their social and political importance was even greater.

Very few law graduates, probably no more than a third of the total, became full-time practicing lawyers. Many pursued other activities, such as livestock raising, mining, and trade, or the priesthood and teaching. The majority were at least part-time, mid-level civil servants. Some tried slowly to climb the bureaucratic ladder or contented themselves with low-level clerical positions, where they could very likely spend the rest of their lives. A handful occupied full-time high bureaucratic posts either in their native regions or in other colonial locales (see Table 2.2).

Practicing lawyers fulfilled a variety of professional functions: preparing deeds and writing wills for wealthy families; designing commercial contracts for local merchants or local and foreign traders; and handling fiscal disputes, criminal cases, or litigation over dowries, entails, inheritances, donations, and land, mining, and property rights, as well as affairs of honor—one of the overriding concerns of Hispanic society.[42] In addition, all lawyers had to spend time serving as *abogados de pobres,* or pro bono attorneys, an obligation many deeply disliked—and tried to avoid, through excuses ranging from the lack of appropriate clothes to the need to handle only paid cases to support their poor families. The Royal Audiencia urged lawyers not to come up with "ridiculous" excuses to avoid the regular visits to jails that, as "advocates of the poor," they were required to make.[43]

Not infrequently, lawyers like Jerónimo Torres, member of a wealthy mining and landowning family from the southern region of Popayán, represented themselves in disputes over lands or mines and did favors for the *cabildo* of their city or for family and friends.[44] Another main occupation of practicing lawyers was handling the legal affairs of the Catholic Church or individual clerics. The convents, monasteries, and Church-administered *colegios mayores* owned properties and mortgages. Thanks to these activities, they constantly sought to collect payment from their many debtors or engaged in litigation over rights to land or other property.[45] Individual clergy needed lawyers when they sought to move up in the Church hierarchy or to negotiate their parish appointments.[46] Priests also relied on lawyers to help them administer their often substantial fortunes and frequent related litigation.[47]

Despite the variety of their activities and clients, most lawyers seem to have found it difficult to accumulate significant wealth through fees for litigation or other full-time legal practices. In 1809, Jerónimo Torres agreed with his brother Camilo's complaints about their unproductive profession. Camilo, also a lawyer, was certainly not destitute and could even lend money to wealthy Bogotá merchants.[48] Yet he was bitter about "the sterile occupation of defending cases over leaking roofs."[49] Similar complaints were voiced by Tunja native Joaquín Camacho, who preferred the increasing frustration of bureaucratic jobs to law practice.[50] Other lawyers who tried to make a living practicing in provinces remote from the capital also complained with even more reason about the pittance they earned.[51]

The profession's limited prospects for economic advancement resulted in part from the generally poor character of New Granada's colonial economy.[52] Yet they seem somewhat paradoxical given New Granadans' high propensity for litigation. Patrician and antimonarchical activist Antonio Nariño Alvarez observed as much in 1797, while in jail accused of conspiracy.[53] In the mid-1790s, the viceroy also complained to the Crown about "the huge number of legal cases ... most of them concerning civil and criminal disputes, filed by the citizens of the city of Tocaima," a little village near Bogotá.[54] Cartagena-based mer-

Table 2.2. New Granada Lawyers in the State Bureaucracy, 1806, by Rank*

	High-Ranking	Middle	Undetermined
Political	5	4	–
Fiscal	7	16	–
Judicial	5	–	–
Clerical	3	2	–
Other	–	–	4
Total	20	22	4

Sources: García de la Guardia, *Kalendario manual,* 57–72; Ots y Capdequí, *Las instituciones del Nuevo Reino de Granada.*

*High-ranking political jobs consisted of governors, *corregidores,* and *tenientes letrados;* middle-level jobs included *tenientes asesores.* High fiscal jobs included *contadores* and *tesoreros* of the Tribunal de Cuentas and the Casa de la Moneda; middle-level fiscal jobs consisted of *administradores, fiscales,* and *asesores* of the Rentas de Tabaco, Aguardientes, Correos, Bulas, etc. High judicial jobs included *agentes fiscales* and *relatores* of the Audiencia. High clerical jobs included *escribanos* of the Real Audiencia and the Tribunal de Cuentas, while medium clerical jobs consisted of *oficiales* of the Contadurías of the Tribunal Mayor de Cuentas. Low-ranking jobs included *meritorios, agregados,* and *padres de menores.*

chant José Ignacio de Pombo was equally concerned over the large number of trials dealing with land rights, which he attributed to the lack of accurate maps.[55]

Apparently not of all these numerous legal conflicts provided income for law graduates. Many were handled instead by *prácticos* or *tinterillos,* legal practitioners who lacked formal training or law degrees.[56] Others were carried out directly by the parties involved. As one lawyer argued, "it is quite uncomfortable to practice law, especially in small cities, because the interested parties take care of their own defense. That is why this profession is not profitable enough."[57] Still other legal affairs were handled by a variety of legal auxiliaries, among them *procuradores* (solicitors) and *escribanos públicos* (scribes and clerks). The former were in charge of drafting *representaciones* (petitions, complaints, and other legal briefs) directed to the authorities, which sometimes, but not always, needed a lawyer's endorsement. The latter, not to be confused with the prestigious honorific officials known as *escribanos de cámara* (special scribes to top state officials or state agencies), witnessed, recorded, and very likely prepared standard legal instruments, including contracts, without lawyers' participation.[58] These lay practitioners and auxiliaries could refer to manuals originally designed to help lawyers in practice.[59]

Faced with this multilayered competition, lawyers ended up moving into other, apparently more lucrative, activities. Many tended to their lands or mines and engaged in commerce. By 1782, Pedro Romero Sarachaga had been *escribano de cámara* of the Royal Audiencia for more than sixteen years but had never received a salary; instead, he made a livelihood out of providing the city of Bogotá with "beef fattened and seasoned on his own haciendas."[60] Jerónimo Torres spent most of his time in mining and commerce; he was in charge of administering his family's gold mine and also had two *compañías de comercio,* or business partnerships, with the wealthy Spanish merchant González de Llorente (to whom his brother Camilo had loaned money). Trading was the major occupation of José Félix de Restrepo, from the northwestern mining region of Antioquia, who, besides teaching at the local seminary in Popayán and holding a minor bureaucratic position, had a profitable partnership with his brother-in-law Miguel María Uribe Vélez trading goods between Popayán and Antioquia.[61] Another Antioqueño lawyer, José Manuel Restrepo, gratefully remembered his own mercantile experience. Just after receiving his law degree in 1808, he was able to do some trading with the help of money provided by his father; otherwise, he recalled with a shiver, he would have had to content himself with making a living as a lawyer.[62]

A large number of lawyers were members of the clergy; they often served as parish priests. About one-third of a sample of 65 priests whose careers are described appear also to have been lawyers. The priesthood presented economic incentives that must have overshadowed those of legal practice.[63]

Teaching law at a university was also a traditional employment for lawyers. This was not a full-time occupation, but rather a complement to other activities. A chair in law also served as a catapult to a bureaucratic career. Law professors had a greater chance of receiving a high-ranking bureaucratic appointment; Mark

Burkholder notes that at least up to the late seventeenth century, law professors were included "as a matter of course on lists of candidates assembled for the use of the Cámara of the Indies when it considered vacancies on the entry audiencias of South America."[64] University chairs therefore were a means to attain "positions of political importance more lucrative than the chair." This prestige is demonstrated by the fact that academic activities and accomplishments were a major item in lawyers' *relaciones de mérito* (curriculum vitae), applications for bureaucratic jobs.[65]

Lawyers regularly updated their *relaciones de mérito,* displaying them as proof of services to the king and thus the basis of virtue, honor, and status.[66] As the *relaciones* attest, joining the bureaucracy was the golden dream of many *letrados* and their greatest source of pride. As John Lynch demonstrates, local lawyers, much like other creoles, sought office for different reasons: "as a career, an investment for the family, an opportunity to acquire capital, and a means of influencing policy in their own regions and to their own advantage."[67] More important, joining the bureaucracy was also a source of honor and prestige—not strictly individual, but extended or passed on to family members. In fact, it seems evident that state service became a vital way—as vital as their respective trade or economic occupation—for dominant social groups to maintain and increase their individual and familial life chances and social status-honor. To join the bureaucracy, however, it was necessary to demonstrate some experience and an appropriate social background. Once one became an insider, great patience and connections were required to obtain promotions.

Lawyers and the Colonial Bureaucracy

Before entering the bureaucracy, a recent law graduate would customarily serve a stint as an unpaid apprentice, or *meritorio,* often in the same agency where one of his relatives served. Subsequently he might pursue some teaching and lend his services to a *cabildo* or city council, not necessarily in his native region, as a *regidor* (councilman), *alcalde ordinario* (mayor, sheriff, and justice of the peace), *síndico procurador* (city solicitor or general attorney), or *asesor* (council's legal adviser). These were mostly honorific jobs that generally carried no salary and were considered somewhat of a burden.[68] At this point, while continuing to teach law if possible, the young lawyer was ready to enter the colonial bureaucracy in the customary lower positions of *oficial secundario, oficial mayor, asesor* of a fiscal monopoly such as the tobacco concession, or *teniente asesor* of a provincial governor. These jobs carried yearly nominal salaries of 400 to 1,000 pesos.

The lower salary was acceptable as long as the job could be performed in a region not far from Bogotá or another major urban center, such as Cartagena or Popayán. Otherwise, better payment was expected. Around the late 1790s, for instance, no lawyer wanted to accept the job of governor-*juez letrado* of the northern city of Mompós, a position that carried a yearly salary of just 500 pesos; by August 1801, the viceroy was authorized to increase it to 1,000 pesos. This salary was attractive even to lawyers with a long bureaucratic trajectory, such as Joaquín

Camacho, who had taught law and served for several years as *teniente gobernador* and *corregidor* in different regions. Camacho was encouraged by a fellow bureaucrat and friend to take the 1,000-peso position of *oficial mayor* (chief clerk) of the new *caja real* (provincial treasury) to be established in the northeastern region of San Gil.[69]

At a later stage in his career, a *letrado* could expect to be appointed to bureaucratic jobs such as *teniente gobernador* of a small province, *corregidor* of a major town, provincial governor or *auditor de guerra* (war auditor) in an important region, or *contador* (accountant) of the Tribunal de Cuentas or a fiscal monopoly such as Bogotá's Administración Principal de Aguardiente. These positions carried a yearly salary of 2,000 pesos. A lawyer could also be appointed to judicial posts, including the much-coveted and highly competitive jobs of *fiscal* or *oidor* of the Royal Audiencia, which by 1816 paid 3,300 pesos a year or, in regions other than New Granada, up to 7,500 or 10,000 pesos.[70] At least 7 lawyers from New Granada held high judicial positions in audiencias outside the viceroyalty in the late colonial period,[71] but it seems that almost any of the mid-level bureaucratic positions could be tempting for most lawyers at any time. Nearly half of the 46 lawyers employed by the late colonial state occupied positions at that level.

Lawyers were also willing to accept jobs that carried no fixed salary but instead depended on the so-called *derechos de actuación*. These were fees proportional to the number and nature of legal services and the signatures endorsing legal documents, which the lawyer provided as *asesor*. Interim appointees to the position of *asesor de gobernador* typically performed these services. In such cases the fees were assessed according to an official tariff, or *arancel*, approved by the royal authorities, which spelled out in great detail the amount to be collected for different activities.[72] Not infrequently, state agencies hired outside lawyers to perform specific tasks for a limited period.[73] Another common situation involved lawyers working as tax farmers and administering, for a share of the profits, state monopolies over alcohol, tobacco, and the postal service. These posts, reflections of the patrimonial component of the colonial state, were normally sold at public auction, with the concessionaire given a percentage of the monies collected on behalf of the Crown instead of a fixed salary.[74]

Lawyers' inclination toward bureaucratic service resulted from the material and cultural incentives derived from such occupations. In material terms, bureaucratic careers were stable and offered steady, sometimes high, salaries or other monetary returns. They also provided power and influence, and offered the aspiring sons and relatives of former bureaucrats an opportunity to gain access to the legal profession and preferential treatment for appointment and promotion (and, therefore, honor and status). This familial right to office even determined the establishment of a sort of dynastic succession in bureaucratic posts.[75]

In cultural terms, bureaucrats were rewarded with access to prestigious noble titles or knighthood in military orders, the right to use particular attire and headgear distinctive of their office, the privilege of meeting the viceroy, and a seat of honor at public ceremonies and rituals. These perquisites increased their individual and familial honor, social prestige, and status.

Local lawyers were active seekers of both patrimonial prerogatives and bureaucratic jobs, and felt entitled to receive them. Both the king's patrimonial servants and professional functionaries performed activities highly valued by society and the Crown itself. As a result, even noble families coveted state service and were willing to contribute their sons to the state ranks. In return for substantial tributes and backing, the Crown was expected to accord these individuals and their families economic, social, political, and cultural privileges. Most of all, elite subjects hoped for the honor to serve the Crown and the king himself.[76]

Chapter 3
Family Networks and Colonial Stability

In their quest for both office and higher honor, some lawyers came to build true family-bureaucratic networks during the eighteenth century. These networks would be challenged by some of the administrative reforms of the late colonial period, the true magnitude and success of which, as well as their impact on subsequent political events in Spanish American societies, are still much debated among historians.[1] This chapter's findings tend to corroborate the historiographical views that the reforms gave way to accommodation and continuity. It shows that the family-bureaucratic networks built by some of New Granada's late colonial lawyers proved resistant to the Bourbon reforms that tried to undo them. In this respect, business continued as usual. However, in practical terms such networks, inconvenient though they seemed to the Spanish Crown, contributed to a high degree of political stability. This is demonstrated through the examination of a subversive incident of the mid-1790s, the Nariño conspiracy. The limited extent to which independence was connected to the Bourbon reforms will not be developed here, but will be further discussed in Chapter 5.

Bureaucratic Promotion and Family Formation

Chapter 2 established that law was numerically the third most important occupation in colonial New Granada and that, because many lawyers became career bureaucrats, their social and political importance was even greater than previously thought. To ensure their rise in the bureaucracy, lawyers behaved cautiously, even to the point that bureaucratic aspirations shaped their family strategies.

It was not wise for an ambitious lawyer to marry until he had secured a good bureaucratic post and could hope to be attractive to the elite women of the city. Conversely, even wealthy, aspiring lawyers found it convenient to marry the daughters or sisters of a well-placed bureaucrat.[2] The lawyer son of a relatively wealthy mineowner, for instance, could thereby gain a foothold in the state bureaucracy. Helped by his own family's economic support and his bride's connections, he could eventually travel to Spain to lobby for a better job. After waiting in Spain for an uncertain number of years, sometimes as many as ten or fifteen, he could return to his native or another colonial region as a *fiscal* or *oidor* (a prosecutor or judge) of a royal audiencia.[3]

If, instead of marrying right after graduation or upon entering the bureaucracy, the dedicated lawyer-bureaucrat waited until he had risen to the position of, say, governor of an important province—which would take, with luck, approximately ten to fifteen years—he could aspire to marry a more prestigious bride, particularly if his own family had enough wealth. The bride might be the daughter of a state official, such as the *corregidor* of an important region or a *contador,* and might also belong to a family of landowners, mineowners, or wealthy merchants. The creole Joaquín Mosquera y Figueroa, scion of a wealthy mineowning family, married into a powerful landowning clan of the region where, after ten years as a bachelor in the middle-level bureaucracy, he served as governor. Years later he became *oidor* in Bogotá, an exceptional case for a *criollo* (creole) in New Granada.[4]

In the case of Mosquera and several other New Granada natives who became *fiscales, contadores,* or *oidores,* being a *criollo* was not an absolute obstacle to rising to the highest bureaucratic ranks.[5] Nonetheless, creoles faced extra difficulty in joining the bureaucracy, especially during the second half of the eighteenth century. José Caicedo y Flórez graduated from law school in 1774. He belonged to the same generation as *oidor* Mosquera y Figueroa, but despite a similar elite background he never gained access to the bureaucratic world. Caicedo was a fifth-generation creole. His grandfather had been an *encomendero,* governor of two provinces, *corregidor* and *superintendente* of two other regions, and a large landholder. His father was also a prosperous landowner but seems not to have occupied high bureaucratic positions. Caicedo's first wife was the niece of a former *contador* of the royal mint of Bogotá, nearly the ideal match for someone in pursuit of a bureaucratic career.[6] His second wife, however, was the daughter of a lawyer of the Audiencia of Bogotá, who was also a wealthy landowner but does not appear to have had any bureaucratic trajectory.[7] As was customary for lawyers, Caicedo y Flórez served as *alcalde ordinario* and *regidor* of the Bogotá *cabildo* during the 1770s and 1780s, but except for a short stint as governor of an unimportant province, he never gained access to any bureaucratic jobs, devoting himself instead to practicing law and ranching.[8] He neither taught law nor occupied even a middle-level position that would accumulate *méritos* toward a bureaucratic appointment. Twenty years after obtaining his law degree, he was unlikely to find major opportunities in the colonial bureaucracy, and probably because of this he became bitter and rebellious.[9]

What is more, Europeans could easily outmaneuver creoles. Those lawyers with close ties to Spain, where most decisions were made and most jobs assigned, could move more quickly and with less expense up the bureaucratic ladder. This will be demonstrated by the case of *fiscal* Alvarez.[10]

Family Networks

Manuel Bernardo Alvarez (maternal grandfather of Antonio Nariño, who would later be jailed for conspiracy and bemoan New Granada's unending litigiousness) was *fiscal* of the Royal Audiencia of Bogotá from 1736 to 1755. He was born

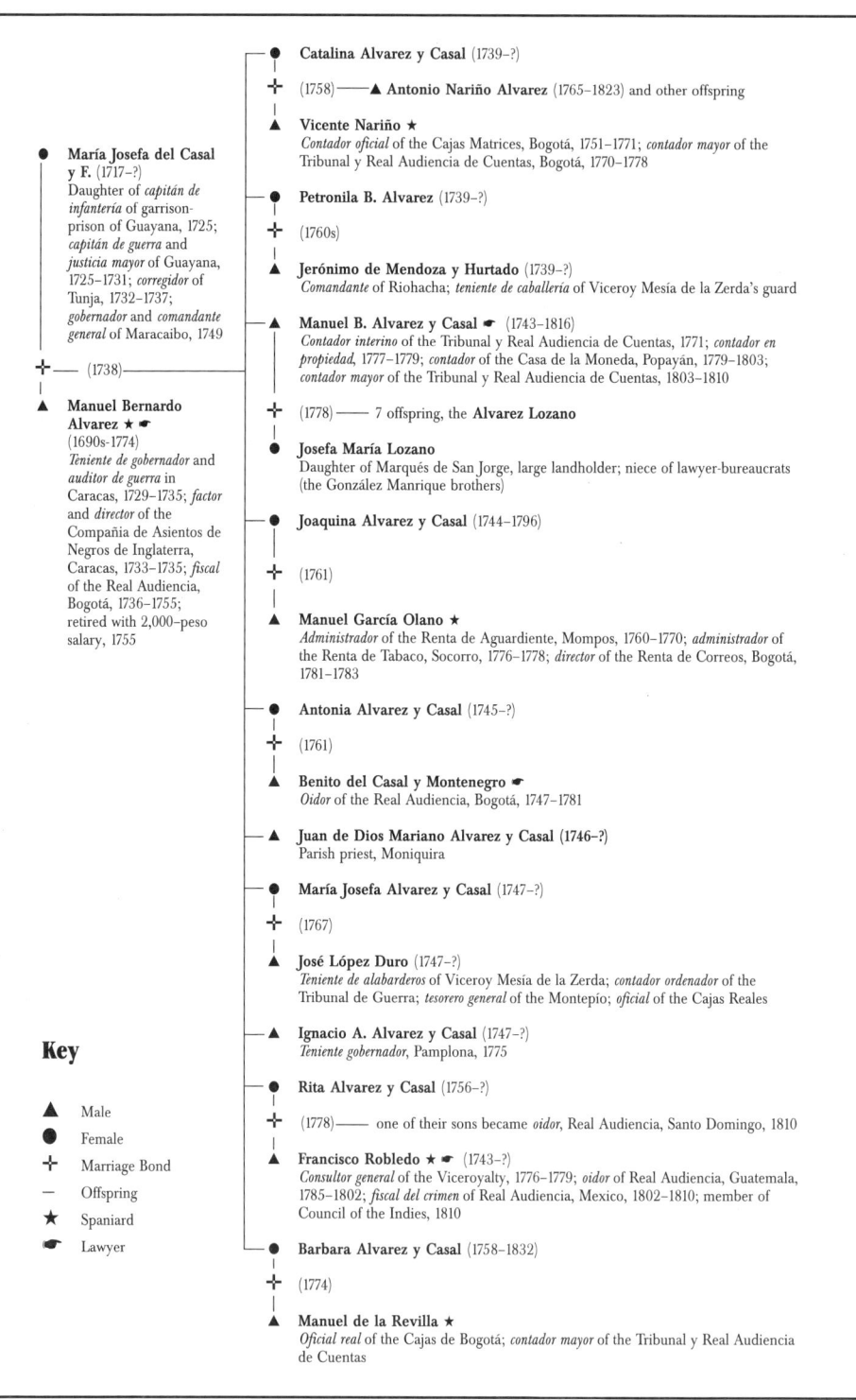

Figure 3.1. The Alvarez Bureaucratic Dynasty (1730s–1810s)

in Spain in the late seventeenth century, and in 1728, two years after graduation and still single, he came to the New World as *teniente de gobernador y auditor de guerra,* a good entry job, in Caracas. In less than a decade, probably through patronage from friends and relatives in his homeland, he rose to the position of Bogotá *fiscal.* Only then did he marry; his bride was Josefa Casal y Freiria, the daughter of a former *corregidor y justicia mayor* of the neighboring city of Tunja.[11] They had fourteen offspring, at least six of whom married important figures in the local economy and politics (see Figure 3.1), becoming, as John L. Phelan has argued, the founders of a true "bureaucratic dynasty."[12]

Lawyers, creole and Spaniard alike, were, in any event, eager to pursue bureaucratic careers. As the examples already offered indicate, that goal determined even their family formation strategies. Still, it was not uncommon for lawyers to marry the daughters of local landowners, mineowners, and, in the late colonial period, merchants—a group on the rise in regions like Cali, Antioquia, and Panama, and presumably also Bogotá and Cartagena.[13] Marrying into elite but nonbureaucratic families placed lawyers in the upper economic ranks of society but, as in the case of Caicedo y Flórez, delayed or endangered their bureaucratic aspirations and chances. Families of fellow bureaucrats were always preferable.

Although government bureaucrats were prohibited by law from marrying female relatives of fellow bureaucrats or having kindred ties with each other, the truth is that after obtaining permission from the Crown, or sometimes in secret, they customarily did just that—married the daughters and sisters of fellow officials. The highest-ranking bureaucrats were related to each other by marriage, which they seemed to consider the best way to consolidate and advance their own careers and those of their family members.[14]

The existence of a small group of high-ranking, interrelated civil servants, tied together through marriage across clans, contradicted the Bourbon theory of government. Along with many other reforms, the Bourbons strove to reduce bureaucratic corruption and nepotism. They prohibited bureaucrats from marrying women from their jurisdiction, so as to maintain a neutral or impartial bureaucracy. But that policy was thwarted by the flexibility with which marriage permits were issued or else was circumvented by bureaucrats in different viceroyalties, where family networks flourished in spite of the official antiseptic measures.[15]

The formidable task of effecting those reforms in the face of such ingrown resistance is exemplified by the lawyer Juan Francisco Gutiérrez de Piñeres, who arrived in Bogotá in 1778 as the Crown's special *visitador* and appointed *regente,* or senior chief of the audiencia. This position, established two years earlier, gave him the mission of enforcing all the Bourbon reforms promoted during these years. With few exceptions, such as the partial dismantling of the Alvarez bureaucratic dynasty, the results of his visit show that local elites had enough material power to frustrate the Crown's attempts to dispossess them of the privileges they had traditionally enjoyed and valued.[16] The hapless *visitador* was run out of Bogotá in 1781 by a tax riot known as the Comunero revolt.

The continuing importance of the colonial state as a source of jobs for local lawyers and their clans up until the end of the colonial period was underscored by the presence of at least one important family network years after Gutiérrez's visit: that of Francisco Vergara y Vela Patiño.[17] Throughout his nearly forty years presiding over Bogotá's Tribunal de Cuentas, this lawyer had established another bureaucratic dynasty that by the 1790s came to dominate vital segments of state and society in New Granada. Vergara's story confirms some of the bureaucratic family patterns referred to in this and previous chapters.

At the age of fifteen, and after having submitted proof of his "legitimate birth and purity of blood," Francisco Vergara y Vela Patiño began studying law in Bogotá, capital of the soon-to-be Viceroyalty of New Granada. The year was 1727. His father, José Vergara Azcárate y Dávila, a thirty-five-year-old widower, had recently become a Catholic priest and was serving in a little parish not far from Bogotá. Don José, four of whose siblings had also embraced religious life, had decided that "after having lost his Gertrudis—his wife, killed along with several of his offspring by a ravaging epidemic in 1719—there was no other refuge but the Church."[18] Numerous other widowers customarily did likewise.[19]

On being ordained as priest in 1723, Don José gave up an *encomienda*, or royal grant of Indian tribute and labor, which he had inherited from his father. He also relinquished the bureaucratic post as *teniente corregidor*, or provincial administrative chief, which he had held in various towns. This position might have led to higher state commissions as well as wealth, power, and prestige.[20] Instead of climbing up the bureaucratic ladder he started on the ecclesiastical one; there, besides some spiritual consolation, one could also find significant material comfort.

Meanwhile, Francisco, Don José's only surviving son, completed his legal studies in Bogotá. In 1734, the year the still-adolescent Francisco was admitted as a lawyer by the Real Audiencia, his father received the last of a series of ecclesiastical assignments: the parish of Socorro, a town of 3,000 inhabitants northeast of Bogotá. In this region of small cultivators of sugar cane and tobacco and artisanal spinning and weaving, Don José accumulated some economic wealth.[21] In such middle-sized parishes, priests benefited from the fees charged for baptisms, burials, weddings, and, more important, the rent of tithes. The priests had to hand over only a small portion of the tithes to the bishop—a portion they further reduced by conveniently altering the collection records.[22] In time, parish priests converted this wealth, becoming large landholders and owners of livestock and slaves.[23]

Don José died in Socorro about 1743, and he must have rested in peace knowing that his son Francisco was by then married and well established in the capital. Fortunately, in 1736 Francisco had married the daughter of José de Caicedo y Pastrana, a wealthy landowner who counted among his other offspring at least two nuns and two priests. The Caicedo family owned extensive lands near Bogotá, along with numerous livestock and even some slaves. In addition to tending to their lands and ecclesiastical careers, several members of the family were *encomenderos* and at least a few became lawyers and state officials.[24] The Caicedos' power, however, was more economic than bureaucratic. Indeed, their lack of bureaucratic influence hindered Francisco's own bureaucratic aspirations.

Francisco hoped to continue a highly valued familial tradition of service to the colonial state—despite his father's disengagement from the bureaucracy.

Francisco's ancestors included an *encomendero* great-grandfather, who also served the bureaucracy as *tesorero*, or treasurer, and provincial governor; and a high-ranking bureaucrat grandfather, who, after buying the position in the mid-seventeenth century, had become a *contador*, or accountant, at Bogotá's Tribunal de Cuentas, the central accounting office.[25] The bureaucratic continuity of Francisco's family was interrupted by the career choices of his uncle and father, whose religious careers weakened the clan's political power. To be sure, the Vergaras' economic well-being was strengthened by the income from Don José's parish and further consolidated when Francisco joined the Caicedo clan. But as Francisco's subsequent career demonstrates, economic power was not enough; bureaucratic influence was vital to promote and maintain elite status.

Fifteen years after graduating from law school, Francisco was weary of tending to Casablanca, his hacienda on the outskirts of Bogotá, and of the series of honorific but usually unpaid jobs *(regidor, procurador, síndico general, alcalde ordinario)* he held in Bogotá's *cabildo*. He may have been frustrated at his failure to recapture his clan's control over a key bureaucratic appointment. Such a position, in addition to its material rewards, would have strengthened his family through political power, the means to dispense patronage, added *méritos* or qualities to obtain future jobs for other family members, honorific treatment, and status.

By the late 1740s, Francisco was preparing to sail for Spain to lobby personally for a bureaucratic appointment, as many American-born Spaniards were obliged to do. By making the journey themselves they avoided the onerous and sluggish brokerage of the Iberian *agentes de negocios,* intermediaries between the Crown and job seekers. Just before he embarked, however—probably through protracted lobbying and large sums of money—Francisco obtained an important commission as *regente contador* of the Tribunal de Cuentas (chief of the viceroyalty's central accounting office). This was the same agency where his grandfather had served decades earlier, blazing a trail that family members could follow. Over the following years, Francisco used his office to promote not only the state's interests but also those of his large family.

Unlike his father, whose marriage and family were cut short by sickness, Francisco would remain married for fifty-two years and produce nineteen offspring. Two of his children became priests, three became nuns, and seven more died before reaching adolescence, a not uncommon occurrence in those years. Several of the rest, including four lawyers, were promoted by their father and became links in a family network within the bureaucracy (see Figure 3.2).[26]

Probably to prepare the ground for the formation of this network, in 1760 Francisco's oldest daughter, Josefa, married one of the highest-ranking members of Bogotá's fiscal bureaucracy: the *tesorero oficial* of the Cajas Reales, Don Antonio de Ayala. A few decades later, by the time of New Granada's 1781 Comunero revolt—a major tax riot that Francisco helped to pacify—two of the four lawyers among Francisco's sons, Felipe and Francisco, Jr., had achieved high-ranking jobs in the fiscal and judicial segments of the bureaucracy. Felipe had spent at

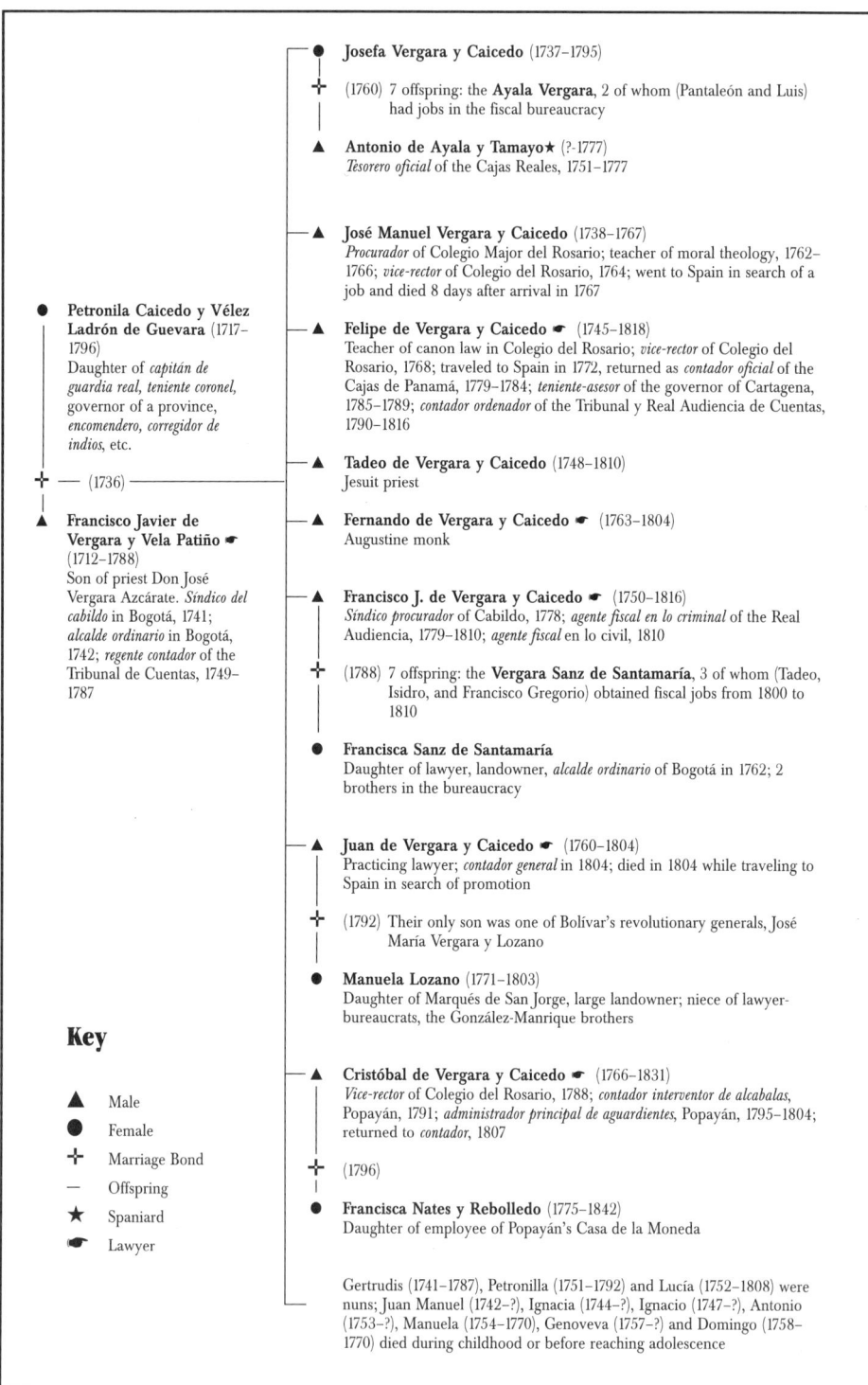

Figure 3.2. The Vergara Bureaucratic Dynasty (1740s–1810s)

least seven years in Spain and, with the help of the Marqués de los Castillejos, his grandfather's former acquaintance, he finally procured jobs for himself and his brother in 1779. He became *contador* in Panama, while Francisco, Jr. was *agente fiscal,* or prosecuting attorney, of Bogotá's Real Audiencia. The fates of their brothers and sisters varied. José Manuel, one of the oldest, had died years earlier, soon after arriving in Spain on a similar bureaucratic pursuit. Another lawyer, Juan, married the daughter of a local noble, the Marqués de San Jorge, and secured a position administering the estate of a wealthy parish priest in a large village. He was allegedly about to receive a high-ranking fiscal job as *contador de hacienda* when he died in 1804, soon after traveling to Spain to secure his appointment.[27] To compensate, two of Francisco's grandsons, the offspring of Josefa and *contador* Don Antonio de Ayala, became officials in the fiscal bureaucracy during the 1790s. Another, a member of the clergy, was appointed by the viceroy to a parish near Bogotá and later served in the Bogotá cathedral.[28] Francisco, Jr. eventually married a member of the influential Sanz de Santamaría family and became part of its network. The Sanz de Santamarías, much like the Vergaras, were active in the administration of the colonial state, from which they derived no small part of their status, prestige, and power.[29]

These clans flourished in the years after the departure of *visitador* Gutiérrez de Piñéres and were still exerting significant clout as late as the 1810s. Felipe Vergara was a senior accountant in the Tribunal de Cuentas, the same fiscal agency where his great-grandfather had served long ago and where his father had served for four decades in the late eighteenth century. Another of Francisco's sons, Cristóbal, was the main administrator and accountant of the tobacco monopoly in the important city of Popayán.[30] Francisco, Jr.'s sons Tadeo, Isidro, and Francisco Gregorio also held jobs in the fiscal bureaucracy,[31] while Francisco and his brothers-in-law were still high-ranking bureaucrats in Bogotá's royal mint and tobacco monopoly.[32] None of these representatives of the creole elite was dislodged from his bureaucratic nest.

What is more, even though the Crown took a dim view of these networks, in practical terms they contributed to a high degree of political stability in the colony. The symbiotic relationship that developed between the state and some local elite groups made the latter generally unsympathetic to antistate activities, although certain local notables were not exempt from temporarily losing their traditional patience and loyalty. The events surrounding Antonio Nariño's trial, for instance, provide evidence of both longstanding loyalty and momentary rebelliousness on the part of elite figures.

Lawyers and Early Political Crisis

During the crisis which took place a decade after the *visita* of Gutiérrez de Piñéres and not long before independence (1794–1795), most of Bogotá's lawyers were supportive of the state and careful to avoid any risk to their bureaucratic careers. They were motivated by not just the fear of being punished, but a desire to secure their individual and familial privilege by joining the state's ranks.

The legal investigations conducted by the audiencia into what one could term "the Nariño conspiracy" originated, not surprisingly, in the testimony of a lawyer and went on to involve numerous members of the local upper class. Among the accused were several young lawyers (Ignacio Sandino, Pedro Pradilla, and Enrique Rodríguez) and recent law-school graduates who were finishing the practical training required for admission as attorneys to the Royal Audiencia (Antonio Cortés, Miguel Gómez, Vicente Huertas, Enrique Umaña, Miguel Valenzuela). (See Table 3.1)[33]

In August 1794, Joaquín de Umaña y López, a twenty-six-year-old native of Tunja who had entered the legal profession just two years before, informed the viceroy of New Granada of the existence of a political plot against the colonial authorities. This lawyer came from a family seemingly lacking any bureaucratic antecedents; he may have been afraid of being charged for not having reported the upcoming plot to the authorities earlier (he had heard about it as early as mid-July) and was probably also eager to gain *méritos* for a future appointment.[34] He pointed to the merchant and *tesorero de diezmos* Antonio Nariño Alvarez, the lawyer and *cabildo* member José Caicedo y Flórez, and the noble landholder José María Lozano y Peralta as leaders of the revolutionary clique. At the same time as Umaña's denunciation, *pasquines* (anonymous libels) were posted in different locations throughout the city. These broadsheets protested against royal taxes and monopolies and referred sarcastically to the "robbery" practiced by the Spanish authorities in the colonies. A group of students at the Colegio del Rosario were denounced by one of its members as the authors of the political leaflets. The students were said to have held meetings with leading local figures in the *colegio* classrooms.[35] Other informants referred to Sinforoso Mutis, a Colegio del Rosario student and nephew of renowned scientist and botanist José Celestino Mutis, as one of the conspirators. The same sources described the translation and alleged distribution of the famous French revolutionary declaration of the "rights of man and the citizen." The man responsible for its translation and printing was Antonio Nariño Alvarez.

Nariño Alvarez was the son of a former royal official in the fiscal bureaucracy, Don Vicente Nariño, who arrived in New Granada in 1751 to serve as *contador oficial* of the Cajas Matrices del Nuevo Reino de Granada. He held this post for nineteen years until he was promoted to *contador mayor* of the Tribunal y Real Audiencia de Cuentas, a job he held at the time of his death in 1778. Seven years after his arrival in New Granada, Don Vicente married the daughter of the lawyer Manuel de Bernardo Alvarez, one of the *fiscales* of the Royal Audiencia and head of a soon-to-be large bureaucratic network (Figure 3.1). Antonio, their third son, became a merchant before the age of twenty and *alcalde ordinario* of Santa Fé at the age of twenty-four. He was appointed to the job of *tesorero general* of the tithes around the same time, in 1789. In 1793 he opened a print shop, a fact that in 1794 got him into a lot of trouble.[36]

The evidence gathered against the conspirators moved the initially skeptical viceroy to order his audiencia to initiate three separate legal investigations. One would deal with the conspiracy in which students and prominent local citizens were supposedly involved; another with the subversive leaflets posted around the city; and a third with the translation of the revolutionary document by Antonio Nariño. Two Spanish *oidores* were put in charge of the first two trials, and a creole native of New Granada, *oidor* Mosquera y Figueroa, handled the last one. Soon after the investigations began, nearly twenty prominent citizens, among them Nariño himself and the lawyers and law students mentioned above, were jailed. Some were sent to Spanish prisons, while others were kept in New Granadan jails. Several spent up to ten years in jail and at least one died nine years after, while still in prison.[37]

Given the fact that various young lawyers were involved, one might have expected some support from the legal profession for its disgraced members, particularly in light of widespread local opposition to the arbitrary procedures of the audiencia.[38] However, with the exception of the strongly supportive stance taken by lawyer José Caicedo y Flórez, the attitude of local lawyers was, to say the least, rather timid. It is clear that, dependent as they were on the state's patronage, they wanted to remain on friendly terms with the colonial authorities.

José Caicedo y Flórez, who had graduated in 1774, was by then forty-seven years old. It is worth remembering that he had a similar elite background and belonged to the same generation as *oidor* Mosquera y Figueroa. Unlike his colleague, however, he never managed to get access to the bureaucratic world, but had to content himself with legal practice and ranching.[39] Twenty years after obtaining his law degree, his bureaucratic frustrations may have made him bitter. Caicedo's favorable attitude toward the lawyers and law students prosecuted by the audiencia, and his denunciations of the arbitrary procedures of the colonial officials, are not surprising if one considers that besides being a powerful

Table 3.1. Lawyers and Law Students Charged with Subversion in 1795

Name	Birth Date	Graduation Date	Birthplace	School
Lawyers				
Pedro Pradilla	1768	1793	San Gíl	Rosario
Enrique Rodríguez	1765	1789	Cartagena	San Bartolomé
Ignacio Sandino	1766	1793	Bogotá	Rosario
Law Students				
Antonio Cortés	1777	?	Ocaña	Rosario
Miguel Gómez	1769	?	San Gíl	Rosario
Vicente Huertas	1767	1796–1800?	Mompós	San Bartolomé
Enrique Umaña	1772	1800	Bojacá	Rosario
Miguel Valenzuela	1770	1796	Girón	Rosario

Sources: AHN, "Médicos y abogados", vol. 3, fols. 132–50; vol. 4, fols. 838–39; vol. 6, fols. 231–43; Pérez Sarmiento, *Causas célebres,* passim; García de la Guardia, *Kalendario manual,* 166, 185; Restrepo Tirado, *De Gonzalo Ximénez de Quesada a Pablo Morillo* (Paris, 1928), 65–98; Pardo Umaña, *Haciendas de la sabana,* 143, 225–36; Guillermo and Alfonso Hernández de Alba, "Galería de hijos insignes del Colegio de San Bartolomé," in Daniel Restrepo, *El Colegio de San Bartolomé* (Bogotá, 1928), 141–39; Eduardo Posada, *Apostillas a la historia colombiana* (Bogotá, 1978), 139–42.

landowner, he had only scant bureaucratic potential and he had little to risk. As a result, his independent behavior diverged sharply from that of other local lawyers, who depended heavily on state support.[40]

In fact, during the 1794–1795 trials José Antonio Ricaurte, Antonio Nariño's defense lawyer, was jailed over the content of a brief he planned to submit to the audiencia in defense of his client. Ricaurte was a former *agente fiscal* of the audiencia and had dedicated himself to legal practice for more than thirty years. He was the first who tried to defend Nariño, in part because the two had family ties.[41] After his detention, practically no other lawyer in town, not even close associates of Nariño's family or the family members of some of the lawyers or law students accused, was willing to assume Nariño's defense.[42]

In August 1795, the wealthy Nariño, all of whose properties had been confiscated, requested the services of at least eight different *abogados de pobres*. The lawyers in question included the young Camilo Torres, a twenty-nine-year-old from the southern region of Popayán, and José Ignacio Quevedo, also in his mid- or late twenties. Having only recently started careers as practicing lawyers, both men refused to come to Narino's aid. The former excused himself, arguing that he was too young, had "scant knowledge," too much work, and too little time to conduct a proper defense. The latter argued that he was overworked and had to conduct paid cases in order to support his family.[43] Thirty-six-year-old Tomás Tenorio, Camilo Torres's uncle, who had been a lawyer for nine years and was currently a middling bureaucrat in pursuit of a better job, also refused,[44] as did two other lawyer-bureaucrats. Francisco Ortíz, *defensor de la Renta de Correos*, argued that he was about to leave Bogotá to fulfil a government commission for the measurement of some lands. Next, and despite the fact that he was related to Nariño's grandfather, José Gíl Martínez Malo, a wealthy landowner and also *alguacil mayor de corte* (sheriff) of the Real Audiencia, pled illness and argued that his public job was an impediment to defending Nariño. Both of these bureaucrats did not seem willing to put their jobs, or the possibilities of a promotion, at risk.[45]

Three other middle-aged lawyers with some bureaucratic trajectory refused the case soon afterward. One was José Ignacio de San Miguel, a lawyer since 1769, who said that he was close to leaving legal practice and returning to his hacienda. The true reason for his refusal may have been his bureaucratic past and expectations.[46] Another was fifty-year-old Eustaquio Galavís, a lawyer for more than twenty-five years. He excused himself by arguing that he had to take his wife, who was very sick, to a climate better than Bogotá's. Galavís, some of whose relatives were also linked to the plot, was a career bureaucrat and former *corregidor* in Tunja.[47]

Even the *procurador,* or solicitor, who ultimately acted on Nariño's behalf ended up quitting due to what he claimed was a sudden illness. He later confessed that he had excused himself from the case "because of fear, for all of the available lawyers had excused themselves from the case."[48] They all must have been afraid of suffering the same fate as the incarcerated defense attorney José A. Ricaurte; their fear extended to the harm that the legal defense of a subversive individual could cause to their future careers. Such a defense did not accrue *méritos,* but rather erased them. This was even more true for lawyers already heavily entrenched within the state bureaucracy.

Of all of these unsympathetic lawyers it is worth highlighting the case of forty-four-year-old Francisco Javier de Vergara y Caicedo, member of the Vergara bureaucratic network, a lawyer for almost twenty years, and at the time of the revolt the *agente fiscal* of the Real Audiencia. He explained that his public post prevented him from defending cases tried by the audiencia, an excuse that may have been true. However, by now we know that there were other reasons to explain his refusal. Vergara, whose background and connections are summarized in Figure 3.2, had held his job since 1779. Both his father and father-in-law were lawyers. The former, who had died six years before, had served for more than forty years as a high official in the Tribunal de Cuentas.[49] The latter was a wealthy landowner and former *asesor* of the Tribunales de Cruzada y Real Hacienda.[50] In addition, his brothers and brothers-in-law held jobs in the colonial bureaucracy.[51] It did not matter that his brother Juan was the son-in-law of the Marqués de San Jorge, along with Antonio Nariño one of the main suspects incriminated, nor that his sister Josefa was the mother of José Ayala y Vergara, Nariño's business partner and closest friend, also jailed for conspiracy. Francisco's bureaucratic commitments took precedence over his brotherly solidarity. Much was at stake for his career and for his relatives, not least among them his own children, who would sooner or later aspire to (and eventually get) jobs in the bureaucracy.[52] This all hints at the supportive role that family bureaucratic networks may have played in times of political crisis.

In the end, the audiencia was reduced to imposing fines to force one of these lawyers, José Ignacio San Miguel, to assume Nariño's defense.[53] Like most of the rest of his colleagues, San Miguel was clearly unwilling to defy the colonial authorities. This fact, along with the various examples noted before, indicates that the colonial state had an overwhelming importance for the lives of the lawyers of New Granada and the advancement and protection of their families.

In the incidents described above, the royal authorities were challenged by a few frustrated lawyers outside of the bureaucracy and by inexperienced and idealistic young rebels, many of whose family members were bureaucratic insiders, as they themselves would become in a few years. These youngsters could be easily repressed, though their presence alerted the state to the necessity to control the number and training of future lawyers. The authorities soon took measures in both areas. The prohibition of partial legal training at the provincial level and the elimination of "dangerous" subject matter (i.e., "public law") from the legal curriculum were enacted in the mid-1790s. These measures, and lawyers' traditional expectation of obtaining state appointments, may have ensured the undeniable loyalty of lawyers to the state.

Had not a serious political crisis affected Spain in 1808, it is likely that for many years to come the lawyers of New Granada would have continued to resist any temptation to oppose the Crown. They would rather make themselves available to the state and be ready to *pretender* (i.e., apply for) "una plaza togada o una auditoria de guerra en cualquier territorio" (viz. a job in an audiencia or an post as an army auditor in any colonial territory), a typical formula in the *relaciones de méritos y servicios* lawyers used to apply for bureaucratic positions. In fact, even many of those involved in the Nariño conspiracy subsequently demonstrated their inclination to support the colonial state and actively seek its patronage. Vicente Huertas, who spent at least a year in prison during 1795, was a faithful subject and accepted royalist appointments during the 1810s.[54] Enrique Umaña, who spent several years in Spanish prisons as a result of the 1795 affair, returned to New Granada in 1809 as *corregidor* of Zipaquira, an important town near Bogotá.[55] As early as 1800, another young conspirator, Antonio Cortés, was serving as an *oficial* in Panama's *aguardiente* monopoly.[56] In 1810 Miguel Gómez Durán, tried and jailed along with Nariño and the rest, was *administrador de aguardientes, bulas y papel sellado* in Socorro.[57] Finally, in 1806 Enrique Rodriguez, jailed until early 1796 and suspended from the legal profession until 1803, and Miguel Valenzuela, who also spent several months in jail, were *fiscal de hacienda* in Cartagena and administrator of the mails in Girón, respectively.[58]

Local elite families traditionally perpetuated and increased their power and status not solely through economic endeavors such as ranching, mining, or trade, but more importantly through college education, ecclesiastical and bureaucratic jobs, and governmental privileges. They deliberately prepared some of their members to join the priesthood and the bureaucracy, the latter through the legal profession and appropriate marriages. In addition, elite clans also strove to display a family history of service to the king, and in so doing developed a symbiotic relationship with the colonial state. In return for state patronage, they reciprocated with as much loyalty as circumstances dictated. Indeed, lawyers were generally unwilling to oppose the colonial state and risk their chances for a prosperous career.

However, some radical changes in the relationship between lawyers and the colonial state took place during the interregnum of the 1790s to the 1810s, forcing some lawyers to opt for extraordinary subversive measures. The following chapter will discuss such changes and detail the participation of lawyers in the independence movement.

Chapter 4
Independence:
A "Revolution from Above"

A full account of the causes of New Granada's independence movement goes beyond the scope of this book. It is nonetheless appropriate to draw some inferences concerning the nature of lawyers' decisive role in achieving independence. The presence of lawyers and other members of the upper segments of colonial society in the revolutionary juntas supremas, or cogovernmental committees, organized in New Granada during the 1810s, particularly the one in Bogotá, was a prime indicator that the early movement for independence was an elite revolution intended to expand creole control over the government to its maximum. Lawyers were traditionally unwilling to oppose the colonial state and risk both their immediate freedom and their future bureaucratic careers. In the 1810s, their attitude changed in response to a crisis in the metropolis that created chaos in New Granada. The lawyers became convinced that, in spite of the extraordinary situation facing the empire and the colonies, the government was unwilling to bargain, reach compromises, or form wider governing coalitions, preferring instead to persecute and repress them. The failure of political bargaining and coalition building thus emerges as a plausible explanation for the rebelliousness of New Granada's lawyers and other elite figures.[1] This chapter's findings also support the view that the revolutions for independence in Latin America were not the unavoidable conclusion of a long-term crisis but resulted, somewhat unexpectedly, from an immediate emergency facing the Spanish monarchy after early 1808.[2] This emergency started with Napoleon's occupation of Spain and his usurpation of the Spanish throne, leading to the establishment of dozens of juntas to take over sovereignty temporarily on behalf of the Spanish king and to organize the resistance against the French. It also caused the election of representatives to the cortes, a parliamentlike body that would meet in Spain. This process, more than anything else, made evident to the creoles their condition as second-class subjects, for the number of representatives they were allowed to send was insignificant relative to the ones elected in Spain itself. All of these factors ultimately pushed creole elites in a revolutionary direction.

Elite Complaints

Thirty-two-year-old Simón Bolívar, soon to become an icon of Latin American independence, wrote a celebrated document in Kingston, his place of temporary exile, on September 6, 1815. Bolívar's document, later known as the Jamaica

Letter, made prophecies for Latin America's future, appraised its contemporary political conditions, and justified the region's current rebellions against the Spanish Crown. Chief among the justifications for rebellion was the exclusion of American-born Spaniards, or creoles, from administration, government, and politics. Bolívar wrote:

> We were cut off and, as it were, virtually removed from the world in relation to the science of government and administration of the state. We were never viceroys or governors, save in the rarest instances; seldom archbishops and bishops; diplomats never; as military men, only subordinates; as nobles, without royal privileges. In brief, we were neither magistrates nor financiers.[3]

He went on to criticize the Spanish reduction of creoles to total passivity and serfdom.

Bolívar's Jamaica Letter echoed long-standing claims found in travelers' accounts, bureaucrats' observations and reports, and elite manifestos and letters, all of which highlighted creoles' animosity toward the Spanish Crown and their desire to hold office. These allusions to creole-peninsular tensions went as far back as 1673.[4]

The study of particular social groups within the creole population that might have resented their exclusion from government and administration offers an opportunity to reexamine creole-peninsular tensions and reevaluate their weight in accounting for Latin America's independence. The legal community of colonial New Granada, much like that of other regions of the Spanish empire, comprised many of the most qualified and eager aspirants to public office. The lawyer-bureaucrat had become a truly central figure of the colonial system, as demonstrated earlier.[5] It thus seems reasonable to assume that lawyers were among the discontented creoles excluded from office, and that this professional group provided substantial support to those who tried to challenge Spain's anticreolism.[6] New Granada's legal community supplied many of the leaders of the 1810s–1820s movement for independence. Lawyers were particularly targeted for persecution; in fact, because of their revolutionary activities, one-fourth of New Granada's lawyers were executed by the Spaniards in New Granada in the 1810s. Yet it is not clear whether political exclusion was the decisive factor that pushed colonial lawyers and other revolutionaries to revolt against the Crown and pursue independence, as contemporary actors and later historians have asserted.[7]

Lawyers and the Revolutionary Juntas

Lawyers were the most conspicuous leaders of the movement for independence that started with the creation of *juntas supremas* in the major cities of the Viceroyalty of New Granada, including Bogotá itself on July 20, 1810.[8] On August 31, 1810, Joaquín Carrión y Moreno, *oidor* of the Royal Audiencia of Bogotá, sent to the Spanish Consejo de Regencia (the council appointed to govern Spain in early 1810 during Napoleon's invasion) a confidential report that included the names of the main leaders of the revolution recently started in New Granada.

Carrión mentioned José Acevedo, *regidor* (councilman) of Bogotá; the *canónigo magistral* Don Andrés Rosillo; Don Baltasar Miñano, *oidor* of the Audiencia of Quito; the royal mint's *contador,* Manuel Pombo, and all of his relatives in Bogotá and Cartagena; the acting *fiscal del crimen,* Don Frutos Gutiérrez; and the two *alcaldes ordinarios* of Bogotá.[9] Carrión and his colleagues in the audiencia had allegedly received news that patrician merchant Antonio Nariño Alvarez, along with the lawyer and priest Andrés Rosillo, *alcalde ordinario* Luis Caicedo, lawyers Joaquín Camacho and Ignacio Herrera, the treasurer of the Reales Cajas (also a lawyer) Pedro Groot, and "many lawyers who aspire to serve posts of *togado [fiscal* and *oidor]* in the Real Audiencia" had been plotting against the colonial authorities since October 1809 (shortly after Quito's elites had rebelled against local authorities and established their own governing junta). Some of these men had actually been jailed in late 1809 and early 1810.[10]

The composition of the Bogotá junta confirms that the lawyers Carrión mentioned were indeed that city's leading activists. Of the junta's six different occupational sectors, all representative of the upper social groups, lawyers were the most numerous (Table 4.1). Delegates from the lower classes, including the many tailors, masons, cobblers, or carpenters that could be found in the city, were conspicuously absent.[11]

Many of these lawyers, and other members of the junta, had not just professional but multiple family ties with other members of the legal profession outside of the junta. These ties suggest that the bulk of New Granada's legal community and its family networks backed the early moves that ultimately led to independence. Indeed, about one-sixth of New Granada's 130 to 150 lawyers were directly or indirectly linked to the Junta Suprema of Bogotá (Table 4.2).

In addition, at least a third of the members of the junta had strong family ties to one another. Thus, for example, soon-to-be military officer Antonio Morales

Table 4.1. Composition of the Junta Suprema of Bogotá, 1810

Occupation	July 27	October 24–25
Lawyers	8	6
Lawyer-priests	2	2
Lawyer-bureaucrats	4	3
Priests	5	4
Bureaucrats	5	3
Military	2	2
Merchants	3	2
Ranchers	2	1
Unknown	4	1
Total	35	24

Sources: Guillermo Hernández de Alba, *Cómo nació la república de Colombia. Documentos* (Bogotá, 1965), 77–80; Gómez, *El tribuno,* 277; García de la Guardia, *Kalendario manual;* Abello Salcedo, "La primera república," 423–53.

Table 4.2. Ties Between the Junta Suprema of Bogotá and the Legal Profession

Junta Member	Relationship: Other Lawyers in New Granada
Lawyers	
Frutos Joaquín Gutiérrez	*Brother-in-law:* Nicolas Ballén de Guzmán, teniente corregidor of La Mesa in 1806
	Half brother: José María Gutiérrez y Caviedes
Ignacio Herrera Vergara	*Son-in-law:* Bernabé Antonio Ortega
	First cousin: Luis Félix Vergara
	Distant cousin: Manuel S. Vallecilla
Luis de Azuola	*Uncle:* Francisco J. de Ugarte
Joaquín Camacho	*Brother:* Manuel Ignacio Camacho
	Brother-in-law: Antonio Martínez Recaman
Camilo Torres	*Brother:* Jerónimo Torres Tenorio
Tomas Tenorio Carvajal	*Uncle:* Jerónimo Torres Tenorio
Manuel Bernardo Alvarez	*Father:* Manuel Bernardo Alvarez Lozano
	Nephew by marriage: José Gíl Martínez Malo
Joseph Sanz de Santamaría	*Son:* Francisco Sanz de Santamaría
	Brother-in-law: Francisco de Vergara y Caicedo
	Brother-in-law: Francisco González Manrique
Juan Francisco Pey	*Brother-in-law:* Manuel de Andrade [lawyer-priest]
Other Nonlawyer Members	
Francisco Morales Fernández	*Father:* Francisco Morales Galavís
	Brother-in-law: Eustaquio Galavís
Antonio Morales	*Brother:* Francisco Morales Galavís
	Nephew: Eustaquio Galavís
Luis Caicedo y Flórez	*Brother-in-law:* Pedro Romero Sarachaga
	Father-in-law: José Antonio Leiva
	Brother-in-law: Joseph Sanz de Santamaría
Antonio Baraya	*Brother-in-law:* Agustín Caicedo Sánchez
José Vicente Ortega	*Brother:* Bernardo Antonio Ortega
	Brother-in-law: José Antonio Ricaurte Rigueiro
	Uncle: Crisanto Valenzuela
	Uncle: Ignacio Herrera Vergara

Sources: Restrepo S. and Rivas, *Genealogías de Santafé*; Hernández de Alba, "Galería de hijos insignes"; Pardo Umaña, *Haciendas de la sabana;* Plazas, *Genealogías de Neiva;* Restrepo Sáenz, "La familia de Nariño"; Arboleda, *Diccionario biográfico; Genealogías de Santa Fé de Bogotá* [1991].

and bureaucrat Francisco Morales were father and son; lawyer José Miguel and priest Juan Bautista Pey were brothers; lawyer-bureaucrat Tomás Tenorio was lawyer Camilo Torres's uncle; lawyer Miguel Pombo was the nephew of bureaucrat Manuel Pombo; and landowner Luis Caicedo and lawyer Joseph Sanz de Santamaría were brothers-in-law. The junta appears to have been a select clique of elite relatives and probably friends.[12]

Lawyers and their relatives were also active in the patriotic or revolutionary juntas created in other regions of the viceroyalty (Table 4.3). By contrast, as

Table 4.3. Lawyers in Other Juntas of the Viceroyalty

Junta (date)	Total Members	Lawyers	Percentage
Socorro (July 1810)	12	4	33.0
First Royalist *Cabildo*, Popayán (February 1811)	22	1	4.5
Cali (February 1811)	29	6	20.6
Cartagena (November 1811)	20	9	45.0

Sources: Zawadzky, *Las ciudades confederadas,* 101, 148; Rodríguez Plata, *La antigua provincia,* 26–27; Posada, *El 20 de Julio,* 257; Lemaitre, *Cartagena colonial,* 126–36.

Table 4.3 also indicates, the presence of lawyers in one of the royalist juntas created to oppose independence was insignificant. Indeed, the twenty-two members of Popayán's loyalist *cabildo* included only one lawyer.[13]

Lawyers' apparent dominance in the several juntas that started the movement to unseat the colonial authorities was bound to affect the extent and nature of that movement.

The 1810 Movement: Independence Without the People

The early movement for independence led by New Granadan lawyers was a true elite revolution. This elitism can be demonstrated by looking at lawyers' social origins, the measures taken by the early revolutionary juntas, and the elites' attitudes toward popular sectors of society.

Lawyers were mostly white male creoles who belonged to families of mineowners, landowners, merchants, and incumbent or former high-ranking military officers and bureaucrats. They rarely, if at all, belonged to mestizo, mulatto, or Indian families, the families of middle-ranking bureaucrats, or workers such as *escribanos* (clerks), *plateros* (silversmiths), or *boticarios* (pharmacy owners). As was established earlier, the narrowly select character of the profession was guaranteed by the demanding standards needed to gain admission to either of New Granada's two law schools.[14]

In addition, after they had occupied generally unpaid positions (*alcaldes mayores, síndicos procuradores, asesores*) in the elite-controlled *cabildos,* teaching law, demonstrating a familial tradition of bureaucratic service, and entering into appropriate marriage alliances with the relatives of at least middle-ranking bureaucrats, law graduates frequently joined the bureaucracy and attained high or middle managerial positions. They thus came to represent the interests of the upper echelons of colonial society, and those of the state itself.

More evidence of elitism can be found in the measures adopted by the Junta Suprema of Bogotá and others.[15] Shortly after its creation, the Bogotá junta issued repeated calls asking people to keep out of the streets and avoid any manifestation of "anarchy." Similarly, it requested that recruits brought to Bogotá by parish priests from neighboring towns disperse, return to their hometowns, and resume their routine activities. It even punished some popular leaders who had urged the junta to jail the viceroy and his wife. The junta also created a series of institutional channels for people to voice their complaints, so that any sort of popular mobilization could be preempted.[16] In each of Bogotá's neighborhoods, or *barrios,* the parish priest, who ordinarily came from an upper-class local family, along with another member of the local elite (either a lawyer, high bureaucrat, or large landholder), were put in charge of hearing people's complaints, making direct popular action or mobilization superfluous.[17]

Containing popular mobilization was also a concern of the juntas created in other regions of New Granada. In the southern city of Cali, near the traditionally loyalist city of Popayán, for instance, members of the junta grew alarmed when black slaves revolted in Raposo, a neighboring mining town. In mid-February 1811, the junta decided "to send a good priest to calm the slave gangs and make them understand that they ought to obey their masters and that if they insist on trying to break from slavery they will face much hardship."[18] On April 8, the junta decided to send two priests to convince the rioting slaves of "the mistake of their illusory freedom, source of infinite private and public disgraces." The junta ordered the priests "to dissuade those miserable people and make them understand that they face ruin if they do not correct their mistakes and go back to discharge their original obligations."[19]

Despite these measures and admonitions, the common people were generally far from docile. An eyewitness account of the events in Bogotá during the last months of 1810 clearly indicates that the treatment given to some of the members of the Real Audiencia, as well as to the viceroy and his wife—held as common prisoners, charged with crimes against society—was largely the product of popular demand, and was only reluctantly agreed to by most members of the "revolutionary" junta.[20] Accounts of the events in other regions also refer to the mobilization of the "lower" people in the early days of the movement. For instance, letters written from Cartagena in the early months of 1811 by Antonio Narváez y Latorre, lieutenant general of the royal army and a leading member of the *junta suprema* formed in that city, indicated the presence of "an infinite multitude of people with machetes, spears, *trabucos* (shotguns), and rifles" and described with alarm how these people "ran through the streets, forced doors and broke into houses, [and] detained some Europeans."[21] In the northeastern region of Socorro, the convent of the royalist Capuchin monks was assaulted by a crowd of *la plebe* (the populace), armed with stones and firearms, who cried "death to the filthy monks!," and insulted them "to the point of threatening them with spears and swords" and "grabbed and pulled out their beards."[22]

Even with these gestures of popular anger, however, it was also apparent that the common people were not willing to die for the revolution. The elite leadership saw that, despite the seemingly spontaneous and somewhat disordered enthusiasm of the masses, the majority of the population (particularly the black slaves, mestizos, *castas,* and Indians) was indifferent or even opposed to independence. Indeed, several Indian groups fought with the Spanish armies against the rebels. This was true of the Indians in the southern region of Pasto and the northern region of Cienaga.[23] Although some slaves from the interior allegedly were offered freedom by their masters if they joined the revolution, many others fought for the Crown. Miguel Tacón, governor of the southern province of Popayán and a staunch Spanish loyalist, reported to the viceroy in May 1812 that "the coastal blacks and those of the Popayán district have never been in favor of their masters, because they regard them as enemies of the king, and that is why blacks have volunteered to defend the government."[24] He noted by contrast that the revolutionary leadership was composed of "almost all of the nobles, the clergy, and the middle classes, all of whom by different means dominate the *plebe* in the volatile areas."[25]

Later evaluations of the revolutionary struggles, made by the elites themselves, attributed the prolongation of the revolution—which lasted more than a decade—to popular indifference. Reports to Congress by lawyer Alejandro Osorio, first minister of war and the treasury, lamented the popular indifference toward the revolution in the late 1810s. The soon-to-be minister of the interior, lawyer José Manuel Restrepo, writing to a merchant in late 1819, echoed Osorio's complaints. He said that in Medellín there was little support for the struggle: "the people are timid, and particularly in this town there is very little opinion in favor of the revolution." He explained the difficulties in consolidating the revolution during the 1810s by stating, "I believe that the republic failed because of the weakness of the new government, the little or nonexistent opinion in its favor and, above all, because people did not want to support it."[26]

Other historical evaluations made by elite descendants referred to the people's lack of involvement with contempt—and relief. One relative of elite revolutionary general José María Vergara Lozano, for instance, asserted that

> our emancipation was carried out, in general, by the most distinguished families, the most educated, the most respectful of law and true freedom, and that is why, in spite of the excesses and mistakes of all revolutions, the republic was organized under the law: *something very different would have occurred if emancipation had been headed by the irresponsible and ignorant populacho.*[27]

The biographies of other key participants in the revolution also emphasized that "the revolution was not carried out by the mass of the people. Just a minority supported the segment of Bogotá's upper classes who promoted the 'revolution.' The majority of the people conformed to and were even happy with the lives they led."[28] To be sure, these were the biased and exaggerated views of aristocratic, nonprofessional historians writing about their ancestors. Yet these views reflect particularly well the elites' self-perception of their commanding roles. The leadership of the dominant social groups is corroborated by research that shows the predominantly elite background of New Granada's high-ranking military officers in the revolutionary and postrevolutionary period.[29] The common people apparently did not play a direct role in triggering the revolution, nor did they furnish as much support as the elites would have wished during its course.[30] In this largely elite-led movement, lawyers are a good example of the reasons and the means by which elite groups ultimately seized the colonial state apparatus.

Alienation and Discontent among Lawyers

There is general evidence of the highly conservative attitudes of the majority of lawyers, both in Spanish America and elsewhere. Even in France, where members of this profession–particularly Parisian lawyers–were massively involved in the ideological struggles that helped bring the Revolution about, having an overwhelming presence (46% of the total) among the deputies of the Third Estate convened in Versailles in May 1789, and rallying to the patriot party, recent research has revealed the lawyers' deep-seated conservatism.[31]

New Granada's lawyers had earlier exhibited conservative attitudes during the Comuneros rebellion, a tax riot in the early 1780s. Lawyers and their relatives helped to negotiate the surrender of the antitax rebels or joined the royal militias organized to fight them. The same attitude emerged during an anti-monarchical plot in 1794–1795. As the previous chapter demonstrated, the young patrician merchant Antonio Nariño Alvarez, leader of the alleged conspiracy, could not find a single attorney to represent him in the city of Bogotá, where half of New Granada's lawyers lived. The city's attorneys were unwilling to contradict the colonial state, whose patronage was vital for the survival and advancement of themselves and their families. Indeed, the eagerness of New Granada's lawyers and their families to pursue all sorts of state jobs and prebends, their relatively significant presence in middle- and upper-level state positions, and their traditional disposition to support the colonial state held steady during the entire colonial period.[32] Nevertheless, much as the alleged plots uncovered during the 1790s seem to have had the active participation of some local *letrados* (priests, teachers, and lawyers), members of the legal profession, in what sometimes appears to be a conservative maneuver, became active during the movement for independence in Spanish America.

After 1810, the legal community's role in the revolutionary movement was far from passive. Indeed, as was suggested above, they led the drive toward independence. Ironically, some of the same lawyers who refused to help Nariño during the 1790s (Camilo Torres Tenorio being the most noteworthy) took their places among the revolutionary leaders of the 1810s. New circumstances determined the radically different stand lawyers took toward the colonial state starting around 1809. They seem to have resented the increasingly limited possibilities of gaining access to, and upward mobility in, the colonial bureaucracy. That is certainly what some lawyers claimed.

Less than a year before the Junta Suprema of Bogotá was established, one of its future members, the lawyer Ignacio Herrera y Vergara, wrote an analysis of the political, economic, and social situation of the colonies. Herrera y Vergara, a forty-one-year-old unsuccessful applicant to bureaucratic jobs, was serving at the time as a law professor at a local *colegio* and as *síndico procurador general* of the Bogotá *cabildo*. He summarized what he claimed was the collective feeling of his fellow lawyers, specifically with regard to their exclusion from key positions in the colonial bureaucracy:

> Americans cannot easily file their complaints before the Crown because of the long distance, and thus the Crown's *oidores* end up becoming sovereign arbiters of the

Americans' property, honor, and lives. Jobs as delicate as these should be entrusted to capable persons. A royal *cédula* issued under Charles III's benevolent kingdom established that applicants to these positions must not be considered unless they are lawyers with at least ten years of practical experience. This wise legislation has never been followed: In the American audiencias we run into many youngsters who have just obtained degrees of *bachiller* at Salamanca, Alcalá, or other universities. With no other knowledge than the principles of Roman Law that they learn in the classroom, with no practical training, and without ever having opened the Laws of the Indies, the largest and most valuable region of the monarchy comes to depend on their decisions. When some perceptive individual questions this situation, it is answered that these youngsters will do for America. And the lawyers born in the Indies, who have grown older working in their trade, see their bureaucratic aspirations delayed, and in order to have their *méritos* recognized have to rely on the favor, efforts, and not rarely the financial ruin of their families. The vast territories of the Indies follow the same banners and are vassals of the same sovereign. Why is it, then, that they are not provided with wise judges and are not given the right to choose those who, on the basis of their services, deserve judicial positions?[33]

At roughly the same time, in late 1809, New Granada was preparing to send envoys to participate in the Junta Central y Gubernativa in Spain. This body had recently decreed that Spanish dominions in America were not colonies but an integral part of the Spanish monarchy with rights of representation. The Bogotá *cabildo* prepared a document for the envoys to carry. Drafted by a creole lawyer, who was assessor of the *cabildo,* it summarized local reasons for discontent and pointed to the exclusion of Spanish Americans from the highest jobs as one of creoles' main concerns.[34]

Envoys sent by Spain to New Granada also reported that creoles or, more exactly, native sons (creoles born in the place where the specific jobs were requested), felt unjustly excluded from the government. In early 1810 the Consejo de Regencia, the small emergency committee gathered after the dissolution of the Junta Central, sent Captain Antonio Villavicencio as an envoy to New Granada with the mission of obtaining New Granadans' allegiance to the consejo and their material support for Spain's war against the French. Villavicencio, born in Quito in 1775, was the son of a Spanish *contador* of the Cajas Reales in that city who bore the title Conde del Real Agrado. During the early 1770s his father married the daughter of *oidor* Verástegui of the Bogotá Audiencia; young Villavicencio was brought up in Bogotá and studied at one of its local *colegios* during the 1780s. There he befriended several of the lawyers who ultimately led the movement in 1810. Because he had migrated to Spain in pursuit of a military career and had connections with these and other members of New Granada's elite, Villavicencio was sent by the Spanish regency to mediate with the unhappy creoles of that region.[35]

Upon his arrival in May 1810, Villavicencio wrote a letter to New Granada's viceroy summarizing the reasons for the *criollos*' discontent. After listing a series of complaints presented by the local elites regarding the fiscal and economic policies of the monarchy, he pointed out:

> one of the oldest complaints of Spaniards and Americans, which still persists, is the oblivion to which have been relegated many virtuous patricians who have served the

fatherland, and who, not having the means to undertake a trip to Spain and lacking patrons, become puppets of the vain hopes with which Spanish business agents [brokers] entertain them, later having to see newly arrived bureaucrats whose youth, inexperience, lack of talents, and other circumstances demonstrate that they were not worthy or appreciated even in Spain from whence they came.[36]

The letter included a list of the frustrated local candidates to public jobs, many of them lawyers native to New Granada and members of the clergy.[37] It also listed a number of Spanish officers and bureaucrats who, along with the lawyers and priests, deserved to be appointed to important bureaucratic jobs or promoted from positions they had held for too long.[38]

It should be recalled that *oidor* Carrión y Moreno's confidential report to the Consejo de Regencia three months later concerning the revolutionary activities of New Granadans also referred to the active role played by *doctores,* or "lawyers who aspired to serve in legal jobs," and had received no such appointments. Finally, shortly after *oidor* Carrión's report, two of these *doctores* themselves wrote a lengthy document justifying the revolt by echoing and elaborating on the foregoing complaints.[39]

All of these contemporary accounts, like most subsequent historical evaluations of the independence movement, refer to the exclusion of local elites from the state bureaucracy as a key cause of the revolution. In addition, they seem to suggest that the jobs lawyers held in New Granada were often not the highest and that upward mobility in the bureaucracy was too slow.[40]

Elsewhere I have indicated how tedious it was for the colonial elites to meet one strategic condition required to get a good job; namely, traveling to Spain.[41] Because of this and other obstacles, only sixteen of the forty-seven permanent *oidores* (i.e., excluding *supernumerarios* and *futurarios*) appointed to the Bogotá Audiencia from 1689 to 1798 were creoles, and only one native son was appointed *oidor* in the Audiencia of Bogotá during the entire eighteenth century.[42] Mark Burkholder and Dewitt S. Chandler have done extensive comparative research to show that although from the late sixteenth century until 1750 many Americans had been appointed to audiencia positions, later these conditions radically changed. From 1751 to 1775, only nine out of sixty-eight new officials named to the American courts were creoles, and between 1751 and 1808 only eleven native sons were directly appointed to their home courts. In consequence, many petitions were sent to the Crown calling for native-son appointments after 1770.[43] These data would tend to support the "exclusion from office" hypothesis in explaining the independence movement. Other evidence calls these justifications into question, or at least qualifies them.

Lawyers and the Late Colonial Bureaucracy

In spite of the claims made by contemporary lawyers and the complaints summarized in Villavicencio's letter, a number of lawyers who became prominent revolutionary leaders actually had highly successful careers in the colonial bureaucracy. Others were closely linked to highly placed administrators or had no further personal ambitions to join the bureaucracy themselves. For example, José María García de Toledo, the most conspicuous leader of the Cartagena junta, was brother-in-law of Joaquín Mosquera y Figueroa, the Audiencia of Bogotá's sole native *oidor*. García's wife was well connected as a sister-in-law of José de Mesía i Caicedo, *oidor* of a Real Audiencia until at least 1795.[44] Given his family background, services to the Crown, and marital alliances, García himself could very probably have become an *oidor* or *fiscal* of a Real Audiencia, had he so desired.[45] Apparently he simply did not aspire to these positions. Indeed, judging by his absence from Villavicencio's letter, García de Toledo, busy with ranching and trade at the time, was not interested in pursuing a bureaucratic career and must have supported the Cartagena junta for other reasons.[46]

Another lawyer in the Cartagena junta with close connections to the colonial bureaucracy was Eusebio María Canabal, acting *administrador principal* of Cartagena's *real renta de aguardientes* (the state liquor monopoly). In the mid-1810s, the Spanish colonial authorities promoted Canabal to *fiscal* of the Real Hacienda, and later to *fiscal* of the Superior Gobierno. Moreover, in 1816 and as late as 1820 he applied, with the viceroy's support, for a "position as *oidor* in Quito, Guatemala, or Caracas."[47] Another member of the Cartagena junta, Ignacio Cavero, could certainly have been interested in a promotion. Nevertheless, Cavero had been an insider in the fiscal bureaucracy for more than twenty years, rising from his original modest job of *oficial segundo* (clerk) of the Secretaría del Virreinato (which he had held in 1789) to the enviable position of *administrador* of Cartagena Customs, which, to the satisfaction of his merchant wife, he still held by 1815.[48]

The presence of lawyer-bureaucrats in other juntas is also revealing. The Socorro junta, for instance, included the *administrador* of the *renta de aguardientes, bulas y papel sellado* (state monopoly on liquor, the pope's edicts, and stamped paper), Miguel Tadeo Gómez; in Cali, José Antonio Dorronsoro, *administrador* of the *renta de aguardientes,* was also an active junta member.[49] Relatives of José Antonio Pérez y Valencia Arroyo, *contador* of the *renta de diezmos* (rent of tithes) in Popayán, led that city's junta.[50]

In several cases, therefore, it seems unlikely that junta activists could have been unhappy about the exclusion of their American-born clan members, or of themselves, from the state's ranks. Even if they did not hold the coveted job of *oidor* or *fiscal,* the bureaucratic posts and prebends they did occupy were among the highest available in their native provinces and the source of much prestige and power. Several lawyers in the juntas appeared dedicated to the *carrera de oficinas* (bureaucratic career) and followed the long tradition of *pretendientes* (applicants) to higher bureaucratic appointments.[51] Several members of the Bogotá junta, to give yet another example, were themselves high officials of the fiscal bureaucracy, a particularly important segment of the colonial state that employed numerous creoles and native sons (see Table.4.4).

Four years before the formation of the revolutionary juntas (and presumably still by the time they were created), about one-third of the lawyers in the district of the Audiencia of Bogotá were employed by the colonial state (see Table 2.2).

At least seven more New Granada lawyers held high judicial positions in audiencias outside the viceroyalty.[52]

The participation of native sons in New Granada's political and fiscal bureaucracy, and the various examples of local lawyers who by the late 1790s and early 1800s were occupying positions as *oidores* and *fiscales* in other regional audiencias, may have been insufficient in the eyes of some, but it gave enough hope to the less successful applicants. Even if discontented or dismayed at the difficulties they would face in climbing the bureaucratic ladder, most lawyers showed a willingness to accumulate *méritos* for a future job in the high bureaucracy by serving as *abogados de pobres;* accepting honorific jobs in the local city councils as *alcaldes ordinarios, asesores, síndicos procuradores;* looking for teaching positions; or holding low-paying jobs as *asesores* or *tenientes* of governors, *corregidores* in small villages, or *oficiales* in the fiscal bureaucracy. This was a colonial tradition.[53]

That this was a common attitude is suggested by numerous examples, such as José Félix Restrepo, Tomás Tenorio, Francisco Vergara Caicedo, and the above-mentioned Eusebio M. Canabal, all of whom had been pursuing bureaucratic careers since the late 1780s and early 1790s and would continue to do so until the 1810s. These and similar cases indicate that patience had always been an essential asset for bureaucratic job seekers. The aspirants' patience was rooted in historical experience; it came from seeing creole friends and relatives become high-ranking officials after years of waiting.[54]

In the meantime, these middle-level lawyer-bureaucrats and other lawyers outside the bureaucracy showed their reluctance to confront the Crown and went about their business as usual. Some made a living through ranching, mining, trade, or the priesthood; many others continued to polish and send *relaciones de mérito* (résumés) to the metropolitan authorities. Some of them never gave up

Table 4.4. The Junta Suprema of Bogotá and the Colonial Bureaucracy

Junta Member	Bureaucratic Position
Manuel Bernardo Alvarez	*Contador mayor,* Tribunal de Cuentas, 1803–1810.
José Sanz de Santamaría	*Tesorero,* Real Casa de Moneda.
Manuel Pombo	*Contador,* Real Casa de Moneda.
Luis Eduardo Azuola	*Contador de resultas,* Tribunal de Cuentas.
Pedro Groot	*Tesorero,* Cajas Reales de Santa Fé, 1806; *tesorero* Junta de Tribunales, 1809.
José Joaquín Camacho	*Corregidor,* Pamplona, until 1808; interim *corregidor,* Socorro, 1809.
José Martín París	*Administrador,* Renta del Tabaco.
Tomás Tenorio	*Fiscal,* Subdelegación General de la Renta de Correos.
Francisco Morales Fernández	*Contador,* Administración Principal de Aguardientes y Naipes.

Sources: García de la Guardia, *Kalendario manual;* Restrepo and Rivas, *Genealogías de Santafé;* Hernández de Alba, *Como nació la república,* 50, 77–80.

hope—not even during the revolution—that they could eventually win the major prize (*oidor*) in the kind of bureaucratic lottery they were used to playing.[55] Moreover, it has been shown that up to the early months of 1809, "the first instinct of leading creoles was to remain loyal to Spain and to await a political accommodation with the metropolis." Many lawyers campaigned to be elected delegates to Spain's Junta Central y Gubernativa that year.[56] Whatever was the primary motivation for lawyers' ultimately revolutionary actions, it evidently stemmed from more compelling motives than their exclusion from government.

Reconsideration of Lawyers' Grievances

Other more urgent factors must have been present to push this ordinarily conservative group to oppose the authorities. The cause is readily found by consulting some traditional sources and closely following the chronology of the events leading to "rebellion." In November 1809 and September 1810, lawyers within the Bogotá *cabildo* wrote two valuable explanations of why they and other elite figures saw it necessary to create governing juntas in the colonies.[57]

The first document, later known and revered as the *Memorial de agravios,* alluded to discrimination against creoles, but its central complaint concerned the number of *vocales,* or representatives, the American colonies had been invited to send to the Junta Central in Spain. In total the colonies were entitled to nine delegates, as opposed to thirty-six from the Spanish peninsular provinces. The document argued that given their territory, population, and wealth, the American colonies deserved a number of *vocales* similar to that of Spain. It offered a formula to complete the twenty-seven representatives the Americans were said to be lacking, and it proposed a substantial salary of between 10,000 and 12,000 pesos (twice the annual pay of a Buenos Aires *oidor*) per individual. The document concluded that if sending the additional representatives to Spain proved too expensive, *cortes generales* (parliaments) could be installed instead in America itself as parallel and juridically equal to the Spanish *cortes,* the traditional but long-dormant parliamentary assembly convened in 1809. The manifesto also insisted on the necessity of allowing the American colonies to follow the example of Quito, which had created a junta *provincial* much like the Spanish ones established in 1808, although it expressed regret for the "sad consequences of the Quito crisis," in which several elite figures had been jailed (and would later be killed).[58] Finally, it argued that the juntas were needed as a means for local society to participate in the government of the "kingless" empire and its colonies and prevent the usurpation of authority by a foreign power, namely, France.[59]

The *Memorial de agravios* was to be sent to Spain with Lieutenant General Antonio Narváez de Latorre, a prominent native of Cartagena who was elected New Granada's only delegate to join the Junta Central y Gubernativa after fierce competition with other eager candidates, several lawyers among them.[60] Narváez's departure was postponed for more than eight months due to the continuing French occupation of Spain. During those months political bargaining between government and elites failed; various of New Granada's local lawyers, priests, and bureaucrats, suspected of wanting to create governmental juntas, were accused of sedition and arrested, and three rebellious young men were summarily executed in late April.[61] The crisis worsened despite the arrival of Villavicencio as mediator in early May. In mid-June the local elites deposed the governor of Cartagena; *cabildo*-led revolts against local officials followed in the southern region of Cali on July 3, and the northeastern region of Pamplona on July 4. On July 10, 1810, elites in the northeastern province of Socorro, claiming that they were about to be "preemptively assassinated" like the many elite figures recently killed in Quito, jailed the recently arrived Spanish governor, and expanded the movement to create juntas, which soon spread throughout the territory.[62]

The September 1810 document, written after several juntas had been organized, offers a detailed chronology of events in the metropolis and the colonies from the time the Spanish juntas and the late Consejo de Regencia were created. It questions the legitimacy of these governing bodies and expresses rage at the idea that both Spain's and New Granada's royal officials should appear willing to "subject themselves to the domination of whosoever came to rule," an allusion to the French.[63] It describes the repressive measures taken by the audiencia and the viceroy during late 1809 and early 1810: removal of Spanish Americans from *corregimiento* jobs; incessant patrol of the cities; jailing and execution of local citizens; removal of rightful *cabildo* members or *regidores* from their seats; and staffing of the city councils with followers of the viceroy. Finally, the document attacks the actions of the Quito authorities against local citizens in late 1809 and questions the nature and activities of the early 1810 Spanish Consejo de Regencia.[64] The Consejo's clearly opportunistic use of American-born envoys such as Villavicencio to appease the colonies, its faked acknowledgment of the "freedom" and "equality" of the American-born Spanish, and its confiscatory measures to support the war against the French were especially abhorred.[65] All these factors, the document concluded, had forced Spanish Americans to withdraw their recognition of the Consejo de Regencia and to take the apparatus of colonial government into their own hands on behalf of the king.[66]

The political crisis in the Spanish peninsula therefore unleashed conditions appropriate for a "revolution from above," led ultimately by lawyers.[67] Lawyers were traditionally unwilling to oppose the colonial state and risk both their immediate freedom and their future bureaucratic careers. The political upheaval and the prosecution of Antonio Nariño Alvarez in 1795 made this evident. If during the 1810s lawyers were willing to participate in the seizure of the state apparatus, they changed only in response to a crisis in the metropolis that created chaos in New Granada. The lawyers became convinced that the government, in spite of the extraordinary situation facing the empire and the colonies, was unwilling to bargain or form wider governing coalitions, preferring instead to persecute and repress its subjects. They were also convinced that in the context of the Spanish crisis their behavior was lawful. Legalistic as they were, this was an important consideration.[68]

The reality of both creole, particularly native-son, exclusion from government and participation in the revolutions for independence seems somewhat more complex than contemporary actors and later historians have asserted.

Creole lawyers' and other elite individuals' active participation in the revolution was not motivated primarily by their exclusion from the colonial bureaucracy or by their difficulties in gaining access to it. Nor was it the logical and unavoidable conclusion of a long-term process of alienation from the Spanish establishment. Their revolutionary mobilization was instead a response to the overwhelming Spanish political crisis in 1808–1810 and the unwillingness of New Granada's government to bargain or to establish a wider interim governing coalition at the time. Those two conditions caused a radical shift (*ruptura*) in their loyalist attitudes and ideas and offered an opportunity for the somewhat hyperbolic expression of long-standing grievances by individual members of the upper social groups. Under ordinary circumstances these grievances would not have been enough to cause revolutionary collective action. Amid the crisis, however, these complaints turned into suitable and timely justifications for a movement to overthrow the highest Crown officials.

Colombia's independence movement started as a "revolution from above." It was led by precisely the upper social groups to which lawyers belonged and by some members of the high state bureaucracy itself. Lawyers and other members of the top echelons of colonial society had traditionally developed a symbiotic relationship with the colonial state. They had benefited, to a greater or lesser extent, from bureaucratic jobs and prebends, particularly fiscal posts and tax-farming positions. As long as the Spanish state was strong and stable, they would take no action against it. But when that state collapsed, creole lawyers and administrators were ready and able to engage in revolutionary maneuvers. Indeed, it became all the more important to take full charge of the colonial state to prevent new arrivals from Europe, either French or Spanish, from taking over. Once in power, such newcomers could break up the kinship and patronage networks that characterized those segments of the bureaucracy, and especially the fiscal apparatus, which for decades had been controlled by local elites.

Chapter 5
Kill All the Lawyers!

This chapter discusses the social and institutional mechanisms that allowed lawyers and other elite individuals to activate and command the early independence movement. Special reference will be made to the elite's capacity for collective action through notable family networks, connections with intellectual peers, former classmates, or fellow bureaucrats throughout the territory, as well as the elite's influence in the local city councils, or *cabildos*. However excluded they may have been from some upper-level offices, creoles had always been intimately involved with local government. Lawyers traditionally used these local councils as catapults for their bureaucratic careers. When a major political crisis arose, the *cabildos* would serve as key committees for the coordination of revolutionary activities and the capture of the state apparatus. This traditional space for sociability and politicking ultimately contributed to the triumph of independence.[1]

Lawyers and Collective Action

Some of the most innovative research on the root causes and progress of Latin America's independence has emphasized the significant revolutionary impact of new forms of "sociability"–*tertulias* and literary clubs, patriotic societies, and the like. These contributed to the development of *mentalités* (collective frames of mind, or *imaginarios*) of a "modern" type among the creole elites of Spain's American colonies. The new *imaginarios,* compared to traditional or "absolutist" *mentalités,* reflected a major transformation in views concerning the constitution of society and the nature of authority; namely, a shift from community orientation to individualism, royal to popular sovereignty, political *pactismo* to contractual relations, and absolute royal rule to the representation of the nation. Besides their major cultural effects, these new attitudes had cataclysmic political repercussions. In a short time, they helped turn the creoles' exalted loyalty to the Spanish king, which characterized this group's early reactions to the 1808 political crisis in the Iberian peninsula, into radical hostility to the throne. By 1810, this major cultural transformation produced a revolution.[2] This revolution, which was not carried out by a particular social class but by a "cultural class," was nothing but a great "cultural mutation."[3]

While cultural and ideological forces helped spark the revolution, it is also necessary to take into account creole elites' specific mechanisms for organizing collective action to overthrow the royal officials of different colonies. The discussion of sociability and *imaginarios* must be supplemented by studies of the ways creoles gathered together and organized collective mobilization. Radical ideas and literary or scientific meetings do not overthrow governments; governments fall as people gather resources, rally, and mobilize. In so doing, society elicits responses from its rulers, and these responses in turn may add further reasons to radicalize, mobilize, and plot.

As Charles Tilly has demonstrated, no matter how discontented a segment of society may become, it cannot engage in collective political action unless its members are part of at least minimally organized groups with access to some resources.[4] New Granada's lawyers certainly had the social, material, cultural, and organizational resources needed to promote such action. On the one hand, they occupied a social position that particularly enabled them to mobilize the elites and their subordinates; on the other, they had the intellectual and institutional capacity to articulate a populist ideology that could attract wide segments of the population, even the popular sectors if need be.

Lawyers' strategic social position included their tight and influential family networks and the connections established among individuals from different regions while studying at the Bogotá law schools. These connections were forged through participating in natural-science study groups created there after the 1780s, or serving together as bureaucrats in the same village or state agency. Another important factor was the capacity of local *cabildos*—of which lawyers and their families were traditionally conspicuous members—to mobilize the lower social groups and coordinate operations with other *cabildos* from distant regions. Several examples of lawyers active in the juntas of the key regions of Cali, Popayán, Cartagena, Socorro, Antioquia, and Bogotá illustrate some of these favorable conditions.

Lawyers Manuel Santiago Vallecilla and Ignacio Herrera y Vergara became the most visible and active links between the southern *cabildos* and juntas of Cali and its neighboring cities and the Bogotá junta.[5] Vallecilla belonged to the core of the *nobleza* and *familias principales* of Cali.[6] He was linked to the Caicedo clan, which along with the Borrero, Barona, Vergara, Ulloa, and Escobar networks was one of the leading upper-class families that led the *junta suprema* ultimately created in Cali.[7] Most of these families included large landholders, mineowners, members of the high clergy, and major merchants who together controlled the Cali *cabildo*.[8] Herrera y Vergara, Vallecilla's contemporary, classmate, and relative, was *síndico procurador* of the Bogotá *cabildo* in 1810, and had married into the influential Ortega Sanz de Santamaría family, an elite local clan.[9] Herrera led a creole faction within the Bogotá *cabildo* in disputes with local authorities concerning attempts by the local viceroy to staff the *cabildo* with his Spanish friends and followers. Herrera also served as Vallecilla's lawyer in a heated disagreement before the local audiencia between Vallecilla and his allegedly corrupt and arbitrary boss, the Spaniard Miguel Tacón, governor of Popayán.[10]

Lawyers Jerónimo and Camilo Torres and their colleague Santiago Pérez de Valencia y Arroyo took advantage of solid family links to coordinate the actions of the Bogotá and Popayán elites and *cabildos*. Besides lawyer Santiago, the Pérez de Valencia y Arroyo clan included Manuel Antonio, a mineowner; Andrés Marcelino, a priest who was part of the local cathedral's hierarchy; and José Antonio, *contador real de diezmos* (royal accountant of tithes). This family was typical of the top clans of Popayán, namely, the Mosqueras, Torres, Valencias, Hurtados, and Arboledas: large family groups of mineowners, landowners, merchants, priests, and lawyers who controlled the local *cabildo*.[11] Family members also had close links to Bogotá's elites. Lawyer Santiago Pérez, in particular, was a close colleague of his former classmate Jerónimo Torres. Important among the members of the mineowning Torres family was Jerónimo's brother Camilo, also a lawyer, assesor of the Bogotá *cabildo,* and active member of the Bogotá junta.[12]

Several lawyers who resided in Bogotá and belonged to or had strong connections with merchant families affected by the Spanish trading policies supplied the links between the Bogotá *cabildo* and the influential *cabildos* of Socorro and its neighboring regions, as well as Cartagena and Antioquia. They included lawyer Joaquín Camacho y Lago, *asesor* of the Bogotá *cabildo* and former bureaucrat in the northeastern regions of Pamplona and Socorro, and his previous classmate, good friend, and legal client, the merchant Miguel Tadeo Gómez Durán, a key bureaucrat from this area.[13] Gómez Durán, administrator of a royal monopoly in Socorro in 1810, was in turn the cousin and trading partner of the Spaniard José Acevedo y Gómez, a rebellious merchant based in Bogotá.[14] Both the lawyer Camacho y Lago, recently removed from his bureaucratic job, and the merchant Acevedo y Gómez, bitter about the loss of merchandise due to the Spanish authorities' refusal to authorize neutral trade to counter a British blockade, provided the contacts between the Bogotá elites and the *cabildos* of the northeast.[15] These *cabildos* were controlled by local elite clans such as the Plata, Ardila, Estéve, Durán, and Valenzuela families. These family groups were apparently led by Gómez Durán, who could recruit a large number of men to fight for the revolution if need be.[16]

Camacho y Lago and Gómez Durán also had a close friendship and continuous correspondence with their former classmate, lawyer Miguel Valenzuela. Valenzuela was *administrador* of the r*enta de correos* (rent of mail) in Socorro's neighboring region of Girón. He also participated in the 1810 movement along with his brother Eloy, Bucaramanga's wealthy parish priest, and his cousins, the young lawyers José Ignacio and Crisanto. Crisanto occupied an important bureaucratic job as *escribano de cámara* of the Bogotá Audiencia and was linked to the prominent Nariño and Ortega clans, which were actively involved with the Bogotá junta.[17]

Young lawyer Miguel Pombo, active in the Bogotá junta of 1810, helped to link the Bogotá and Cartagena elites through his influencial uncles: Manuel Pombo, former official of Cartagena's *consulado* and current *contador* of Bogotá's Casa de la Moneda (mint), and José Ignacio Pombo, founder, member, and ideologue of Cartagena's *consulado*. The juntas of Cartagena and Bogotá were further connected through lawyers José María García de Toledo, the prominent rancher and trader who was José Ignacio's colleague in the Cartagena *consulado,* and José María del Castillo y Rada. Castillo y Rada was a relative of Lieutenant General Antonio Narváez y Latorre, New Granada's representative-elect to the Spanish *cortes*. Before returning to Cartagena after finishing law school, Castillo y Rada had spent more than ten years in Bogotá. There he married, in 1804, a member of the Rivas family, a wealthy and influential local clan that supported and financed independence, and befriended the colleagues who would lead the Bogotá junta. Having conveniently moved back to Cartagena in 1809, the year before the juntas were first organized, Castillo y Rada, along with his younger brother and fellow lawyer Manuel, was active in the ensuing revolutionary incidents.[18]

Finally, lawyer and bureaucrat Pedro Groot formed a bridge between the Bogotá *cabildo* and the merchant elite of Antioquia. Groot was Bogotá's acting *tesorero* of the royal Board of [fiscal] Tribunals, and was a trading partner of Antioquia's merchant families Pérez de Rublas (Arrublas) and Corral. These families, whose sons Groot had sponsored when they came to study in Bogotá, led the juntas created in Antioquia.[19] Some other Antioqueño lawyers and merchants later active in the revolution, particularly José Manuel Restrepo, also developed extensive contacts in Bogotá through natural-science study groups established during their school years. The members (marked with * in Table 5.1) of these tightly knit groups of elite intellectuals returned to their native regions and, spread throughout New Granada as they were, eventually assisted in communications between the different *cabildos* and juntas.[20]

In sum, the independence movement was facilitated by a tight network of bureaucrats, merchants, and lawyers from the upper social groups, closely linked through friendship, business, family, bureaucratic, and intellectual ties. They may have shared *imaginarios* and probably belonged to the same "cultural class." More significant was the fact that they, their relatives, and friends controlled the *cabildos,* or city councils, and thereby could promote and coordinate collective action throughout the territory.

The *cabildos* struggled to maintain their relative economic independence and to become active regulatory bodies of local life. Not infrequently they disputed with colonial bureaucrats the right to police the local economy and society. These city councils certainly had influence over the popular sectors (economically dependent on the *cabildo*'s members and the *cabildo* itself), whom, with the help of local parish priests, they could convoke–and hope to control–with relative facility.[21] Influence over the common people also was made possible by the *cabildo* leaders' appeal to the populist ideology of "creolism."

The idea of common membership in a "creole society" was a unifying abstraction (perhaps the only one) that could bring together, on the one hand, the leaders of the independence movement–the rich landowners, merchants, mineowners, different sectors of the clergy, and incumbent bureaucrats; and on the other, the popular sectors, composed of the much-feared blacks, mestizos, and Indians.[22] To the elites it seemed not to matter much that some of their close relatives and immediate ancestors were European-born Spaniards.[23] In the midst of a serious political crisis in the metropolis, the elites appeared willing to create a common front against the local viceroy and his followers by appealing to the slowly growing feeling of creolism.

To develop among as many people as possible a common sense of "creole" identity, the elites used engaging metaphors and a new political language (e.g.,

Table 5.1. Lawyers and Other Elite Figures Who Helped to Link New Granada's Main *Cabildos* for Independence

Nature of Relationship		Name	Birthplace	Birth Date	Graduation Date or Activity	*Cabildos* Linked
1. Relatives, classmates, lawyer-client	1 {	Manuel Santiago Vallecilla	Cali	1766	1793	Cali
		Ignacio Herrera y Vergara	Cali	1769	1797	Bogotá
2. Brothers	2 {	Camilo Torres Tenorio	Popayán	1766	1794	Bogotá
		Jerónimo Torres Tenorio	Popayán	1771	1799	Popayán
3. Close friends	3 {	Santiago Pérez de Valencia y Arroyo	Popayán	1773	1803	
4. Close friends, lawyer-client	4 {	Miguel Tadeo Gómez Durán*	San Gil	1770	Bureaucrat	Socorro
		Joaquín Camacho y Lago*	Tunja	1766	1792	Bogotá-Tunja
5. Friends	5 {	Miguel Valenzuela*	Girón	1770	1796	Girón
6. Brothers	6 {	Eloy Valenzuela*	Girón		Priest	Bucaramanga
7. Cousins	7 {	Jose Ignacio Valenzuela	Gambita	1772	1804	Bogotá
8. Brothers	8 {	Crisanto Valenzuela	Gambita	1776	1803	Bogotá
9. Nephew-uncles	{	Miguel Pombo Pombo*	Popayán	1779	1805	Bogotá
		Manuel Pombo Ante	Popayán	1769	Bureaucrat	Bogotá
	9 {	José Ignacio Pombo Ante	Popayán	1761	Merchant	Cartagena
10. Friends	10 {	José María García de Toledo	Cartagena	1769	1792	Cartagena
		José María del Castillo Rada	Cartagena	1773	1802	Bogotá
11. Family-representative and partner	11 {	Pedro Groot y Alea	Bogotá	1755	1780	Bogotá
		José María Arrubla y M.	Antioquia	1780	Merchant	Medellín
		Juan del Corral†	Mompós	1778	Merchant	Medellín
12. Member of study groups linked to *†	12	José Manuel Restrepo	Envigado	1781	1808	Medellín

Sources: Restrepo y Rivas, *Genealogías de Santafé*; Zawadzky, *Ciudades confederadas*, 101; Arboleda, *Diccionario biográfico*; Escorcia, *Desarrollo social, político y económico*; Ortega Ricaurte, *Proceso histórico del 20 de Julio*, 26–28; "Torres y Tenorio, Jerónimo," 144–46; Martínez Delgado, *Noticia biográfica*, 106–7, 123, 263–94; Rodríguez Plata, *La antigua provincia del Socorro*, 173–75; Gómez, *El tribuno*, 221–25; Caballero, *Diario de la independencia*, 223; McFarlane, "Economic and Political Change in the Viceroyalty of New Granada," 304; García de la Guardia, *Kalendario manual*, 76; Jiménez Molinarez, *Linajes cartageneros*, 2:7; Guerra, "José Nicolás de Rivas, 343–66; Patiño Millán, "Factores de unidad en el Nuevo Reino de Granada," 105; Uribe and Alvarez, "El parentesco y la formación de las élites en la provincia de Antioquia," 92; Restrepo, *Autobiografía*; Garrido, *Reclamos y representaciones*, 36–54.

common membership in a "single family," resistance to "300 years of slavery"), and a series of modern symbols (e.g., the tree of liberty, the title of citizen).[24] The local oligarchy also appealed to the lower sectors with promises of popular sovereignty, "mass political participation" in the election of representatives to *juntas provinciales,* and opportunities for the development of economic activities (distilling *aguardiente* and processing tobacco) that up to then the Spanish monopolies had prohibited. Laws of free birth, and the abolition of both the slave trade and selected taxes–later much regretted–were also aimed at enlisting the lower social sectors in the swelling republican armies.[25] The opportunistic elites, using the *cabildos* (some now transformed into juntas), managed to magnify their protest against the undeniable majority presence of recently arrived Spaniards in many top positions, a situation that was not new, nor sufficient to provoke a revolt.[26]

The *cabildos,* therefore, served well the interests of the leaders of the 1810 "revolution from above." That revolution, however, did not follow the smooth course of an affair among friends and family, but soon degenerated into a bloody anticolonial war. In the meantime, though they could not hide their deep internal disagreements, the elites tried to establish a new institutional order.

Early Institutional Reforms and Internal Disputes

Between 1810 and 1815, the same local elites who had led the *juntas supremas* were busy writing constitutions and designing institutional reforms. They also spent precious time settling internal quarrels.[27] The most critical of these pitted the province of Cundinamarca, home of the most traditional and aristocratic families of the colonial period, as well as the most important central institutions of the Spanish colonial state, against the so-called Provincias Unidas de la Nueva Granada, a union organized in November 1811 that comprised nearly all of the rest of the provinces.[28] The quarrel revolved around Cundinamarca's reluctance to give up the considerable resources of its *Casa de la Moneda* and its desire to continue being the center of bureaucratic life, as it had been during the colonial period.[29] This conflict between Cundinamarca and the rest of the provinces produced the earliest clusters of political factions. Most of the provincial lawyers aligned with the "Provincias Unidas," whereas the lawyers of Cundinamarca (many of them with long bureaucratic trajectories in the colonial state) supported the government headed by Antonio Nariño Alvarez and his relatives, particularly his uncle, the lawyer and experienced colonial bureaucrat Manuel Bernardo Alvarez y Casal.[30]

Despite these disputes, the elites also held a series of congresses and constitutional conventions in the different regions during the first half of the 1810s (Table 5.2). These congresses demonstrated their highly legalistic proclivities and produced constitutions and diverse other measures that eventually hindered the full restoration of Spanish control. Lawyers were once again in the front line, although they were more numerous in the constitutional gatherings of Cundinamarca than anywhere else and were less important in a few regions, like Tunja, where they were overshadowed by other sectors, mostly priests.[31]

The rapid enactment by the revolutionaries of numerous local, provincial, and national political constitutions during the early 1810s represented the beginnings of a new postcolonial state.[32] These documents were not merely theoretical achievements; they implied practical consequences, such as the actual implementation of local elections, no matter how restricted.[33] More important, they also brought about the participation on an equal footing of formerly dissimilar regions and eliminated various political and economic institutions that—sometimes in theory, other times in practice—were replaced by new judicial, legislative, and political institutions. All of this disrupted the administrative routines formerly followed by the Spaniards and complicated Spain's efforts to regain military and political control over the colony.

Taxation was a clear example of the difficulties that the Spanish authorities faced during the second half of the 1810s due to the institutional changes introduced by the revolutionaries. A report published by the Spanish authorities during the *reconquista* of Cartagena complained that the revolutionaries' "flamboyant" economists thought that it was easy to abolish and create new revenue sources, which they did without actually being able to collect the new taxes.[34] The Spaniards therefore had to carry out a painstaking reorganization of state institutions while simultaneously engaging in fierce repression of the revolutionary movement.

Expansion of the Movement

During the 1810s and early 1820s, all of New Granada became a military battleground. The revolutionary leaders radicalized their demands; if initially they had declared their desire to govern on behalf of the absent Spanish king, later, starting with Cartagena in November 1811, region after region (Tunja in December 1811 and December 1813, Antioquia in May 1812 and August 1813, Cundinamarca in July 1813) openly fought for complete autonomy from the home country. The Spanish monarchy, restored in 1814, in its turn stubbornly tried to hold on to power, ultimately taking a hard line.

The Crown first offered a combination of rewards to cities or individuals who appeared loyal to the king. Loyal towns were promoted to the rank of "noble and loyal" or "faithful" cities; loyal individuals were rewarded with the Order of Isabella the Catholic, special medals, and bureaucratic jobs. In addition, amnesties and pardons were granted to the revolutionaries in December 1812, May 1816, December 1817, and March 1819.[35] However, the Crown generally considered severe repressive measures to be more effective.[36] Large armies were brought from overseas, and a serious military campaign was launched in late 1815 through the second half of the decade.[37]

This campaign made possible the return to Bogotá, six years after its expulsion, of the Royal Audiencia, which had functioned in Cartagena and Panama from March 1812 until late 1816.[38] It also determined the execution of a large number of lawyers whose revolutionary influence was deemed too threatening. Many of these lawyers, while engaged in conflicts against the Spaniards and amongst themselves, had helped to introduce the institutional reforms outlined

Table 5.2. Participation of Lawyers in Institutional Reforms, 1810–1815

Signatories of	Total	Lawyers	Percentage
Constitution of Cundinamarca March 30, 1811	41	15	36
Declaration of Independence of Cartagena November 11, 1811	20	9	45
Provincias Unidas of New Granada's Union Proclamation November 27, 1811	5	4	80
Constitution of Tunja December 9, 1811	87	1	1
Reformed Constitution of Cundinamarca April 17, 1812	60	26	43
Constitution of Antioquia May 12, 1812	19	0	0
First National Congress, Villa de Leiva October 4, 1812	11	10	90
Constitution of Cartagena June 15, 1813	34	10	29
Declaration of Independence of Cundinamarca July 16, 1813	46	13	28
Constitution of Mariquita June 21, 1815	13	1	7
Reformed Constitution of Antioquia July 6, 1815	5	3	60

Source: Pombo and Guerra, *Constituciones de Colombia*, vols. 1 and 2, passim; García de la Guardia, *Kalendario manual.*

earlier, which seriously disrupted Spanish administration and control of New Granada.

After their arrival in Bogotá in 1816, the Spanish military commanders, headed by General Pablo Morillo, established war tribunals to examine locals' recent activities. Lawyers were a favorite target of these trial-like processes, following which many of the guilty were summarily executed. Indeed, at least twenty-eight of the numerous individuals executed by the Spaniards in the 1810s were lawyers—close to one-fourth of the entire legal community at the time (Table 5.3). The executed belonged to key elite families throughout New Granada. Some were relatives of high-ranking bureaucrats; others were members of the families of wealthy merchants, landowners, or mineowners. Of the lawyers executed, Manuel Bernardo Alvarez y Casal was the oldest at seventy-three, and thirty-year-old José León Armero the youngest. José María Lombana, twenty-eight, died in prison, allegedly from ill treatment. The executed were evenly distributed by region, although Cartagena, Tunja, and Bogotá, each with four, lost the most, followed by Popayán and Cúcuta, each of which lost three. Most of these lawyers had graduated in the 1780s and 1790s. The newest members of the profession had graduated in 1807, 1808, and 1809. None of those executed had graduated after 1810.[39]

Lawyers were clearly favorite targets of the Spanish repression. Thirty-three-year-old Benedicto Domínguez, who had entered the legal profession in 1809, denied that he was a lawyer during his interrogation by Commander Pablo Morillo. He knew that Morillo was especially harsh with the members of this profession, whom he blamed for the revolution.[40]

Indeed, in March 1816, General Morillo had reported to the Spanish Ministry of War that to contain the ongoing revolutionary avalanche, Spanish lawyers must be sent to New Granada to replace the local ones.[41] Meanwhile, Morillo created two antirevolutionary tribunals, the *Consejo de Purificacion* to try the suspected revolutionaries, and the *Junta de Secuestros* to confiscate their properties.[42] As the data in Table 5.3 indicate, he tried to eliminate as many local lawyers as possible.[43]

It was not uncommon, however, to replace severe physical punishment, even death sentences, with fines. The most likely candidates to benefit from this treatment were, of course, those able to pay. Although General Morillo vehemently defended himself against such charges, it was said that bribes played a major role in sparing punishment for some of the revolutionaries.[44] Social connections and friendship were also useful in obtaining pardon.[45] On the other hand, many of the lawyers who were neither pardoned nor killed were punished in other ways: jailed, conscripted into the royal army, banned from the profession, and/or their properties confiscated.[46] A few others took advantage of the situation to reaffirm their loyalty and obtain bureaucratic jobs and promotions. Some even took positions in the *Consejo de Purificación* and *Junta de Secuestros,* which had prosecuted their colleagues so harshly.[47]

Rewards, pardons, and deals notwithstanding, Spain's repressive treatment of lawyers incurred a high cost. It made the surviving members of the elite all the more determined to expand the revolution until it succeeded.[48] It also contributed to a degree of revolutionary unity, which had been elusive in the previous years, when internal disputes had consumed much of the revolutionaries' time and resources. Given the need to respond to the Spanish military campaign, those intra-elite quarrels were abandoned, and local elites at the head of large armies finally defeated the Spanish military in the early 1820s.[49]

Lawyers' leadership in unleashing revolutionary collective action was facilitated by the dominant role that they and their families traditionally played in the city councils, or *cabildos*. The *cabildos* helped them mobilize both elite and popular sectors; they were also the vehicles through which the elites articulated the revolutionary ideology of "creolism." Consisting of the rejection by Spanish Americans of continental Spaniards' exclusive right to rule, "creolism" was opportune, expedient, and populist. Under the close supervision of the elites, all ethnic and social groups were expected to add their individual grievances and

Table 5.3. Lawyers Executed during the Spanish Antirevolutionary "Terror"

Lawyer	Birthplace	Date	Admitted to Bar	Executed
Alvarez y Casal, Manuel Bernardo	Bogotá	1743	1769	1816
Ardila, Antonio	Socorro	?	?	1816
Armero, José León	Mariquita	1786	?	1816
Ayos, Antonio José	Cartagena	1764?	1789	1816
Benítez Plata, Emigdio	Socorro	1766	1793	1816
Caicedo de la Llera, Francisco A.	Cali	1765	1790	1816
Caicedo y Cuero, Felipe Joaquín	Cali	1773	1798	1813
Camacho Rodríguez, José Joaquín	Tunja	1766	1787	1816
Cañete, Manuel	Cúcuta	?	?	1815
Castillo, Manuel	Cartagena	1781	1804	1816
Dávila, José María (Antioquia)	Rionegro	?	1807	1816
Díaz Granados, Miguel	Cartagena	1772	1794	1816
García de Toledo, José María	Cartagena	1769	1792	1816
García Rovira, Custodio	Bucaramanga	1780	1809	1816
Gutiérrez, Frutos Joaquín	Cúcuta	1770	1796	1816
Gutiérrez Moreno, José Gregorio	Bogotá	1781	1804	1816
Hoyos, Joaquín de	Antioquia	1773?	1798	1816
Lombana Cuervo, José María	Bogotá	1781	1804	1816*
López de Tagle, Juan Elías	Cartagena	1777	1804	1819
Matey de Piedri, Juan Nepomuceno	Cúcuta	1766	1806	1816
Niño, Juan Nepomuceno	Tunja	?	?	1816
Peña y Valencia, José Gabriel	Pamplona	?	?	1816
Pombo Pombo, Miguel	Popayán	1779	1805	1816
Torres Tenorio, Camilo	Popayán	1766	1794	1816
Umaña López, Joaquín	Tunja	1768	1793?	1816
Ulloa Campo, Francisco Antonio	Popayán	1766	1808	1816
Vargas, Ignacio de	Charalá	1771	1794	1816
Vásquez, José Cayetano	Tunja	?	?	1816

Sources: García de la Guardia, *Kalendario manual,* 57–72; Restrepo S. and Rivas, *Genealogías de Santafé;* Hernández de Alba, "Galería de hijos insignes del Colegio de San Bartolomé"; Páez Courvel, "Precursores, mártires y próceres," 476–94; Jiménez Molinares, *Linajes Cartageneros;* Arboleda, *Diccionario biográfico y genealógico;* Plazas, *Genealogías de la provincia de Neiva;* Nicolas García Samudio, *Reconquista de Boyacá en 1816* (Tunja, 1916).

*Died in jail.

dissatisfactions to this broad ideological "melting pot" of American complaints. Lawyers contributed their bureaucratic frustrations, which alone were not new or sufficient to cause a revolt. They then proceeded to lead the elite creole capture of high state jobs.

In trying to take over the state apparatus, lawyers and their elite peers produced much social and institutional disruption. Socially, they presided over the mobilization of unruly masses of Indians, black slaves, and *castas*. Having disrupted the traditional regional hierarchies, they also facilitated the rise of provincial sectors to leading political positions. Institutionally, they distorted traditional administrative arrangements and routines, created new offices and taxes, and enacted numerous bodies of legislation. The social and institutional chaos they helped unleash earned them the decided enmity of the Spanish Crown which, along with attempts to pardon, negotiate, and conciliate, savagely repressed them, particularly after the restoration of King Ferdinand VII in late 1814. Subsequently, their elite families, friends, and supporters, overcoming ideological and social differences, deepened the revolution and brought it to completion. The radicalization of the creole elites resulted, therefore, not just from the "mobilizing" force of a new political language and *imaginarios,* but as a response to physical repression on the part of the Crown. Repression, probably more so than ideas, gave the creole elites their resolve to expand the revolutionary movement.

In the process of deepening the revolution, the revolutionary elites helped erode the traditional regional and social hierarchies that had characterized colonial society. They thus opened the way to the participation of new social forces in politics and state management. In the long run, this meant that the state, from which elites and their families traditionally derived the significant status-honor they were intent on maintaining, slipped away from their exclusive control.

Chapter 6
Changing Generations and Regions in the 1820s

As one examines the social characteristics of New Granada's postcolonial lawyers, who were among the key state officials administering and shaping the postcolonial state, the generational, regional, and social changes become apparent. Political patterns similar to ones observed in other Spanish American regions also emerge. A largely civilian political scene continued to prevail, even in the midst of frequent military conflicts over control of the state, and political participation on the part of the "middle sectors" appears to have been intense.[1] It also becomes clear that understanding the colonial background is essential to make sense of the true nature of postcolonial social changes and political conflicts, many of which were the direct result of both the erosion of the social stratification prevailing in the colonial period and the way postcolonial society regarded the state.[2]

The Early Postcolonial Bureaucracy: Senior and "Transitional" Lawyers

Although they do not in themselves explain the nature of early postcolonial politics, significant generational changes in political leadership did occur after independence. Soon after the rebels' decisive military triumph against the royal armies in 1819, young members of the legal profession began to play a central role in New Granada's postcolonial state bureaucracy and in Congress. What can be labeled a "transitional generation" of high-ranking lawyer-bureaucrats and congressmen emerged. This socially mixed generation significantly displaced the senior colonial lawyers who had furthered independence but, for various reasons, did not gain access to leading positions in the postcolonial state, a continuing source of status-honor avidly pursued by the members of the legal profession. The transitional generation consisted of a group of lawyers trained between 1805 and 1819, who therefore spent their formative years within the context of the independence revolution (see Appendix 3). Two-thirds of the forty to fifty individuals who entered the legal profession in these years became public functionaries and/or members of parliament. One could add to this generation the even younger group of nearly sixty more lawyers who graduated during the 1820s, two-thirds of whom also became state officials or congressmen.

This young generation filled the early republic's most important and strategic public positions for a variety of reasons. As we may remember, a significant number of the senior colonial lawyers who had promoted independence–about a quarter of the total legal profession–were killed during the 1810s (Table 5.3). Another 10–15% died of old age shortly before or after independence (see Appendix 2). Others never entered the new bureaucracy; instead, they retired to their estates and devoted themselves to agriculture, or spent their time in other activities.[3] Several more were simply excluded from the bureaucracy owing to their antirevolutionary views. There was reluctance in the high spheres of government to appoint those senior lawyers who, in the opinion of the new state officials, had cooperated until very recently with the Spanish authorities. Only lawyers "de un patriotismo a toda prueba" ("proven patriotism") were eagerly appointed to state positions by the Consejo de Gobierno.[4] In addition, not a few lawyers, probably including several of those who dropped out of the historical records (see Appendix 2), chose to emigrate.[5] Only one small group of senior lawyers–in many respects, a new, postindependence reincarnation of the upper colonial bureaucrats–reached high administrative positions.[6] But even these few senior colonial lawyers in the high bureaucracy vanished from the political scene due to death, retirement, and other causes in the 1820s and early 1830s. The bureaucratic ground was mostly left to younger members of the profession.

The earliest examples of young lawyer-bureaucrats in top state positions include Estanislao Vergara Sanz de Santamaría and Alejandro Osorio. Vergara was handpicked by General Bolívar to be the first minister of the interior of the government established in New Granada after the triumph of 1819. A twenty-nine-year-old lawyer he was the grandson, son, nephew, cousin, and brother of former high colonial bureaucrats (see Chapter 3, and Figure 3.2 on the "Vergara Bureaucratic Network, 1740s–1810s").[7] He and several of his relatives continued in the bureaucratic footsteps of their traditional colonial family.[8] The new minister of war and fiscal affairs was also a twenty-nine-year-old lawyer, Alejandro Osorio, son of either a colonial artisan or an artist. Although he was from a middling social background–his mother ran a bakery–Osorio was linked to traditional Bogotá families such as the Caicedos (see Appendix 4). Probably thanks to their sponsorship, he too was handpicked by the victorious military commanders to serve as a minister.[9]

Nineteen of the other twenty-seven lawyers who were given high bureaucratic jobs after the 1821 Congress of Cúcuta also belonged to this transitional generation (see Table 6.1).[10] Whereas the senior lawyers among the early bureaucrats were appointed mainly as judges, the transitional lawyers were generally given more politically strategic jobs, such as secretary of the interior or intendant of key regions like Cundinamarca, site of the state's administrative capital of Bogotá.[11] Throughout the decade new law graduates garnered more and more positions which, along with the ongoing displacement of the senior lawyers, greatly strengthened the power of the younger generation.[12] Not all of these youngsters were democrats at heart, as some historians have argued; a number of transitional aristocrats, like their seniors, favored authoritarian politics.[13]

Besides the significant generational change outlined above, important changes also occurred in the civilian composition of the bureaucracy and the regional

Table 6.1. New Granada Lawyers in High State Jobs, 1821

Position	Name	Birthplace	Provincial/ Aristocrat*	Admitted to Bar / Age
Secretaries of State				
Hacienda	J. M. Castillo	Cartagena	Aristocrat	1802 / 48
Interior	J. M. Restrepo	Antioquia	Provincial	1808 / 40
Judges				
Alta Corte	Félix Restrepo	Antioquia	Provincial	1786 / 61
	J. M. Cuero	Cali	?	1806 / 43
Corte Suprema	Miguel Tobar	Cundinamarca	Aristocrat	1809 / 39
	Diego F. Gómez	Socorro	Provincial	1820 / 35
	Nicolas Ballén	Cundinamarca	Aristocrat	1797 / 50
	Antonio Viana	Honda	Aristocrat	1793 / 52
	Joaquín Ortíz	Buga	Aristocrat	1794 / 54
	Alejandro Osorio	Cundinamarca	Aristocrat	1811–17 / 31
	Ignacio Herrera	Cali	?	1797 / 52
Fiscales				
Alta Corte	Vicente Azuero	Socorro	Provincial	1817 / 34
Corte Suprema	Ignacio Márquez	Boyaca	Aristocrat	1817 / 28
	Vicente Borrero	Cali	?	1808 / 33
Councilors				
Intendente	Francisco Soto	Pamplona	Provincial	1810 / 32
	Agustín Barona	Cali	?	1804 / 41
	Henrique Rodríguez	Cartagena	?	1789 / 56
	Estanislao Vergara	Cundinamarca	Aristocrat	1813–17 / 31
Governor	Manuel J. Ramírez		?	1804 / 38
	Ignacio Muñós	Cartagena?	Provincial	?
	Salvador Camacho	Casanare	Provincial	1820 / 30
	Estevan Díaz G.	Cartagena	Aristocrat	1806 / 41
	Ildefonso Méndez	Cartagena	?	1811 / 37
	Bernardino Tovar	Cundinamarca	Aristocrat	1819 / 35
	Juan B. Valencia	Pamplona	?	pre-1806 / 45
	José María Baloco	Cartagena	?	1821 / 36
Other Jobs				
Contador General	José Sanz de Santamaría	Cundinamarca	Aristocrat	1790 / 55
Contador Auxiliar	Francisco Ugarte	Cundinamarca	Aristocrat	1810 / 34
Oficial Mayor Secretaría Interior	Casimiro Calvo	Cundinamarca	Aristocrat	1808 / 37

Sources: Gaceta de la Ciudad de Bogotá, nos. 126 and 127, December 1821; García de la Guardia, *Kalendario manual; Actas Cúcuta,* 744–55.

*Definitions of these terms can be found in the Introduction, Chapter 1, and text below between notes 29 and 83.

origins of both bureaucrats and military officers. These changes further help us to make sense of early postcolonial politics and state-building.

Conflictive Coexistence of New Granada's Lawyers with the Venezuelan-dominated Military

Both the protracted war for independence and the creation of an expedient politico-military union among several colonial regions produced significant social and political changes. The few colonial lawyers left in New Granada and their new transitional colleagues had to share the political scene with a considerable number of soldiers and military officers. The latter were mostly Venezuelans.

In spite of various divisive factors of an administrative, geographic, and ethnic nature, during the 1810s Venezuelans and New Granadans combined their military might to defeat the Spanish.[14] Their de facto cooperation turned into a formal constitutional pact, arranged during congresses held in 1819 and 1821 in Angostura (today Ciudad Bolívar), a village located in Venezuela's eastern province of Guayana, and Cúcuta, a village in northeastern New Granada near the border with Venezuela.[15] Of the seventy-one members of the 1821 Constitutional Congress in Cúcuta, forty-two were New Granadans and twenty-eight Venezuelans (one delegate was a lawyer from New Spain, today Mexico).[16] Lawyers, priests, and military officers comprised two-thirds of the delegates, with lawyers being the most numerous. They represented 59 percent of the New Granada delegation, and almost one-half of the entire Congress. New Granadan lawyers also participated actively in subsequent congresses (see Tables 6.2 and 6.3).

Priests were less well represented in New Granada's congressional delegations and the bureaucracy in general. Nevertheless, although the Church's power had diminished during the early postcolonial state, the clergy retained considerable ideological power. Priests were influential in decision making, the actual government of the state, and disputes among political factions.[17] Factional struggles, however, were usually perceived not as disputes between civilians and the clergy, but as a contest between the civilian and military sectors for control of the state apparatus.

Table 6.2. Regional Origin and Occupation of Delegates to the Congress of Cúcuta, 1821

Region	Lawyers	Priests	Officers	Other	Total
Venezuela	7	9	5	7	28
New Granada	25	3	0	14	42
New Spain	1	–	–	–	1
Total	33	12	5	21	71
Percentage	46	17	7	30	100

Sources: Actas Cúcuta; Gaceta de Colombia, October 14, 1821.

Table 6.3. Occupation of Delegates to Greater Colombia's Early Parliaments

Congress	Lawyers	Officers	Priests	Unknown	Total
1823	28	9	5	47	89
1824	27	5	5	37	74
1825	30	1	9	47	87
1826	26	4	7	49	86
1827	26	2	4	100	132

Sources: *Actas Congreso 1823, Actas Cámara 1824, Actas Senado 1825;* Pérez Perdomo, *Los Abogados en Venezuela; Gaceta de Colombia,* October 14, 1821; January 9, 1825; January 15, 1826; January 7, 1827.

The dynamic of the anticolonial war led to the creation of an army that far outnumbered colonial forces.[18] During most of the 1820s, the army consumed a great part of the state's revenues, seriously contributing to the fiscal crisis. In 1825, for example, military spending still accounted for more than two-thirds of the 15.5-million-peso national budget, 5.5 million of which represented deficit spending.[19] This level of spending deeply worried civilian sectors, who started to clash with the army.

Civilian-military disputes paralleled and combined with mutual antipathies between New Granadans and Venezuelans, which first surfaced in the mid-1810s and intensified thereafter.[20] The army's officer ranks were composed of a greater number of Venezuelans than New Granadans. The predominance of Venezuelan officers was widely resented, so much so that by the mid-1820s, according to a contemporary observer, the New Granadans felt that their territory was becoming a "colony" of the Venezuelan military.[21] Many of the Venezuelan officers were upwardly mobile nonwhites promoted because of their heroism, and who now outranked members of the white New Granadan elite.[22]

The sheer size of the army, its effects on the state's budget, and its social and regional composition turned into a major source of conflict between the civilian political elite and the army.[23] From the outset, the high bureaucracy of the new state reflected the civilian-military split. This bureaucracy, appointed by the 1821 Constitutional Congress or by Generals Bolívar and Santander themselves, was composed of a competing mix of lawyers and military men (Table 6.4).[24]

As Table 6.4 indicates, numerous military officers from both regions were given high-level bureaucratic jobs. In addition to the appointment of a general as one of the secretaries of state, generals and colonels were also at the head (as *intendentes*) of six of the seven *departamentos*. All of the provincial governors were members of the military,[25] and officers were given numerous municipal-level posts. The military's high share of power remained unchanged until almost the late 1820s, principally because ongoing military operations in New Granada until 1823, and in Peru until 1826, demanded active military involvement.[26]

Following the colonial tradition of pursuing jobs in the bureaucracy to increase one's individual and familial status, lawyers were the military's strongest

Table 6.4. Civilians and Military Personnel in High State Positions, 1821

Position	New Granadan Military	New Granadan Civilian	Venezuelan Military	Venezuelan Civilian
President	0	0	1	0
Vice president	1	0	0	1
Secretary of State	0	3	1	0
Departmental intendant	1	1	5	0
Intendant's councilor	0	3	0	3
Provincial governor	7?	0	8?	0
Governor's councilor	0	8	0	1*
Senators	2	13	5	7
Justices and *fiscales* of high courts	0	12	0	11
Total	11	40	20	23

Sources: *Actas Cúcuta; Gazeta de la Ciudad de Bogotá,* nos. 126 and 127, December 1821; Pérez Perdomo, *Los abogados en Venezuela.*

*Other data from Venezuela, where seven more lawyers should have filled these jobs, are missing.

competitors for state positions. Fourteen of the New Granadan lawyers who participated in the Cúcuta Congress were appointed to high bureaucratic positions, and three were also elected to the future Senate. Another fifteen lawyers from this region who did not attend the 1821 Congress were also appointed to bureaucratic jobs. Six more were elected to the Senate, and in fact, eleven of New Granada's sixteen senators were lawyers.[27] In all, approximately thirty-five New Granadan lawyers were among the sixty civilians who were given high-ranking state positions at the 1821 Congress and/or soon afterwards (see Tables 6.1 and 6.4). Several more lawyers entered the state ranks later in the decade.[28]

Various of the aristocratic lawyers in this group and nearly all of the provincials pushed for the demilitarization of the state apparatus in the late 1820s. By then, major changes had taken place in the social background of New Granada's lawyers. Such changes were perhaps even more significant than the generational shifts, or the regional and civilian-military changes and ensuing tensions.

Upward Mobility Unleashed by Independence: The Rise of the "Provincials"

The wars of independence and the attendant political upheavals inaugurated a process of upward mobility for formerly marginalized individuals and regions. This mobility translated into wider access to educational institutions and state employment for new sectors of the population. Unlike the senior colonial lawyers or young aristocrats, many of the new law graduates and bureaucrats came from families or regions that did not have a history of high bureaucratic service nor, therefore, high status-honor during the late colonial period.[29]

Several factors promoted the entry of nontraditional and nonelite individuals into law schools. A law issued by the Congress of Cúcuta determined that children of fathers who had died fighting for independence would be educated free of charge in primary schools and colleges.[30] Although the state's fiscal crisis limited the number of fellowships for poor applicants, several examples suggest that this law was in fact enforced.[31] At the same time that some economic obstacles to education were reduced, moral and ethnic restrictions were also lifted gradually. From as early as 1822, the authorities began to receive petitions to admit individuals of illegitimate birth into law school and to grant them degrees.[32] In 1823, Congressman Isidro Arroyo complained to the executive authorities that the local Colegio Mayor "has not wanted to receive one of his sons...arguing that he had not submitted all of the customary documents to prove his legitimate birth." Arroyo claimed that the real obstacle to his son's admission was that the applicant was a *pardo*. The Consejo de Gobierno decided that, although it was indeed necessary to prove the applicant's legitimate birth, race could not be considered an obstacle, because "by the constitution and new regulations of Colombia, public institutions must be common and open to every class in society."[33] Laws granted citizenship rights to Indians and afforded them fellowships to enter educational institutions,[34] and a contemporary later remembered that Indians and mulattos were gradually admitted into the schools.[35] The decline of racial restrictions throughout the 1820s made it possible to count a least a few "ilustrados indígenas" ("illustrious Indians") like Rafael María Vásquez among the local lawyers who graduated in the early 1830s.[36]

Restrictions based on legitimacy were eventually abolished in the mid-1820s as well. A law enacted in 1825 granted "illegitimate sons" the right to enter a colegio and to obtain a law degree.[37] Despite opposition by clergymen in Congress, after months of debate the law was approved by the legislators on the grounds that "the constitution does not exclude anyone, even illegitimately born people, from enjoying the rights of citizenship...it has established equality, and the legislature cannot overrule it."[38] In practice, this restriction seems to have lingered on a bit longer. In 1832, the national director of education complained to the minister of the interior that students were opposing the admission of Ruperto Anzola as a classmate because of unspecified motives "characteristic of an aristocratic government rather than an equality-based republican one." Nevertheless, he also agreed that Anzola should prove his "legitimidad y buenas costumbres" ("legitimate birth and good customs").[39] Progress was therefore not steady, but liberalization was undoubtedly taking place in an educational arena that customarily confirmed the social standing of traditional colonial elites.

The same liberal trend affected bureaucratic appointments, also a traditional source of social honor and prestige in the colonial era. Many of the lawyers and other individuals who entered the bureaucracy in the 1820s owed their appointments to the most important new sources of social mobility: their own personal service in the independence movement or their family ties to former members of that movement. The 1821 law mentioned above honored those who died for the "fatherland" and provided aid to their widows, orphans, and parents. In addition to free education, the law entitled such families to state jobs,[40] and in fact, numerous bureaucrats appointed during the 1820s owed their jobs to their own revolutionary merits or those of their relatives rather than to elite social backgrounds or connections.[41] In addition, Congress also favored the entry into the bureaucracy and politics of individuals whose ethnic origin would have been an obstacle during the colonial period. In May 1823, for instance, Congress responded to a member's question as to whether or not color hindered one's right to be elected to Congress. This question was especially pertinent, given that all congressmen were then white. The reply was that nonwhites were absent only because of their widespread illiteracy, itself the product of colonial restrictions on access to education. The House of Representatives then added that the new constitution "does not make any distinction based on one's *casta* or color for the provision of public jobs."[42]

Nobility was another previous prerequisite for high office that fell into disregard. In early 1823, Congress rejected a petition for the reestablishment of Caracas's Colegio de Abogados. It argued that the colegio's colonial tradition of demanding noble birth of its members contradicted the principles of the postcolonial state, which dictated that "appointments to the Republic's court system [should be given] to any lawyer available as long as he is recommended by his intellectual and moral competency."[43]

Again, change was slower to come for those of illegitimate birth. Even the progressive vice president Francisco de Paula Santander hesitated to allow free access to the bureaucracy for individuals of illegitimate birth, either because he did not want to anger the clergy or because some "modern" leaders like him were still strongly imbued by the traditional colonial mentalities.[44] Nonetheless, the social composition of both the legal profession and the high bureaucracy was changing.

Upward social mobility was not entirely absent during the colonial period, when the sons of modest bureaucrats had the opportunity to become lawyers and rise in social status. However, as Chapter 2 demonstrated, law graduates who lacked the appropriate social background or high bureaucratic connections tended to remain in low bureaucratic jobs or spend their lives as modest practicing lawyers with limited possibilities for economic and social advancement.

The revolution altered this rigid situation. Not only did the mere adoption of a republican constitutional system increase the number of official positions to be filled, but even the positions previously entrusted to traditional families were occupied by upwardly mobile individuals. One example of social mobility is Vicente Azuero, a former classmate of Vice President Santander. Azuero was the brother of Juan Nepomuceno Azuero, parish priest of Anolaima, a small town outside Bogotá. The Azuero brothers came from a provincial family, none of whose members occupied high positions in the colonial bureaucracy or had any claims to superior social status resulting from old *encomiendas* or noble titles.[45] However, they were both active revolutionaries. Juan, like several other priests, was jailed in 1809 on suspicion of participating in the plot to create revolutionary juntas. After his release, he was active in the 1810 junta and the revolutionary and republican congresses convened during the 1810s and 1820s. Vicente also participated in those congresses, was jailed by the royal authorities in the late 1810s, and escaped in 1819. After occupying a fiscal position and serving as a member of the patriots' Junta de Secuestros (confiscations), he attended the Congress of Cúcuta, where he led the opposition against the senatorial appointment of Antonio Nariño Alvarez, a Cundinamarca aristocrat.[46] During the Congress Azuero played an active role in designing legislation and was subsequently appointed *fiscal* and justice of the Alta Corte. He later ran unsuccessfully for the presidency.[47]

In the same group as Azuero was Francisco Soto, who came from a family without bureaucratic history or noble background but who had also accumulated revolutionary merits.[48] After the Cúcuta Congress, he was named *asesor* of the military intendant of one of New Granada's four *departamentos*. He later became *fiscal* of the highest court, and shortly afterwards secretary of state for fiscal affairs. Like Azuero, he was also an active congressman and a visible leader of the antimilitary political faction in which several Socorro and Pamplona natives were active.[49]

In general, these natives of Socorro and neighboring Pamplona, with the conspicuous exception of Azuero, did not establish family alliances with individuals from the traditional colonial elites as a way to foster their bureaucratic future.[50] The upward mobility of this group was based mostly on their revolutionary merits. They also profited from the public position of their friend and fellow Socorrano, Vice President Santander, who was himself also an upwardly mobile figure.[51] General Santander (1792–1840) was a native of Cúcuta. His father was a middling bureaucrat and relatively wealthy landowner, and his maternal grandfather an inconspicuous colonial official and small property owner. His maternal uncle, lawyer and priest Nicolás Omaña, was a member of Bogotá's ecclesiastical hierarchy, a law professor, and an active revolutionary. Under his sponsorship Santander studied law, but during the 1810s, because of the revolution, he dropped out of law school and joined the army. As vice president and acting president during most of the 1820s, Santander came to occupy the most strategic bureaucratic position in the postcolonial state. Besides presiding over the administrative organization of the early state, he supervised most appointments to bureaucratic jobs, often promoting his friends.[52]

Azuero and Soto, along with lawyers Diego Fernando Gómez Durán and Angel María Flórez, were the most prominent leaders of the antimilitary and antiaristocratic faction known to its rivals during the 1830s as the "jacobins," or the *partido Socorrano*.[53] Their friend, lawyer Joaquín Suárez Serrano, was also an active member of the Socorrano group, although he died prematurely in 1832 without having achieved bureaucratic prominence. Some contemporaries from other regions were integrated into Socorrano political circles in the late 1820s and early 1830s, including lawyer Salvador Camacho Naranjo, a native of the remote eastern Casanare plains. There were many more like him, most of them still unstudied, with roughly the same provincial and social backgrounds. The group continued to grow throughout the 1820s and 1830s (see Appendix 5).[54]

A younger generation of Socorranos, like lawyers Florentino González and José Pascual Afanador and young student Pedro Celestino Azuero, who shared a similar "provincial" social background, joined the antimilitary campaigns led by Azuero, Gómez, Soto, and the others. Provincial law students who graduated in the mid- and late-1820s and belonged to nonelite Bogotá and Tunja families–Miguel Larrota, Romualdo Lievano, Mariano Ospina Rodríguez, Ezequiel Rojas, Juan N. Vargas, and Rafael María Vásquez–and several Antioqueños–José Duque Gómez, José María Latorre Uribe, Miguel Uribe Restrepo, and Wenceslao Zulaibar Santamaría, some of whom belonged to wealthy but nonaristocratic families–also joined the antimilitary struggles led by the "partido Socorrano." All came from families without a high bureaucratic trajectory or claims of noble birth. They identified with each others' social origins, shared common experiences, and developed strong social bonds as classmates, thus becoming almost a "second kin group."[55] Another common factor was that they generally did not come from traditionally powerful regions.

Paralleling the progressive social changes listed above, another major transformation occurred in the relative distribution of political weight and power among New Granada's regions. During and after the 1821 Congress of Cúcuta there was a marked tendency toward the equal participation of territorial units. This probably reflected both the dynamics of the independence war and the elites' desire to use top bureaucratic positions as a means to build multiregional coalition governments able to achieve much-desired stability, countrywide acceptance, and legitimacy.[56] Regions like Bogotá, Cartagena, and Popayán that during the colonial period had been centers of military, bureaucratic, educational, and commercial activity now found themselves competing for state jobs with provincial regions considered relatively insignificant in a bureaucratic sense. Besides Socorro in the northeast, the latter included Antioquia, in the northwest, and, a little later, Neiva to the south. Natives of these regions began to receive equal consideration for high bureaucratic service in the central government. This de facto pattern of regional upward mobility, which from 1821 onward brought natives of nontraditional regions to the highest ranks, was codified into law in 1824 with legislation that abolished distinctions across localities and regions, which in the colonial period had been organized hierarchically into Spanish cities, villages, Indian towns, parishes, and mestizo settlements.[57]

As a result of those changes, the regional origins of the individuals staffing the upper bureaucracy were modified substantially. Cartagena in the north, Bogotá in the center, and Popayán in the south were the traditional sites of the bulk of the state bureaucracy and military, as well as of economic and religious life. Members of elite local families tended to occupy most of these jobs. These regions were better entrenched in the state apparatus than the rest of the Viceroyalty, rendering their societies somewhat more "honorable", prestigious, and aristocratic than the rest (Table 6.5).[58]

The wars of independence, however, demanded the full participation of all of the regions. By the early 1820s, revolutionary merits had been accumulated by regions outside the traditional aristocratic orbit. These merits translated into ac-

Table 6.5. Distribution of Colonial Bureaucratic Jobs by Town

Town	Jobs	Percentage
Bogotá	184	21.6
Cartagena	82	9.6
Popayán	58	6.8
Honda*	31	3.6
Panama	29	3.4
Mompós	27	3.1
Socorro/Pamplona/San Gíl/Vélez	24	2.8
Santa Marta	21	2.4
Antioquia/Medellín	19	2.2
Zipaquirá*	10	1.1
Neiva	9	1.0
Cali	9	1.0
Tunja*	5	0.5

Source: García de la Guardia, *Kalendario manual.*

*Also within Bogotá's orbit.

cess for their natives to a bureaucratic share in the central institutions of the postcolonial state.

Socorro was a region of small cultivators of sugar cane and tobacco and artisanal spinning and weaving northeast of Bogotá.[59] It was among the pioneers in the formation of revolutionary juntas in 1810, and found itself at the outset of the postcolonial state with a vice president acting chief executive (General Santander); a *fiscal* soon to be justice of the Alta Corte de Justicia (Vicente Azuero); a justice in one of the three highest courts of appeals (Diego Fernando Gómez); and an *asesor* in one of the four *departamentos,* soon to be secretary of fiscal affairs (Francisco Soto).[60]

In Antioquia, a mountainous region northwest of Bogotá, economic and social life during the colonial era revolved around gold-mining, commerce, and some agriculture. Antioquia's families not only lacked a tradition of bureaucratic service, but a titled nobility was practically nonexistent.[61] There were no educational establishments, and intellectual life was rather limited. Antioquia's elite families thus concentrated on trade and mining instead of intellectual activities or the bureaucracy. After independence, however, natives of this wealthy region were appointed secretary of the interior (José Manuel Restrepo) and president of the Alta Corte (José Felix Restrepo), and several more were named as diplomatic agents.[62] By the beginning of the 1830s, Antioquia also had various native sons employed as secretaries of state and top bureaucrats (see Chapter 9).

Elites from Antioquia and Socorro were as well positioned within the high state bureaucracy as those from the central region of Bogotá, and in an even better strategic position than their counterparts from the aristocratic regions of

Cartagena, Popayán, and their satellites (see Table 6.1).[63] In the 1830s, as a new generation of lawyers from the nontraditional regions of Neiva and Mariquita came of age, politics and the bureaucracy were further penetrated by provincials.[64] To be sure, all of these provincials competed for state jobs and social prestige with numerous aristocrats.

Traditional Lawyers and Traditional Regions

Lawyers from the aristocratic camp had social backgrounds and regional origins significantly different from those of the antimilitary provincial group described above.[65] They all came from and resided in Cundinamarca (and Tunja), Popayán, and Cartagena, regions of central importance during the colonial period. In addition, they belonged to family networks of noble ancestry, wealth, and, especially, bureaucratic experience, both in the clerical and secular sectors—traditional markers of superior status-honor. Several such families even held titles of nobility (e.g., Marqués de Surba y Bonza, Marqués de San Jorge, Marqués de Torre Hoyos, Condes de Pestagua y Santa Coa). Others had been offered such titles and declined them; for instance, in 1805 several individuals were nominated to obtain *títulos de Castilla* but, not wanting to spend the significant amount of money these titles entailed, refused them. Whether they had titles or not, their families often held substantial land grants *(composiciones)*, which could be traced back for centuries as appendices to grants of Indian labor, or *encomiendas*. Finally, and more important, their ancestors and close relatives, or those of their wives, were connected to the high-ranking clergy and/or had occupied high-ranking colonial posts as governors, accountants, or treasurers of the Tribunal de Cuentas or the royal mint, administrators of state monopolies, and *oidores* or *fiscales* of a royal audiencia (see Appendix 4).[66]

Membership in the Church hierarchy and colonial state bureaucracy, a historically undervalued source of social preeminence, was, as I indicated earlier in this work, determinant of social superiority. Being part of the Church and state ranks was not merely a source of material benefits, such as stable income and power, but also afforded prestige, deference, and honor, all of which entitled its possessors to a higher status or "right to pride."[67] This right, as Chapter 2 demonstrated, was not merely individual, but was extended or passed on to family members. Honor thus became both a personal and familial affair, achieved by bureaucrats and passed on to their kin.[68] Therefore, a fair number of the "aristocrats" we are dealing with were not an aristocracy of titled nobles or gentry in the European sense, but rather individuals and families (sometimes of relatively modest wealth) connected to high-ranking bureaucratic circles.

These features were true of the older colonial survivors, members of the transitional generation, and younger figures alike.[69] Aristocratic lawyers within the transitional generation included the members of the Domínguez clan from Bogotá—Benedicto, José María, and Mateo—and Bogotá natives Estanislao Vergara, Manuel María Alvarez Lozano, Francisco Morales Galavís, Casimiro Calvo Ortega, and José Arce de León. Their social origins are described briefly below.

The Dominguez family descended from a colonial governor and an accountant of the Tribunal de Cuentas. The individual members cited above and their relatives married members of traditional clans: the descendants of the Marqués de Torre Hoyos; the Espinosa Prietos who, in turn, descended from a high official in Bogotá's royal mint; and the Martínez Malos, who were linked to a high member of the royal audiencia.[70] Lawyer Francisco Morales Galavís, who graduated in 1808, was descended on both sides of his family from high colonial bureaucrats. He married a member of the wealthy Caicedo y Sanz de Santamaría family who could trace her ancestry to *encomenderos* in regions neighboring Bogotá and was linked to a judge in the audiencia.[71]

We already know that Estanislao Vergara and Manuel María Alvarez Lozano also descended from members of notable bureaucratic networks (Chapter 3, Figures 3.1 and 3.2). The final two examples among the Bogotanos are Casimiro Calvo Ortega and José Arce de León. The former was a maternal grandson of an administrator of Bogotá's aguardiente monopoly, and his wife was the daughter of San Cristóbal's colonial governor. Arce de León was the son of a *contador* of the Tribunal de Cuentas and married into the prestigious Sanz de Santamaría clan.[72] Socially equal to all of these were several natives of the Tunja region, particularly lawyers Antonio Malo and Narciso Casanovas Neira, who graduated in 1811 and 1820, respectively.[73] Cartagena natives Eusebio María Canabal, Joaquín José Gori, and José Angel Lastra, who graduated in the same years, belonged to this group as well.[74] An important clique of Popáyan natives headed by Joaquín Mosquera y Arboleda, Antonio Carvajal y Tenorio, and José Manuel Hurtado, all of whom were trained during 1806 and 1810, was also part of the "aristocratic" circle.[75] Finally, as was mentioned above, a series of younger figures trained during the 1820s joined the "aristocratic" ranks as time went on, including Ramón Villoria, José Antonio Arroyo, Antonio Plazas, and José María Mendoza Morales (Appendix 4).[76]

As was customary among a segment of the colonial aristocracy, many of these youngsters decided to devote themselves to their lands and businesses instead of bureaucratic careers. Others were excluded from the new bureaucracy due to their earlier failure to embrace the cause of independence and their subsequent opposition to republican practices.[77] But, as could be expected, several others gained access to high state jobs during the 1820s and 1830s. They were facilitated by the fact that, on top of their excellent social connections, they and their relatives also possessed revolutionary merits. After all, independence had started as, and to a large extent remained, an elite movement spearheaded by top-ranking colonial bureaucrats and their families.

Some less aristocratic but still illustrious lawyers joined these aristocrats, especially through marriage to their daughters or sisters. The most representative examples of this situation were lawyers Alejandro Osorio, José Ignacio de Márquez, and Rufino Cuervo, whom some historians have presented as ascending to high social positions based solely upon their intellectual abilities.[78] Other reasons help explain the entry of these lawyers into high bureaucratic circles alongside aristocrats. Osorio, son of an artist and a bakery owner, married the daughter of a lawyer from a traditional family related to Antonio Nariño Alvarez

(Chapter 2). Osorio thus became a sort of foster son to some of the elite families of Cundinamarca. Besides his relationship to the Nariño, Ortega, and Ricaurte clans, he was also close to the socially prominent Caicedo clan, whose patrician, General Domingo Caicedo, helped to save his life during the Spanish terror and addressed Osorio as "mi amadísimo Alejandro" ("my beloved Alejandro"). Osorio served as a high-level bureaucrat at various times during the late 1810s, early 1820s, and 1830s; although his industrial ventures (a cotton mill in which he invested in 1836) were not much of a success, he became wealthy through the legal practice that consumed most of his time. He was an active senator as well.[79]

José Ignacio de Márquez (1793–1880) descended from families devoted to mining in Ramiriquí's (Tunja) neighboring regions and was the son of a farmer from this area. After becoming a lawyer in the mid-1810s he participated in the Cúcuta Congress of 1821, where he joined ranks with some "jacobin" provincials in attacking the Church's educational privileges, demanding the suppression of understaffed conventos, and supporting freedom of the press regarding religious topics. During the 1820s he was a law professor, and after occupying high judicial positions he was appointed chief executive (intendant) of his native region. With a promising bureaucratic career under way, in 1827 he married a daughter of the Marqués de Surba y Bonza, a rich landowner. He allegedly wanted to devote himself to farming the lands of his father-in-law but ended up returning to the bureaucracy. There he increasingly aligned himself with the aristocratic group which he favored during his 1837–1841 presidency.[80]

Rufino Cuervo (1810–1853), whose mother was a first cousin of Márquez's mother, was the son of an unsuccessful merchant but benefited from the fact that his uncle Nicolás had been an influential revolutionary priest. After five years in high judicial jobs, he married the daughter of a former accountant (*contador*) of the colonial Tribunal de Cuentas. His new wife was the niece of high colonial bureaucrats and wealthy landowners.[81] Although during the mid-1820s Cuervo publicly sympathized with the "provincial" antimilitary group, by the end of the decade he was leaning toward the more authoritarian aristocratic creed. In September 1828, Popayán aristocrat Rafael Mosquera summed up this transformation in a letter to then-dictator General Bolívar:

> Rufino Cuervo has been quite helpful to us under the new circumstances. He is an enthusiastic man, quite sensible and somewhat weak: thus you know to what extent we can count on his character and that it is easy to make him commit himself.... He resents his former friends, because General Santander and Soto wished to charge him with the crimes of the [opposition newspaper] *Bandera Tricolor*. Cuervo has taken a new attitude *[una nueva forma],* and his stay here [in Popayán] seems to me quite important ... therefore you must excuse me if my patriotism makes me insist that he be allowed to remain in this city.[82]

Like Cuervo, Osorio and Márquez experienced major social transformations in the 1810s and 1820s. The three became characteristic "aristocrats," representing a sort of bridge for traditional colonial elite groups who renewed their social and political prominence by forming family alliances with these successful public officials.

These relationships were not quite the same as the marital alliances typical of the late colonial bureaucrats, which were generally aimed at advancing one's career by marrying the daughter of an important colonial official. These young lawyer-bureaucrats were already among the top state ranks, and they married daughters or sisters of individuals who at the time did not occupy positions in the state bureaucracy. Rather, the brides' traditional families were the ones who looked forward to marrying into the families of the new bureaucrats, probably as a way to ensure that their traditional status would not be lost now that the revolution had altered the criteria for access to the state bureaucracy and brought to power a series of nontraditional figures. In contrast, the young bureaucrats' choice of spouse was based on the economic position and social status of the bride, which sooner or later might become more important than family linkages to the state bureaucracy. This consideration was doubtless a result of the turmoil and unsettled circumstances of the early republican period; although not yet culturally superior, wealth became more reliable during those years than bureaucratic connections.[83]

In sum, through the 1820s one can discern significant generational, regional, and social changes among the members of the legal profession and the high-ranking clerical and secular bureaucracy. To the dominance of the younger generations was added the distinction of an upwardly mobile group of provincial lawyers who began to compete with their aristocratic colleagues for political prominence. In spite of tensions among these two groups, an open confrontation between them did not take place at that time. Instead, during the second half of the 1820s, the New Granadan–Venezuelan/civil-military disputes obscured the internal conflicts that resulted from the radical transformation of the social and regional balance of power within New Granada.

It was not until the 1830s when, having dissolved the union with Venezuela and expelled the latter's armies, the two socially diverse segments of New Granada's ruling civilian elite clashed with each other. Even then, however, their disputes took a military form only in exceptional cases. For the most part, they occurred peacefully within both the "public sphere of civil society" and the parliamentary institutions of the new state. The following chapter will illustrate some of these confrontations, while noticing too the continuing dynamic transformation of both the aristocratic and provincial sectors.

Chapter 7
Politics and the "Public Sphere of Civil Society," 1820s–1830s

Starting in the 1820s, the provincial and upwardly mobile sectors of New Granada's elite appeared more inclined to liberal ideas than were their aristocratic peers. However, the dominance of the military, and Venezuelan officers in particular, seems to have pushed some of New Granada's aristocrats to join forces with provincial elites for an antimilitary crusade. This crusade also became a campaign against Gran Colombia, New Granada's union with Venezuela and Ecuador. Thus, the reciprocal social differences between the heirs of New Granada's colonial aristocracy and the provincials now competing with them for control of the high state bureaucracy were temporarily muted by the presence of a common enemy.

Once that enemy was defeated, the intra-elite status tensions among New Granadans finally came to the surface. Those tensions were further compounded by qualitative transformations facing both segments of the postcolonial elite. In effect, the 1830s witnessed a dual change bound to increase political and social stress: Antioquia's provincial elite, the wealthiest of the postcolonial period, was gradually assimilated into aristocratic social circles and ideology. But, while the aristocrats' power was thus augmented, other provincial elites continued to expand. The regions of Neiva and Mariquita illustrate this expansion and show that provincial groups remained powerful, politically active, and a challenge to aristocratic dominance.

The tensions surrounding this social process did not take an intense military character at first. Like the disputes of the 1820s, such tensions mostly consisted of skirmishes over elections, constitutions and laws, the definition of the voting rights of citizenship, and the character of local and regional government. The different segments of the struggling postcolonial elite armed themselves with rifles and machetes only on occasion. For the most part they fought through newspapers, ballots, and parliamentary means. Confrontations primarily took place within an exploding political and electoral arena and an expanded public sphere.

The "Public Sphere" in New Granada

Recent scholarship has reawakened interest in the forgotten history of nineteenth-century elections and citizenship in Latin America. Such works forcefully argue against the stereotypical view of Latin America's early republics as lawless lands ruled by men on horseback (*caudillos*) supported by competing private armies of subordinate peasants. From very early on, elections to the presidency, parliament, and other political bodies were a decisive component of power and legitimacy. To a large extent, it was because of electoral disputes and disagreements over constitutional reforms and citizenship rights that political instability prevailed and civil wars recurred.[1] This argument is substantiated by an examination of the emergence of the "public sphere of civil society" in Latin America.

Decades ago German philosopher Jürgen Habermas discussed the emergence of a "bourgeois" "civil public sphere" in seventeenth-century England and eighteenth-century France. This sphere was a domain between state and society where first literary and journalistic and, later, openly political activities were pursued by diverse groups of people. As time passed, such activities helped to counterbalance the power of absolutist states. The protagonists were "capitalists" (merchants, bankers, entrepreneurs) and "scholars" (doctors, priests, officers, professors, and jurists) who engaged in journalistic and literary activities. They also developed new venues (clubs, cafes, salons, academies, lodges, philanthropic associations, *tertulias,* and so on), making it possible for individuals to mold "public opinion" and influence the state's policies.

I have shown elsewhere that, as in Europe, the social segments responsible for the "public sphere of civil society" that emerged as early as the late eighteenth century in the Spanish colonies were originally a limited circle of cultural elites: noblemen and aristocrats, high-ranking bureaucrats, clergy, professionals, professors, and students. In the 1790s, the public sphere over which they presided was still incipient. But, with the opening of the world of competitive politics and the parallel expansion of journalism, it became substantial in the 1820s and 1830s.[2] As was the case in France and elsewhere, in Spanish America lawyers, both aristocrats and provincials, played a central role in creating this sphere and contributing to its expansion.[3] Their disputes with each other and with various other segments of society over the character of the state, elections, and the rights of citizenship, especially suffrage, attest to these circumstances. These disputes also reflect the chasm separating provincial from aristocratic factions and the changing balance of power.

Civilian-Military Tensions in the Confusing 1820s

During the 1820s, a group of lawyer-bureaucrats founded and contributed to numerous newspapers intended to mold "public opinion," one of their favorite concepts.[4] In their newspapers and public speeches they increasingly demanded the demilitarization of the state. In 1825 and 1827, antimilitary views were voiced by newspapers like *El Conductor, La Miscelánea, La Bandera Tricolor,* and the official *Gaceta de Colombia*. Several others printed during the second half of the 1820s, including *El Zurriago* and *El Meteoro,* vigorously advocated constitutional ideals and voiced the antimilitary views of New Granada's *letrados*. In the same period, cultural and philanthropic associations were organized by some elite circles, while students in Bogotá's Colegio de San Bartolomé established literary and political clubs whose antimilitary inclinations led to the establishment in this school of a so-called *república democrática*.[5]

Not all of the individuals behind the antimilitary press or societies were upwardly mobile provincials. Several young aristocratic lawyer-journalists shared their views,[6] as did other aristocrats whose economic interests were affected by the continuous marches and countermarches of large and predominantly Venezuelan armies across New Granada. This was especially the case among Popayán's landowning and merchant elites, who were plundered by armies marching south.[7] Landowners of the central region of Cundinamarca, such as aristocratic General Domingo Caicedo and his landowning family, felt likewise.[8] Others, including the wealthy and traditional Tunja lawyer Antonio Malo, were further annoyed by the scandalous behavior of soldiers in small cities and probably also resented the way in which the army contributed to the demise of the social and ethnic hierarchies of colonial society.[9]

Army officers were in turn incensed by the "yearnings of priests and lawyers" who wanted to reduce the military to the "condition of slaves."[10] General Bolívar himself complained about Santander's lawyer-inspired administration's attempt "to destroy even the military's pride."[11] These disputes turned into journalistic, electoral, and constitutional confrontations over redefining the character of the postcolonial state and the composition of its bureaucracy.

Newspapers, elections, laws, and constitutions were ultimately geared not only toward shaping the form of the state but also assuring control over the bureaucracy by one's own group. As has been demonstrated for nineteenth-century Brazil, and is likely to have occurred in Mexico, New Granada, and elsewhere, elections and the state were important means to render patronage and perpetuate individual and familial dominance.[12] For postcolonial elites, the state remained a vital source of power and steady income worth fighting for. This was even more so in a society like New Granada, whose stagnant economy failed to produce other alternative sources of livelihood.[13] Moreover, as in the colonial period, the continuing pursuit of honor and social prestige through state service was no less important than material benefits. In fact, many of the competitors for state jobs could have made a good living for themselves and their families independently. Mere material interests do not seem to have driven them to fight for control over state service; at least in the short run, the acrimonious political debates among factions seem to have derived, first and foremost, from jealousy over access to power itself, individual and familial status-honor, prestige, and recognition.

The most heated of the early legal and electoral intra-elite debates concerned the revision of the 1821 constitution.[14] This revision became urgent as a means to resolve a political crisis over the Senate's impeachment of Venezuela's military commander, General José A. Páez. The union's chief executive, General Bolívar, was sympathetic to Páez. He not only cleared him of charges that he raided civilian homes to draft military recruits, but also introduced a series of state reforms that aroused the hostility of Vice President Santander and other New Granadans.[15] Santander and some of his plutocratic provincial friends from the region of Antioquia were also enraged by Bolívar's accusations that they had misappropriated British loans.[16]

By 1826, Bolívar had become the symbol and leader of what provincial New Granadans termed a military faction. The upwardly mobile lawyers around Santander especially resented the likelihood of either a military dictatorship or a monarchy headed by the Venezuelan general. This would certainly have implied a halt to nontraditional elites' access to power, constitutionally and legally sanctioned in 1821 and thereafter, which had enabled provincials to climb the bureaucratic and educational ladders. The most probable beneficiaries of a strong, centralized, Bolívar-headed state would be those lawyers and military officers close to the *Libertador* and, by extension, their regions and families. In New Granada these lawyers and military men were predominantly aristocrats. They included Major Joaquín Barriga, Colonel Tomás Cipriano de Mosquera, and Generals Pedro Alcántara Herrán, Francisco de Paula Vélez, José María Ortega, Joaquín París, José María Vergara Lozano, and Antonio Morales Galavís; Bogotano lawyers Estanislao Vergara Sanz de Santamaría, José Miguel Pey, Alejandro Osorio, and Manuel María Alvarez Lozano; and Cartagena lawyers Eusebio María Canabal and José María del Castillo y Rada. All of these officers and *letrados* were natives of Cundinamarca, Popayán, and Cartagena and came from high status-honor colonial circles (see Appendix 4).[17] Some of them likely hoped to regain for themselves the former predominance of their aristocratic ancestors to counterbalance the growing social and bureaucratic might of the nontraditional individuals and regions who had benefited from the relative dispersal of power under the early postcolonial state.

At the same time, of course, some aristocrats were antimilitary and sided with the provincials. Joaquín Mosquera, Jerónimo Torres, Miguel Tobar, Antonio Malo, Francisco Cuevas, and José I. de Márquez were among the aristocratic jurists who eventually decided to set aside their grievances with the upwardly mobile lawyers and join them, for the time being, in their anti-Bolivarian, antimilitary, and anti-Venezuelan campaign.[18] They considered it more urgent to dissolve the union with Venezuela and reduce the army than to confront and stop the threatening rise of their provincial New Granadan peers. These aristocrats advocated the civilian and "republican" ideal and promoted a federal (decentralized) government, which seemed to them the most effective means to disassemble both the union and the army.[19] They would take part in a socially heterogeneous coalition that, during the convention that revised the 1821 constitution and afterward, tried to oppose the projects of the pro-Bolívar authoritarians.[20]

The constitutional convention celebrated in New Granada's northeastern city of Ocaña in early 1828 became the arena in which authoritarian and republican factions finally radicalized and came to a decisive clash. This constitutional dispute presaged numerous subsequent conflicts over electoral issues, local administration, and the rights of citizenship, especially suffrage. In the meantime, journalistic polemics and even physical actions against journalists and printing presses continued.[21]

Disputes over Elections, Constitutions, and Citizenship in a Heated Public Sphere

The elections to the Ocaña convention were meticulously planned, and the results were favorable to the electorally savvy procivilian provincial faction headed by Santander.[22] Santander disenfranchised most of the military to weaken the power of his opponents.[23] To the further dislike of Bolívar, Santander had himself elected representative to the convention, after successfully campaigning to change the law that prohibited his election.[24] One-third of the delegates elected to the Ocaña convention along with Santander were lawyers, with an even number of provincials and aristocrats (see Table 7.1).

At the meeting, the pro-Santander and pro-Bolívar blocs promoted alternative projects for a new constitution, in the midst of vociferous threats from the Bolivarian military.[25] The group that clustered around Santander was formed by a mixture of moderate aristocratic and upwardly mobile provincial lawyers. It advocated strengthening the separation of powers and creating provincial assemblies, which were expected to play an active role in regional administration and in the appointment of each region's public officials.[26] The pro-Bolívar group was led by aristocratic lawyer José María del Castillo. He was joined by fellow Cartagena lawyer and priest Anastasio García Frias and lawyer Joaquín José Gori, as well as several Ecuadorian and Venezuelan delegates.[27] These men declared themselves enemies of a "democracia tumultuosa" and favored a strengthened central executive power with limited regional participation in government.[28] Facing the impossibility of having their project approved by the Santander-controlled convention, Bolívar's more recalcitrant followers abandoned the meeting, forcing its dissolution in June 1828. Shortly afterward, in late August, Bolívar, supported by a number of city councils, assumed dictatorial powers. He invited a group of aristocratic lawyers to join the newly created Consejo de Estado, an advisory body consisting of all the ministers of state, representatives of the key geographic regions, and clerical and military representatives.[29] The vice presidency was suppressed and the incumbent, General Santander–probably to neutralize his local political influence–was appointed Greater Colombia's diplomatic representative to the United States.[30]

During his tenure, Bolívar dissolved the numerous municipal councils that had been established in the mid-1820s under Santander.[31] His cabinet ministers made further attempts to do away with the republican form of government, promoting the return of a monarchical system.[32] They despised and feared popular elections because they could lead to disorder and also because, as one of them said, "all our evils have resulted from the ambition to rule, and as long as there are elections there will be a powerful incentive for ambitious people."[33]

These aristocrats hoped that their promonarchical efforts would be furthered by yet another constitutional congress summoned by Bolívar himself to legitimate the regime. The congress met in Bogotá in January 1830. Unlike the tumultuous 1828 convention in Ocaña, it consisted of a relatively small and homogeneous group dominated by aristocrats.[34] The small size and aristocratic

Table 7.1. Composition of the Ocaña Convention, 1828

Origin	Lawyers	Military	Unknown	Total
New Granadan	19	3	20	42
Venezuelan	6	4	11	21
Ecuadorian	–	–	8	8
Unknown	–	–	3	3
Total	25	7	42	74

Sources: Guerra, *La Convención de Ocaña;* Rogelio Pérez Perdomo, *Los abogados en Venezuela* (Caracas, 1981).

dominance were due to new electoral rules, adopted in late 1828. These rules provided for relatively wide enfranchisement so that even peasants, under the influence of conservative aristocratic hacendados, could vote. Suffrage was also given back to the military, which voted under the careful direction of pro-Bolívar officers.[35] The new electoral rules reduced the number of regional representatives as well, making the congress more exclusive.[36] More important, for the provincials, many of their leaders were involved in an assassination plot against Bolívar in late 1828. At the time, they were in hiding or exiled and thus could not stand for election.[37]

As in earlier congresses, lawyers and military officers were again the key protagonists. These two groups each represented almost a quarter of the assembly's members. A military representative, General Antonio J. Sucre, presided over the proceedings. Bolívar's supporters were believed to dominate both groups. However, some moderate aristocrats played key roles in dissolving the union and establishing a civilian government (see Table 7.2).

The regions of the Gran Colombian union were unevenly represented at the congress, and some refused to send delegates.[38] The "admirable" congress, as it was later called, formed by a small and not very representative group of individuals, therefore had little legitimacy and even fewer hopes of creating a stable government acceptable to all of the regions' elites. When Bolívar resigned the presidency in frustration in March 1830, the congress was forced to appoint a temporary president and vice president amid noisy cries from young students who, as had become customary in Colombia's expanding public sphere, sat in the galleries as observers.[39] The short-lived rule (May-September 1830) of the two moderate aristocrats chosen by the congress (Popayán lawyer Joaquín Mosquera and Cundinamarca General Domingo Caicedo) was plagued by regional division and military revolts in Venezuela and Ecuador. Indeed, during the second half of 1830 a rapid process of regional separatism definitively ended the Gran Colombian union. Venezuela and Ecuador rejected the new constitution adopted by the congress in April 1830 and proceeded to form independent states.[40] To top off these events, a new military takeover occurred in New Granada a few months afterward.

The new military government was headed by Bolivarian General Rafael

Table 7.2. Composition of the Constitutional Congress, 1830

Regional Origin	Number	Occupation	Number
New Granadans	34	Lawyers	12
Venezuelans	9	Military	11
Ecuadorians	10	Priests*	7
Total	53	Merchants	4
		Undetermined†	19
		Total	53

Sources: Arboleda, *Historia contemporánea,* 1:19–20; Pérez Perdomo, *Los abogados en Venezuela; Gaceta de Colombia,* January 10, 1830.

*Two of these were also lawyers.
†The occupations of the Ecuadorian delegates are unknown.

Urdaneta. As had been the case with Bolívar's own dictatorial government, Urdaneta's coup was favored and sponsored by aristocratic segments of New Granada's elite at odds with their fellow procivilian aristocrats. The aristocratic lineage of Bolívar's and Urdaneta's followers is clearly demonstrated by their strong family linkages to the high-ranking colonial bureaucracy.

Urdaneta was also encouraged to take power by Bogotá's city council, which included the most authoritarian members of the city's aristocratic elites to which the general himself was closely tied. Though he was away from Bogotá during most of the independence war and retained strong ties to Venezuela's Zulia region, which he represented in Congress, Urdaneta married into the prestigious Vargas París family of Bogotá. He had lived in Bogotá intermittently since 1804 with his uncle, Martín Urdaneta, who had been *contador mayor* of Bogotá's colonial Tribunal de Cuentas.[41] Indeed, the ancestors of several of the aristocratic Bogotanos who had supported Bolívar's 1828 dictatorship and were now supporting Urdaneta's coup had served in the Tribunal de Cuentas, the viceroyalty's highest fiscal agency during the colonial period (Table 7.3).[42] These offspring of the colonial regime were not prepared for a republic, nor were they accustomed to novelties. Used as they were to exercising authority and accumulating honor for themselves and their families, various members of Bogotá's aristocracy could not entirely stomach the ascent to power by the plutocratic provincial elites from Antioquia, nor much less other rabble-rousing provincial sectors. Their support for Bolívar first and later Urdaneta seems to have reflected a struggle to maintain status-honor in the colonial sense; that is, the social prestige derived from service to the Crown and the colonial state. The Bogotá aristocracy was unwilling to surrender its monopoly over the state bureaucracy, power, and panache without putting up a fight.

Urdaneta's takeover was also supported by members of Cartagena's aristocracy and some of the leading clans of the southern city of Cali, near Popayán.[43]

Table 7.3. Family Ties Between the Colonial Tribunal de Cuentas and Bolívar's and Urdaneta's Dictatorships, 1828, 1830

Late Colonial Contadores	Relationship	Supporters or instigators of Bolívar's and/or Urdaneta's dictatorships
Gregorio Domínguez	Granduncle	Pedro Domínguez Hoyos
Martín Urdaneta	Uncle	Rafael Urdaneta
Felipe Vergara	Uncle	Estanislao Vergara
Antonio J. Caro F.	Brother	Rafael Caro F.
Manuel B. Alvarez C.	Father	Manuel B. Alvarez L.

Sources: García de la Guardia, *Kalendario manual,* 161–63; Restrepo and Rivas, *Genealogías de Santafé,* 21–22, 212, 316–18; Arboleda, *Historia contemporánea,* 1:50, 56–57, 88–89, 124; González, *Memorias,* 132.

Though it may seem odd, it was equally supported by a couple of wealthy provincials from Antioquia: the Santamaría brothers, Raimundo and Julián. These two acted separately from the mainstream merchants and mineowners of their region, their relatives included, all of whom were politically closer and socially affined to Santander's provincial group. The Santamarías, in any event, anticipated a shift in political and social allegiances, which later became common among their wealthy peers from Antioquia.[44]

After Urdaneta's short-lived dictatorship (September 1830 to May 1831), an uneasy coalition of provincial elites and moderate aristocrats took over and set out to rearrange the state and politics. The coalition's armies, under provincial Generals José H. López and José M. Obando, eventually overthrew both General Urdaneta and his politically extreme aristocratic friends. They then pushed for the discharge of a part of the old Bolivarian military.[45] All of the pro-Bolívar aristocrats were removed from the cabinet; like the Consejo de Estado, it was soon filled with provincials.[46] Elite provincials, including General Santander—who had been exiled with others in late 1828—were welcomed back to the country in the midst of public protests by their supporters against what was labeled an oppressive "aristocracy." Protests centered mainly on traditional colonial families from Cartagena, Popayán, and, in particular, Bogotá. Families from these areas had recently supported both Bolívar's and Urdaneta's irregular governments.[47]

The provincial agenda was supported and legitimized by yet one more constitutional congress—exclusively New Granadan—which met in October 1831.[48] The number and characteristics of its delegates were a result of pressures from the provincial sectors. Once again they redefined voting rights by reducing the voting age, increasing the number of representatives, and excluding (aristocratic-led) *jornaleros* and *sirvientes* from voting.[49] In this way the congress managed to ensure the election of a good number of provincials (Table 7.4). These included several radically republican young lawyers (ages 27 to 36) who had graduated as recently as the late 1820s and early 1830s (Table 7.5).

The mixed presence of moderate aristocrats and provincials in the governments of the early 1830s contributed to some peace and stability. But social changes in the composition of aristocratic and provincial groups and the eventual alteration of the balance of power brought about new sociopolitical tensions during the rest of the decade.

The "Antioqueños" and the Emerging Balance of Power

Thanks to their economic power, derived from both their merchant and mining activities, the Antioqueños became highly influential in New Granada's postcolonial society and politics. One example, Francisco A. Zea, presided over the 1819 Angostura Congress that laid the basis for the union with Venezuela and Ecuador. He was later elected vice president, and in 1822 was sent as a diplomatic envoy to Europe, with the particular mission of negotiating loans from British financiers.[50] After Zea's premature death, two more Antioqueños, the wealthy Manuel A. Arrubla and Francisco Montoya, were sent to England in 1824 to obtain new loans for the Gran Colombian union.[51] Vice President Santander, acting chief executive from 1821 to 1827, also favored important Antioqueños, like Juan de Dios Aranzazu and Alejandro Vélez, and bestowed on them high bureaucratic commissions, thus adding political power and social

Table 7.4. Regional Composition of Lawyers at the 1831 Constitutional Congress

Provinces	Delegates	Lawyers	Provincial
Tunja	14	5	3
Bogotá	13	7	2
Socorro	10	4	4
Antioquia	8	3	3
Cartagena	7	3	–
Pamplona	4	1	1
Neiva	4	2	2
Mariquita	4	2	–
Panama	3	–	–
Santa Marta	3	–	–
Mompós	3	1	1
Riohacha	1	–	–
Casanare	1	–	–
Total	75	28	16

Source: Arboleda, Historia contemporánea, 3:111–12; Gaceta de Colombia, April 14, 1839.

honor to the already considerable economic affluence enjoyed by individuals from this region.

During the 1820s the Antioqueños—particularly the Sáenz, Santamaría, Lorenzana, Montoya, Campuzano, Echeverri, Uribe Restrepo, Arrubla, Villa, García, Zea, and Gutiérrez de Lara families—had risen to become the most important and wealthy merchants and mineowners of New Granada. They traveled frequently to Jamaica on trading ventures, were the first to establish trading houses in Europe, and were the largest producers of gold in the nineteenth century, displacing the traditionally dominant mineowners of Popayán.[52] The Antioqueños not only had profitable businesses in their own region, but also established mercantile activities in Bogotá, where they became important landholders and established ties with local families.[53]

Several Antioqueños married into Bogotá's landowning and noble families in the late colonial period and during the independence years. A representative case is José María Arrubla Martínez (1780–1816), who stayed in Bogotá after studying at the Colegio de San Bartolomé, devoted himself to trade, and married the daughter of a local high bureaucrat in 1803. His brother, Manuel Antonio Arrubla (? –1864), also married into the wealthy Bogotano Domínguez del Castillo clan.[54] In 1818, the Antioqueño lawyer José Joaquín Gómez Hoyos, owner of large estates in Bogotá and Antioquia, married the widow of the noble Bogotano Jorge Tadeo Lozano, Marqués de San Jorge, and settled in the town of Funza, neighboring Bogotá.[55] Another example is merchant and industrialist

Table 7.5. Young Lawyers at the 1831 Constitutional Congress

Name	Province	Admitted to Bar	Age in 1831
Alandete, José María	Cartagena	1832	*
Camacho, Manuel A.	Mariquita	1827	28
Cañarete, Manuel	Mompós	1827	30
Cantillo, Manuel A.	Bogotá	1825	35
Ciprián Cuenca, Domingo	Neiva	1827	30
Gómez Barrientos, Estanislao	Antioquia	1827	33
Landínez, Judas T.	Tunja	1825	27
León, Juan H.	Cartagena	1835	30
Lievano, Romualdo	Bogotá	1827	34
López Aldana, Fracisco de P.	Bogotá	1828	30
Rojas, Eleuterio	Tunja	1827	28
Salgado, Manuel A.	Cartagena	1832	36
Vargas, Inocencio	Socorro	1824	33

Sources: GNG, April 14, 1839; GNG, June 22, 1845; Arboleda, Historia contemporánea, 1:111; Restrepo and Rivas, Genealogías de Santafé.

*His recent appointment to the bar makes it likely he was a young man.

Luis Montoya—brother of merchant Francisco and Colonel José Manuel—who married the daughter of Pantaleón Sanz de Santamaría, a member of one of the most aristocratic clans of Bogotá.[56] There were several other similar cases.[57]

In the late 1820s, these newcomers—who lacked the status-honor and pedigree of traditional colonial bureaucratic family-networks—did not generally exhibit the exclusionary and authoritarian political preferences of the aristocratic Bogotanos whose clans they had recently joined. In fact, several Antioqueños participated alongside their provincial peers in the main political gatherings and the antimilitary political campaigns of the late 1820s.[58] Some merchants of the region (e.g., Juan de Dios Aranzazu, Manuel A. Jaramillo, Francisco Montoya, and Manuel J. Arrubla), for instance, attended the 1828 Ocaña convention. In it, they exhibited a moderate attitude that was not altogether acceptable to provincial leader Santander, yet was far from open support for the aristocratic Bolivarian group.[59] Indeed, the subsequent (September 1828) assassination attempt against Bolívar was allegedly sponsored by Antioqueños.[60]

The plot was planned at the Bogotá store of Antioqueño merchant Wenceslao Zulaibar Santamaría. Zulaibar's coconspirators included a number of Antioqueño merchants—Alejo Pérez, Gabriel Echeverry, Alejo Santamaría Bermúdez and his uncle, Antonio Santamaría Isaza—who were probably reacting to recent measures that restricted the region's gold trade. Antioqueño merchants conducted import-export trade with Jamaica by using gold that they mostly smuggled out of New Granada. Thus they were undoubtedly hurt by Bolívar's decree of March 15, 1828, prohibiting the export of gold out of the country without first taking it to the mints of Bogotá or Popayán, or obtaining special licenses to mint it locally. This decree also established military checkpoints in Antioquia and Chocó to carry out extensive searches of travelers' baggage.[61] Bolívar rightly suspected that a group of influential citizens of Medellín, the capital of Antioquia, was behind the plot. The same group was behind the local military revolt headed around the same time in Rionegro, a village east of Medellín, by Bolívar's former supporter José María Córdova.[62] Bolívar imposed heavy fines on some of these individuals,[63] while those accused of plotting against his life were tried and executed.[64] Among the plotters were several provincial law students from other regions, as well as young provincial lawyers trained in the mid-1820s.[65] In any case, except for the conspicuous exception of Antioqueño lawyer José Manuel Restrepo, Bolívar's cabinet minister, most provincial lawyers from Antioquia and other regions were politically sympathetic to Vice President Santander, and several of them participated in the plot against Bolívar. Despite the repression and fines they endured because of their anti-Bolívar activities, a significant part of the Antioqueño elite continued to resist Bolívar's rule and, later, also opposed the short-lived dictatorship of his follower, General Urdaneta.[66]

This Antioqueño group was regarded as a key variable in the structure and balance of power. Members of Antioquia's elite continued to be considered a threat by the short-lived authoritarian governments of this anarchical period. In August 1830, several of the most powerful anti-Bolívar Antioqueño merchants—the Montoya and Arrubla brothers—were ordered out of the country, and new persecutions followed in early 1831.[67] However, over the course of the 1830s the Antioqueños were spared further problems under the more stable presidency of provincial General Santander (1832–1837). They continued to accumulate political power during the shakier presidency that followed, that of aristocratic lawyer José I. de Márquez (1837–1841).

After the defeat of the pro-Bolívar sectors in 1831 and the installation of a provincial-aristocratic coalition government presided over by Santander, the influential Antioqueño group continued to rise to the highest bureaucratic ranks. The cases of Juan de Dios Aranzazu and Alejandro Vélez Barrientos demonstrate as much. Aranzazu (1793–1845), a member of a wealthy Antioqueño family that possessed large landholdings and a trading house in Maracaibo, attended parliaments during the 1820s and was sent to Venezuela on diplomatic missions in 1830. Vélez Barrientos, who had established business connections in Europe during 1823 and was a member of an important merchant family, served as consul general in the United States from 1826 until 1829. Both men returned to Colombia to carry on their private business. They served as governors of Antioquia and attended constitutional congresses during the late 1820s and early 1830s and later took up cabinet appointments and served in the Consejo de Estado.[68]

Other examples of high-ranking Antioqueño bureaucrats include the Restrepos—lawyers Félix and José Manuel—who also held key bureaucratic jobs during the 1820s and 1830s. Miguel Uribe Restrepo, a nephew of Félix, declined the post of economics minister offered to him by Santander in 1836. Another interesting example is Juan María Gómez Pastor (1798–1850), a close friend of Aranzazu and Vélez, who was ambassador to Brazil, treasurer of Antioquia in the early 1830s, and ambassador to France in 1834. Later he was named a general and became the top Antioqueño in the army. He became military chief of Antioquia in late 1840 and was also a cabinet minister. His close friend, the Antioqueño lawyer Juan Antonio Pardo, was a diplomatic agent in Peru until 1845, undersecretary of the interior and foreign relations during the late 1840s, and cabinet minister in the 1850s.[69] Several members of the Antioqueño Sáenz Montoya clan also served as consuls in London during the 1840s, and their London-based commercial firm was in charge of paying Colombia's diplomats in Europe.[70]

These influential bureaucrats, and the Antioqueño merchant and mineowning families to which they belonged, promptly used their position in Congress to pass measures favorable to the administration of their local affairs and their region's mining and financial activities. Indeed, the Antioqueños had already demonstrated their strength in May 1830, during the anarchical period that preceded the formation of the provincial-aristocratic coalition, when they achieved Antioquia's recognition as the sixth separate province of New Granada, carving it out of Cundinamarca.[71] Subsequently, they obtained the modification of decrees regarding the trading of gold in 1832, pressed for the creation of a local mint in 1833, obtained the creation of a regional court of appeals in 1834, and benefited from the 1835 law freeing the amount of interest to be charged on loans.⁷² Later, under a period of aristocratic regimes (1837–1849) begun by Márquez, various other merchants from the region, several of whom were lawyers, also used their state connections to obtain important contracts for the export of tobacco (see Figure 9.1).⁷³ Moreover, as late as the 1850s the ministries of foreign relations, interior, and war continued to operate out of buildings in Bogotá that belonged to Antioqueño merchants, from whom the state leased them.⁷⁴

As they became entrenched in business, the upper social circles of the capital, and in politics, the Antioqueños gradually found more affinity with the moderate aristocratic clique than with the provincials who were their closest allies in the recent past.⁷⁵ Indeed, the prosperity of their own businesses and their active intervention in state management during the 1830s and beyond made them wish more than ever for order, stability, firm authority, and restricted access to the state. Radical republicanism of the sort some had advocated in the late 1820s was no longer vital for their survival and advancement. From political liberalism, they began to tend to conservative politics. Thus, the Antioqueños slowly converted to a variation of the kind of exclusionary state-building project that they had in part revolted against in the late 1820s.⁷⁶ This process of aristocratic conversion paralleled what Hugo Nutini's study of the Mexican case and Eul-Soo Pang's work on Brazil's nobility have illustrated so well: the renewal of aristocratic groups by the incorporation of plutocratic segments of society over time.⁷⁷

The Antioquenos' aristocratic conversion was sealed in 1836–1837 with Márquez's victory in the presidential elections, due largely to their support. The 1836 elections were, as usual, accompanied by heated journalistic disputes. The government-sponsored "constitutionalist" press generally supported President Santander's favorite candidate, provincial General José M. Obando, citing his strength, energy, and military experience.⁷⁸ Márquez's followers, in turn, launched *El Imperio de los Principios,* a newspaper published in Bogotá but with subscribers in several other cities and towns. This paper stressed Márquez's patriotism, experience, and civilian orientation, and rejected the government's intervention in favor of Obando.⁷⁹ The intense press disputes again demonstrated that persuading the public was a central concern of both political factions. One newspaper even referred to public opinion as the "world's queen," evidence of the unquestionable advancement of New Granada's "public sphere"–for which a public aware of and engaged in critical political debates is vital.⁸⁰ Shaping public opinion, however, is never an easy task. In the end, Márquez's aristocratic and Obando's provincial followers seemed to have reached a stalemate.

The final results indicate that the electoral power of the aristocratic and provincial factions was fairly evenly balanced in the key provinces of Bogotá, Cartagena, and neighboring Mompos, and in the northeastern region of Vélez. Other regions presented conspicuous exceptions. The most important was, not surprisingly, Antioquia, whose elites almost completely shifted their allegiance to the aristocratic camp. More than 80 percent of electors in that region (8.5 percent of the national total) supported Márquez. Thanks to this support and to the backing of his native province of Tunja, which was endowed with the country's second largest number of electors (14.5 percent of the total), Márquez won a plurality (39 percent of the total).[81] In an indication of continuing provincial strength, however, Obando also obtained a significant number of the divided provincial votes.[82] Since no candidate received a majority, the election had to be determined by Congress in 1837. Despite allegations from the provincial ranks as to the unconstitutional nature of his election–since he was the country's incumbent vice president–Márquez was declared the victor.[83]

The conversion of plutocrats to the aristocratic ranks touched not only Antioquia natives but also the region's adoptive sons, including future minister and president Mariano Ospina Rodríguez, a former law student and native of the central region of Cundinamarca. After spending several years in Antioquia under the protection of powerful families there, Ospina became a key advocate of "conservative" politics in the late 1830s and thereafter.[84] We must not forget, however, that this process of aristocratic renewal was accompanied by a parallel growth of the provincial elite, which remained a challenge to aristocratic control.

The Provincials of Neiva and Other Regions

During the second half of the 1830s, the provincial Socorrano group was joined in its resistance to aristocratic expansion by an active cluster of upwardly mobile lawyers, made up of mostly marginal figures from Bogotá and Tunja. Romualdo Lievano and Rafael María Vásquez are representative cases. Lievano, a native of the little town of Fusagazuga, was described by a contemporary as an "hombre de modesta condición" ("a man from modest background"). After returning from exile in the early 1830s, he occupied high judicial jobs, ran a small shop, and practiced law in Bogotá.[85] Vásquez, an Indian from Bogota's neighboring town of Funza, was described by his contemporaries as an individual of "modesta fortuna" ("modest means"). He escaped persecution in the late 1820s by becoming a priest; he later became a lawyer and, as was common among provincials, worked as a full-time professional educator during the early 1830s. He also joined the opposition's clique,[86] which included a significant cluster of individuals from the regions of Neiva and neighboring Mariquita.

The southern-central region of Neiva, located between Bogotá and Popayán, had a scant presence in the colonial bureaucracy (approximately 1 percent of the total jobs in the viceroyalty; see Table 7.5). Like their contemporaries in Antioquia, Neiva's colonial elites devoted themselves to other endeavors. The region's main economic activities revolved around small-scale agriculture, ranching, and some mining.[87] Lawyers also represented an important segment of Neiva's middle sectors and elites.

An example of the late colonial generation of provincial lawyers linked to this region is José María Lombana, the son of a small Bogotá-based merchant. Lombana's admission to law school in Bogotá was originally denied during the 1790s because of the alleged illegitimate birth of his mother.[88] Eventually, however, he entered law school and became a lawyer in 1805. After graduating he settled in the thriving rural region of La Plata, a small town in Neiva not too far from aristocratic Popayán. Here he devoted part of his efforts to developing a cacao plantation. Cacao planters seem to have made a good living; passing through Popayán, mules loaded with cacao traveled from La Plata all the way to gold-rich Antioquia, where hot chocolate made from cacao was an important staple of the local diet.[89] Lombana must have accumulated some wealth, for he was considered eligible to marry into an influential local family. His wife was from La Plata's Buendía clan, a landowning family that also had ties with other local lawyers, including the influential and politically active José María Céspedes.[90] Lombana died during the wars of independence in 1816 but left offspring in Neiva.

Like an increasing number of individuals from provincial families in the 1830s, three of Lombana's sons—Cayetano, Ramón, and Vicente Lombana Buendía— profited from the boom in provincial education and the laxity of the provincial-sponsored plan of legal studies adopted in 1832 and 1835 (see Chapter 8). Cayetano became a doctor, and Ramón and Vicente lawyers. Ramón graduated in 1836 and became a middling bureaucrat at the Ministry of Economy in 1837. Vicente finished his studies in 1833; in addition to practicing and teaching law, he worked as a small shopkeeper, doctor, and politician from the mid-1830s on.[91] In fact, Vicente perfectly fit the mocking description in the aristocratic press of a "two-year" *doctor* in both medicine and law.[92]

Colonial Neiva did have a few aristocratic lawyers, such as Andrés José Iriarte Rojas, son of one of the region's governors. After teaching law and serving in low bureaucratic jobs, he became *fiscal* of the Quito Audiencia in 1799, where he died in 1809. Part of his family remained in Neiva and, much like Lombana's, his relatives, particularly his nephew Joaquín Gómez Iriarte, received legal training. Gómez Iriarte became an active conservative congressman and politician during the postcolonial period.[93]

Nevertheless, the majority of lawyers that Neiva produced in the late 1820s and the 1830s seem to have come from families more like Lombana's than Iriarte's. Examples included Domingo Ciprián Cuenca (1801–1850), of seemingly modest background. He had practiced law since 1827 both in Bogotá and in the little town of Purificación, part of Neiva at the time. Cuenca reinforced his provincial tendencies by marrying the sister of fellow lawyer Angel María Flórez (1802–1836), who under General Santander had served as governor of Vélez, his native region.[94] Another example was Bernardo Herrera Buendía (1812–1887), an 1834 law graduate who descended from apparently prosperous landowners. Herrera was a first cousin of the Lombana Buendía brothers and in 1838 was *oficial tercero* in the Ministry of Economy, where his cousin Ramón served. That year Herrera married a daughter of the high-ranking and authoritarian-minded Antioqueño bureaucrat José Manuel Restrepo, director of the local mint. This marriage probably saved him from losing his job in retaliation for his support in 1837 of Obando's anti-aristocratic presidential campaign. It probably also kept him from participating in the civil war of the late 1830s, a conflict that at least one of his cousins openly supported.[95] Perhaps helped by his father-in-law's close connections with Antioqueño merchants (Figure 9.1), Herrera practiced business in Bogotá and became a prosperous lawyer; however, he was not entirely coopted by the aristocrats. In addition to supporting Obando, he remained an active member of the *progresista* group, later the Liberal party, through the 1840s and beyond.[96] The Manrique Gaitán brothers, Eladio and Eloi, their brother-in-law Laureano Gaspar Díaz Sánchez (1810–1878), who graduated during the 1830s, and 1836 law graduate Andrés Durán González were also part of Neiva's provincial elites. They all came from families of middling provincial proprietors, lacking in aristocratic credentials or high bureaucratic colonial background. It might be said that they represented a sort of middle class, although some prosperous landholders were not altogether absent from the group. Little is known yet about their family strategies, but we do have some information about their careers. They became practicing lawyers in Bogotá and Neiva, as well as active liberal politicians, congressmen, law professors, and bureaucrats during the 1830s.[97]

The same trajectory was typical of some lawyers from little towns in the neighboring province of Mariquita. Prime examples are Eujenio Castilla, Manuel Murillo Toro, and Patrocinio Cuellar, modest provincial students from a little *villa* called Chaparral, which only became an official town (*cantón*) of the province in 1837, perhaps thanks to their influence.[98] Castilla's family activities are obscure. All we know is that the family lived and married in rural Chaparral and that one of Eujenio's uncles, a parish priest in Neiva, was active in raising funds for the creation of a local *colegio* and probably contributed to the education of his nephew.[99] Murillo, who had served during his adolescence as scribe for Ignacio Gutiérrez Vergara's aristocratic relatives in Bogotá, was referred to as a "poor student in need of material support," "offspring of a modest family," and from a "poor cradle." He was educated in a provincial *colegio* under the sponsorship of a local priest. Like Castilla, he later traveled to Bogotá, where both eventually became lawyers, bureaucrats, and active opposition politicians during the late 1830s and 1840s. Indeed, Murillo became one of the most active participants in the anti-aristocratic War of the *Supremos* (1839–1842), when he joined at least three of the different revolts.[100]

A hegemonic project of state and society could not develop in early postcolonial Colombia. In the late 1820s confrontations between, on one hand, New Granada's upwardly mobile (provincial) groups, supported by wealthy mining entrepreneurs and merchants from the region of Antioquia, and, on the other, aristocratic sectors linked to traditional colonial circles from Cartagena, Popayán, Bogotá and Tunja, impeded the consolidation of the Gran Colombian union established in 1821. The aristocratic groups were not monolithic; an important segment joined the provincials in an attempt to dissolve the union of New Granada with Venezuela and Ecuador and demilitarize the government, to avoid social disorder and damage to their properties by "foreign" (Venezuelan) armies. The confrontation in question took the form of constant constitutional gatherings, elections, coups, and countercoups, not to mention intense journalistic disputes in a more or less open public sphere. In the end, the union would be dissolved, the army reduced, and a provincial-aristocratic coalition government established under civilian control from 1832 to 1837.

The state continued to provide status-honor to traditional aristocratic sectors, but also benefited the upwardly mobile provincial elites. These groups would share power as long as necessary, but given the social changes both sectors began to undergo, new crises were bound to emerge soon. The aristocratic renewal in the late 1830s and the parallel strengthening of elites from Neiva and other marginal regions were at the root of these crises. As the following chapter will indicate, educational policies toward law schools added still another critical area of competition among the two sociopolitical sectors.

Chapter 8
Legal Education: The Making of Bureaucrats and Citizens

Legal training and the law were significant ideological tools during the colonial and the postcolonial periods. The historical records leave no doubt that the education of lawyers was a key instrument for state-building, and that the conflicts over its reform reflected diverse visions of state and society on the part of socially antagonistic groups.

Colonial Background

The colonial state, the Catholic Church, and elite groups were all very concerned about the character and mechanics of legal education. The state and Church in particular competed for the regulation and control of the educational process. The Church had more effective control over legal education than did the state until the late colonial period, when the Crown encroached upon Church privileges and tried to gain control over the "production" of lawyers. However, royal administrators soon had to turn their attention to more pressing issues, leaving the Church again in command.

The underlying reasons for the state's interest in legal education changed constantly. Initially, during the 1760s and 1770s, the state's attempt to regulate legal education was part of a larger absolutist effort to neutralize and curtail the power of the Church in all spheres of civil life. Later, from the mid-1790s on, state intervention, framed within the anti-French conservative reaction taking place in the Iberian peninsula, was aimed at curbing the political activism of rebellious young law students. Like Church privileges before, this activism was perceived as a threat to the power of the Crown.[1]

During the early 1770s, colonial authorities introduced some reforms aimed at increasing state intervention in legal training and changing the heavily religious nature of the courses offered. Bogotá's Royal Audiencia tightened educational standards in response to *fiscal* Moreno y Escandón's allegations that the Dominicans were granting the degree of *doctor* in law with scandalous facility. In August 1770, in addition to reiterating that no degree of *licenciado* or *doctor* should be given before the degree of *bachiller* (earned after five years of study), the Royal Audiencia also increased from two to three years the period of practical training (*pasantía*) required for admission to legal practice. On July 22, 1771, the Crown issued a *cédula* ratifying the five-year study requirement and increasing the period of practical training from three to four years.[2]

Further reforms were introduced in the late 1770s. A Junta de Estudios composed of the local archbishop, a royal *visitador,* the *fiscales* of the Royal Audiencia, and the directors of the two *colegios mayores* and the university was created in 1778 to enhance state supervision of legal education.³ In 1779, reflecting the Crown's perception of legal studies as a means to train royal servants, the Junta ordered both of Bogotá's *colegios mayores* to offer, in addition to two years of canon law and two years of Roman and Spanish civil law, a year-long course in "public law, the learning of which, although very useful and convenient, has always been ignored in this kingdom."⁴ Classes in public law had a secular orientation and included principles of political institutions, international law, and *derecho natural* (natural law), all of which pertained to the affairs and functioning of the state.

As a result of this innovation, in September 1780 the *fiscal* instructed the Colegio Mayor de San Bartolomé to open the competition (*oposición*) for a professorship in public law. He appointed a local lawyer to teach this subject in the interim.⁵ Relatively few students attended the new course initially, perhaps because they were afraid of angering the local clergy, and in 1782 the instructor temporarily appointed by the *fiscal* resigned.⁶ Regardless, classes in public law seem to have gained acceptance in the 1790s.⁷ Soon, however, the state was forced to change its course.

In 1795 the local authorities, following similar measures taken in Spain the year before as part of the conservative reaction aroused by the French Revolution, banned the teaching of public law and substituted it with courses in *derecho real* (Spanish national law).⁸ This happened soon after a noisy series of trials of several of Bogotá's law students, who were jailed and exiled by the local audiencia under suspicion of participating in a pro-French political plot (see Chapter 3).

Shortly afterward, the local authorities also decided to prohibit the teaching of law courses in other than the two Bogotá *colegios*. Provincial students were discouraged from attending law classes at their regional seminaries, and after 1796 these classes were not accepted toward law degrees in Bogotá.⁹ In addition, "royal censors" were established in 1802 to guarantee the elimination from all courses of "any doctrine against the authority and privileges of my Crown" and any teaching favorable to regicide.¹⁰ All of this indicates the growing power of the state over a system of legal education which, less than three decades before, had been under the exclusive control of the Church. Nevertheless, the state was unable to take away the Church's exclusive degree-granting privileges.

During the period between the *fiscal* Moreno y Escandón's initial efforts to increase the state's control over legal education in the late 1760s and the mid-1790s, when some of the measures adopted under his sponsorship were reversed (e.g., instruction in public law), other forms of political agitation had been shaking New Granada. The tax reforms introduced during the late 1770s and early 1780s by a Bourbon administrator sent from Spain, *visitador* Gutiérrez de Piñéres, unleashed a major popular uprising, the Comunero revolt, in 1781. The significant threat to political stability this movement represented forced the Crown to change its secularizing direction. In effect, the Crown relied on the Church, which remained highly influential among the popular masses, to quell the revolt.¹¹ On top of this, the Comuneros forced some modernizing bureaucrats like Moreno y

Escandón to leave New Granada[12] and obliged the Crown to direct its efforts at reforming the local military, sacrificing educational reform.[13]

Moreno y Escandón's departure undoubtedly contributed to slowing down the projected reforms, particularly the proposed creation of a public university. For more than a decade he had been the most active promoter of educational reform. Besides tightening the requirements for obtaining law degrees, increasing the duration of lawyers' practical training, introducing new subject matter into the curriculum, and organizing a state-directed Junta de Estudios, the *fiscal* led the creation of the first public library in New Granada in 1777. He also pioneered the introduction and teaching of modern mathematical and astronomical theories.[14]

It has been widely argued that Moreno y Escandón's efforts helped to produce a new generation of local intellectuals, who went on to play an active role in the independence movement in the 1810s.[15] Elsewhere, I have questioned the early revolutionary commitment of an important segment of these intellectuals, the enlightened colonial lawyers.[16] Far from being prorevolutionary, educational reforms contributed to independence mostly in the way they helped to alter New Granada's balance of power. In effect, the reforms increased the alienation of a segment of the local Church, making it available and willing to participate in a "revolution from above" ignited by elite priests, law school professors, and students (see Chapter 4).[17]

Furthermore, the history of the reforms shows that despite its growing encroachments upon the educational powers of the Church, the state lacked the ability to implement its policies effectively. For more than four decades the colonial authorities were unable to implement the core of the *fiscal*'s proposals, in particular the creation of a public university. This failure resulted from the combination of factors mentioned earlier and an alleged lack of funds. Moreno insisted that the properties confiscated from the Jesuits, along with the current funds employed in education, a segment of the rent of tithes, and part of the revenues coming from the royal salt mine monopoly would suffice. The Crown, accepting the Dominicans' allegations, disagreed.[18]

In reality, the main obstacle to educational reform was not financial but rather the continuing legal maneuvering of the Dominicans.[19] They saw legal education—and college education in general—as a means to advance the overall interests of the papacy, maintain the political and social presence and influence of the clergy, and reinforce the clerical mentality of colonial society. The reproduction of the Church's own ranks and membership also benefited from training that emphasized canon law. The strength of this training was reflected in the fact that many colonial lawyers also became priests, and vice versa.

New Postcolonial Institutions and the Decline of Clerical Influence

Primary, secondary, and professional education were among the first concerns of New Granada's postcolonial state.[20] In addition to creating several primary schools during the 1820s, the new ruling elites also promoted and regulated secondary education.²¹ In the 1820s, the government, exercising the traditional right of *patronato* (supervision of the Church), undertook dramatic policies: On July 5, 1820, it assumed direction of all existent *colegios,* most of which were then controlled by the Church; on October 1820, it issued a provisional education plan; and on July 18, 1821, the Congress of Cúcuta enacted a law requiring that each province have at least one *colegio* or *casa de educación*.²² Demonstrating the strategic importance the elites attributed to legal education, other measures and countermeasures, specifically concerning law schools, were adopted in several stages: in late 1826 and 1828, during the early and mid-1830s, in the early 1840s, and, finally, in the late 1840s. Some of these measures will be outlined below.

Along with the October 1820 provisional plan of studies that regulated the content of legal education in existing institutions, the 1821 law provided, to the extent possible, for the projected provincial *colegios* (which were assigned the confiscated properties of small monasteries–*conventos menores*²³) to offer law classes. Finally, the law allowed for all provincial law courses to be accepted toward law degrees in the "universities" (Art. 3), although only one university remained in existence–the Dominicans' St. Thomas.²⁴ Heated disputes accompanied this legislation, which, like similar efforts in the colonial period, represented the beginning of another long series of reforms and controversies surrounding legal education.²⁵ These debates involved not only the Church and state but also emerging political factions and, later, political parties.

Creating the provincial *colegios* as provided for in the 1821 law was not an easy undertaking. The provincial elites were caught in a series of disputes with the local clergy concerning the transference to the new *colegios* of the monasteries' properties and funds. Throughout the early 1820s and 1830s, the buildings and rents of suppressed monasteries were sought by different localities intent on becoming the site of a *colegio*.²⁶ These localities disputed each other and lobbied before the central state for the privilege of being selected as the location for their province's *colegio*.²⁷

During the first half of the 1820s several such *colegios* were founded and their directors and professors appointed by the executive power (initially the president, later the provincial governors).²⁸ The government's appointments were legitimated by following the traditional procedure of *oposición,* a public contest among candidates that was the custom during the colonial period. In a reversal of tradition, however, the government now reserved the right to make the final determination.²⁹

Despite the state's new power over *colegios,* the fact that most of them carried religious names–San José, San Pedro Apostol, San Carlos, San Simón, Santa Librada, San Juan Nepomuceno–indicated the continuing clerical influence. Not a few of the *colegios*' directors and professors were members of the clergy.³⁰ They were not regarded as state employees, suggesting a certain ambiguity as to whether education was considered to be a state (public) or a private affair.³¹ Regardless, this trend of state intervention in the creation of *colegios* and the appointment of their staff indicated the growing strength of the postindependence state over the Catholic Church in the area of education, and the increasingly public character attributed to this activity.³²

By the mid- to late 1820s several of the new *colegios* had opened their doors, and a few taught law classes. However, the truly significant expansion in the provincial teaching of law took place during the 1830s and 1840s, when even small parish schools applied for authorization to teach law courses that counted toward degrees.[33] This trend was spawned by legal measures sponsored in 1832 by a provincial group of lawyers who tried to curtail the powers of both aristocratic sectors and the central authorities.[34] Nevertheless, the central government retained the power to authorize law classes in the *colegios,* thus making sure that the provincial assemblies established in the early 1830s would not have a say in this matter.[35] In addition, through the Dirección General de Instrucción Pública, established in 1826 as a special division within the Ministry of the Interior, the central state supervised and promoted public *certámenes* (honors examinations). The state began to use these exams as an opportunity to disseminate republican propaganda. It also exerted supervision over the content of courses taught at the provincial level.[36]

Besides the provincial *colegios,* three state universities were organized during the 1820s. One, the Universidad Central, was created in Bogotá in 1826. It was not a fully separate and independent institution, but rather based its curriculum on the subjects already taught at the two local *colegios* (San Bartolomé and Nuestra Señora del Rosario) plus a few additional new courses. The Bogotá *colegios,* despite their formal university membership, continued to function semi-independently, retaining their own directors and professors, controlling their budgets, and maintaining their old names. Thus, throughout the first half of the nineteenth century their status and autonomy remained ambiguous and disputed.[37] The Universidad del Cauca, created in the southern region of Popayán in late 1827, absorbed the local *colegio* and by 1828 was teaching law courses. Another school, the Universidad de Magdalena e Istmo, was opened in Cartagena, absorbing the local *colegio seminario* and beginning classes in November 1828.[38] The state participated in the appointment of the universities' directors and faculty, selected, like the *colegios',* by the process of *oposiciones.* This did not translate into the establishment of fully secular institutions, for several among the universities' faculty were also members of the clergy.[39]

All of these universities were under the formal control of the state and were subject to tight vigilance. Yet, this did not prevent the local elites from exercising a significant degree of autonomy in their management and ideological orientation.[40] The universities were given the right to issue academic degrees, which tended to reinforce the regions' educational autonomy. It also ended the Dominicans' exclusive control over degrees; the monks issued their last degrees in 1826, and their University of St. Thomas was finally closed.[41] At last, in contrast to its failure during the colonial period, the state was able to establish public universities.

State intervention also determined which subjects were to be taught in schools. The resulting changes in postcolonial education had four major consequences. First, they helped reinforce the state's republican project and the decentralizing trend of the 1830s. Second, while not making legal education altogether secular, they nevertheless advanced an antireligious posture. Third, the reforms prepared the ground for the upsurge of free trade during the mid-nineteenth century. Finally, they also led to the production of a large number of lawyer-bureaucrats. Each of these undertakings reflected not only the state's efforts to shape legal education according to certain political needs, but also the increasing intra-elite disputes between upwardly mobile groups of provincial lawyers and the aristocratic sectors that had dominated in colonial society.

Public Law, "Universal Legislation," and the Bentham Controversy

During the early 1820s the Colombian elites opted for a constitutional and republican form of state. The content of legal education was undoubtedly considered a contributing ideological factor to the establishment of such a system. The 1821 law that provided for provincial *colegios* indicated, in fact, that in addition to the traditional courses in civil and canon law, a course on *derecho natural de gentes* (public law, constitutional doctrines, rights of citizenship) should be taught in each of the projected provincial schools.[42] This course proved controversial owing to the tensions it ultimately provoked between secular and clerical visions of state-building.

Dealing with such delicate matters as the nature of political authority, the role of legislatures, and the duties of rulers toward their subjects, this revolutionary course was reinstated in Bogotá during the independence period. The class, briefly taught in the 1780s and early 1790s until the colonial authorities banned it, was offered again during the 1810s and through the 1820s in at least one of Bogotá's local *colegios*. The course taught the enlightened political doctrines of Montesquieu, Rousseau, Heinecio, Filangieri, Beccaria, Bentham, and other progressive and liberal thinkers. These readings as well as the instructor himself, young lawyer José I. de Márquez, praised the virtues of the republican form of government, discussed citizenship and its duties, advocated equality of all citizens before the law, and rejected the existence of coloniallike "ligas, cofradías y hermandades" ("lay confraternities and religious brotherhoods").[43]

With the conspicuous exception of San Gil, a town near Socorro, the class was not taught in any of the new provincial *colegios* until the 1830s, but it caused intra-elite disputes from early on.[44] Most of the conflicts concerned the works of Jeremy Bentham, which were the main texts for this and related courses in Bogotá. The textbooks became sources of discord after several observers deemed them inappropriate.

In New Granada, the introduction of Bentham's works as required textbooks for classes in *derecho público* and "legislative science" came by way of a decree in October 1825. The measure proved to have a long-lasting impact.[45] Its author was Vice President Santander, who introduced a systematic *plan de estudios* (official curriculum) the following year. Santander led the provincial professors put in charge of the new law classes. His plan provided for a six-year program of legal studies leading to a doctorate.[46] In addition to the customary courses in Roman and canon law, which suffered little transformation,[47] law schools were required to teach "political, constitutional, and international law" (i.e., public law), political economy, and two other innovative subjects: "principles of universal legislation"—which was generally combined with the public law classes—and "administrative science and principles of statistics." Bentham's works were listed as required reading for these classes.[48]

Santander's educational measures soon gave rise to political controversies between Church and state and among the emerging political factions. Sufficient academic attention has been paid already to the disputes surrounding the use as textbooks of Bentham's legal treatises, which some considered contrary to religious dogma. The adoption of Bentham's works caused the gradual alienation of an important sector of the Catholic Church from the provincial segment of the political elite—soon to emerge as the Liberal party. It resulted in an alliance between the Church and the aristocrats, soon to become Conservatives.[49]

Bentham's works remained in the curriculum until March 12, 1828, when President Bolívar issued a decree banning the controversial textbooks.[50] The next day, the general instability of the country, resulting from controversies between civilians and the military, a constitutional crisis, and several recent incidents in Bogotá involving local students, provincial journalists, and the military, led Bolívar to assume extraordinary constitutional powers. Under these powers he was allowed to take any measure required to arrest the prevailing "internal chaos."[51] Vice President Santander, public law professor Vicente Azuero, and political economy professor and lawyer Francisco Soto, Bolívar's opponents, were away from Bogotá at the national constitutional assembly in Ocaña. Soon after the convention disbanded, Bolívar adopted additional measures designed to court the support of the Catholic Church. In August, he suspended the constitution and, in the midst of continued street protests by Bogotá's students, assumed dictatorial powers.[52]

Shortly afterward, as described in the previous chapter, in a culmination of a long political crisis that had begun around 1826, several of Bogotá's law students, lawyers, and law professors were involved in a failed attempt on Bolívar's life. Because of "the disgraceful participation in it [the plot] by some young college students," and since their conduct was allegedly rooted in "the political sciences that have been taught to students," on October 20, 1828 the government ordered Colombian universities "to suspend for the time being the courses of principles of universal legislation and public-political law, constitutional law, and administrative science." Instead of these courses, the teaching of the "fundaments and apology of the Roman Catholic religion" was to be emphasized. The government's resolution stated that the students were too young to be exposed to dangerous doctrines they could not well comprehend, and that "the evil has increased considerably because of the authors used to illustrate the teaching of the principles of legislation, such as Bentham and others, who alongside brilliant doctrines also contain many doctrines contrary to religion, morality, and the people's tranquility, of which we have received painful examples and warning signals."[53]

Bolívar's main adviser for the adoption of these measures was Antioqueño lawyer José Manuel Restrepo who, in his diary and letters to friends, expressed his conviction that the current legal education, particularly Bentham's doctrines, led the young men to conspire against the government. Restrepo encouraged his Antioqueño relatives and friends not to send their sons to study in Bogotá, but rather to choose the more conservative anti-Benthamite University of Cauca in Popayán. In a letter written to Antioqueño merchants Sinforoso García and Pedro Sáenz on October 14, 1828, Restrepo noted: "I have been told that you and Sáenz were thinking about sending your sons to this capital so that they could continue with their studies. The studies are so bad, though, and the youths' corruption is such, that some students were among those involved in the attempt to assassinate the *Libertador* [Bolívar] this 25th of September. Therefore, I would venture to advise you not to do such a thing, and to leave your sons without any education, rather than to see them turn into immoral, impious, and corrupt people, which is what they will learn to be in this capital."[54]

The political activism of law students, then as during the 1790s, provoked fierce state intervention in legal education. This time, however, the conflicts not only reflected tensions between state and civil society or between Church and state, but also fanned intra-elite disputes. In fact, the state's reaction was led by a coalition of authoritarian centralists who represented a segment of aristocratic lawyer-bureaucrats, the high Church, and the pro-Bolívar military. Together, these groups were opposed to the growing insurgency led by Santander's provincial faction, several of whose members, including the vice president himself, were sent into exile for alleged participation in the plot against Bolívar.

While exiled in Europe, Santander met the elderly Bentham, who wrote letters on his behalf.[55] Upon his return to New Granada in 1832, Santander led the way for the reintroduction of Bentham and public law into the legal curriculum.[56] Breaking away from the recent centralizing and authoritarian trend, the provincial faction—within a wider coalition government—also promoted legal education at the provincial level.[57] Public law and Bentham were now taught in the provincial *colegios* as well as in Bogotá's law schools. This corresponded not only to Santander's individual wishes, but also to a "constitutionalist" campaign sponsored by the coalition government of provincials and moderate aristocrats formed in the early 1830s to curtail the power of the army.[58]

The campaign consisted of the publication in several regions of "constitutionalist" newspapers, official publications that printed the most important resolutions of the regional and national authorities as well as "articles promoting good political principles and the advantages of the republican system, thus rectifying and unifying public opinion."[59] These newspapers were published for several years in key regions such as Cundinamarca, Boyacá, Antioquia, Cauca, and Cartagena. At least one copy of every regional newspaper was distributed in each of the region's towns and read publicly by the local *jefe político* or the town's mayor. It was probably also expected that the people would further disseminate the news after attending church, or in the marketplace, *pulperías, chicherías,* and other informal gatherings.[60] The provincial/aristocratic ruling coalition then in place considered an intensive process of civil reeducation and the molding of public opinion in favor of civilian-led political life to be a major priority. If the public at large was to be reeducated it was all the more important that law students learn new public law doctrines such as Bentham's.

Opposition to Bentham during the 1830s stemmed from a segment of the coalition led by the *director de estudios,* Antioqueño lawyer José Manuel Restrepo, and composed of other high bureaucrats and clergy. Opposition was fueled too by the new Catholic Societies organized in 1838, intolerant aristocratic political leaders of several regions, and pious aristocratic members of the Senate.[61] In spite of this resistance, the teaching of public law according to Bentham continued until 1840, by which time the aristocrats, led by President José I. de Márquez (1837–1841), were increasing their hold on the state and were ready to shape legal education according to their conservative interests.

New Conservative Anti-Benthamite Reaction

In May 1840, a few days after former President Santander's death, the aristocratic government, facing a provincial military revolt issued a new reform of legal education that again changed its ideological direction. Although this reform preserved courses in public law, it eventually eradicated Bentham's teachings.[62] Further measures banned the teaching of any doctrine contrary to the New Testament and the Constitution.[63] Additional reforms against "antireligious" teachings plus a new comprehensive program of studies were introduced in early 1842. By this time Márquez had been succeeded by an aristocratic general, Pedro Alcántara Herrán (1841–1845), and the insurgent political faction formerly led by Santander had been defeated by the government in a bloody civil war fought from late 1839 through 1842.[64] During the war provincial law professors favorable to Bentham and alleged to have supported the rebellion were persecuted.

In late 1840, thirty-year-old Benthamite lawyer José Duque Gómez, professor of public law and acting director of Bogotá's Colegio del Rosario, was tried and jailed after one of his classes was deemed subversive.[65] His colleague Florentino González, former professor of public law at Bogotá's Colegio de San Bartolomé, not only was vetoed by the government as recently elected director of the capital's other law school, the Colegio del Rosario, but was jailed along with several other provincial law professors and practicing lawyers.[66] They managed to escape, but their persecution marked the beginning of the conservative changes in legal education.[67]

The government shut down Bogotá's *colegios* during the civil war until mid-1841, when hostilities were receding.[68] It then formulated a sweeping modification of the legal curriculum. In a report presented to the Congress late in 1841, Minister of the Interior Mariano Ospina Rodríguez explained the government's reasoning by arguing that young law students trained in Bentham's and other abstract political theories "only think about legislating and governing." In light of the very few available government jobs, he added, "there will be a great number of people ready to try to overthrow the established order so as to take over the public jobs from which they deem themselves to have been unjustly excluded."[69]

As Ospina's report makes clear, the traditional tendency of New Granadans to live 'honorable lives' by holding public jobs was now defined in a different way. The term *empleomanía* was used by the minister to suggest college graduates' dangerous dependency on the bureaucracy. This tendency, along with the teaching of subversive doctrines in law schools–where most *empleomaniacos* could be found–were blamed for the recent war. From being a source of status-honor, state careers and doctrines were beginning to be perceived as a source of instability and even a deplorable "vice."

In 1842, under the leadership of Ospina Rodríguez, the government further checked the teaching of subjects regarded as dangerous and directed legal studies into a more conservative and "practical" direction.[70] Political theory yielded to the practical study of contemporary Colombian legal statutes, with emphasis placed on court rules and procedures. Courses dealing with abstract "general principles" of universal legislation, constitutional law, and administrative science were replaced by courses in concrete statutes, including the Constitution and administrative norms and regulations.[71] For the first time, courses in commercial law, civil procedures, and criminal procedures were made available.[72] The only theory class that remained was political economy which, along with the traditional history of Roman law, the authorities apparently regarded as uncontroversial and practical in nature.

The 1842 measures also increased the state's control over the appointment of law school faculty.[73] Ospina put an end to the *oposiciones,* the system through which provincials received their appointments and tenure in the mid-1820s and early 1830s, and which allowed them to remain in their jobs during the aristocratic regime of the late 1830s.[74] In 1844, the government even invited the Jesuits to return.[75] Initially invited to pursue missionary work in remote areas of the country, Jesuit fathers rapidly became active educators in various urban centers.[76]

In what was largely a repetition of the process of the late 1820s, the aristocratic governments of the early 1840s tried to reduce the political activism of law students while strengthening ties to the Catholic Church.[77] Yet, even under the new plan many students trained in Bogotá during the 1840s continued to study the prohibited subjects. As one student later said, the government's efforts to make young people conservative made them instead rebellious, pro-Benthamite, anti-Jesuit, and radically liberal "hasta la extravagancia" ("to the extreme").[78]

In sum, the struggles surrounding the teaching of Bentham and public law from the 1820s to the 1840s reflected deepening intra-elite confrontations. These struggles soon shaped the alliance between most high members of the Catholic Church and the authoritarian, centralizing, and aristocratic lay politicians who in 1849 formally created the Conservative Party. The process of institutionalizing politics through the formation of formal parties channelled the educational disputes, especially those around Bentham. Such disputes continued into the second half of the nineteenth century, becoming a hallmark of inter-party confrontation and a pervasive topic of academic discussion.[79]

Intense intra-elite controversies like the ones surrounding the teaching of public law and Bentham did not affect the new course on political economy, also introduced in the 1820s. This fact confirms that intra-elite disputes were not so much over economic doctrines and interests, but rather an ideological reflection of tensions over the power, prestige, and status-honor derived from control over high-ranking bureaucratic jobs (ultimately alleged to have provoked *empleomanía* and instability). To explain this fact it is necessary to go back to the 1820s and notice what occurred with respect to other components of the postcolonial legal curriculum.

New Contents and Purposes:
Building a Republic of Free-Trader Citizens

Along with the reintroduction of public law, the teaching of political economy as one of the required courses for law students in Bogotá's Colegio Mayor de San Bartolomé in 1824 was viewed as a major innovation.[80] Political economy had been written about and discussed by local intellectuals in the 1810s and before but had never been taught in schools.[81]

In 1823, an unknown local author who signed his work simply as "G.P.P." and who likely was a merchant wrote and sent to the government a brief treatise on political economy that advocated the abandonment of state protectionism but also criticized the liberal doctrines of Jean Baptist Say and Jeremy Bentham.[82] This did not keep the government from adopting Say's *Tratado de economía política* as a textbook in the new course to be taught in the local law schools.[83] The course was introduced in Bogotá in late 1824 and taught for the first time by "provincial" lawyer Francisco Soto, who in addition to being a law professor was also an employee of the local court of appeals and later the country's *director de crédito público* (director of the state's public credit office).[84] Soto, a close associate of Vice President Santander, remained in charge of the political economy class until late 1828, when he was forced into exile.[85] The course was not offered again until 1832 when, with Soto now returned from exile and serving as economics minister, it was reinstated under the professorship of Ezequiel Rojas, Soto's disciple.[86] Rojas was also a provincial exiled in the late 1820s and was to become the most successful and prosperous of Bogotá's practicing lawyers during the 1830s. Using Say's textbook, he continued teaching political economy until at least the mid-1840s.[87]

During the 1830s, official "constitutionalist" newspapers praised the "science" of political economy based on the works of Say and also Adam Smith. It became a standard course in law schools throughout New Granada, taught by professors who belonged mostly to provincial circles.[88] As opposed to other courses, political economy was spared serious attacks by the aristocratic faction or the Church and was kept as part of the curriculum even during political crises.[89] Since its subject matter was considered scientific, academic consensus on the need to teach political economy reigned among the various political factions. This consensus was so strong that during the 1830s and 1840s, despite the pragmatic protectionism observed by New Granada's ruling elites, even outstanding conservative figures hesitated to approve economic subsidies and state monopolies that "did not conform to the lessons of political economy" that they had recently learned at the universities.⁹⁰ As proof of the ideological impact of legal education, law schools from the 1820s to the 1850s, with full elite support, produced several generations of free-traders. Indeed, intra-elite disputes rarely revolved around the teaching of economic doctrines or the adoption of specific tax laws, tariff regulations, or labor acts. Unlike the conflicts that occurred in Mexico or Peru, New Granada's elites, provincials and aristocrats alike, seemed to agree on economic doctrines and policies, first pragmatically protectionist and later liberal.⁹¹

New Courses and New Lawyers: Administrative Science and Bureaucratic Training

Santander's 1826 plan also called for the introduction of "administrative science"—a field that has received almost no scholarly attention—as another required course for law students. Its introduction into the legal curriculum, and its actual teaching from the mid-1830s on, suggests that some of the ruling elites were interested not just in the secularization of society and education, the formation of good citizens through the spreading of constitutionalist republican ideals, the diffusion of free-trade doctrines, or even in simply training good practicing lawyers. Rather, they were intent on producing a crop of state servants—true "mandarins," "cameralists," or state administrators. In this they certainly followed the customary practices of other countries.⁹² More important, they drew on a long colonial tradition that saw legal education as the training ground and springboard for honorable lives in state service.

Provincials eager to compete for the status-honor derived from state service were enthusiastic about the "science of [public] administration." The class was taught for the first time at Bogotá's Colegio del Rosario by provincial lawyer José Duque Gómez from the early 1830s until 1840, when he was jailed on charges of fueling an ongoing civil war. Thereafter, it was taught by his colleague Manuel Cañarete.⁹³ By the mid-1830s, several provincial law schools began to offer classes in administrative science.⁹⁴

Following the provisions of Article 169 of the 1826 plan, law professors of the 1830s, along with regional and local bureaucrats, based their courses on an 1812 treatise on administrative science written by the Frenchman Jean Charles Bonnin.⁹⁵ Bonnin's text, even if mildly monarchist and tending toward political rather than administrative issues, still represented an improvement over the administrative manuals used by colonial administrators up until the eighteenth century.⁹⁶ By 1840, three local lawyers had published texts more appropriate to local conditions.

Even after aristocrats succeeded in passing conservative restrictions on teaching in 1842, these local works became standard textbooks. They sought to dismantle the colonial "patrimonial" state and implement an increasingly "bureaucratic" state, offering practical guidance on how to conduct an efficient public administration in a tripartite republican government. They set rules regarding the appointment and rotation of bureaucrats and the issuing of regulations. They also stressed the necessity of granting equal access to public jobs, preferring elective over appointive positions at different administrative levels, eliminating privileges and subsidies, and granting administrative autonomy to the country's different regions.[97] For reasons yet to be determined, by 1849 these texts were out of print and unavailable. A younger generation of professors and "mandarins," comprised of several of the lawyer-bureaucrats who had come of age during the 1840s, had to improvise its own textbooks.[98]

The Abundance of Lawyers Trained in the New Sciences

The impact of administrative and other new sciences can be better gauged in the context of changes in the rank and file of the legal profession during the 1830s. The educational reforms of the 1820s and 1830s contributed to the rapid rise in the number of lawyers. Since many came from nontraditional backgrounds, this increase tended to strengthen an insurgent group of upwardly mobile provincials and in the long term shifted the balance of power to their advantage. Moreover, this process allegedly heightened the demand for state jobs (now increasingly labeled *empleomanía*), a matter of great concern for all political factions and especially the aristocratic government of the early 1840s (see Table 8.1).[99]

The rapid growth in the number of lawyers was not entirely planned. Part of it was the result of the Dominicans' reaction to their loss of educational and degree-granting privileges in 1826, to which they responded by generously issuing degrees in their last days.[100] Regional pressures inspired by the provincials also led to the opening of additional training centers from the mid-1820s through the 1830s, increasing the opportunities available for a legal education.[101] Finally, the laws issued during the early 1820s and the provisions of the 1826 plan combined with competing interpretations of the 1830s laws (and the reluctance of the provincial-controlled Congress to modify them) to open additional opportunities for the graduation of even more lawyers. Indeed, some of these laws allowed students to take several courses in a single year *(cursos simultáneos),* thereby significantly abbreviating the legal training period. *Cursos simultáneos* had been forbidden during the colonial period but became common by the early 1820s

Table 8.1. Number of Law Graduates in New Granada, 1790–1850

Years	Graduates
1790–1806	61
1810–1819	27
1820–1829	62
1830–1839	198
1840–1849	272

Sources: García de la Guardia, *Kalendario manual; Gaceta de La Nueva Granada,* 396, April 14, 1839; 453, May 17, 1840; 575, September 11, 1842; 608, March 30, 1843; 676, April 21, 1844; 747, June 22, 1845; *Gaceta Oficial,* 1030, March 4, 1849; 1031, March 18, 1849.

and 1830s.¹⁰² They continued to be criticized by government officials and ridiculed by writers in the 1830s, but nothing was done to correct the problem until the law of May 16, 1840 absolutely prohibited the practice.¹⁰³

Authorities were unable to contain the seeming avalanche of law graduates. The alleged lack of qualified candidates for public service in the 1820s might explain the flexibility with which legal degrees were awarded for almost two decades in order to meet the demands of the republican bureaucracy, the new judicial system in particular.¹⁰⁴ Internal struggles among the elites in the 1820s and 1830s impeded attempts to pass stricter standards for obtaining legal degrees. In fact, the successive confrontations between civilians and the military in the 1820s, and between provincials and aristocrats in the mid- and late-1830s, led indirectly to a sharp increase in the number of lawyers in New Granada.

The abundance of lawyers was compatible with the projects of the antimilitary coalition of provincial and moderate aristocrats intent on curtailing authoritarian rule by increasing the potential pool of legally trained civilian politicians. In addition, provincial figures, who strongly influenced education during the 1820s and 1830s, undoubtedly benefited from the enhanced opportunities for social mobility through public jobs on the basis of education, not birth.¹⁰⁵ These lawyers, who soon after graduation became congressmen and active political leaders in regions and localities all over the country, helped the provincial group counterbalance the traditional power of the aristocratic sectors. The provincial faction under the leadership of Professor Vicente Azuero was also active in the transfer of administrative powers away from the center, thus increasing the need for qualified administrators at the regional and local levels.¹⁰⁶

The need for qualified state administrators was so widely felt that even aristocratic figures, generally opposed to the proliferation of lawyers (their potential competitors for status-honor), supported the training of lawyer-bureaucrats.¹⁰⁷ After all, New Granada's legal and political culture had always embraced *letrado* bureaucrats. For example, as director of Bogotá's Colegio del Rosario in 1833, aristocratic lawyer José María del Castillo y Rada requested executive authorization to initiate the teaching of administrative science in his *colegio*'s law school.¹⁰⁸ Even Minister of the Interior Mariano Ospina Rodríguez, an advocate of practical over theoretical knowledge who worried about the bureaucratic ambitions of lawyers and sponsored the conservative reforms of 1842, played a role in augmenting the number of lawyers trained as state administrators.

A former Benthamite provincial who took part in the 1828 plot to assassinate Bolívar, Ospina took refuge in Antioquia, where he served as secretary to the provincial governors Alejandro Vélez and Juan de Dios Aranzazu in the 1830s. While performing his bureaucratic duties in Antioquia, Ospina appears to have relied on Bonnin's text on administrative science. The treatise had been sent to him around 1830 by his former professor and political ally Vicente Azuero.¹⁰⁹ In addition to using it for practical purposes, Ospina taught administrative science at Antioquia's provincial *colegio* in the 1830s and undoubtedly helped spread Bonnin's ideas throughout the school.¹¹⁰ During those years Ospina, who was in reality a bourgeois, joined his Antioqueño friends in converting to the aristocratic cause. After becoming minister of state in 1841, he expressed strong complaints against the dangerous bureaucratic pretensions of lawyers trained to and obsessed with "gobernar y legislar" ("governing and legislating"). However, shortly after a series of conservative educational measures had been implemented according to his advice in 1842 and 1844, Ospina sent another report to Congress with a somewhat different tone. It praised "the universities' teaching of administrative law and administrative practices" and expressed the hope that "men thus trained for public careers will be prepared not just to hold judicial positions, but also political and municipal office."[111] After all, Ospina, like some of his aristocratic friends, seems to have had difficulty moving out of a colonial mindset that valued state careers as the logical outcome of a legal education. It appears, therefore, that even the conservative-minded members of the elite were intent on training a fair number of lawyers—as long as the graduates refrained from excessive political speculation—for the honorable and very "practical" task of public administration.[112]

Despite the pragmatic orientation of their training, however, students of the 1840s continued to speculate, philosophize, and plot. This group became known as the "generation of 1848," and it included new law professors who replaced the provincials who were exiled or died in the early 1840s (e.g., Duque Gómez in 1841, Azuero in 1844, Soto in 1846). This generation sponsored a new series of educational changes, discussed elsewhere, which contributed to the larger "liberal revolution" in 1849 and beyond.[113]

Confrontations over the rhetoric and practice of legal education were pervasive in New Granada from the 1810s to the 1840s. At first, the dominant practices and discourses were exclusively in the hands of the Catholic Church, which had long enjoyed hegemonic control over education. They then fell progressively under the control of the republican central state. State intervention in legal education helped reinforce the republican project and the decentralizing trend of the 1830s, advanced an antireligious agenda, prepared the ground for the upsurge of free trade during the mid-nineteenth century, and led to the production of a large number of lawyer-bureaucrats.

The state tried to shape legal education according to its political needs, but intra-elite disputes between upwardly mobile groups of provincial lawyers and the aristocratic sectors that had dominated colonial society made it impossible—even during the long period of aristocratic governments (1837–1849)—for any segment of the ruling elite or the central state itself to exert clear hegemony over the schools and curricula and, through them, over civil society.

This chapter closed with a cycle of conservative reforms in the early 1840s. In the long run, however, several components of the reform of legal education (i.e., expansion of provincial instruction, teaching of political economy) seem to have benefited the provincial liberal sectors, leading to an increase in the number of upwardly mobile lawyers and the spread of liberal principles. The educational changes of the 1840s and the subsequent success of the liberal sectors can be better understood in the context of the civil war fought during the late 1830s and early 1840s, and against the background of the transformation experienced by the provincial ranks during those years. These themes are discussed in the last two chapters of this work.

Chapter 9
The War of the *Supremos*

New Granada's first nationwide civil war of the postcolonial period was fought during the late 1830s and early 1840s. This war represented the most manifest and radical confrontation between the provincial and aristocratic elites. It further polarized these two groups and laid the foundations for the formal emergence a few years later of two political factions: the Liberal and the Conservative parties. These parties fought several more civil wars and continue to dominate Colombia to this day. This chapter discusses the origins, nature, and outcome of the war. It reiterates the interrelation, noticed by recent scholars, between civil wars and electioneering.[1] It also confirms the thriving character of New Granada's public sphere, reflected in intense journalistic debates and new forms of political sociability. More important, as the alleged bureaucratic origins of the war are discussed, one sees again the intimate links between status-honor and public office, and the social tensions derived from it.

The War of the *Supremos*

In 1840–1841, several of New Granada's provinces, including Vélez, Tunja, Mariquita, and some parts of Neiva, staged a series of *pronunciamientos* or military revolts against the central government. The revolts were led by high-ranking officers, referred to as *jefes supremos*. The *supremos* were colonels or generals who had served under Santander, during whose 1832–1837 government they were given regional military commands or governorships.[2] The conventional view is that the rebellion was a typical expression of the sort of *caudillo* politics that many Latin American countries experienced during those years. In the words of a recent historian, "the 1840 revolution was but a military revolt. It is appropriate to consider it as the last militarist attempt in New Granada's history."[3] This interpretation overlooks the social groups and factors underlying the regional rebellions. The *supremos* were not alone and were not acting for "militaristic" reasons. Their revolts were triggered, accompanied, and advised by provincial lawyer-bureaucrats stationed in their regions who, facing what they saw as attempts by an "aristocratic government" to exclude them from bureaucratic power and status-honor, decided to rebel. Specifically, these lawyers were responding to several major concerns: the exclusion or removal of provincials from several strategic positions in the civilian bureaucracy and the officer corps; the transfer of several lucrative government contracts from provincials to aristocrats; and, finally, the electoral frauds supposedly perpetrated by the government in recent elections.

The provincials were particularly incensed by a series of administrative and military appointments that replaced provincial lawyers, priests, and officers with aristocrats. First, there was the 1837 firing of two provincial lawyers (F. González and L. M. Lleras) from high-ranking jobs within government ministries and their replacement by aristocrats (I. Gutiérrez Vergara and J. M. Galavís). This was followed by the indirect removal of a dissident aristocratic lawyer, Francisco Ugarte Azuola, from the accounting office because of his support for provincial General Obando's presidential candidacy in 1837. Second, the removal of the governor of Vélez, Colonel Thomas Murray, was resented and resisted by a bureaucratic network of local provincial lawyers, as was the appointment of aristocratic lawyer José María Galavís to the governorship of Neiva, where some provincial networks were also dislodged. The state-influenced appointments of priest García Paredes as treasurer of Panamá's Cathedral and Mariano de Quintana as parish priest of Charalá, as well as the appointments of aristocratic lawyers Narciso Casanovas and Mateo Domínguez as justices of Socorro's high court of appeals, were equally rejected by the provincial press in the late 1830s. The provincial papers also opposed the transfer of *Doctor* Juan N. Gómez (nephew of Socorrano lawyer Diego F. Gómez), who was accused of publishing an article offensive to the Vatican's diplomatic envoy, from Bogotá's government to remote Casanare province. They also criticized the veto of provincial lawyer Florentino González as director of Bogotá's Colegio del Rosario, as well as the appointment of Antioqueño Colonel Anselmo Pineda to a military commission in Cartagena to replace a protégé of Santander. Other cases that caused controversy included the transfer of provincial General Antonio Obando from the Ministry of War in July 1838, and of Colonel Tomás Herrera from the *jefatura militar* (military command) of Panamá in late 1839; the appointment of former Bolivarian General Pedro Alcántara Herrán as secretary of the interior and foreign relations in early 1838, and his command of the government troops at Pasto in late 1839; and the appointment of aristocratic Colonel Juan María Gómez to the *jefatura militar* of Antioquia in 1840.[4]

Besides these changes in bureaucratic, ecclesiastical, and military posts, which alienated provincial leaders all over the country, there was also a dispute regarding the cancellation of a ten-year contract for the exploitation and administration of the state salt deposits in Muneque. The contract had been granted in 1835 to an individual associated with provincial General Juan N. Moreno of Casanare. It was prematurely terminated in 1838 under alleged pressure from aristocratic Tunja lawyer and Senator Antonio Malo (Appendix 4) and the wealthy leader of the religious society known as La Católica, Ignacio Morales, who managed other salt deposits in the neighboring region of Chita.[5]

Individuals close to aristocratic circles also benefited from the sale of 60,000 *arrobas* of government-monopoly tobacco for exportation. This deal was handled by the wealthy Antioqueño merchant Francisco Montoya and his relatives, especially young lawyer Jorge Gutiérrez de Lara, husband of Montoya's niece. It was followed by several more sales that turned Montoya into the wealthiest export-import merchant of the 1840s and launched his firm, Montoya Sáenz y Cía., which dominated the business world of New Granada for more than a decade.[6] This firm formed part of an endogamic network of Antioqueño merchants and lawyers and had close connections to high-ranking pro-aristocratic bureaucrats (see Figure 9.1).

In sum, however, provincial unhappiness about exclusion from appointive office appears to have been more decisive in triggering the revolt than the few explicit incidents of exclusion from economic gain. Bureaucratic grievances were further compounded by provincial allegations of governmental electoral fraud in the controversial vice-presidential elections of 1838.

Increasing Polarization of Provincials and Aristocrats over Elections

Besides bureaucratic and economic complaints, provincial grievances centered on the 1838 vice-presidential elections, which the provincial candidate lost. The elections gave rise to organizational and journalistic campaigns by the aristocratic and the provincial factions that had an additional polarizing effect and were accompanied by heated disputes over alleged electoral fraud.

On the eve of the vice-presidential elections in May 1838, a segment of the aristocratic elite led by the wealthy Bogotano Ignacio Morales organized the Sociedad Católica.[7] This association opened branches in the southern regions of Cali, Pasto, and Popayán, calling for a restoration of religious influence in New Granadan society and politics. La Católica, as it became known, also presented successful candidates for the approaching elections to Congress and the provincial assemblies.[8] The association symbolized the renewal of overt intra-elite ideological clashes over the religious question, which continued through the 1840s. However, it soon became a nuisance to Morales's fellow aristocrats in power, because it took away votes from governmental candidates. More important, the society's fanatical stance—which alienated even the local archbishop—added unwelcome fuel to the original popular protests against closing small convents in Pasto that led indirectly to the great civil war of 1840–1842. Later, when the overwhelmed government itself appealed to religious arguments to bolster its power, relations between La Católica and the ruling elite would improve.[9]

La Católica had its provincial counterpart in the Sociedad Democrática Republicana de Artesanos i Laboradores Progresistas. This association was organized by the lawyer Lorenzo María Lleras, one of the editors of *Bandera Nacional,* a vocal opposition newspaper. The Sociedad Democrática was founded on June 17, 1838, shortly before the July vice-presidential election, and established branches in Santa Marta, Cúcuta, Buga, Bogotá, Tunja, and neighboring towns.[10] In spite of its name, few artisans had a say in the management of the society, which was rather a political tool of provincial lawyers—namely the Socorranos Francisco Soto, Vicente Azuero, and Florentino González; Juan Nepomuceno Vargas, Ezequiel Rojas, Rafael Eliseo Santander, and Lorenzo M. Lleras, from Tunja and Bogotá; and Neiva native Vicente Lombana Buendía (see Appendixes 5 and 6).

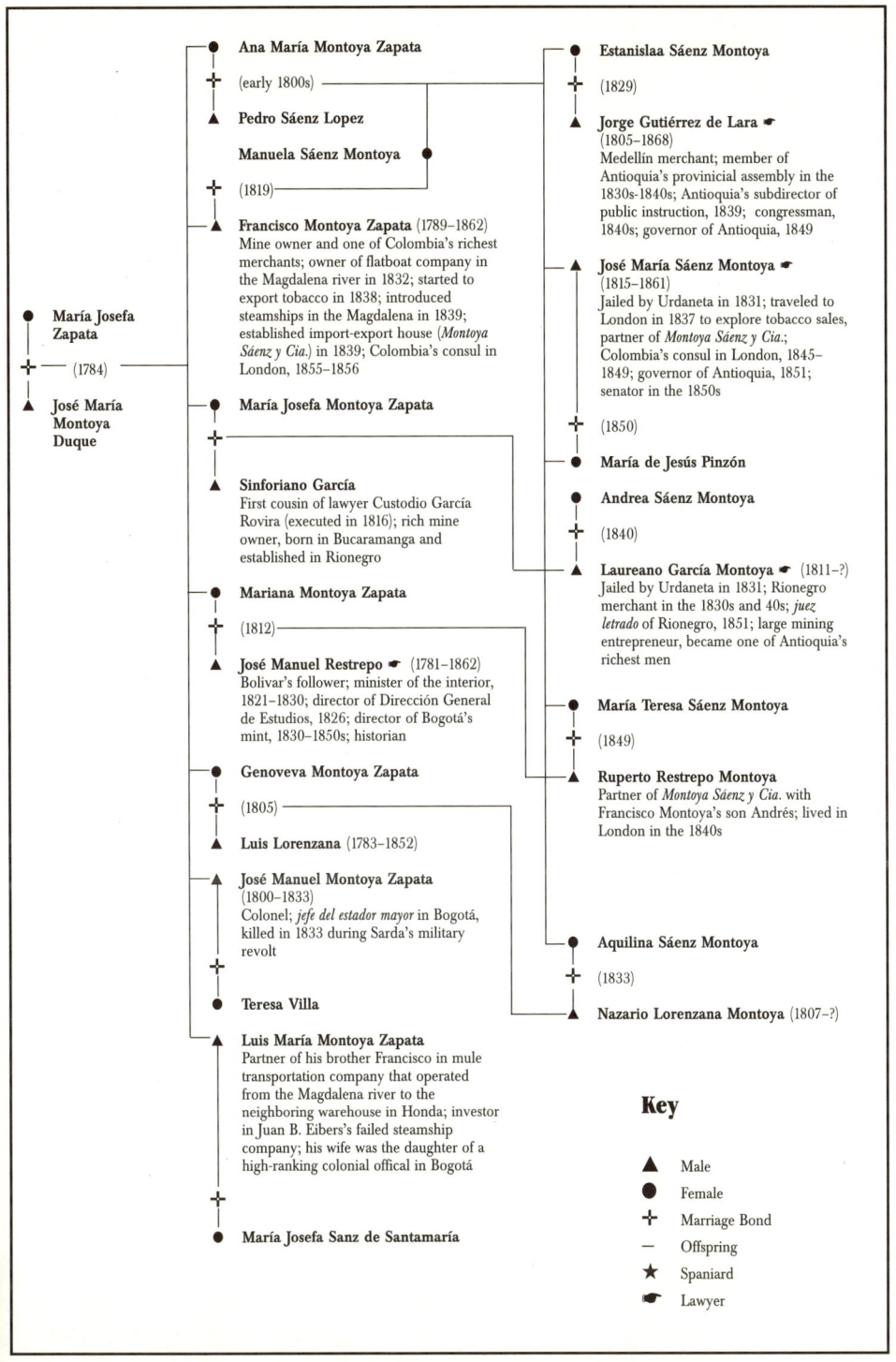

Figure 9.1. The Montoya Sáenz Clan, a Network of Antioqueño Businessmen, Lawyers, and Bureaucrats (1820s–1850)

These and other elite provincials tried to spur the political participation of the popular classes, insisting that such participation was the only way to halt the establishment of a coloniallike aristocratic government.[11] The recently appointed minister of war, aristocratic General Tomás C. Mosquera, and some young conservative supporters reacted to those claims by launching a newspaper that portrayed the provincial leaders as political opportunists whose unemployment or lack of bureaucratic success was the only motivation for a sudden interest in the masses. Mosquera and his followers claimed to be the true "friends" of the people, hence the title of their paper, *El Amigo del Pueblo* (Friend of the People).[12]

In the end it seems that the provincials were less successful than the religious aristocrats and the governing clique in attracting the favor of the masses, in part due to opportunistic laws aimed at increasing popular support for the aristocratic candidate. For example, a law favoring the popular distillation of liquor was passed by the government shortly before the elections. The June 29, 1838 law banned the state's liquor distillation monopoly and allowed the distillation of *aguardiente* under license. In Bogotá alone 520 *chicherías* and 120 *pulperías* benefited from the measure, which had been requested all over the country since the early 1830s.[13] Aristocratic candidate General Domingo Caicedo defeated provincial Socorrano lawyer Vicente Azuero in the elections.

This victory proved to be even more controversial than the 1837 election, which had brought aristocratic lawyer José Ignacio Márquez to the presidency. Continuing New Granada's tradition of chronic electoral disputes, the provincials, who had themselves been accused of fraud not long before, charged the aristocrats with electoral fraud in several regions,[14] claiming that the military vote was being manipulated by the incumbent government. The aristocratic newspaper *La Bandera Negra* responded that, if anything, it was the provincials who had a tradition of manipulating the military vote and supporting military enfranchisement whenever they could control the way the troops would vote.[15]

Despite this heated response, the provincials went on to charge that a group of provincial lawyers in the region of Neiva who were known Azuero supporters had been arbitrarily jailed and kept from participating in the elections.[16] The social profile of this region's lawyers has been discussed (see Chapter 7); however, the political background of their participation and that of other provincials in late 1830s opposition politics is worthy of further examination. The cases of Neiva and Vélez should suffice as examples.

Opposition Politics in the Late 1830s and the Provincial Decision to Rebel

Previous chapters of this book focused on an active group of provincial lawyers, the Socorranos. They led the antimilitary struggles of the 1820s and presided over the coalition formed with moderate aristocrats under General Santander in the early 1830s. Along with these aristocratic allies, the Socorranos and other provincial figures comanaged the state until Márquez succeeded Santander in 1837 and started to push them aside. During the second half of the 1830s, the Socorrano group was joined in resisting the government's exclusionary efforts by an active cluster of upwardly mobile lawyers from the regions of Neiva, Mariquita, and Casanare, and by several marginal figures from Bogotá, Tunja, and also Vélez. The political alignments of all of these individuals corresponded to their nontraditional social status. With few exceptions, their aristocratic classmates and *paisanos* joined the group dubbed the *retrogrados,* more commonly referred to as *ministeriales* (i.e., occupants of the government or *ministerio*), the soon-to-be Conservative party.[17] The provincials, on the contrary, joined the *progresista* group, soon to become the Liberal party.[18] As a result, they suffered directly from the Márquez administration's offensive against provincial political networks.

Soon after his inauguration, Márquez appointed as governor of Neiva twenty-nine-year-old aristocratic Bogotano lawyer José María Galavís, the nephew and foster son of lawyer and high colonial bureaucrat Eustaquio Galavís (Appendixes 1 and 4).[19] Young Galavís's presence in Neiva very likely upset the local provincial political network presided over by lawyer José María Céspedes, the uncle of the Lombana Buendía brothers (see Chapter 7 and Appendix 5). Céspedes had until recently occupied high-ranking bureaucratic positions in Neiva, where he had also been a small entrepreneur and an influential politician. As early as 1831, Céspedes appeared to have enough clout to act as mediator between the dictatorship of Urdaneta and the provincial armies that opposed it; subsequently, in 1833 under Santander, along with his son-in-law José María González Suárez, he was given a government concession to build a bridge in the growing city of La Plata, a thriving urban center not far from Neiva. He also occupied at different times the jobs of judge and governor.[20]

Galavís's arrival threatened Céspedes's position and the political influence of his peers. In 1838 Governor Galavís allegedly ordered the mayor of Neiva to jail several local lawyers and *electores*–the Manrique brothers and their brother-in-law Laureano Gaspar Díaz–who were expected to vote for the provincial vice-presidential candidate Vicente Azuero.[21] In late 1839 Galavís was also accused of both interfering in the election of deputies to the provincial assembly and forcing the assembly to nominate him for a second term as governor.[22] This allegedly caused a protest rally, or *asonada.* Therefore it is no surprise that all of Neiva's provincial lawyers sided in parliament with Socorrano lawyer Vicente Azuero's oppositionist clique. Some of them and their families, including the young law student Angel Maria Céspedes, son of former Governor Céspedes, joined the rebel armies during the subsequent civil war.[23]

A similar situation occurred in the cacao and coffee region of Vélez.[24] During the Santander presidency the governorship of Vélez had been in the hands of lawyer Angel María Flórez Camacho, a member of the provincial group. Under Flórez Camacho, Indian lawyer and priest Rafael M. Vásquez was appointed director of the provincial *colegio,* a job he continued to occupy after Flórez's premature death in late 1836 and during the subsequent governorship of Irish Colonel Thomas Murray, an ally of the provincials.[25]

The progovernment press alleged that Márquez's subsequent removal of Murray from the governorship had disturbed the *camarilla política* (political clique) headed by the "unpalatable priest" (*indigesto cura*) Vásquez, and by

Murray's successor, lawyer José Nicolás Escobar, whom the government also removed and indicted shortly afterward.[26] Indeed, the rebellion that exploded in Vélez in 1840 was attributed by the minister of the interior to the bitterness of "a half a dozen men who for quite a while have taken over the province's public jobs and, wishing to continue their bureaucratic monopoly but not having the support of the incumbent president... organized a rebellion."[27] Among the members of the Vásquez-Escobar clique were the local treasurer Camilo Rivadeneira, a former law student who gave the rebels access to the local treasury; Congressman Juan Azuero; and the local judge, lawyer Francisco de P. Vargas, who was jailed in February by government officials and charged with complicity in the revolt.[28]

From 1837 until 1839, these provincials had attempted different strategies to oppose Marquez's government (e.g., motions of impeachment, requests of investigations, bills increasing the decentralization of power, proposals for constitutional amendments, critical journalistic pieces). They had faced the stubborn opposition of aristocratic congressmen such as lawyer José María Mendoza Morales, scion of Bogotá's and Tunja's most traditional colonial families (Appendix 4). Rather than impeach Márquez as the provincials wanted, Mendoza Morales instead proposed an investigation of the crimes committed by former president Santander against his political enemies. This originated angry debates in Congress, which allegedly contributed to the worsening of Santander's health and his eventual death.[29]

In region after region the provincials now decided to go to war, perhaps following General Santander's recent invitation to exert the "sacred right to rebellion." Their decision also reflected the controversial remarks of Socorrano lawyer Vicente Azuero, who in the provincial outlet *El Correo de la Razón* predicted an imminent crisis and urged a "revolution of ideas."[30] The revolution, however, went far beyond the mere discussion of ideas. Following are examples of the most important military revolts. Each case will highlight provincial lawyers who inspired, sympathized with, joined, or directed the successive uprisings which will, as far as possible, be discussed in chronological order (see Appendix 5).

Lawyers and the *Supremo* Revolts

The initial *supremo* revolt began in January 1840 and was led by provincial General José María Obando, who gathered a rebel army of Indians, peasants, and slaves in the Pasto and Patía regions south of Popayán, the scene of recent protests over the closure of local convents. He was joined by twenty-five-year-old lawyer José Ignacio Piedrahita, an 1839 law graduate from Buga, who served as Obando's secretary. Other recruits included young law graduate Pedro Antonio Medina and Angel María Céspedes Buendía, twenty-two-year-old son of lawyer José María Céspedes, the former governor and displaced provincial political boss of Neiva. Angel María, a doctor in law, was first cousin of various of the lawyers from Neiva (see Chapter 7), including the Lombana Buendía brothers, and eventually became General Obando's son-in-law. In mid-1841, along with Piedrahita and General Obando himself, he fled New Granada after Obando's defeat at the battle of La Chanca.[31] But by then, several other natives of Neiva had also risen up in arms. Among these was lawyer Andrés Durán González, an 1836 law graduate. Durán's father was a landowner and a former governor of Neiva in the early postcolonial period. Andrés was also a landowner, an "hombre rico" (rich man), active in politics. He was a member of Neiva's provincial assembly and a congressman even before his graduation as a lawyer, and he accompanied the rebel forces in battles fought in Neiva in early 1841.[32] Neiva's rebel troops at the time were commanded by Colonel Pedro A. Sánchez, a relative of Neiva lawyer and congressman Laureano Gaspar Díaz Sánchez, one of the opposition *electores* detained in that region in 1838 by aristocratic Governor Galavís.[33]

The revolt led by Colonel Vicente Vanegas in Vélez in February 1840 was started by Congressman Juan Azuero and former Governor José Nicolás Escobar, a thirty-one-year-old lawyer. Escobar had graduated in 1837 and was a classmate of provincials active like himself in opposition politics, among them Ruperto Anzola and Eugenio Castilla (Appendix 5).[34] Escobar and Azuero were accompanied by the "indigesto cura" and lawyer Rafael Vásquez, director of the local *colegio,* who was alleged to be the soul of the local revolt.[35] Local judge Francisco de Paula Vargas, an 1834 law graduate, also took part and was soon imprisoned under charges of complicity.[36]

Casanare's July 1840 revolt counted with the tacit support of provincial lawyer Julián Beltrán, a native of the town of Pore, who discretely resigned the local governorship days before Colonels Mariano Acero and Juan N. Molina rose up in arms. Another influential provincial lawyer from Casanare, Salvador Camacho Naranjo, was arrested and expelled from the country, most likely for participation in the rebellion.[37]

A more straightforward role was played by law graduate Miguel Larrota in Tunja's September 1840 revolt. This rebellion was commanded by Colonel Juan José Reyes Patria, who was a cousin of Juan N. Escobar, one of the lawyers active in the Vélez revolt.[38] Larrota, son of a local *escribano,* served as governor of Tunja while it was under rebel control, and was also *auditor de guerra* of the combined rebel forces of Vélez, Tunja, and Socorro, which marched against Bogotá in October 1840.[39] These forces appointed lawyer-priest Vásquez as their chaplain[40] and were led by Colonel Manuel González, whose private secretary was twenty-four-year-old lawyer Manuel Murillo Toro, from the little town of Chaparral (see Chapter 7). Murillo Toro had written articles denouncing President Márquez and, until recently, had been the *oficial mayor* of the House of Representatives.[41] Colonel González had originally taken up arms in Socorro in September, receiving the cooperation of young Manuel María Ramírez, former director of Cúcuta's *casa de educación,* who had graduated as a lawyer three months earlier and eventually served as treasurer of the province of Pamplona under the rebels. In the capacity of *secretario de la intendencia general,* Ramírez later joined the armies of the Atlantic coast commanded by *Supremo* Colonel Francisco Carmona, who rebelled in October with support from Cartagena lawyers Andrés Level Goda, Antonio F. Falquez, and Blas Núñez.[42]

When the combined forces led by Colonel González against Bogotá were defeated in November 1840, lawyer Murillo Toro headed towards his native region of Mariquita, where less than two months later Colonel and Governor José María Vesga, allegedly alienated by a personal encounter with President Márquez, rose up in arms. Like González, Colonel Vesga appointed Murillo Toro as his private secretary.[43] Vesga was soon defeated and went to join Antioquia's rebel troops under Colonel Salvador Córdova. Murillo Toro headed north and eventually enlisted in rebel Colonel Francisco Carmona's Cartagena forces, where he served as *auditor de guerra* in 1841.[44]

The revolt started in Antioquia by Colonel Salvador Córdova in September 1840 was finally backed by his lawyer cousin Governor Francisco A. Obregón, a follower of Santander who had been reluctant to join at first. Córdova also received active cooperation from twenty-four-year-old lawyers José María Facio Lince, a Medellín native "de familia pobre" (of a poor family) who had recently graduated and was working as a primary-school teacher, and Juan N. Pontón, an 1836 graduate who practiced law and worked as a professor at the local *colegio*, and who happened to be a brother-in-law of General Santander. Pontón served as governor of the province until the defeat of the rebel forces in May 1841, after which he was jailed, fined, and eventually exiled. Facio Lince was also expelled.[45]

In early 1841, rebel forces continued fighting in the southern areas neighboring Popayán and Cali. An elite lawyer of Cali, twenty-five-year-old Manuel Dolores Camacho, eventually decided to support the local forces, a rather unusual decision given his high social standing.[46] By July 1841 the rebels were also defeated there, and the remaining battles occurred for the most part in the northern region under Carmona. After several setbacks, and not before imposing a naval blockade on Cartagena that could only be defeated with British cooperation, Carmona eventually decided to accept an amnesty in early 1842. This amnesty concluded the war and determined the final exodus of Murillo Toro to Panama, where he joined his colleague Rafael M. Vásquez, who had arrived earlier to participate in a local secessionist movement. Taking advantage of the prevailing chaos, this movement started in November 1840 and ended with another amnesty, in April 1842.[47]

Early Antirevolutionary Responses and Progovernmental Stands

To help put down the early military revolts in Pasto and Vélez, which threatened to expand to other regions, the congressional opposition proposed constitutional reforms to weaken the executive and increase provincial power and autonomy.[48] Led by General Santander and provincial lawyers Vicente Azuero, Florentino González, and Ezequiel Rojas, the opposition also proposed generous amnesties to appease the rebels and forgive any crimes with which General Obando might be charged, including the alleged masterminding of the assassination of independence hero General Sucre back in 1830. But these amnesties were voted down in April 1840, after heated parliamentary debates during which surfaced many of the animosities accumulated between provincials, or *progresistas,* and aristocrats, or *ministeriales*. Some of these hostilities had to do with the allegedly comparable way former President Santander had put down some military revolts against his own government in the early 1830s, including the unlawful execution of political enemies. Most, however, were related to recent bureaucratic and electoral grievances, and they reflected status-honor clashes over the control of the state apparatus.[49]

The aristocratic group that defeated the amnesty proposal was led by lawyers Antonio Malo and young Manuel Torcuato Silva, from Tunja and neighboring Chiquinquira, respectively, two areas traditionally controlled by aristocratic groups.[50] Several other lawyers from the Tunja region also opposed the amnesty, among them the Franco Pinzón brothers, sons of an influential colonial *escribano* who had been the leading political boss *(gamonal)* of Guateque, a little town close to both Tunja and Bogota.[51] The anti-amnesty group also included traditional Bogotanos like lawyer Alejandro Osorio, former law student Rafael Alvarez Lozano (from the colonial bureaucratic family described in Figure 4.1), and lawyer Uldarico Leiva Caicedo, member of the traditional Caicedo clan and son of colonial lawyer José A. Leiva, who served in the Spanish antirevolutionary tribunal of *secuestros* (confiscations) in the 1810s (see Appendixes 1 and 4).[52] More important, the aristocrats were led by the traditional elites of Popayán, headed by Don José Rafael Mosquera, a first cousin of the Mosquera clan described in previous chapters. Mosquera was joined by thirty-two-year-old lawyer Manuel M. Mallarino, a leading young congressman and *ministerial,* trained, as most of his classmates were, at the pious University of Cauca in Popayán.[53]

Mallarino became a wealthy landowner but did not seem to have possessed any clear aristocratic credentials.[54] He belonged to the first generation of lawyers trained during the 1830s in the orthodox university recently created in the city of Popayán, soon to be known as the bulwark of Colombian conservatism.[55] Several of Mallarino's classmates belonged to some of the most traditional families of Popayán and its neighboring towns, but others like him seem to have come from nonaristocratic backgrounds and to have joined the *ministerial* group for reasons other than their lineage. They joined it perhaps because their training, freed of Benthamite and other sensualist ideas, rich in subjects like *derecho natural* and *moral,* and carried out in a traditional region isolated from the political effervescence of Bogotá, made them natural conservatives. But even more likely, they joined the aristocrats because they depended on the patronage of Popayán's traditional elites: the slave-owning Mosqueras, Arboledas, Carvajales, Hurtados, and Arroyos, who exerted hegemonic control over the affairs of this mining region.[56] This was clearly the case for modest students like Palmira native Vicente Cárdenas. He was an orphan brought to Popayán at the age of sixteen to serve as secretary to wealthy Don Rafael Arboleda, professor of literature at the local university. Arboleda sponsored Cárdenas's legal studies, and after Cárdenas became a lawyer in 1833 he helped him find several jobs in the national and regional bureaucracy (secretary of the Consejo de Estado, secretary of the governor of Buenaventura, *fiscal* of Popayán's court of appeals, governor of Pasto, etc). Had Cárdenas been born in Neiva or Socorro, probably he would have joined the provincial group and its local networks. But his training with the sons of Popayán's slave-owning aristocracy, and the patronage he received from it, turned him into a devout *ministerial* for the rest of his life.[57] Many Caucanos, from Popayán, Buga, and neighboring regions like Pasto, followed Cárdenas's political inclinations. Several of them were well entrenched in the local bureaucracy and enjoyed high status-honor in Popayán society (see Table 9.1).

Among the *ministerial* lawyers of the Cauca region it is worth highlighting the Sanclemente Domínguez brothers (Ramón and Manuel A.), Jorge Juan Hoyos Cabal, and the Martínez Escobar brothers (Francisco, Carlos, Rafael, and José Vicente), all of whom belonged to the dominant local clans of Buga, a southern town not far from Popayán. The head of the Martínez Escobar clan, for example, was colonial lawyer Pedro Vicente Martínez y Cabal, Buga's wealthiest landowner. The leading member of this family during the 1840s was young José Vicente Martínez, doctor in jurisprudence, congressman, and one of the wealthiest import-export merchants of New Granada. He had married a sister of Clímaco Ordóñez, another important progovernment lawyer linked to the northern regions of Girón and Pamplona, where the government also had active supporters. Both Martínez and Ordóñez, besides being relatives and trading partners, were influential congressmen and major financial contributors to the government's cause, and certainly they must have led the progovernment traditional families of Buga, Pamplona, and Girón.[58] In addition, Martínez and his brother-in-law Ordóñez would later be the key negotiators of the settlement of New Granada's English debt, which was eventually completed in 1845.[59] They seem to fit the trajectory of plutocratic Antioqueños, or for that matter other Latin American plutocrats, assimilated into aristocratic groups over the years.[60] All of the above-mentioned lawyers from Buga and Giron were leading *ministerial* bureaucrats during the 1840s and beyond, reaching positions as ministers of economy, justices of the regional court of appeals, and even, in the case of Mallarino and Manuel Sanclemente, vice president and president of Colombia, respectively.[61]

With the support of traditional or plutocratic elites from Bogotá, Tunja, Buga, Pamplona, Girón, Popayán, and neighboring regions, as well as the backing of the thriving Antioqueño elites and several young lawyers and congressmen from Cartagena (Table 9.2), the government defeated an amnesty project in May 1840 and continued fighting the rebels and their parliamentary allies.

The War Expands

Opposition leader Santander died days after participating in the congressional debates and witnessing the rejection of the amnesty law. Shortly afterward, to the annoyance of the provincial group, a project honoring Santander's memory was opposed by several of the aristocrats mentioned above.[62] This opposition was offset by the victory of a provincial candidate in the presidential primary of mid-1840. Socorrano lawyer Vicente Azuero, again a candidate, obtained a plurality of the vote, with governmental candidate General Herrán a close

Table 9.1. Cauca Lawyers Who Supported the Government during the *Supremos* Civil War, 1840

Name	Birth Date	Admitted to Bar	Occupation
Jaime Arroyo Hurtado	1815	1839	Judge; *fiscal,* Court of Appeals
Vicente Cárdenas	1811	1833	Justice, Court of Appeals
Juan Antonio Castro	1807	1832	Justice, Court of Appeals
Francisco J. Chaux	1811	1836	Judge in Quibdó
Cayetano Delgado	1814	1835	Trade?/Farming?
Jorge Juan Hoyos Cabal	1812	1835	Congressman; Minister of Economy
Manuel V. López	–	1836	*Relator,* Court of Appeals; legal practice
Manuel María Mallarino	1808	1831	Congressman
Francisco Martínez Bueno†	–	1834	Governor
Carlos Martínez E.	1817	1837	Legal practice
Francisco Felipe Martínez E.	1811	1834	Legal practice
José Vicente Martínez E.	1810	–	Merchant; congressman
Rafael Martínez E.	1813	1839	Legal practice
José Cayetano Mazuera	1809	1833	Landowner
Manuel María Muñóz	1806	1837	Judge in Popayán
Antonio Olano	1809	1832	Legal practice
Zenón De Pombo O'Donnell	1805	1832	Justice, Court of Appeals
Ramón Rebolledo†	1810	1833	Justice, Court of Appeals
Ramón A. Sanclemente	1812	1836	Congressman
Manuel A. Sanclemente	1813	1837	Congressman; legal practice

Sources: GNG, April 14, 1839; May 17, 1840; September 11, 1842; Aragón, *La universidad del Cauca;* Arboleda, *Diccionario biográfico; El Observador,* March 1, 1840.

†Executed by the rebels in 1840 and 1841

runner-up. As the provincial press predicted, Herrán became a heroic figure ("agrandado") when the government chose him to put down the early military rebellions in the south.[63] The 1841 Congress had to decide between Azuero, Herrán, or a third candidate, Cali General Eusebio Borrero (see Appendix 5).

Probably as a way to press Congress into choosing Azuero, the revolt of the provincial groups—initially confined to Vélez and the areas neighboring Popayán—deepened in late 1840 under the leadership of Santander's heir, General Obando. Instead of helping him, the expanded revolt probably cost Azuero the presidency and provoked harsh repression against the provincial group. But despite the government's repressive efforts, the imposition of forced loans on several regions, and support for the government by local and foreign capitalists, the revolt could not be contained so quickly.[64] As outlined above, numerous

Table 9.2. Cartagena Lawyers within the *Ministerial* Group, 1840–1842

Name	Birth Date	Admitted to Bar	Occupation
Lázaro Ramos	1809	1835	Congressman
Manuel del Río	1809	1835	Congressman
Nicanor del Portillo	1811	1835	Congressman
Ramón Benedetti	1806	1835	*Relator*, Court of Appeals
Aquilino Alvarez	1804	1830	Justice, Court of Appeals
José M. Vivero	1811	1834	*Fiscal*, Court of Appeals

Sources: *El Argos,* April 8, 1838; *El Observador,* April 15, 1840; May 24, 1840; *GNG,* April 14, 1839.

provincial lawyers and military figures continued to fight for over two years, becoming quite threatening at times.

The serious threat posed by the united troops of Vélez, Socorro, and Tunja in late 1840, for example, forced a change of cabinet and the temporary removal of President Márquez from his post thanks to pressures from provincial leaders in Bogotá, including Socorrano lawyers Soto, González, and Azuero.[65] Subsequently, the rebel troops reached the outskirts of Bogotá and almost occupied the city.[66] The rebels were eventually defeated with the help of battalions made up in part of young students from Bogota's most distinguished families ("de las principales familias bogotanas" or "de la más distinguida sociedad"). The students were aided by the aristocratic Sociedad Nueve de Enero (Society of the Ninth of January), led and financed by young lawyer José Antonio de Plaza (Appendix 4).[67] To further incite popular support in the effort to put down the rebels, the entire city was mobilized in a "gran semana" (great week) of religious processions. Government forces were exhorted to follow the example of wealthy Tunja landowner Colonel Juan José Neira, whose role in saving Bogotá became legendary. Neira left his large hacienda, which, like many others, had been ransacked by the rebels and, probably after recruiting some of his own peons, led troops that put the rebel forces on the run, thus sparing the city.[68]

In spite of Neira's decisive victory in Bogotá, other regions continued to come under fire, especially Antioquia, Neiva, Mariquita, and the Atlantic coast. In addition, the secessionist movement that erupted in Panama in November 1840 declared the independence of this region. Not just the provincials but several aristocratic Panamanian lawyers joined the movement motivated by local circumstances (i.e., fiscal bankruptcy of the local treasury). Although triggered by the general situation facing New Granada, Panama's situation was a case apart.[69]

One revolt exploded after another, and although some were rapidly put down and partial amnesties granted to the rebels, the war dragged on.[70] Though weakened by the rebel military threats and the forced removal of the president, the government did not give up. It continued to gather funds, obtaining support from other nations like Ecuador and, later, England, and to recruit troops to fight the rebels.⁷¹ It also launched a campaign of repression against key provincial lawyers and their families, deemed the instigators of the rebellion.

An example of this repression is provincial Antioqueño lawyer José María Duque Gómez who, as mentioned in the previous chapter, was imprisoned by the government in late 1840 and accused of instilling subversive doctrines in his public law class at a Bogotá colegio. During October and November Duque Gómez told students in his "science of legislation" class that, because there was a civil war going on, the revolutionary armies' confiscations could not be considered, in strict legal terms, crimes of "theft." He argued that the government itself had confiscated horses from several families, going on to explain that although an amnesty law promulgated in 1832 had exonerated any political crimes committed by General Obando, he continued to be persecuted, giving him further motive to rebel.⁷² Duque Gómez paid for these lectures with a sentence of three years in jail. He subsequently escaped, but died soon after.⁷³ In the meantime, his fellow Antioqueño plutocrats-turned-aristocrats continued to support the repressive government.⁷⁴

Fleeing the government's persecution, Vicente Lombana Buendía, a member of the provincial group from Neiva and assistant director of Bogotá's Colegio del Rosario, left Bogotá in September 1840, shortly before several of his peers were detained. He traveled to the neighboring town of Villeta and, because of his sudden departure, was charged with abandoning his job. Although he provided medical justifications for his absence, the government later expelled him from Bogotá.⁷⁵

In late 1840, as the insurgent armies were poised to take Bogotá, a group of provincial lawyers was preemptively arrested and charged with supporting the rebels. In addition to Francisco Soto, Salvador Camacho Naranjo, Florentino González, Lorenzo M. Lleras, and Juan Nepomuceno Vargas, this group included Vicente Azuero, the candidate who received the most votes in the 1840 presidential primaries. Azuero and his fellow provincials were detained until February 1841, when a Bogotá judge ordered their release. At this point the provincials were physically assaulted by a mob of Bogotá artisans and workers, who demanded their reimprisonment.⁷⁶

The Pueblo Against the Provincials

It was not just the government and distinguished aristocrats, but also the common people who moved against the provincial rebel leaders. Since before the war, artisans had supported the government. In early 1839, for instance, Bogotá's Catholic Society persuaded more than 300 artisans to sign petitions demanding proreligious educational reforms, opposed by the provincials. The reforms were soon approved.⁷⁷

According to a young witness sympathetic to the provincials, the riots that demanded their reimprisonment were headed by members of "las clases ordinarias" (the working classes), including a *toreador* (bullfighter), an *albañil* (bricklayer), and a *placera* (market vendor). The latter caused particular scandal when she threw her underwear into the air, screaming that it was for the men in government "que no supieran apretarse bien los calzones" ("who did not know how to tighten up their pants").[78] Among the rioters were several other women, who carried pocket knives and stones and accompanied a large group of "hombres de baja estofa" (marginal or low-life men). They belonged to those social sectors probably the most affected by the government's forcible draft imposed to fight the rebel armies.[79] The rioters considered the government negligent in the pursuit of public peace, as evidenced by the recent release of the provincials. The masses marched to the residence of the provincial leader and presidential candidate Vicente Azuero, who surrendered to them after the door and windows of his house were broken in.[80]

Crowds marched all over the city. A member of the clergy, "al frente de unos cuantos harapsos y mujerzuelas" ("leading a few low women and people dressed in rags"), led several groups in the frenetic persecution of other provincial elites whom the mob wanted back in jail. These groups assaulted the homes of the judge who had released the rebels and of President Márquez himself. Their actions resulted in the capture of several of the recently released provincials, as well as some of their relatives and followers. The riot was slow to subside because, perhaps at the instigation of local capitalists or members of the government itself, "bastantes depósitos de aguardiente" ("abundant supplies of liquor") had been placed at different points "para el consumo gratuito de la plebe" ("for the masses to drink"). In addition, the same witness notes, reflecting the pejorative tone toward the common people characteristic of some contemporary intellectuals, "gran parte de la *soldadesca* fraternizaba con el *populacho*" ("a fair number of *soldiers* fraternized with the *little people*"), helping to prolong the riot.[81]

As the popular riot, or *pueblada,* made clear, the provincial lawyers were far from being a part of *el pueblo*. Nor did they enjoy popularity among the lower classes of Bogotá; after failing to mobilize these classes against the government through the short-lived Sociedad Democrática Republicana de Artesanos y Laboradores Progresistas (1838), they now faced the masses' direct physical opposition.[82] The common people, including Bogota's growing body of artisans, remained progovernment then and during almost the entire decade of the 1840s.[83] This was also the case in Medellín and several other regions.[84] Provincial efforts at popular organization were to bear fruit only after renewed attempts during the late 1840s. Until then the common people, including artisans, backed the aristocratic government.

The protracted military struggle of the *Supremos* and their civilian allies against the government represented not a confrontation between the common people and the elite but rather an internal confrontation between provincial and aristocratic elites–groups with diverse social status, but elites nonetheless.

Further Government Repression

Several weeks later, on March 14, Congress struck Azuero from the list of candidates in the presidential run-off vote. The assembly confined the election to the two progovernment candidates, Generals Herrán and Borrero, and chose Herrán after two rounds of voting.[85] Once in office, Herrán and his cabinet ministers, especially Antioquia's adoptive son Mariano Ospina, would lead further persecutions of the provincials, while Azuero prepared himself for exile. The repression that the government unleashed in order to contain the subversive movement even affected some influential lawyers linked to aristocratic circles. For instance, Antioquia native José María de Latorre Uribe, a justice on Bogotá's local court of appeals, was charged with being too lenient in sentencing rebels. In March 1841, he abrogated the sentences of several rebels who had been condemned to death, arguing that "estando el país en una verdadera guerra civil, el poder judicial era incompetente para conocer la causa de los rebeldes cojidos en Bellavista" (as the country was suffering a true civil war, the judiciary did not have any jurisdiction over the rebels captured in Bellavista). After the Senate indicted Latorre, the Supreme Court then sentenced him to three years in prison and imposed a heavy fine paid in part by the forced sale of his house.[86] Following this episode, Ospina wrote to Herrán that it was as important to punish lenient judges as the criminals themselves.[87]

The war concluded in early 1842 with the defeat of the rebels in the north. Some were granted amnesty but had to leave the area and settle in Panama, where a pardon had also been granted to the members of the local secessionist movement.[88] Although it was ultimately lenient toward the northern rebels, the government subjected a select group of provincials living in Bogotá and other cities to a final series of repressive measures in December 1841, expelling them from the cities where they lived or exiling them from the country entirely (Table 9.3).[89] Probably in this way the government expected to rid itself of the ambitious job- and status-seekers who allegedly plotted the war.

Excursus on Empleomanía

According to the government, the provincials' so-called *empleomanía* and their "futiles motivos de puestos" ("futile job motivations") were the cause of the war.[90] Colombians' aspiration to bureaucratic jobs was not new; in the colonial period, as we have seen, status-hungry local lawyers favored bureaucratic careers over any other occupation (Chapter 2). Since the late 1820s, however, individual members of the aristocratic elite, probably as a way to discourage their potential competitors, had began to launch isolated criticisms against the continuing preference for "la carrera de los empleos" (bureaucratic careers).[91] Surprisingly, however, one of the first critical articles on *empleomanía* was written in 1833 by provincial lawyers–Florentino González and Lorenzo M. Lleras–who mirrored similar discussions launched in Mexico in 1827 by liberal priest José María Luis Mora.[92] By the late 1830s, widespread and systematic assaults on *empleomanía* were commonplace. Rather than an adequate source of status-honor, critics charged, public job-seeking was becoming a pathological tendency.

On the eve of the War of the *Supremos,* Cerbeleón Pinzón, a *ministerial* lawyer from Vélez who wrote a treatise on constitutional law, criticized the pref-

Table 9.3. Examples of Provincial Lawyers Exiled Abroad or Expelled from Bogotá and Other Cities following the War of the *Supremos*

Means of Expulsion	Admitted to Bar	Place of Exile	Returned to Colombia
Exiled abroad			
Salvador Camacho Naranjo	1820	Venezuela	1842?
Florentino González	1832	Europe	1845
Miguel Larrota		Venezuela	1848
Vicente Lombana Buendía	1833	Europe	mid-1840s
Francisco Obregón	1827	Caribbean/Italy	late 1840s
José Ignacio Piedrahita	1840?	Ecuador	Never
Juan N. Pontón	1836	?	Never
Manuel María Ramírez	1840	Venezuela	1849
Francisco de P. Vargas	1834	?	Never?
Rafael M. Vásquez	1832	Ecuador	Never
Expelled to other cities			
Ruperto Anzola	1839	La Palma	1845
Vicente Azuero	1817	La Mesa	Never[a]
Manuel D. Camacho	1837	?	1844?
Manuel Cañarete	1827	Anolaima	1845
José María Facio Lince	1840	?	1845?
Romualdo Lievano	1825	El Guamo	1843
Lorenzo M. Lleras	1836	Ibagué	1842
Manuel Murillo T.	1836	Panamá	1844
Francisco Soto	1810	Cúcuta	Never[b]
Juan N. Vargas	1824	?	1845

Sources: Arboleda, *Diccionario biográfico,* 353; Restrepo Sáenz, *Gobernadores de Antioquia,* 2:261, 271, 407; Monge, "El Doctor Rafael María Vásquez," 718–28; *GNG,* April 14, 1839; September 11, 1842; April 21, 1844; June 22, 1845; *La Bagatela,* August 15, 1853, 53; Ramírez Monreal, "Manuel María Ramírez," 53–60.

[a]Died 1844.
[b]Died 1846.

erence for "la profesión de los destinos [públicos]," arguing that it turned elections into a life or death struggle.[93] Later he also published a textbook on ethics in which he attacked the "vice" of living from public jobs. He argued that

> the mania of searching for public jobs is one of our many political evils . . . to this mania one can attribute the heated elections, the citizens' division into bloody factions, the dangerous and overpowering influence of government, partisan hatred and animosity, and some of our revolutions and constant turmoil. This mania also causes an increase in the number of public jobs and rising public expenditure, which brings no benefit but rather much harm to the nation.

His conclusion was that moral philosophy should instill a rejection of "la inclinación funesta a subsistir de empleos" (the terrible proclivity to subsist on public jobs).[94]

In 1840–1841, progovernment newspapers and state officials targeted *empleomanía* as the cause of the provincials' revolt.[95] Provincials were equally critical of *empleomanía*, perhaps as a way to dismiss the charges against them.[96] Years later, in any event, the origin of the War of the *Supremos* and several more of the nineteenth century's numerous civil wars continued to be attributed to *empleomanía*, which some contemporary academics have come to consider a cultural bias of Latin Americans.[97]

Throughout this book we have seen the importance of state service for colonial elites. I have insisted that the concept of honor was linked to participation in the state bureaucracy, toward which elite individuals oriented their family strategies.[98] During the postcolonial period, state jobs remained important both as a source of status and as a mechanism for economic security. But without the Crown to mediate and decide how such jobs were to be distributed, local elites had to settle by themselves, through elections and other republican mechanisms, the conflicts derived from the need to staff governmental positions in the midst of competing bureaucratic ambitions. These conflicts did not merely involve the spoils of government; underlying the bureaucratic ambitions of different groups were manifest social conflicts.

Contrary to the prevailing orthodoxy that has denied the existence of social conflicts behind the struggles between New Granada's political factions and, later, its political parties, I have argued that there was indeed a social pattern underlying postcolonial political divisions and conflicts, including those of the late 1830s.[99] It was not a pattern of class conflict or conflict over the means of production, however, but rather a pattern of status conflict, or conflict over the means of administration.

Max Weber asserted that individuals "do not strive for power only in order to enrich themselves economically. . . . Very frequently the striving for power is also conditioned by the social 'honor' it entails."[100] Colonial society had in great part been stratified by "status," which went hand in hand with the monopolization of ideal and material goods and opportunities—including the opportunity to get a legal education and enter the high ranks of the bureaucracy. Within these colonial "status circles" there were visible tendencies toward intermarriage or endogamy (Chapter 3 and Appendix 1), and the preferential opportunities for state employment grew into a monopoly of key offices for the members of these increasingly closed family groups or networks. Their members were for obvious reasons opposed to democratic practices such as provincial education and elections, which for them meant increasing opportunities for upwardly mobile provincial elites to qualify and compete for state service. Even more important, democracy meant a free market in state jobs and a breakdown of their monopoly over the main source of traditional honor, prestige, and power. That is why many aristocrats like the Bogotano Vergara and Alvarez clans (Figures 3.1 and 3.2) favored an end to elections, the restriction of regional participation in government, dictatorial governments, and a return to monarchical rule, as well as the possibility of establishing protectorates under foreign nations to help restrain electoral contests.[101]

Some of these aristocratic clans accepted a short-lived power-sharing arrangement in the early 1830s, but after a while they tried to reshape the state bureaucracy by favoring their peers and excluding upwardly mobile individuals. The result was the War of the *Supremos,* which represented a serious clash between the aristocratic sectors who had dominated the colonial bureaucracy and were now increasingly encroaching upon the state apparatus, and those regional elites who rose to bureaucratic power after independence and refused to let themselves be pushed aside.

As Chapter 7 argued, these two groups did not clash earlier because their attention was diverted to more urgent conflicts with foreign regions and foreign armies. However, the common front they created for this fight was short-lived, and with the Venezuelans gone, aristocrats and provincials eventually faced each other in the 1830s. Although the war they fought was motivated by the immediate bureaucratic and electoral grievances listed above, these grievances occurred in a context of increasing encroachment upon the state apparatus by New Granada's aristocratic (and sometimes wealthier) sectors (Appendix 4). Besides pitting the two sides in a confrontation over the spoils of government, the war also carried characteristic status-honor overtones.[102]

Those overtones can be seen in the provincials' 1837 claims, ridiculed by the aristocratic press, that the Santander-led opposition to the Márquez government was comparable to that sustained in the United States by former President Andrew Jackson against what they termed the *aristocracia mercantil* (merchant aristocracy)[103] This argument suggests that by the late 1830s, as had occurred in Mexico and elsewhere, the traditional aristocracy derived from noble titles or colonial officeholding was merging with a newer aristocracy based on economic wealth, of which the alliance between Antioqueños (as well as businessmen from Buga and Giron) and traditional groups was an indicator.[104] However, although provincials claimed to be opposing a vaguely defined *aristocracia mercantil,* status grievances were probably more pervasive than economic grievances at the time. Many provincials were small merchants themselves and some had become quite wealthy; their fight seems to have been directed primarily at traditional colonial families who wanted to continue monopolizing the state apparatus, rather than at groups in control of the economy or the "means of production."

In memoirs written in 1900 to exalt his father's deeds, the son of a high-status Bogotano bureaucrat of the 1840s highlighted these status connotations while summarizing the prevailing mood among Bogotá's opposition in 1838. According to him, "los Pombos, los Caicedos, los Mosqueras y otras *familias ilustres,* eran blanco puesto a la inquina de aquellos *plebeyos de nuevo cuño.* Ya desde 1831 se habia gritado por las calles: muera la aristocracia y la dinastía" ("the Pombos, Caicedos, Mosqueras, and other traditional families were the target of opportunistic plebeians. Since 1831 people had screamed in the streets: Down with aristocracies and dynasties!").[105] Similar anti-aristocratic protests were witnessed in other regions during the 1839–1842 war. As a descendant of aristocratic President Márquez recalled:

> in Cartagena after 1839 the opposition started to agitate and mobilize. Already by the celebrations of Christmas Eve, the population was divided into two factions . . . the Chambacú group, which included the government's friends and most of the city's distinguished people, and people from Pozo, made up of the popular classes and the opposition who, by means of antisocial ideas, wished to attract the people to their party. This last group used as its symbols red ribbons with inscriptions such as: *Muera la aristocracia!,* all of which brought to the city great consternation.[106]

In an account that focused more on economic than status aspects, the contending factions were described in mid-1840 by Antioqueño cabinet minister Juan de Dios Aranzazu as the "perdularios contra los industriosos, . . . las plebes contra las clases elevadas . . . el salvaje, contra el hombre civilizado" ("rabble rousers against the industrious . . . the plebeians against the high classes . . . the barbarian against civilized man").[107] But in Antioquia itself rebel newspapers published verses against what they characterized as a "turba aristocrática maligna" ("evil aristocratic clique"). The provincial press was particularly enraged against the "four families" who allegedly considered New Granada as their patrimony; although the names were not given, we can safely assume the Caicedos and Mosqueras were two of the four.[108] Finally, constant critiques were published against an ambiguously defined "aristocratic dominance" over the 1840 Congress, which voted down the amnesty projects.[109] All of this suggests that the dispute for "jobs," which was real, hid more serious social (status-honor) contradictions, yet to be explored in further historical research into regional and local politics.

Chapter 10
The "Liberal Revolution": A Friendly Affair

This chapter summarizes the political developments following the War of the *Supremos* and examines the social transformations of the groups that formed the Conservative and Liberal parties. These parties, still dominant in Colombian politics today, were formally established in 1849. In the late 1840s and through the early 1850s they promoted a "liberal revolution," the nature of which will be discussed here as well.

Political Demise of the Provincial Elites

The political power of the provincial *(progresista)* group identified in previous chapters dwindled as a result of the *Supremos* civil war. After the war the government passed a constitutional amendment, drafted by Popayán aristocrat Rafael Mosquera, providing for a strong executive. The amendment took away from the provincial assemblies the power to participate in the appointment of regional governors, who would in the future be named freely by the president. It also ended the right to nominate justices to the regional courts of appeals. These officials would now be nominated by the Supreme Court and appointed by the president himself without the intervention of the congressionally appointed Consejo de Estado. The amendment also enfranchised workers *(jornaleros)* and servants *(sirvientes)* as long as they had a yearly income of 150 pesos. This measure likely increased the power of large landholders and other patrons in regions like Bogotá, Tunja, and Popayán, who controlled the way their workers voted. Issued in the "name of the Father, the Son and the Holy Ghost," the constitutional reform also increased the power of the Church by reestablishing Catholicism as the country's official religion. Around the same time, the government approved the return of the Jesuits to Colombia. Finally, the new charter made parish (primary) elections less frequent, ordering them to take place every four, instead of every two, years.[1] All of these reforms went against many of the proposals that provincials had upheld in the late 1820s and 1830s, including their quest for the decentralization of power, provincial autonomy, secular education, and regular elections.[2]

In addition to curtailing the power and ideals of provincial elites, Congress banned internal travel without a passport, prohibited the unlicensed possession of firearms, placed all heavy weapons under government control, and condoned the arrest and indefinite exile of anyone deemed even slightly threatening to the public order.³ In early 1842, dozens of provincial officers were excluded from the army.⁴ By then, the government had already expelled several key provincial lawyers from Bogotá and other cities, or from Colombia entirely. Most of these opposition figures remained out of politics until the mid-1840s (see Chapter 9, Table 9.3).

Further accelerating the decline of the provincials, some of the faction's main leaders and ideologues followed Santander to the grave in the mid-1840s. Vicente Azuero and Francisco Soto, Socorranos who along with Santander had led the group of insurgent provincial lawyers since the 1820s, passed away in the mid-1840s. The former died in 1844 at the age of fifty-seven. He spent his final years away from politics and devoted to the care of a small sugar cane plantation that he owned in Bogotá's neighboring lowland town of La Mesa.⁵ Soto died in 1846, also at age fifty-seven, after having spent his last years in his native city of Cúcuta, performing minor municipal bureaucratic services.⁶ Several more provincial lawyers died during the *Supremos* war or, somewhat mysteriously, dropped out of the historical registers afterward, probably because they remained abroad, died, or completely withdrew from public life following the war.⁷

Other provincials who did not altogether disappear from the public scene withdrew from politics and busied themselves with professional activities, business, teaching, or agriculture. In fact, several lawyers who escaped persecution during the 1840s devoted themselves to legal practice and business, through which a few accumulated significant economic wealth. Some examples include Domingo Ciprián Cuenca, Bernardo Herrera Buendía and, especially, Ezequiel Rojas.⁸ The latter became very rich, representing local magnates of all political affiliations in and out of court. By 1840 Rojas already owned land in Miraflores, near Tunja, and lent money to local merchants. Soon after the war, he continued lending his services to rich aristocratic merchants, including Buga native José Vicente Martínez.⁹ Rojas was deemed the best, and perhaps most prosperous, of Bogotá's practicing lawyers. During the 1850s he was rich enough to lend money even to wealthy Antioqueño merchants like Francisco Montoya (Figure 9.1). In addition to practicing law, loaning money, and administering his valuable properties, Rojas taught liberal political economy at a local university.¹⁰

Most provincials, however, eked out a modest living through secondary-school teaching, small-scale agriculture, unpretentious legal practices, and related endeavors. Lorenzo María Lleras, for one, returned from his short exile in 1842 to direct Bogotá's Colegio del Rosario and later began his own private *colegio,* "Del Espíritu Santo," which was successful for a short while.¹¹ Manuel Cañarete, a forty-year-old lawyer from Mompós, supported his large family before the *Supremos* war by teaching, practicing law, and engaging in trade. He subsequently alternated between his legal practice and farming.¹² Salvador Camacho Naranjo, Romualdo Lievano, and Juan Nepomuceno Vargas, who were punished during the war but returned to their activities shortly afterward, were also among the modest legal practitioners who barely made a living. Lievano sold his small shop in 1842 and went to the little town of El Guamo to practice law. Later, he moved back to Bogotá and continued his practice without as much success as his peer Ezequiel Rojas.¹³ His close friend Salvador Camacho Naranjo practiced and taught law after returning from his short exile in Venezuela. He even remained in Congress as an opposition senator from the marginal province of Casanare during a good part of the 1840s. He certainly did not become rich from these activities; to support his numerous family, he sent his sons to work and rented rooms at his Bogotá house to provincial students attending local *colegios* or the university.[14]

From time to time, some of the surviving old provincial lawyers and military officers (e.g., J. N. Vargas and R. Lievano, and Generals Antonio Obando and José María Mantilla) held *tertulias* in Camacho's house where, surrounded by admiring young law students, they must have nostalgically remembered past glories and lamented their failed political projects. Participants in these gatherings probably also commented on the increasing number of street children *(chinos)* and artisans in the city, and complained about the return of the Jesuits in 1844, and the city's many beggars, mounting filth, and insecurity. They must have also reflected, with some envy or even rage, on the economic success of a few of their provincial peers and the Antioqueño merchants involved in tobacco deals and exports. They may even have discussed the beginnings of a colonizing rush toward the lowlands *(tierras calientes)* northwest and southwest of Bogotá, the region their peers Azucro, Cañarete, and others moved to after the war ceased in the early 1840s.[15]

Outside of Bogotá, provincial lawyers followed a professional course roughly similar to that of Camacho and his friends. A representative case is that of Neiva's provincials, several of whom left the bureaucracy and politics and devoted themselves to arduous legal practice in small towns.[16] The professional competition faced by all lawyers was becoming fierce.

Changes in the Composition of the Profession, Career Paths, and Values

The legal profession grew tremendously during this period. In particular, the number of legal practitioners increased considerably; it doubled in Antioquia between 1839 and 1845, almost doubled in Cundinamarca (and Neiva), and increased by a third in Cauca. In the following four years the total number of lawyers devoted to legal practice, as opposed to those devoted to the bureaucracy and other activities, further increased by almost 60 percent, twice the pace of growth of the profession's general membership (see Table 10.1).

To make things worse, the lawyers described above practiced in provincial settings where competition from tinterillos and *pleiteros* may have significantly reduced their potential income. On top of this, they faced growing social uneasiness over *rabulismo* (lawyer-instigated litigation) which, to be sure, was neither a new or exclusively provincial phenomenon, but a long-standing nationwide problem.[17] More important, the bureaucracy, a traditional alternative to legal practice, became much harder to reach.

Whereas the number of legal practitioners increased significantly, the overall number of lawyers entering the bureaucracy experienced a relative decline. From 1839 to 1845 the number of lawyer-bureaucrats rose by 52 percent; over the

Table 10.1. Number of Lawyers and Evolution of Their Activities in 1839, 1845, and 1849

Year	Region (Judicial District)*	Number of Lawyers	Activities		
			Legal Practice	Bureaucracy	Other
1839	Antioquia	20	6	7	7
	Boyacá	25	11	9	5
	Cauca	67	33	14	20
	Cundinamarca	130	52	41	37
	Guanentá	41	24	11	6
	Magdalena	48	26	14	8
	Total	331	152	96	83
	Percentage		(45.9%)	(29%)	(25%)
1845	Antioquia	37	12	14	11
	Boyacá	43	15	18	10
	Cauca	84	45	20	19
	Cundinamarca	154	90	46	18
	Guanentá	45	20	19	6
	Magdalena†	53	24	23	6
	Istmo	11	2	6	3
	Total	427	208	146	73
	Percentage		(48.7%)	(34%)	(17%)
1849	Antioquia	38	17	13	8
	Boyacá	68	41	20	7
	Cauca#	70	44	14	12
	Cundinamarca	175	114	48	13
	Guanenta	51	34	14	3
	Magdalena#	57	35	17	5
	Popayán	54	29	19	6
	Santa Marta	25	9	14	2
	Istmo	19	7	10	2
	Total	556	330	169	57
	Percentage		(59.3%)	(30%)	(10%)

Sources: GNG, no. 396 (April 11, 1839); GNG, no. 747 (June 22, 1845); GNG, no. 1029 (March 4, 1849); GNG, no. 1030 (March 11, 1849); GNG, no. 1031 (March 11, 1849).

* Some of these districts were made up of both traditional cities and provincial areas. For instance, Cundinamarca included Bogotá plus several towns in today's Neiva and Tolima; Guanenta included Socorro, San Gil, Girón, Pamplona, Vélez, Chiquinquira and all of these cities' neighboring towns.
† The original district was divided into two. Istmo (today's Panamá) was separate from Magdalena.
# The original district was divided into two. Cauca was separate from Popayán and Magdalena was separate from Santa Marta.

next four years the increase was just 15 percent, or half the pace of growth of the entire legal profession itself (see Tables 8.1 and 10.1). This suggests that not only were provincial lawyers generally prevented by the ruling aristocracy from joining the bureaucracy, but the state's overall capacity to absorb the large number of new lawyers from all social backgrounds was also becoming narrower. Other than having the very limited opportunity to serve in one of the *juzgados letrados de hacienda* or *del circuito* (local and circuit judgeships) introduced to several localities through the 1830s and 1840s, or in the few high-ranking judicial jobs available, new lawyers' access to the state bureaucracy became a less feasible career path.[18]

In addition, although state positions were hardly spurned, the cultural prestige of belonging to the state bureaucracy was declining. As already noted during the 1840s and 1850s, attacks against so-called *empleomanía* became widespread. Service in the state ranks, formerly seen as an honorable and eminent activity, was not just deplored in public speeches, official reports, and the press (see Chapters 8 and 9), but was even ridiculed in public comedies.[19] One such comedy depicted the pitiful Don Nicasio, a career bureaucrat who, to keep his job, switched political orientations as quickly as governments followed one another. Dismayed about the impending end of his career he told his wife, who was worried at their two demanding offspring:

> What do you wish, my dear? The job, or rather, keeping the job, does not leave us any time for family, as God would have wished. How sad is *empleomanía!* Slaves enjoy, at least, their freedom of thought; journeymen have independence, they count on tomorrow and may know how to guide and support their offspring. I have spent thirty years as a state employee, and have never been able to save four *reales*. I have kissed impure hands, have flattered hateful men, have cried many deceptions, have suffered many humiliations. But, I am to blame because from the time I was a young boy I became attached to public office and never learned how to work. What can I do now?

In the comedy's final lines, Don Nicasio's wife reflected on the need to "teach our sons any practical occupation" to avoid their becoming public employees.[20] This same lesson was already being taught in manuals on morality and ethics published since the early 1840s.[21]

Lawyers, both aristocrats and provincials alike, were materially and morally compelled to look for career options other than the state bureaucracy. In spite of its harshness and competitiveness, legal practice and the marketplace in general now appeared as unavoidable and eventually attractive alternatives. But the economy would have to undergo radical transformations to absorb the entire and ever-growing population of lawyers, not to mention the large masses of the unemployed.[22] These transformations were about to take place, again under the active leadership of lawyers, and with the timely cooperation of groups from all political inclinations and social origins.

The Provincial Comeback

The twelve-year rule (1837–1849) of the conservative aristocratic elites, which had started with lawyer José Ignacio de Márquez's presidency (1837–1841) and followed with General Herrán (1841–1845), ended in personal and ideological divisions. Added to the fact that the provincial group was never completely suppressed, such divisions resulted in a provincial political revival.

Having sealed the defeat of the provincials during the *Supremos* war and successfully passed centralizing and proclerical amendments to the constitution, General Herrán handed power over to his father-in-law, Popayán native General Tomás C. de Mosquera (see Appendixes 1 and 4). Mosquera won the 1845 election without a provincial challenge. He defeated two other candidates close to the aristocrats who, over the years, would become yet more divided as a political group.[23]

By the time of Mosquera's victory most of the provincials had been amnestied. As the cases mentioned earlier in this chapter illustrate, they were starting to return to Bogotá from the foreign countries or provincial towns to which they had been exiled.

Even before the exiles' return, a handful of provincial figures continued to perform bureaucratic jobs of some importance in the early 1840s. The most noteworthy example was Socorrano Diego Fernando Gómez Durán. Perhaps because of the low profile he kept during the war, during which he continued to administer his Fusagasuga *hacienda,* the aristocratic governments allowed Gómez to serve as a justice of the Supreme Court.[24] Like provincial lawyer and senator Salvador Camacho Naranjo, his was an exceptional case. Most other provincials had to wait until the second half of the 1840s to enter the public sphere and join the top echelons of the state bureaucracy.

Along with the new generations of law graduates, the returnees soon became active in New Granada's public sphere. Critical journalism, as usual, was key among their activities.[25] The reemerging provincial press came to include outlets such as *La Noche* (1844–1845), *El Siglo* (1847–1848), *La América* (1848), *El Censor* (1848–1849), *El Aviso* (1848–1849), and *El Alacrán* (1849).[26] These and others were, for the most part, weekly newspapers, edited by senior and young lawyers alike, with cooperation from radically romantic and liberal young law students.[27] Discussing politics was one of these papers' main concerns, but mere talk was not sufficient for these determined individuals.

The rehabilitated exiles soon resumed their participation in actual electoral politics, traditionally one of provincial lawyers' favorite activities. Upon returning from his brief exile, for example, Camacho Naranjo, now over fifty, immediately joined the Senate. As in the 1830s (see Tables 7.2, 7.4, and 7.5), politics, particularly parliamentary politics, also continued to captivate younger law graduates. While seeking now to engage in mercantile ventures as well, the new generation embraced politics enthusiastically. For example, at the age of thirty, the key revolutionary activist Manuel Murillo Toro, a participant in three *Supremos'* military revolts, returned from Panama in the mid-1840s and settled in Santa Marta.[28] He later joined a company intent on renewing the steamship navigation of the Magdalena River, an activity conducted intermittently by different entrepreneurs from 1825 to 1847.[29] With the help of friends he made during his exile in Panama, he was elected to Congress in 1846 and went to Bogotá. Later, along with his congressional activities, he published a business-oriented newspaper, *La Gaceta Mercantil,* in Santa Marta (1847–1848).[30] Thirty-six-year-old lawyer and medical doctor Vicente Lombana, who owned a pharmacy before the war forced him out of the country, also came back from Europe in 1845. Two years later he joined the House of Representatives and resumed his business activities.[31] Forty-year-old lawyer Florentino González, the young radical who plotted against Bolívar back in 1828 and was later exiled under accusations of complicity with the *Supremos,* also returned to Bogotá in 1845 to dedicate himself to trade, journalism, and politics. As we shall see, he somewhat unexpectedly joined Mosquera's aristocratic government. Of these three provincials, Murillo and González became the most radical advocates of liberal reforms in the late 1840s and early 1850s.

The "Liberal Revolution"

Despite the preceding examples, the liberal changes experienced in mid-nineteenth-century New Granada were not the ideological patrimony of the provincials. Mosquera's aristocratic administration promoted the first liberal reforms as early as 1847. Furthermore, as had been the case with liberal educational policies adopted in the late 1840s, some aristocrats converged with the provincials and were eager to introduce liberal reforms. For instance, conservative Senator and lawyer Climaco Ordoñez, a wealthy merchant linked by marriage to the family of a high-ranking colonial bureaucrat, sponsored a key liberal bill, the 1848 law abolishing the tobacco monopoly. This bill was also backed and promoted by conservative law graduate Mariano Ospina and aristocrat Julio Arboleda.[32] Conversely, a few provincials opposed a full economic liberalization, the most telling case being that of lawyer Ezequiel Rojas himself. Rojas's favorable views on liberal political economy did not keep him from opposing the abolition of the state's tobacco monopoly.[33] On the whole, however, most provincials and a fair number of conservative aristocrats supported President Mosquera's liberal political economy.

Mosquera's cabinet was initially composed of mostly nonliberal aristocrats or their protégés. Its leading members were Popayán's former *ministerial* lawyer Manuel M. Mallarino, minister of foreign relations and public works and a young protégé of Rafael Mosquera, the president's cousin; and Bogotano lawyer Alejandro Osorio, minister of the interior, a protégé of the Caicedo clan and an outspoken anti-free trader.[34] To carry out heterodox ideas that neither of the two was entirely ready to help implement, and to the surprise and annoyance of both former *ministeriales* and *progresistas,* Mosquera invited Socorrano lawyer Florentino González to accept the position of finance minister in September 1846.[35]

González, as mentioned, had just come back from his European exile, during which his mercantile occupations (he operated a *casa de comercio* or shop in Paris) turned him into an even more ambitious and clearly probusiness lawyer. As one young contemporary put it, González was "thirsty for fame and power, coveted wealth, and was friendly with capitalists and businessmen."[36] Soon after arriving in Bogotá, perhaps helped by his French experience and his in-laws' connections with the wealthy lawyer-merchants Clímaco Ordóñez and Miguel Saturnino Uribe, he became an import merchant himself, entering into business partnerships with aristocrats like his former classmate (and, until recently, personal enemy) José Vicente Martínez, Ordoñez's closest partner and relative by marriage.[37] He also wrote editorials in local newspapers that proposed modernizing liberal economic policies.[38] In 1847, as a cabinet minister, González helped reform New Granada's fiscal administration by advocating a radical lowering of import duties (on flour, rice, grease, furs, shoes, iron, and some textiles), which anticipated the liberalizing trend of the early 1850s.[39]

The 1847 tariff modification and other reform proposals (i.e., reforming the tithe, reorganizing the treasury, improving currency supply, tightening control of the salt monopoly) earned González the admiration of wealthy aristocrats, including Popayán natives Julio Arboleda and Lino de Pombo. Along with a group of young liberals, these leading conservatives even promoted González's candidacy to the presidency in 1848.[40]

The tariff modification, however, also earned González (and the government) the enmity of Colombia's artisans. In late 1847, backed by two Bogotano lawyers—Cayetano Leiva Millán, also an *escribano público,* and Juan Evangelista Durán—they organized societies (later known as Sociedades Democráticas de Artesanos, the Democratic Society of Artisans) to press Congress for the law's abrogation.[41] Artisans had supported the aristocratic governments of the late 1830s and 1840s and turned down invitations to join the provincial faction, with whose members they even had physical confrontations in several regions (Chapter 9). But now, facing the liberal reforms promoted by Mosquera and his business-oriented peers, they claimed to have gained a new awareness as to which elite social group might truly uphold their material interests; namely, the provincials. They thus flocked to the support of the provincial group, backing their candidate, General José Hilario López, in the forthcoming 1849 presidential election. Although a member of the new Liberal party, López was expected to repeal the liberal tariff law.

Artisan support proved vital in securing López's victory and was courted by the activism of a socially heterogeneous generation of young law students and recent law graduates. These young intellectuals (individuals like Francisco Eustaquio Alvarez, Carlos Martín, Próspero Pereira Gamba, Antonio M. Pradilla, Medardo Rivas, Januario Salgar, José María Samper, and several more of those listed in Table 10.2) were welcomed into the artisanal societies as educators during 1848, 1849, and 1850. To the ultimate dislike of many members, they turned the societies into political clubs to serve the Liberal Party.[42]

Redefinition of the Political Factions: Rebellion of the Young "Mandarins"

The return of the provincial leadership to power in 1849 was thus to a great extent spearheaded by a new generation of young lawyers trained during the 1840s. Provincial ideologue Vicente Azuero, one of their law professors, had predicted years earlier that his young protégés would come to control the state apparatus during the late 1840s and after.[43] In fact, some of them did join the state ranks, while several others became political activists. Along with the young, technically trained bureaucrats ("mandarins"), they rebelled against the expectations of the aristocrats who, as a previous chapter illustrated, had shaped their legal training in a "practical," conservative direction.[44] Rather than following in the footsteps of their conservative mentors, they set out to radically transform the status quo. They started by eliminating several of the remaining fiscal features inherited from the colonial period, and looked for ways to turn the state apparatus into a steward and promoter of the marketplace. Numerous other liberal reforms (i.e., May 15, 1850–complete freedom of education; May 18, 1850–expulsion of the Jesuits; May 21, 1851–abolition of slavery) were introduced subsequently under their sponsorship and pressure.

Among these radically liberal young lawyers were several descendants of provincials. Brothers Manuel and Joaquín Suárez Fortoul were sons of provincial lawyer Joaquín Suárez Serrano, a radical antimilitary Socorrano of the late 1820s.[45] Brothers José María and Miguel Samper Agudelo were sons of a small landowner and merchant from the little town of Honda, in the Mariquita region northwest of Bogotá. Their father lost his properties after participating in the *Supremos* war to avenge his own brother, a rebel lieutenant colonel killed in battle.[46] Brothers Guillermo, Nicolás, and Próspero Pereira Gamba were sons of moderate lawyer Francisco Pereira and in-laws of their father's close friend, provincial lawyer Salvador Camacho Naranjo, one of the opposition leaders exiled after the war.[47] Camacho Naranjo's own son, lawyer Salvador Camacho Roldán, also formed part of this group. So did Anibal Galindo, son of a colonel, small merchant, and landowner in the region of Ibague who was executed by the government during the *Supremos* war, and brothers Eustacio and Domingo Buendía Durán, offspring of a middle-class family from Neiva's neighboring town of La Plata and younger cousins of Vicente Lombana Buendía, a provincial exiled after the war.[48] All of these radical youths were the offspring of modest lawyers, small merchants and landholders, and military officers. In addition, a fair number of their ancestors or relatives had taken part in the provincial struggle against the aristocrats during the late 1820s and the 1830s, for which several had paid with their lives or fortunes (see Table 10.2).

The new generation of young liberal activists was not an exclusively provincial circle. It was also composed of several individuals whose ancestors were traditional aristocrats or allies of aristocrats. Three representative examples of rebellious aristocrats were young lawyers Camilo Antonio Echeverri, Joaquín Pablo Posada, and Jose María Vergara y Tenorio. The first was the son of the wealthy Antioqueño merchant and mineowner Gabriel Echeverri, who had ex-

Table 10.2. Sample List of Young Radical Law Students and Lawyers Active in the Revival of Provincial Political Projects in the Late 1840s and Early 1850s

Name	Birth Date	Graduation Date	Birthplace
Francesco Eustaquio Alvarez	1827	1848	Gigante (Tolima)
Domingo Buendía Durán	1829?	1850s	?
Salvador Camacho Roldán	1827	1847	Nunchia (Tunja)
Camilo Antonio Echeverri*	1828	1850s	Medellín
Anibal Galindo	1834	1852	Coello (Tolima)
Narciso Gómez Valdez	1824	1845	Leiva? (Tunja?)
Ramón Gómez	1832	1850s	Tenza (Tunja)
Santos Gutiérrez	1820	1847	Cocuy (Tunja)
Carlos Martín Gaitán	1826	1845	Bogotá
Rafael Núñez Moledo	1825	1845	Cartagena
Guillermo Pereira Gamba	?	1848	Cartago?
Nicolás Pereira Gamba	1824	1845	?
Próspero Pereira Gamba	1830	?	Bogotá
Santiago Pérez	1829	1850s	Zipaquirá
Felipe Pérez	1836	1850s	Sotaquira (Tunja)
Manuel Pombo??	1827?	1847	Popayán
Joaquín Pablo Posada*	1825	1850s	Cartagena
Antonio María Pradilla	1822	1847	Barichara
José María Rivas*	1822	1847	Rionegro (Antioquia)
Medardo Rivas*	1825	1847	Bogotá
José María Rojas Garrido	1824	1847	Agrado (Neiva)
Octavio Salazar	1830	1850s	?
Januario Salgar	?	1847	?
José María Samper Agudelo	1827	1848	Honda (Tolima)
Miguel Samper Agudelo	1825	1846	Guaduas (Tolima)
Manuel Suárez Fortoul	?	?	?
Joaquín Suárez Fortoul	?	?	?
Ricardo Vanegas	1822	1843	Vélez
Jose María Vergara y Tenorio*	1823	?	Bogotá

Sources: Restrepo and Rivas, *Genealogías de Santafé;* Arboleda, *Diccionario genealógico y biográfico;* Ospina, *Diccionario biográfico y bibliográfico; GNG,* no. 1029 (March 4, 1849); *GNG,* no. 1030 (March 11, 1849); *GNG,* no. 1031 (March 11, 1849); Otero Muñóz, "Bocetos biográficos," 217–20; Samper, *Historia de un alma;* Galindo, *Recuerdos históricos;* Rivas, *Los trabajadores de tierra caliente;* Camacho Roldán, *Mis memorias;* "Una sesión de la Escuela Republicana" (Bogotá, 1850).

*From aristocratic background and connections.

tensive kinship and commercial ties to other members of the conservative Antioqueño elite and gave financial backing to the aristocratic governments of the early 1840s.[49] The second, who was to become a committed pro-artisan socialist in the early 1850s, was the son of aristocratic Cartagena General Joaquín Posada Gutiérrez, a loyal Bolivarian in the 1820s who fought the provincial rebels during the *Supremos* war.⁵⁰ The third was the son of the well-known Bogotano lawyer Estanislao Vergara, who was linked to colonial bureaucratic clans and promoted authoritarian projects during the 1820s and 1830s.⁵¹ Justo Arosemena, Rafael Caicedo y Cuero, José María Malo Blanco, Teodoro Valenzuela, and several other lawyers were also part of this group of young aristocrats turned Liberal sympathizers during the late 1840s and early 1850s.⁵²

These and other aristocrats' identification with the provincials went beyond their common belief in liberal economic doctrines. They also shared the new entrepreneurial mentality that downplayed the significance of bureaucratic careers as an expression of *empleomanía*. Instead, they valued the business drive observable among the new and old generations alike. This common antibureaucratic frame of mind started to blur the status differences between individuals and families with or without a colonial bureaucratic tradition, gradually eroding one of the key social differences between aristocratic and provincial elites discussed throughout this work. As this occurred, reciprocal status-honor differences declined and the true class affinity of the two groups began to surface.

This growing class affinity may help explain why, after the slow transformation they themselves experienced during the 1840s, some mature aristocrats joined the rejuvenated liberal provincial group. Three interesting cases were those of lawyers Francisco Javier Zaldúa and Rafael Rivas Mejía and former law student José Caicedo Rojas. From 1842 until 1844, Zaldúa served the victorious aristocratic government as governor of the former rebel region of Socorro, with whose traditional elites he established family ties. At that time Zaldúa was apparently penniless, despite his descent from "muy notables familias" (a fine family) and his father's distinguished colonial bureaucratic career. After leaving the governorship, he ran a prosperous legal practice during the 1840s. Perhaps helped by his Socorrano ties, his disappointment with the increasingly centralist and authoritarian nature of the 1837–1849 aristocratic regimes, or his perception of the probusiness stance of the renewed provincial clique, he gradually shifted from the *ministerial* camp, joined the bloc that created the Liberal party in 1849, and became an active Liberal militant.⁵³

Rivas Mejía also served in a high-ranking bureaucratic job within the aristocratic government that won the *Supremos* war, a victory he openly celebrated. He descended from one of the richest landowning families of Bogotá and was a nephew of aristocratic authoritarian lawyer José María del Castillo y Rada, a Bolívar supporter and cabinet minister.⁵⁴ During the early 1840s, after personal disputes with President Herrán, Rivas Mejía resigned from the bureaucracy, devoted himself to running a *trapiche* (sugar mill) in the lowlands neighboring Bogotá, and leaned more and more toward the Liberals, whom he joined during the 1850s. His young brothers, lawyers Medardo, Ricardo, and José María, followed Rafael's inclinations, eventually joining the Liberal party.⁵⁵

Finally, José Caicedo Rojas, nephew of aristocratic General Domingo Caicedo and a law student during the 1830s, fought alongside the government's armies during the *Supremos* civil war and occupied bureaucratic jobs afterward. During the 1840s, however, he also shifted toward the nascent Liberal party. This was perhaps due to ideological reasons, although the fact that he was fired from the bureaucracy in the mid-1840s may have been a more powerful motivation. In addition, he established social connections with provincial groups when he married the sister of the radically liberal Suárez Fortoul brothers.[56]

More important was the fact that for all of these Liberal aristocrats, "status" confrontations with the provincials were no longer central. The quest for the spoils of government and the honor and power derived from bureaucratic service were now overshadowed by the fascination of agrarian and trading ventures, in which several Conservatives participated as enthusiastically as Liberals. This entrepreneurial drive was magnificently described in the memoirs of one of the young Liberals, lawyer Rivas Mejía's younger brother Medardo. Medardo became one of the many "trabajadores de tierra caliente," that is, a colonizer of the lowlands between Bogotá and the Magdalena River, which in the late 1840s and early 1850s were quickly covered by sugar cane *trapiches,* cacao and tobacco plantations, and merchant houses.[57]

In contrast to the aristocrats listed above, at least some of the young lawyers who joined the ranks of the Conservative party tended to be from unassuming provincial families. They seem to have pursued aristocratic patronage and were ideologically driven by their devout Catholicism.[58] But except in matters of religion and, to a lesser degree, educational ideas, their agenda did not differ much from that of their Liberal counterparts; certainly, their differences as to how to structure New Granada's political economy were becoming insignificant.[59]

New Alliances and the Social Nature of the Emerging Political Parties

The 1846 advent of Socorrano lawyer Florentino González to the cabinet of an aristocratic government, the artisanal support for a provincial Liberal candidate, and the activism of young lawyers—both provincials and aristocrats—within artisanal societies, were signs that New Granada's political factions were being redefined during the second half of the 1840s. These factions, which paradoxically turned into formal political parties in 1848–1849 just when their members were starting to converge socially and ideologically, were no longer relatively clear-cut groups of "aristocrats" and "provincials" struggling primarily over bureaucratic jobs and status-honor.[60] Provincials and aristocrats mingled socially with each other, and as *empleomanía* fell under intense criticism and other sources of social prestige opened up, the state lost its traditional appeal. Furthermore, intra-elite status confrontations receded as class struggles pitting a united provincial/aristocratic elite against subaltern social groups began moving to the forefront in the mid-1850s.

The new alliances between provincial Liberals and aristocratic Conservatives followed a series of significant economic transformations: a short-lived financial bubble that ended precipitously with the ruin of some local tycoons in Bogotá in the early 1840s;[61] the slowing down and ultimate failure of 1830s experiments in economic nationalism and proto-industrialism;[62] and, more important, the emergence of expanding economic opportunities derived from the initial settlement of grievances with foreign bankers, which determined the reentry of New

Granada into the English financial markets in the mid-1840s. Expanding economic opportunities were also tied to the emergence of a tobacco export economy, which triggered the subsequent colonization of *tierras calientes* and promised increasing economic opportunities and profitable returns.[63] Within this modified economic context, liberalism (except for its anticlerical components, which were radically rejected by most Conservatives) represented an attractive program for virtually all of the elites.

In 1849, however, the old-time provincial Liberals and the Conservatives' former aristocratic leadership engaged in a dispute that became legendary and added to the idea that a "liberal revolution" had occurred. The Liberals were accused of having physically, with the help of hordes of knife-wielding artisans, coerced the parliament to elect General López as the country's new president. The two rival candidates, lawyers Rufino Cuervo and Joaquín J. Gori, represented the now divided forces of the *ministerial* or aristocratic group.[64] With López in power, the old provincials allegedly proceeded to fire aristocrats from high-ranking bureaucratic positions.[65] There is some truth to these accusations, but these and other Liberal-Conservative confrontations were far from the clear status struggles of the past, nor were they open intra-elite class struggles. They resulted from the logical tensions arising from the long exclusion of the old Liberal leadership from state power.

A certain social gap between the leaders of the Liberal and Conservative parties seems to have persisted for a while. A number of these leaders were members of the provincial and aristocratic groups that had clashed in the late 1830s and still faced tense relations. But in general, both parties' membership was now more socially mixed and generally converged in pushing for the liberalization of the economy and the state (e.g., disassembling state monopolies, lowering tariffs, decentralizing bureaucratic administration and education, abolishing both slavery and the death penalty). This liberalization was not the product of a revolution fought by upwardly mobile merchants against aristocratic and unwilling landowners, nor was it the exclusive creation of Liberal activists. If it was a "bourgeois" revolution at all, the bourgeoisie that presided over it was a bipartisan group.[66] Its most direct beneficiaries included prominent Conservative aristocrats.

The revolution directly benefited, to mention just one, the dominant Antioqueño group, which had so actively backed the recent aristocratic governments and obtained concessions, contracts, and bureaucratic positions during the late 1830s and 1840s. Now, despite losing the monopoly over tobacco exports and transportation that they had briefly enjoyed in the second half of the 1840s, Antioqueño merchants and mineowners substantially expanded their businesses and profited from the long-awaited abolition of taxes on gold exports. This measure, for which they had fruitlessly lobbied since the early 1830s, was eventually decreed in 1851.[67] It thus comes as no surprise that lawyer and merchant Jorge Gutiérrez de Lara, an Antioqueño linked to the most influential business network of this region (Figure 9.1), eventually supported López's election and was subsequently appointed to the governorship of Antioquia. Furthermore, the very wealthy Antioqueños linked to Gutiérrez de Lara actively opposed a short-lived Conservative revolution against General López supported by pious elites within their region in 1851.[68]

A United Social Class Emerges

In addition to their convergence regarding the liberalization of New Granada, the leaders of both parties tightly closed ranks before major popular threats. Notable among such threats were mounting artisan-supported banditry and an artisan-backed military coup. Both these situations were countered by a determined and united front of former aristocrats and provincials. The united elites seem to have realized that underneath the status-honor differences that caused them to confront each other for so many years lay similar material interests—namely, the common interests of an upper social class made up of high-ranking bureaucrats, proprietors, professionals and intellectuals, merchants, and landholders.

The first threat that brought together former provincial and aristocratic groups in Bogotá took the form of banditry. In the early 1850s several upper-class homes and businesses were burglarized. The properties in question included the store of rich Spanish merchant Juan Alcina and the Bogotá homes of leading citizens, among them provincial lawyer Florentino González and his wife, Bernardina Ibañez; the elderly Josefa Fuenmayor; wealthy aristocrat Andrés Caicedo Bastidas and his wife, Evarista Quijano y Caicedo; and the sisters Concepción and Mercedes Prieto Espinosa, members of a traditional Bogotá family. At least one convent, San Agustín, was also raided.

In late April 1851, thirty-five-year-old José Raimundo Russi, native of the small town of Leiva (Boyacá), was jailed along with three Bogotá mill workers.[69] The workers and *Doctor* Russi, alleged leader of the criminal band, were charged with the assassination of their friend, blacksmith Manuel Ferro. They were supposedly afraid that Ferro would denounce several recent thefts their "gang" had carried out seemingly on behalf of the artisans' community.[70]

Young Russi, a failed school owner and teacher,[71] was also an eccentric, presumably able, and popular lawyer. He was particularly liked among the lower social classes, thanks to his work as a pro bono defense attorney. His clients included some of his codefendants and their relatives. More important, the flamboyant Russi had served as secretary of the artisans' Sociedad Democrática, in which post he was instrumental in the election of President López, whom he was said to accompany on frequent walks up the promenade in front of Bogotá's cathedral.[72] He also took part in commissions made up of artisans and young provincial lawyer-activists, like Carlos Martín and José M. Samper, who in early 1850 visited the president to demand the expulsion of the Jesuits from New Granada and to promote other radical liberal measures.[73]

Neither Russi's popularity and influence among the artisans, nor his acquaintance with young liberal activists and support for López's election, were enough to obtain a presidential pardon. A pardon was requested, on humanitarian and

Christian-philosophical grounds, by over 200 petitioners. The protests of Russi's many followers, including radical young attorney Joaquín Pablo Posada and his in-laws, brothers Ignacio and Francisco Morales Montenegro, were similarly unsuccessful. They contended that Russi was innocent of all charges, but the government faced pressure from a bipartisan "meeting" of local *poderosos* (magnates and merchants), who needed a scapegoat and a moralizing spectacle to contain social thievery.[74]

Former aristocrats were not the only ones to ask for the execution of Russi and his alleged subordinates. Their deaths were demanded by former provincials like lawyer Florentino González, victim of some of the thefts and organizer of the *poderosos'* April 29 meeting. The death penalty was vehemently defended at the trial by *fiscales* Benigno Guarnizo and Francisco Eustaquio Alvarez, two attorneys from the provincial liberal group.[75] The executions were ultimately approved by President López himself, who not only supported the jury law under which Russi and his peers were tried but also refused any pardon.[76] Even popular literature written at the time shared the general consensus on Russi's culpability and contributed to vilify him.[77] It could be argued that all of these individuals, as well as the jury (which included Francisco Londoño, a black artisan and one of Russi's former companions) and writers of the period acted under the conviction that Russi and his accomplices were guilty. Be that as it may, several contemporaries and later historians have asserted that the evidence of Russi's guilt was neither solid nor sufficient. According to these critics, it was the tense social atmosphere and pressure from property owners that ultimately determined Russi's execution.[78] Provincials and aristocrats, in the midst of a tense social scene, were closing ranks against their common enemies from the popular classes. Russi may have been a tragic scapegoat.

There are several indications that provincials gradually distanced themselves from the popular classes, their recent political allies, and turned toward their original nemesis, the aristocratic sector. By July 17, 1851, the date of Russi's execution, eight months had passed since the radical young provincial lawyers and law students had left the artisanal societies that had helped them to elect General López. Their latest project was an eccentric political club for radical intellectuals, the Escuela Republicana. Here, along with rebellious young aristocrats, they freely engaged in exalted rhetorical exercises in Christian (but anticlerical) socialism and communism, while under their compliant eyes their former artisan "friends" were being abused or, as in the case of Russi and his accomplices, persecuted and exterminated.[79]

As artisans became even more threatening, the young provincials soon turned to active and open hostility toward the craftsmen and other ordinary people and, subsequently, against their military allies. In this provincials were not alone, of course. There is evidence that they were closing ranks with aristocrats, as the two sectors perceived that their mutual material interests were under threat not just from social criminals but also from insurgent armies assisted by the artisan leagues.

The threat posed by the popular sectors finally took the form of a successful coup, led in mid-April 1854 by a radical coalition of anti-free trade artisans under *maestro* (master craftsman) Miguel León and military troops led by General José María Melo.[80] The coup followed a series of confrontations between angry artisans and congressmen who had voted against tariff increases. Popular riots also occurred in Bogotá's commercial districts, ending in several deaths and the severe beating of elite provincial lawyer and former cabinet minister Florentino González.[81] In addition to those clashes, some army officials were edgy over congressional measures to weaken the military and try General Melo, commander of Bogotá's garrison and champion of military prerogatives, for the murder of a soldier.

In response to the coup, numerous individuals from both the former provincial and aristocratic groups and the two political parties took up arms, organized joint battalions, and fought fiercely against "the dictator" Melo.[82] Very few lawyers supported Melo and his troops. Fifty-two-year-old Francisco A. Obregón, who presided over Bogotá's Democratic Society of Artisans and served as the new regime's secretary general and minister of economics, was one.[83] Another exception was young socialist idealist Joaquín Pablo Posada, who edited the *4 de Abril*, the military regime's newspaper, and participated in military combat alongside General Melo and his artisan-backed troops.

The final battle between the two sides was fought in Bogotá eight months after the coup, on December 4, 1854. The joint antirevolutionary forces organized by the elites and well financed by merchants and capitalists from all over New Granada defeated Melo and the people's troops. Virtually all members of the artisans societies, especially in Bogotá, were placed under arrest. General Melo, over 300 artisans, and several other supporters, including Posada (who had been injured in combat), were subsequently exiled.[84] The artisans were sent to forced labor camps in Panama; only two returned alive. The threat represented by the coup sealed the bipartisan alliance of the now closer aristocratic and provincial elites.[85]

Following the War of the *Supremos* the provincial group dwindled, as its leaders died or were sentenced to exile. The survivors returned to the public sphere a few years later and were joined by a younger generation of innovative lawyers from provincial and aristocratic backgrounds alike. This group soon proceeded to form the Liberal party and, having penetrated and gained the electoral support of artisan leagues, took over the presidency in 1849. They then pushed for the liberalization of New Granada's economy, society, and politics. The economic liberalization, however, was not accomplished exclusively by the Liberal party; it also had the support of a good number of the party's former political rivals. Its "Liberal" nature is therefore questionable, given that members of the newly created Conservative party eventually also backed it. The "bourgeois" lineage of these economic reforms is also controversial. Aristocrats, from both the young and old generations, were equally active in promoting them. The mid-nineteenth century saw the emergence of a coalition of traditional and provincial elites in favor of sponsoring a free-trade economic "revolution," which resulted from an ultimately unstoppable trend supported by almost all elite sectors of society—merchants, mineowners, and landowners alike.

Behind the union of provincials and aristocrats lay radical changes in the way elites conceived of and approached the state apparatus. From a source of power and status-honor, the state had begun to turn into a basis for stigmatization. Those wishing to join it at all costs were now catalogued as *empleomaniacos*, described as suffering from the disease of public office and the inability to engage in productive activities. The cure for this disease was readily available in the form of expanded economic opportunities, which made it unnecessary for educated individuals and others intent on increasing their power and prestige to pursue bureaucratic careers. Elite lawyers from all sectors seized the new opportunities.

The rediscovered economic homogeneity derived from these entrepreneurial opportunities and endeavors considerably diminished the mutual status differences of the past, and further sealed the social union of the provincials and aristocrats. This class union was reflected in their common struggle against bandits and insurgent artisans.

Conclusion

This study disputes the long-held belief that postcolonial Latin America was exclusively dominated by *caudillos*. It also questions the widespread idea that constitutions and elections were meaningless and that postcolonial social mobility was limited. More interesting, it addresses another cherished stereotype: that Latin American societies and cultures have always been state-oriented[1] and, as a result, Latin Americans have unalterably been avid seekers of state patronage and state jobs; or, in nineteenth-century words, they have been *empleomanos*. Finally, it challenges two sets of ideas concerning postcolonial political conflicts and affiliations: first, that they followed economic patterns; and second, that they did not follow any social pattern at all, but were random and/or personalistic.

Instead of looking at *caudillos*, this study focuses on lawyers to understand New Granada's social and political history in the critical years from about 1780 to 1850. The lawyers of this period comprised a select segment from elite and middling backgrounds alike. The collective history of their lives thus illustrates the economic, ethnic, and cultural characteristics of those various social sectors. Moreover, since many lawyers strove to follow bureaucratic careers, the study of their activities affords us valuable information not only about the shape of society and social relations, but also about the nature of state-society interactions. This is especially pertinent to a momentous and turbulent long period like the Age of Revolution, a time of intense reform of state structures, revolution, civil war, and efforts at reconstruction. This period witnessed the formation of new state and social institutions and spaces, including the gradual liquidation of the colonial caste regime, the rise of a public sphere of civil society, and the parallel creation of a system of political parties. In all of these processes, lawyers and their families played central roles.

This book shows that elite colonial families perpetuated and increased their power and status not solely through economic endeavors such as ranching, mining, or trade. In addition to these activities, they avidly pursued college education, ecclesiastical and bureaucratic jobs, and government privileges. They deliberately prepared some of their members to join the priesthood and the bureaucracy, the latter through the legal profession and appropriate marriages. Even noble families coveted state service and were willing to contribute their lawyer sons to the state ranks. Serving the Crown was a major source of individual and familial status-honor. Elite clans strove to display a family history of service to the king; in so doing, they developed a symbiotic relationship with the colonial state, within which they built family-bureaucratic networks well into the regime's last days. In return for state patronage, lawyer-bureaucrats in and out of such networks reciprocated with as much loyalty as circumstances dictated. In fact, lawyers were generally unwilling to oppose the colonial state and risk their chances for a prosperous career.

Given that lawyers made up a good proportion of the state's bureaucratic ranks, the Crown and the colonial state attributed great importance to law schools and legal education. Whatever lawyers were trained to do and think directly affected the functioning of the state. To assure that their training was free of politically inconvenient doctrines was therefore critical to the Crown, which sought to control law schools and to censor the curriculum. However, the Crown seemed unable to displace the Church and gain full control over legal education, and it could not contain either the massive participation of lawyers in New Granada's subsequent movement for independence.

The active participation of creole lawyers and other elite individuals in the revolution was not motivated by the content of legal education. It was not the inevitable result of their exclusion from the colonial bureaucracy or their difficulties in gaining access to it, nor was it the logical conclusion of a long-term process of alienation from the Spanish establishment. Revolutionary mobilization was rather a response to Spain's overwhelming political crisis and the Spanish Crown's unwillingness to discuss the formation of wider governing coalitions. When the state collapsed, creole lawyers and administrators were thus ready and able to engage in revolutionary maneuvers, a mobilization that resulted in a "revolution from above."

The role of lawyers in unleashing revolutionary collective action was facilitated by the dominant position they and their families traditionally held in local city councils. These councils were instrumental in mobilizing both elite and popular sectors. They were also the vehicle through which elites articulated the opportune, expedient, and populist ideology of creolism, and the base from which they went on to capture the state apparatus.

In trying to capture the state and its booty, lawyers and their elite peers produced much social and institutional disruption. Socially, they presided over the mobilization of unruly nonwhite masses. Having disrupted the traditional regional hierarchies, they also facilitated the rise of provincial sectors to leading political positions. Institutionally, they distorted traditional administrative arrangements and routines, created new offices and taxes, and enacted numerous bodies of legislation. The social and institutional chaos they helped to unleash earned them the enmity of the Spanish Crown, which savagely repressed them, killing over a fourth of the entire legal profession. The elite families, friends, and supporters of these lawyers, overcoming regional, ideological, and social disputes, deepened the revolution and brought it to completion.

It is now obviously mistaken that elections and constitutions in postcolonial Latin America were meaningless and social mobility limited. As early as the 1810s and through the 1820s, significant generational, regional, and social changes were evident among the members of the legal profession and the high-ranking clerical and secular bureaucracies. To the dominance of the younger generations was added the distinction of an upwardly mobile group of provincial lawyers. Through legal mechanisms and elections, and occasionally through military means, provincials began to gain political prominence in competition with their colleagues from traditional colonial families. These aristocrats were reluctant to forfeit the status-honor they had gained through individual and familial service in the colonial state.

Neither the aristocrats nor their competitors could establish a hegemonic project of state and society during those years. In the late 1820s, provincial groups supported by wealthy mining entrepreneurs and merchants from the region of Antioquia fought aristocratic sectors linked to traditional colonial circles from Cartagena, Popayán, Bogotá, and Tunja. These conflicts impeded the consolidation of (Gran) Colombia, the 1821 union with Venezuela and Ecuador. Neither group was monolithic; an important segment of aristocrats joined the provincials to dissolve the union and demilitarize the government. A provincial-aristocratic coalition then governed New Granada under civilian control from 1832 to 1837.

Having dissolved the union and expelled Venezuela's armies from New Granada, the two segments of New Granada's ruling civilian elite began to clash. Even then, however, their clashes took a military form (coups and countercoups) only in exceptional cases. For the most part, they occurred peacefully within the "public sphere of civil society" and the new state's parliamentary institutions. Their confrontation more commonly took the form of constitutional gatherings and elections, not to mention intense journalistic disputes in a more or less open public sphere.

These disputes did not reflect clear-cut economic differences or class struggles among provincials and aristocrats, nor were they random conflicts; the confrontation was determined predominantly by status-honor tensions over control of a traditional source of prestige: the high state bureaucracy. Throughout the early postcolonial period, the state continued to provide status-honor to traditional aristocratic sectors. As was outlined above, however, it also benefited upwardly mobile provincial elites. All would share the spoils as long as necessary, but with the social changes both sectors started to undergo, crises and attempts at excluding opponents were bound to emerge. The aristocrats' cooptation of plutocratic sectors from New Granada's northwestern mining region of Antioquia in the late 1830s and the rise of the Neiva, Mariquita, and other marginal elites were at the root of these crises, which were aggravated by disputes over the nature of legal education.

Confrontations over the discourse and practice of legal education were pervasive in New Granada from the 1810s to the 1840s and beyond. State intervention in legal education helped reinforce the trend toward republicanism and decentralization, encouraged an anticlerical agenda, and prepared the ideological ground for the free-trade policies of the mid-nineteenth century. Through the state, the two segments of the elite tried to shape legal education according to their political needs. However, growing internal disputes over some of these objectives made it hopeless—even during a long period of aristocratic governments (1837–1849)—for any segment of the ruling elite or for the central state itself to exert clear hegemony over the schools and curriculum and, through them, over civil society.

In the long run, the reform of legal education benefited the provincial liberal sector, leading as it did to a growing number of upwardly mobile lawyers and the spread of liberal principles. The tensions over legal education and the ultimate success of liberalism were intimately linked to New Granada's first nationwide civil war, fought during the late 1830s and early 1840s. According to the government, the provincial lawyers' *empleomanía* and their "futiles motivos de puestos" ("futile arguments over jobs") were the cause of the war. This would confirm the alleged state-centered nature of New Granadan society.

Colombians' aspiration to bureaucratic jobs was not new; it was a cherished tradition inherited from the colonial period. What *was* new in the postcolonial period was the gradual development of a negative attitude toward this tradition. Since the late 1820s, individual members of the aristocratic elite, probably as a way to discourage potential competitors, had launched isolated criticisms of those who pursued "la carrera de los empleos" ("the career of public office"). A few elite provincials themselves also attacked this proclivity. Nevertheless, widespread and systematic assaults on *empleomanía* did not occur until the late 1830s. By then, rather than an adequate source of status-honor, public job-seeking was allegedly becoming a pathological tendency. Despite provincial claims to the contrary, the War of the *Supremos* and several others of the nineteenth century's frequent civil wars were attributed to *empleomanía*. Underlying this scramble for the spoils of public office was the struggle of two socially and culturally (but not economically) diverse social groups for status-honor.

In colonial and early postcolonial Latin America, elites craved the authority, respect, and prestige that surrounded high-ranking state servants. To a large extent, when unavailable, the "authority of wealth" could be compensated for by the authority of public office. Even when available, wealth and the power resulting from it appear to have been insufficient to satisfy honor-starved individuals and families, who eagerly pursued the superior status-honor accruing from state service.[2] Only when more or less massive political competition ultimately made the state available to all–even talented or electorally savvy rabble rousers–the significance of a state job dramatically changed. The mere fact of their accessibility through democratic mechanisms like elections robbed such jobs of their status, a trend reflected in the coining of pejorative expressions like *empleomanía*. It was at that point that wealth gained a new cultural prominence. Being wealthy was largely perceived by elite individuals and families as an end in itself, intrinsically worthwhile and culturally advantageous, regardless of the absence of control over any political office.

In New Granada, new attitudes toward the superiority of wealth and gain over honor followed the 1840–1842 *Supremos* civil war. In this war's aftermath, the provincial group of lawyers competing for control of the state apparatus dwindled, as its leaders died or were sentenced to exile. Several returned to the public sphere a few years later and were joined by a younger generation of innovative lawyers from both provincial and aristocratic backgrounds. Together, they took over the presidency in 1849 and pushed for the liberalization of New

Granada's economy, society, and politics. Behind the union of provincials and aristocrats lay radical changes in the way elites conceived of and approached the state apparatus. From a source of power and status-honor, the state had turned into a basis of stigmatization. Those wishing to join it at all costs were now seen as plagued by a true disease, the disease of living from public office and being unable to engage in productive activities. The cure for this affliction was readily available in the form of expanded economic opportunities, which made it unnecessary for educated individuals and others intent on increasing their power and prestige to pursue bureaucratic careers. Elite lawyers from all sectors seized the new opportunities and increasingly expressed their desire for material gain over honor.

The rediscovered economic homogeneity derived from these entrepreneurial opportunities did away with the mutual status differences of the past and further sealed the social union of aristocrats and provincials. This class union was reflected in the struggle of the two groups against common enemies—bandits and insurgent artisans—and was facilitated by the social mingling of provincials and aristocrats.

In several of his insightful works, Tulio Halperín Donghi forcefully argued that postcolonial Latin America experienced the "militarization" of state and society and the "ruralization" of the bases of political power.[3] Some of this was generally true, but postcolonial Latin American societies and states were much more complex than these simple categories suggest. To be sure, military bosses crowded the social and political landscape, but lawyers, journalists, and politicians did, too. Rural landlords were economically and socially prominent, but so were independent urban professionals, businessmen, and bureaucrats. A more nuanced explanation of both the social and political history of the period in question requires that we take a new look at these social sectors and examine their dynamic interactions. It also demands that we discard the traditional dichotomy between colonial and modern historiography and try to understand the two periods' cultural and social crossovers.

Chronological Outline

Presidents, Chief Executives, and Dictators

Year	Name, Occupation, Regime's Nature
1819–1828	Simón Bolívar (President elect), Army General
1821–1827	Francisco de P. Santander (Vice President, acting President), Army General, Provincial, coalition with all aristocrats
1828–1830	Simón Bolívar (Dictator), Army General, Aristocratic
1830	Joaquín Mosquera (President), Lawyer, Aristocratic, coalition with provincials
1830–1831	Rafael Urdaneta (Dictator), Army General, Aristocratic
1831	Domingo Caicedo (Vice President acting as chief executive), Army General, Aristocrat, coalition with provincials
1831–1832	José M. Obando (Vice President acting as chief executive), Army General, Provincial
1832–1837	Francisco de P. Santander (President), Army General, Provincial, coalition with moderate aristocrats
1837–1841	Jose Ignacio de Márquez (President), Lawyer, Aristocratic
1841–1845	Pedro Alcantara Herrán (President), Army General, Aristocratic
1845–1849	Thomas C. Mosquera (President), Army General, Aristocratic
1849–1853	José Hilario López, Army General, Provincial

Some Significant Events and Dates

1760s–1780s	Fiscal Moreno y Escandón leads efforts to create a public university and reform legal education.
1778–1784	Visitor and Intendant Juan Francisco Gutiérrez de Piñerez leads fiscal reforms that provoked popular upheaval.
1780–1782	Comuneros Revolt in northeastern New Granada.
1794–1795	Antonio Nariño and a group of lawyers and law students jailed and tried for publishing *The Rights of Man* and posting subversive leaflets in Bogotá.
1810	Junta Suprema of Santafé, formed in Bogotá, July 20–21, 1810.
1810–1816	*Patria Boba* period. Provincias Unidas of Nueva Granada fight civil war against Cundinamarca. Civil confrontations facilitate Spanish reconquest.
1816–1819	Spanish *Reconquista* under General Pablo Morillo. Royalist forces restore Spanish power over viceroyalty of New Granada.

Chronological Outline

1819	Battle of Boyacá. Patriotic forces defeat royalist army. This was the turning point in Colombia's independence.
1819	Patriot congress meets at Angostura, Venezuela.
1821	Congress of Cúcuta writes a constitution for Colombia.
1826	Santander's Plan of Studies, first major educational program in independent Colombia, is enacted.
1826	Dominicans' University of St. Thomas ceases to exist.
1826–1828	Public universities open in Cauca (Popayán), Magdalena e Itsmo (Cartagena), and Cundinamarca (Bogotá).
1828	Constitutional Congress meets in Ocaña ("Ocaña Convention").
1828	Opponents try and fail to assassinate Bolívar.
1828–1830	General Bolívar declares dictatorship.
1828–1832	Vice President Santander goes into exile in Europe and the United States.
1830	General Bolívar installs Admirable Congress (Congreso Admirable) in Bogotá.
1830	Antioquia established as a new Province.
1837	Sociedad Democrática Republicana de Artesanos i Laboradores Progresistas established under provincial leadership.
1838	Sociedad Católica created under aristocratic leadership.
1839	Closure of small convents provokes popular riot in Pasto, southern Colombia.
1840–1842	Nationwide civil War of the *Supremos*.
1840	*Supremo* rebels stage a siege on Bogotá forcing changes in government.
1847	Sociedad Democrática de Artesanos organized under provincial leadership to press for abrogation of liberal tariff law. Young law students join to serve as educators.
1847	Liberal tariff reform introduced under finance minister Florentino González.
1849	Election of Liberal general José H. López causes clashes in congress.
Late 1840s	Liberal party formally established late during the decade.
Late 1840s	Conservative party formally established late during the decade.
1850	Escuela Republicana, radical liberal club, created by young students who abandon artisan societies.
Early 1850s	Bandits terrorize Bogotá neighbors. Popular lawyer José Raimundo Russi alleged to be the bandits' leader is executed in 1851 along with several artisan accomplices.
1853–1854	Artisan riots to protest congress vote against increasing tariffs.
1854	General Jose M. Melo leads artisan-backed coup.

Appendix 1
Background and Trajectory of Some of New Granada's Colonial Lawyers

1. Alvarez Alvarez, Manuel Bernardo. **Born:** Madrid (Spain), 1658. **Admitted to bar:** 1726. Spanish ancestors of undetermined occupation; he came to America in the late 1720s to serve in the bureaucracy; in the late 1730s, while a *fiscal* in the Bogotá Audiencia, married daughter of Tunja's *corregidor*, former captain and *justicia mayor* in Guayana, and future governor and general commander of Maracaibo; several of his offspring married high-ranking bureaucrats (see Figure 3.1).

Teniente gobernador and *auditor de guerra* in Caracas, 1729–1735; *factor* and *director* of the Compañía de Asiento de Negros de Inglaterra in Caracas, 1733–1735; *fiscal* of Bogotá's Real Audiencia, 1736–1755; retired in 1755; died in 1774.

2. Alvarez Casal, Manuel Bernardo. **Born:** Bogotá, 1743. **Admitted to bar:** 1769. Son of Manuel B. Alvarez Alvarez, *fiscal* in the Bogotá *audiencia* (see previous entry); in 1778, while a *contador* in Bogotá's Tribunal de Cuentas, married the daughter of the Marqués de San Jorge, one of Bogotá's largest landowners; some of his offspring were congressmen during the postcolonial period.

Interim *contador* of Bogotá's Tribunal de Cuentas, 1771; *contador* of Bogotá's Tribunal de Cuentas, 1777–1779; *contador* of Popayán's mint, 1779–1803; *contador mayor* of Bogotá's Tribunal y Real Audiencia de Cuentas, 1803–1810; executed by the Spaniards in 1816 at the age of 73.

3. Arango Echeverri, Pantaleón. **Born:** Medellín, 1765. **Admitted to bar:** 1796. Son of lawyer, and nephew of parish priests in several towns of Antioquia. Married a woman from Girón (Socorro region) whose background is uncertain.

Teniente gobernador and *teniente asesor* of Antioquia's governor in the 1790s; practicing lawyer in early nineteenth century; became a medical doctor and practiced medicine after 1810; interim justice of Antioquia's court of appeals in the 1830s; *juez letrado del circuito* in Santa Rosa, Antioquia, in the early 1840s; practicing lawyer during the mid-1840s.

4. Ayarza, José Ponceano. **Born:** Portovelo, 1774? **Admitted to bar:** 1803. *Pardo,* son of Portovelo's wealthy captain of *pardo* militia; two of his brothers, Pedro and Antonio, were also sent to study in Bogotá.

After protracted litigation, from the mid-1790s on, was eventually admitted to the bar. Appointed justice of Panama's court of appeals in 1839. Further trajectory unknown.

5. Azuola, Luis Eduardo. **Born:** Bogotá, 1764. **Admitted to bar:** 1791. Grandson and son of colonial *tesoreros de cruzada;* married granddaughter of an *oidor*.

Became *tesorero de cruzada; contador mayor* of the Tribunal y Real Audiencia de Cuentas,

1790s to early 1800s; *primer contador de rentas,* 1805; *contador general de hacienda* and *director general de rentas* during the 1810s; appointed interim secretary of economy, 1821. Died in 1821.

6. Ballén de Guzmán, Nicolás. **Born:** Bogotá, 1771. **Admitted to bar:** 1797. Brother-in-law of *fiscal del crimen* of the Real Audiencia; in 1803 married a Spanish woman of undetermined background.

Teniente de gobernador in La Mesa, neighboring Bogotá, during the late colonial period; delegate to Cúcuta Congress, 1821; appointed justice of Bogotá's Court of Appeals in 1821. Died in 1822.

7. Caicedo y Flórez, José. **Born:** Bogotá, 1748. **Admitted to bar:** 1774. Son of largest landowner in the Saldaña region, near Neiva; nephew of *escribano* of Bogotá's Real Audiencia; married daughter of lawyer who was large landowner in Bogotá and Engativa; brother of Luis, an important landowner and leader of the Bogotá *junta,* and Fernando, first postcolonial archbishop of Bogotá; father of Domingo Caicedo, postcolonial general and vicepresident.

Was briefly colonial governor of a province; occupied honorific jobs in Bogotá's *cabildo;* was suspended from the legal profession in the mid-1790s because of his solidarity with Antonio Nariño Alvarez, suspected of conspiracy. Died in 1803.

8. Caicedo y Sánchez, Agustín. **Born:** Ramiriquí, 1777. **Admitted to bar:** 1806. Son of Tunja landowner; brother of two priests, one a parish priest of Guacheta; brother-in-law of colonial military officer Antonio Baraya.

Appointed *juez letrado de primera instancia* in Soatá, Tunja, but seems not to have assumed this or any bureaucratic jobs during the postcolonial period; probably devoted himself to tending his lands in Soatá, where he lived in the 1830s and mid-1840s.

9. Camacho Rodr. y Lago, Joaquín. **Born:** Tunja, 1766. **Admitted to bar:** 1792. Son of lawyer Francisco Camacho y Solórzano; married a close relative; had four brothers (one, Fernando, was a priest, another, Manuel Ignacio, a lawyer), and three sisters. One brother married the sister of a local bureaucrat (García Olano, Figure 3.1); a sister married lawyer Antonio Martínez Recamán.

Law professor mid-1790s; *teniente gobernador* in Tocaima for seven years during the 1790s and early 1800s; *corregidor* in Pamplona from 1805 to 1808; interim *corregidor* in Socorro, 1809; *asesor* of Bogotá's *cabildo,* 1808–1810; member of Junta Suprema's *Gracia y Justicia* section in 1810; Tunja's representative to revolutionary congresses in 1811–1812; member of the Botanical Expedition, contributor to *El Semanario, El Diario Politico,* and *El Argos.* Executed by the Spaniards in 1816.

10. Campo y Rivas, Manuel del. **Born:** Cartago, 1750. **Admitted to bar:** 1773. Grandson of large landowners in Bogotá; grandnephew of at least three priests; remained single and eventually joined Franciscan order; became *caballero* of King Charles III's order.

Interim *consultor* of the Holy Inquisition in Cartago, 1774; *maestre de campo* in Cartago's militia, 1775; *teniente asesor* of colonial governors; *oficial real* and *corregidor* in the late 1770s and during the 1780s; *oidor* in Guatemala's Audiencia after 1793; *oidor* of Guadalajara's Audiencia after 1802; *alcalde del crimen* and *oidor* of Mexico's Real Audiencia in 1805 and 1810, respectively; served as *presidente* of the Audiencia and member of the Casa Imperial under Iturbide. Died in 1830.

11. Cavero, Ignacio. **Born:** Mexico, 1756. **Admitted to bar:** 1786. Brought to New Granada in 1789 by Viceroy Caballero y Góngora, his alleged relative; married Teresa Leguina from Cartagena, who later ran a shop that sold "géneros de Castilla" (Castillan textiles); traveled to Jamaica in 1815 to get weapons for rebels.

Administrador of the Renta de Tabaco in Cartagena, 1790–1792; *administrador* of Cartagena's Aduana from 1802 until at least 1815; interim *contador* of Santa Marta's Cajas Nacionales, 1821–1822; justice of Magdalena's Court of Appeals from the mid-1820s until at least 1830. Died in 1834.

12. Galavís, Eustaquio. **Born:** Bogotá, 1745. **Admitted to bar:** 1770. Son of Spanish captain; nephew of Bogotá's colonial archbishop; in 1778 married a daughter of the Marquis of San Jorge; brother-in-law of *contador* of Bogotá's Renta de Aguardiente; foster father of postcolonial lawyer José María Galavís (Appendix 4).

Corregidor in Zipaquirá and Ubate, 1771; *juez conservador* in salt mines of Zipaquirá, 1774; *corregidor y justicia mayor* of Tunja, 1784–1789. Died in 1810.

13. Gaona de la Bastida, Francisco. **Born:** Bogotá, 1730s. **Admitted to bar:** 1755. Son of Spanish captain of infantry under King Philip V, and later *sargento mayor* in Bogotá during 1740s; father-in-law of chemist Juan José D'Elhuyart and of lawyer José Caicedo y Flórez (see above).

Procurador and interim director of Bogotá's Colegio del Rosario; large landowner in Bogotá. Does not seem to have occupied any bureaucratic jobs. Died in 1799.

14. García de Toledo, José María. **Born:** Cartagena, 1769. **Admitted to bar:** 1792. Son of wealthy landowner who was *contador* of the Holy Inquisition in Cartagena; grandson of Andrés de Madariaga, Conde de Pestagua; married in 1793 to the daughter of Bogotá's *administrador* of Alcabalas; his wife's sisters married, respectively, an *oidor* of the Bogotá Audiencia and the wealthy Antioqueño merchant José M. Arrubla. Was himself a rich import-export merchant and landowner.

Fiscal of the Juzgado de la Comandancia General, Cartagena, 1794; *teniente consul* of the Tribunal Real del Consulado; first president of Cartagena during the 1810s; member of Cartagena's constitutional assembly, 1812; governor of Cartagena, 1814. Executed in 1816.

15. González Manrique, Antonio. **Born:** Bogotá, 1744. **Admitted to bar:** 1767. Son of *presidente* of New Granada during the late 1730s; brother-in-law of Bogotá's Marquis of San Jorge; one of his nieces married former *fiscal de lo criminal y de lo civil* of Bogotá's Real Audiencia in 1805, later to be *fiscal* of Mexico's Audiencia.

Relator of Bogotá's Real Audiencia in 1806.

16. González Manrique, Francisco. **Born:** Bogotá, 1747. **Admitted to bar:** ? Brother of Antonio González Manrique, *relator* of the Real Audiencia (see previous entry). Married daughter of a local lawyer and landowner; father-in-law of *fiscal* of Bogotá's Audiencia, later *fiscal* of México's Audiencia.

President of Real Acuerdo de Justicia during the early 1810s. Subsequent career undetermined. Probably died in the early 1800s (according to José M. Caballero, *Diario,* 176, died in 1816).

17. Groot, Pedro. **Born:** Bogotá, 1755. **Admitted to bar:** 1780. Son of one of Bogotá *cabildo*'s 1780s *regidores* and *fiel ejecutor;* married daughter of *oidor* Benito Casal y Montenegro, granddaughter of *fiscal* Manuel B. Alvarez (Figure 3.1).

Milicias' captain, 1776–1779; member of Compañía de Caballeros Corazas organized to fight Comunero rebellion, 1781; Bogotá *cabildo*'s *procurador general* and *alcalde de primer voto,* 1777, 1782; *Asesor* of Bogotá's *cabildo,* 1782; *tesorero oficial* Popayán's Cajas Reales, 1787; *contador oficial* Popayán's Cajas Reales, late 1787–1790s; *tesorero* of Bogotá's Cajas Reales, 1806; *tesorero* of New Granada's Junta de Tribunales, 1809.

18. Gutiérrez de Piñerez, Germán. **Born:** Mompós, 1776. **Admitted to bar:** 1799. Son of 1770s royal bureaucrat working in Mompós; married niece of Spanish army's General Antonio Narváez y Latorre, New Granada's elected delegate to Spain's Junta Central y Gubernativa; settled in Cartagena in the 1790s.

19. Herazo y Mendigaña, Lucas. **Born:** Bogotá, 1749. **Admitted to bar:** 1774. Son of Spaniard who was *tesorero* of Santa Cruzada; married a member of the Rivas clan, a wealthy landowning family from Bogotá and Cartago. Was himself very wealthy.

Corregidor de naturales in Chocó and Neiva during the 1770s; governor of Neiva from 1789 to 1793. Died in 1807.

20. Herrera Vergara, Ignacio. **Born:** Cali, 1769. **Admitted to bar:** 1797. Son of Spaniard of unknown occupation who settled in Cali; maternal grandson of lawyer and landowner who occupied honorific positions in Cali's *cabildo;* married member of Bogotá's Ortega Sanz de Santamaría clan, granddaughter of former *administrador* of Bogotá's Real Renta de Aguardientes, and daughter of lawyer who was *teniente corregidor* in Zipaquirá.

Occupied honorific positions in Bogotá's *cabildo* during the early 1800s; practicing lawyer and advisor of Cundinamarca's centralist government during the 1810s; law professor and member of the Supreme Court in the 1820s and early 1830s; congressman during the 1820s; retired in 1834. Died in 1840.

21. Iriarte, Andrés José de. **Born:** Timaná (Garzón), 1755. **Admitted to bar:** 1780. Son of former colonial governor of Neiva, 1742–1743, and occupant of honorific jobs in Timana's *cabildo;* maternal grandson of *maestre de campo;* one sister became a nun and one brother a priest; rest of siblings married into families of La Plata and Garzón, in the Neiva region.

Professor of public law in Bogotá's Colegio Mayor de San Bartolomé, 1782; *asesor* of Bogotá's Casa de la Moneda, 1799; appointed *fiscal* of Buenos Aires's Audiencia, 1798; *fiscal* of Quito's Audiencia, 1806. Died in 1809.

22. Martínez y Cabal, Pedro Vicente. **Born:** Buga, 1762. **Admitted to bar:** 1788. Son of a Spaniard of undetermined background. Married Rosalia Escobar y Rivas, daughter of lawyer Miguel Escobar and sister of lawyer Tomás Escobar. Had six offspring, four of whom became lawyers (José V., Francisco F., Carlos, and Rafael). Became one of Buga's wealthiest *hacendados.*

Procurador general, alcalde ordinario, and *regidor* of Buga's colonial *cabildo;* member of Cauca's 1822 electoral assembly; governor of Cauca briefly in the early 1830s; devoted himself to tending his haciendas. Died ca. 1844.

23. Martínez Malo, José Gíl. **Born:** Bogotá, 1752. **Admitted to bar:** 1782. Descendant of Spanish *oidor* and relative of Santa Marta's colonial bishop; linked to the Alvarez dy-

nasty (Figure 3.1); married into the wealthy landowning and merchant clan of the Rodríguez de la Serna. Became a wealthy landowner himself in Bogotá.
Alguacil mayor of the Real Audiencia in the early 1800s.

24. Martínez Recamán, Antonio. **Born:** Bogotá, 1753. **Admitted to bar:** 1753. Son of *escribano de cámara* of the Tribunal y Real Audiencia de Cuentas; married daughter of a lawyer and political boss in Tunja.
Defensor of the Juzgado de Difuntos in Bogotá, 1784; *asesor* of the Cajas Reales in Bogotá from 1783 to at least 1787. Probably died in the 1790s or early 1800s.

25. Moreno y Escandón, Francisco A. **Born:** Mariquita, 1736. **Admitted to bar:** 1758–59. Son of Spaniard who came as *teniente gobernador y justicia mayor* of a region in Chocó, and later became a mineowner in Mariquita; in 1759 married the sister of a high-ranking member of the clergy, niece of a former bishop of Guatemala; at least four of his five siblings became lawyers, two of whom (Francisco Javier and Santiago) were high-ranking bureaucrats, and another parish priest of Tuta, near Tunja; had seven offspring, at least two of whom married wealthy landowners and merchants from Bogotá.
Fiscal protector de indios after 1766; *juez conservador* of the Rentas de Aguardiente y Tabaco after 1767; *defensor* of the Renta de Diezmos, 1766–1780; *fiscal civil* of Bogotá's Real Audiencia, 1770–1778; *fiscal del crimen* of the Real Audiencia, 1776–1781; *fiscal* of the Lima Audiencia, 1781–1785; *oidor* of the Lima Audiencia, 1785–1789; *oidor* of the Chile Audiencia, 1789–1792. Died in 1792.

26. Moreno y Escandón, Francisco J. **Born:** Mariquita?, 1740s. **Admitted to bar:** 1768. Brother of Francisco Antonio, Miguel, and Santiago (see previous entry).
Oidor of the Manila Audiencia, 1788; *alcalde del crimen* and *oidor* in the Lima Audiencia; *regente* of the Quito Audiencia; president of the Alta Cámara de Justicia of Peru under General San Martín, 1821.

27. Moreno y Escandón, Miguel. **Born:** Mariquita, 1740s. **Admitted to bar:** 1766. Brother of Francisco Antonio, Francisco Javier, and Santiago (see other family entries).
Does not appear to have occupied bureaucratic jobs; was in the mining region of Chocó in 1806, where he died in 1815.

28. Moreno y Escandón, Santiago. **Born:** Mariquita, 1748. **Admitted to bar:** 1776. Brother of Francisco Antonio, Francisco Javier, and Miguel (see other family entries); in 1778 married daughter of the *contador* of Bogotá's Royal Mint.
Was briefly *agente fiscal* of the Real Audiencia; *corregidor* in a small region in the late 1770s. Further trajectory undetermined.

29. Mosquera Figueroa, Joaquín. **Born:** Popayán, 1747. **Admitted to bar:** early 1770s. Second-generation creole, member of landowning and mineowning family. Two brothers were rich mineowners, another was high member of Church hierarchy. In the mid-1780s married daughter of former *contador* of the Inquisition, and sister of rich Cartagena lawyer, merchant, and landowner Jose María García de Toledo (see above). His nephews Joaquín, Tomás, Manuel María, and Manuel José became key figures of postcolonial New Granada's political and ecclesiastical elites.
Assistant lieutenant to the governor of Popayán, 1774; *auditor de guerra,* 1774; assistant lieutenant to the governor of Cartagena, 1778; governor of Cartagena, 1785; *oidor* of Bogotá's Real Audiencia, 1787; *alcalde del crimen* and later *oidor* of the Mexico Audiencia

after the mid-1790s; *visitador* and *regente* of Caracas's Audiencia, 1803; member of Spain's Suprema Junta de Gobierno, 1809; member of Spain's Consejo de Regencia, 1810; minister of the Spanish Consejo de Indias, 1814. Died in Spain in 1830.

30. Ortíz Nagle, Joaquín. **Born:** Buga, 1767. **Admitted to bar:** 1794. Maternal grandson of Irish merchant; son of merchant who traded in the Chocó region and owned 50 slaves, and who later went bankrupt; while a practicing lawyer, married daughter of a former *justicia mayor* in Tunja; owner of hacienda El Salitre, in the Bogotá plains, which he sold to Antioqueño merchant in the 1820s; his two sons, José Joaquín and Juan Francisco, became lawyers and occupied some bureaucratic jobs in the postcolonial period.

Practicing lawyer during the 1790s and early 1800s; congressman and member of the Supreme Court from the 1820s until the early 1830s; practiced law during the 1830s; was refused a retirement pension the late 1830s. Died in 1842.

31. Pey, José Miguel. **Born:** Bogotá, 1763. **Admitted to bar:** 1789. Son of Spanish *oidor* who served in the Bogotá Audiencia from the 1750s to the 1780s; brother-in-law of high-ranking priest.

Director of Bogotá's Casa de la Moneda after 1821; nominated to High Martial Court, 1825; minister of war of Urdaneta's dictatorial government, 1830; retired with 1,000-peso pension in 1834. Died in 1838.

32. Pombo, Miguel. **Born:** Popayán, 1779. **Admitted to bar:** 1805. Grandson of a Spaniard of undetermined occupation who settled in Popayán; nephew of wealthy merchant settled in Cartagena and of former *tesorero* of Cartagena's Consulado, later to be *contador* of Bogotá's Casa de la Moneda.

Member of Bogotá's botanical expedition; *teniente gobernador* in Bogotá, 1811, when he translated the U.S. Constitution and published a profederalist pamphlet; *fiscal* of Cundinamarca's Tribunal de Gobierno y Hacienda in the early 1810s; delegate to Cundinamarca congresses, 1812–1813; executed by the Spaniards in 1816.

33. Restrepo, José Félix. **Born:** Envigado, 1760. **Admitted to bar:** 1786. Son of a seemingly well-to-do landowner or merchant from Medellín; had two brothers who were parish priests in towns of Antioquia; one of his sisters married wealthy Antioqueño merchant Miguel M. Uribe Vélez; he married in 1788 into the Sarasti family headed by a Spaniard of unknown occupation resident in Popayán.

Professor of philosophy in Popayán from 1782 until the early 1810s; *juez de balanza* in Popayán's Casa de la Moneda after 1787; interim *asesor* of Popayán's governor, 1791–1792; interim governor and *subdelegado general de rentas* in Popayán, 1800; pledged allegiance to the king and requested bureaucratic jobs in the mid-1810s; delegate to the Cúcuta congress, 1821; justice of the Alta Corte de Justicia from 1821 until his death; professor of philosophy in Bogotá, 1822; member of the Consejo de Gobierno during the 1820s; appointed to the Consejo de Estado in 1830. Died in 1832.

34. Ricaurte y Rigueiro, José Antonio. **Born:** Bogotá, 1748. **Admitted to bar:** early 1770s. Son of colonial lawyer; married daughter of career bureaucrat who served several times as governor of Popayán (1760–1761, 1766–1771, 1777), and later as *superintendente* of Bogotá's Casa de la Moneda, and *contador principal* and *administrador* of Bogotá's Renta de Aguardientes, 1779–1780s; linked to influential Ortega, Nariño, and Mesa clans.

Solicitador fiscal (agente fiscal) of the Audiencia after 1777; *juez general* of the Reales

Rentas, 1786; practicing lawyer for more than three decades; defended Antonio Nariño in the mid-1790s and was jailed. Died in jail in 1804.

35. Rodríguez Saturio, Henrique. **Born:** Cartagena, 1765. **Admitted to bar:** 1789. Son of Spaniard of undetermined occupation.

Fiscal of the Real Hacienda in Cartagena in 1796; *asesor* of Cartagena's government, 1814; appointed to diplomatic mission in England in mid-1810s, declined; *teniente asesor* of Magdalena's *intendente,* 1821; justice of Magdalena's Court of Appeals, 1825; practiced law in Cartagena during 1830s. Died in late 1830s or early 1840s.

36. Romero Sarachaga, Pedro. **Born:** Spain, 1735. **Admitted to bar:** 1764. Son of a Spaniard of unknown occupation; arrived in New Granada in the 1740s; married a sister of lawyer José Caicedo y Flórez (see above); became large landholder who supplied most of the beef for the city of Bogotá.

Performed honorific jobs in the Bogotá cabildo during the 1760s; *consultor* of the Holy Inquisition, 1771; *escribano de cámara* of the Real Audiencia from 1766 until at least 1782; *secretario contador* of the Real Junta del Montepío de Ministros, 1806. Died in 1813.

37. Sanmiguel, José Ignacio. **Born:** Honda, 1740s. **Admitted to bar:** 1768. Son of Pedro Sanmiguel Ramírez, seemingly a Spaniard, of unknown occupation; married Rosalía Cacho, from obscure family; his son Victor Félix became lawyer and served as interim *fiscal* of the Quito Audiencia.

Consultor of the Holy Inquisition in Cartagena; *defensor* of the Renta de Diezmos; *corregidor* of Mompós in the 1780s; forced to be pro bono lawyer for Antonio Nariño in the mid-1790s; governor of Neiva, 1805; *teniente letrado y corregidor* of La Mesa, neighboring Bogotá, 1817; interim justice of the postcolonial Supreme Court, 1825, 1831. Died in 1834.

38. Sanz de Santamaría, Francisco J. **Born:** Bogotá, 1722. **Admitted to bar:** 1740s. Son of colonial captain who served as *corregidor* in several towns neighboring Bogotá, and possessed large landholdings in Bogotá and its neighboring regions (haciendas Márques, El Boque, Venta de Sopo, Meusa, Hatogrande, Yerbabuena, Aposentos, etc.); son-in-law of royal *contador;* brother of at least two priests who served in parishes in the Tunja and Bogotá regions; brother-in-law of Marqués de Surba; in 1752 married a descendant of the founder of Bogotá's mint; had at least nine offspring, some of whom became, or married, high-ranking colonial bureaucrats.

Held honorific jobs in Bogotá's *cabildo* in the 1750s; *asesor* of the Tribunales de Cruzada y Real Hacienda; large landowner in the Bogotá plains; died in the early 1780s.

39. Tenorio y Carvajal, Tomás. **Born:** Popayán, 1758. **Admitted to bar:** 1786. Grandson of mineowner in the Chocó region; son of individual who occupied honorific jobs within Popayán's *cabildo;* brother of *oidor* in the Quito Audiencia; one of his daughters married lawyer Estanislao Vergara in the 1810s (see Appendix 4 and Figure 3.1).

Professor of canon law in a Bogotá *colegio* during the colonial period; *fiscal* of the Renta de Correos; interim *agente fiscal* of Bogotá's Real Audiencia; occupied interim jobs in the early postcolonial courts of appeals. Died in 1827.

40. Tordesillas, Francisco. **Born:** Bogotá, 1740?. **Admitted to bar:** 1763. Seemingly son of Spanish captain; brother of lawyer-priest Ignacio (see other family entries); one of his sons, José, served as *corregidor* in different places, including Socorro (1801).

Traveled to Spain in pursuit of appointment; remained there for a long time and spent most of his patrimony; was appointed *corregidor* of Tunja in 1789; traveled back to New Granada in 1790 and died while on the Magdalena River.

41. Tordesillas, Ignacio María. **Born:** Bogotá, late 1730s. **Admitted to bar:** 1761. Brother of lawyer Francisco (see entry).

Served as parish priest of Gacheta from the 1760s to 1780 and in the cathedral of Bogotá afterwards; was large landholder in Bogotá, owner of *haciendas* Fusca, El Común, and probably others.

42. Torres Tenorio, Camilo. **Born:** Popayán, 1766. **Admitted to bar:** 1794. Son of mineowner and large landholder in Neiva, Popayán, and the Pacific coast; nephew of *oidor* of Quito's Audiencia; in 1802, while a practicing lawyer and *asesor* of Bogotá's Casa de la Moneda, married member of the influential Ricaurte Terreros clan, a member of which had founded Bogotá's Casa de la Moneda.

Practicing lawyer after the mid-1790s; *asesor* of Bogotá's Casa de la Moneda after 1799; executed in 1816.

43. Torres Tenorio, Jerónimo. **Born:** Popayán, 1771. **Admitted to bar:** 1799. Brother of lawyer Camilo Torres (see entry).

Merchant, had *compañias de comercio* with Spanish merchant González Llorente, one of Bogotá's richest; Senator, 1821–1828; member of committee for liquidation of Colombia's debt; director of Popayán's Casa de la Moneda, 1825 on; member of committee for reorganization of education, 1826; member of Bolívar's Consejo de Estado, 1828; diplomatic envoy to France; *contador general de hacienda*. Died in 1839.

44. Umaña López, Joaquín. **Born:** Tunja, 1768. **Admitted to bar:** 1792. Seemingly son of middling landowner from Tunja; brother of member of Tunja's 1811 constitutional congress; married into the Araos family of unknown background; his brother married into the Neira family, a wealthy landowning clan from Tunja.

Practicing lawyer in Bogotá in 1794, denounced to the authorities the political conspiracy of that year; practiced criminal law and was leading political boss in Tunja in the late 1790s and early 1800s; *fiscal* of the Representación Nacional in Tunja, 1812; served honorific jobs in the local *cabildo* during the early 1800s; executed in 1816.

45. Umaña Barragán, Enrique. **Born:** Bojacá, 1772. **Admitted to bar:** 1800. Son of largest landowner in the regions of Bojacá and Tequendama, neighboring Bogotá; in 1805 married in Europe the daughter of a Spaniard, former captain of the royal army; his wife had become a merchant in the early 1800s.

Jailed and sent to Spain in mid-1790s; promptly released, became a lawyer shortly afterwards and remained in Europe studying mineralogy; returned to Bogotá as *corregidor* of Zipaquirá, 1809; appointed *gobernador político* of Bogotá and *intendente* of Cundinamarca in 1821 and 1825, respectively; soon afterwards left the bureaucracy and spent his time taking care of his *haciendas* and doing research on mineralogy.

46. Valenzuela Conde, Crisanto. **Born:** Gámbita, 1776. **Admitted to bar:** 1803. Cousin of lawyer Miguel Valenzuela, *administrador* of Girón's Renta de Correos (see below); in 1806 married a member of Bogotá's Ortega Sanz de Santamaría clan, granddaughter of former *administrador* of Bogotá's Real Renta de Aguardientes, daughter of lawyer who was *teniente corregidor* in Zipaquirá, and sister of lawyer Ignacio Herrera's wife (see above).

Escribano de cámara of Bogotá's Real Audiencia from 1804 until 1810; *agente fiscal* of the Sala de Justicia, and secretary of Cundinamarca's first congress; delegate to congresses during the 1810s; secretary of foreign relations in the mid-1810s; executed by the Spaniards in 1816.

47. Valenzuela Mantilla, Miguel. **Born:** Girón, 1796. **Admitted to bar:** 1796. Cousin of Crisanto, *escribano* of the Real Audiencia (see previous entry); brother of Bucaramanga's parish priest, Eloy, who owned the road between Bucaramanga and Pamplona in the late colonial period; married Micaela Mutis y Consuegra, from the family of priest and scientist José C. Mutis; one of their sons became governor of Pamplona during the late 1830s.

Administrador of Girón's Renta de Correos in the early 1800s; *juez letrado* of the cantón of Girón, 1826. Died in the mid-1840s.

48. Vallecilla Caicedo, Manuel. **Born:** Santiago Cali, 1766. **Admitted to bar:** 1793. His father and maternal grandfather occupied honorific positions in Cali's *cabildo* and were probably landowners in this region; his siblings married into branches of Cali's influential Caicedo clan; married one of his nieces.

Corregidor of Mariquita in 1803; in the early 1800s served as *teniente asesor* and *auditor de guerra* of Popayán's colonial governor; delegate to the Junta Superior de Gobierno of the Ciudades Confederadas del Valle del Cauca, 1811; governor of the province, 1814. Executed by the Spaniards in 1816.

49. Vargas Tavera, Ignacio. **Born:** Bogotá?, 1771. **Admitted to bar:** 1794. Married Ignacia París y Ricaurte, daughter of Bogotá's *administrador de tabacos* (José Martín París); had three offspring, one of his daugthers married postcolonial General Rafael Urdaneta, another General José María Melo; his son, José Vargas París, became general in postcolonial period.

Corregidor in Turmeque, 1806; defense lawyer for *oidor* Juan Hernández de Alba in revolutionary period.

50. Vergara y Vela Patiño, Francisco J. **Born:** Bogotá, 1712. **Admitted to bar:** 1734. Son of former *teniente corregidor* in small towns during the 1710s, who later served as parish priest in Topaga during the late 1720s, and in Socorro from 1735 to 1740; in 1736 married a member of Bogotá's Caicedo clan, daughter of a former captain of the royal guard, *teniente coronel,* governor of a province, *encomendero,* etc.; several of his offspring became high-ranking bureaucrats (see Figure 3.2).

Occupied honorific positions in Bogotá's *cabildo* in the early 1740s; became *contador* of the Tribunal and Real Audiencia de Cuentas in Bogotá from 1749 to 1787. Died in 1788.

51. Vergara Caicedo, Felipe. **Born:** Bogotá, 1745. **Admitted to bar:** 1766. Son of lawyer Francisco Javier Vergara y Vela Patiño and brother of Fernando, Francisco Javier, and Juan Vergara Caicedo (see below).

Law professor during the 1760s; *contador oficial* of Panamá's Cajas Reales, 1779–1784; *teniente-asesor* of Cartagena's governor, 1785–1789; *contador ordenador* of Bogotá's Tribunal y Real Audiencia de Cuentas, 1790–1816. Died in 1818.

52. Vergara Caicedo, Fernando. **Born:** Bogotá, 1763. **Admitted to bar:** mid-1780s. Son of lawyer Francisco Javier Vergara y Vela Patiño (see above), brother of Felipe, Juan, and Francisco Javier Vergara Caicedo (see below).

Law professor during the 1780s; occupied honorific jobs in Bogotá's *cabildo* during the 1790s; declined job of *teniente de gobernador y auditor de guerra* in Popayán in the late 1790s; became a monk in the early 1800s and died shortly afterward.

53. Vergara Caicedo, Francisco Javier. **Born:** Bogotá, 1750. **Admitted to bar:** 1777. Son of lawyer Francisco Javier Vergara y Vela Patiño, brother of Felipe, Juan, and Fernando Vergara Caicedo; in 1788, while *agente fiscal* of the Real Audiencia, married a member of Bogotá's influential Sanz de Santamaría clan, daughter of lawyer, landowner, and member of Bogotá's *cabildo;* some of his offspring became influential bureaucrats during the postcolonial period (see Appendix 4's entry for Estanislao Vergara).

Occupied honorific jobs in Bogotá's *cabildo* in the 1770s; *agente fiscal* of the Real Audiencia from 1779 until the early 1810s. Died in 1816.

54. Vergara Caicedo, Juan. **Born:** Bogotá, 1760. **Admitted to bar:** early 1780s. Son of lawyer Francisco Javier Vergara y Vela Patiño and brother of Felipe, Fernando, and Francisco Javier; in 1792, while a practicing lawyer, married daughter of Bogotá's Marqués de San Jorge, a large landowner.

Practiced law during the 1780s and 1790s and died in 1804 while traveling to Spain in pursuit of a bureaucratic appointment.

55. Viana, Antonio. **Born:** Honda, 1769. **Admitted to bar:** 1793. Son of Cartagenero merchant and mineowner who settled in the region of Honda, becoming one of the wealthiest individuals there; his mother was a relative of Viceroy Villalonga; his maternal grandfather had been *procurador general* and *oficial real* in Popayán; in the early 1800s married the granddaughter of José de Mesa Armero, the most important landowner of the Mariquita region in the mid-eighteenth century; brother-in-law of rich merchant linked to Honda, who became minister of economy under Bolívar.

Asesor of the colonial governor of Antioquia in the early 1800s; justice of the court of appeals of Cundinamarca after 1821; member of Congress during the 1820s. Died ca. 1839–1840?

Sources: Gustavo Arboleda, *Diccionario biográfico y genealógico del antiguo departamento del Cauca* (Bogotá, 1962); Gabriel Arango Mejía, *Genealogías de Antioquia y Caldas,* 2 vols. (Medellín, 1973); José María Caballero, *Diario de la independencia* (Bogotá, 1974); Hernán Clavijo Ocampo, *Formación histórica de las elites locales en el Tolima,* 2 vols. (Bogotá, 1993); Rufino and Anjel Cuervo, *Vida de Rufino Cuervo y noticias de su época,* 2 vols. (Paris, 1892); Carlos Cuervo Márquez, *Vida de José Ignacio de Márquez,* 2 vols. (Bogotá, 1917); Ivan Flórez de Ocariz, *Genealogías del Nuevo Reyno de Granada,* 2 vols. (Bogotá, 1995) [1674]; Antonio J. García de la Guardia, *Kalendario manual y guía de forasteros en Santafé de Bogotá . . . para el año 1806* (Bogotá, 1988) [1806]; María C. Guillén de Iriarte, *Nobleza e hidalguía en el Nuevo Reino de Granada. Colegio Mayor de Nuestra Senora del Rosario,* 2 vols. (Bogotá, 1994); Ignacio Gutiérrez Ponce, *Vida de don Ignacio Gutiérrez Vergara y episodios históricos de su tiempo (1806-1877)* (London, 1900); Guillermo and Alfonso Hernández de Alba, "Galería de hijos insignes del Colegio de San Bartolomé," in *El Colegio de San Bartolomé,* ed. Daniel Restrepo (Bogotá, 1928), 141–439; William Jaramillo Mejía, *Real Colegio Mayor y Seminario de San Bartolomé. Nobleza e hidalguía. Colegiales de 1605 a 1820* (Bogotá, 1996); Gabriel Jiménez Molinares, *Linajes Cartageneros,* 2 vols. (Cartagena, 1951–1958); Joaquín Ospina, *Diccionario biográfico y bibliográfico de Colombia,* 3 vols. (Bogotá, 1927–1939); Juan F. Ortíz, *Reminiscencias* (Bogotá, 1907); Camilo Pardo Umaña, *Haciendas de la sabana* (Bogotá, 1988); Francisco Plazas, *Genealogías de la provincia de Neiva* (Bogotá, 1985); Pastor Restrepo, "Titulos nobiliarios en la gobernación de Cartagena de Indias," *Boletín Historial* 11, 108–111 (March-June 1947): 3–34; José M. Restrepo and Raimundo Rivas, *Genealogías de Santafé de Bogotá* (Bogotá, 1928); *Genealogías de*

Santa Fé de Bogotá, new ed. expanded by Mons. José Restrepo Posada et al., 5 vols. (Bogotá, 1991–1995); José M. Restrepo Sáenz, *Gobernadores y próceres de Neiva* (Bogotá, 1941); idem, "Gobernantes de Cundinamarca," *BHA* 35, 407–408 (September-October 1948): 473–505; "Gobernantes de Pamplona," *BHA* 36, 411–413 (January-March 1949): 97–129; idem, *Biografías de los mandatarios y ministros de la Real Audiencia (1671–1819)* (Bogotá, 1952); idem, "La provincia del Socorro y sus gobernantes," *BHA* 61, 476 (June 1964): 321–78; José Restrepo Posada and Bernardo Sanz de Santamaría, "Osorio," *BHA* 56, 651–653 (January-March 1969): 119–30; idem, "Vargas," *BHA* 58, 678–680 (April-June 1971): 269–309; Ulises Rojas, *Corregidores y justicias mayores de Tunja y su provincia desde la fundación de la ciudad hasta 1817* (Tunja, 1962); Leonidas Scarpeta and Saturnino Vergara, *Diccionario biográfico de los campeones de la libertad de Nueva Granada, Venezuela, Ecuador y Perú* (Bogotá, 1879); Roberto Tisnes, *Neogranadinos en las órdenes nobiliarias* (Bogotá, 1990); José M. Uricoechea, "Noticias genealógicas," *BHA* 58, 675–677 (January-March 1971), pp. 33–101; Julio C. Vergara y Vergara, *Don Antonio de Vergara y Azcárate y sus descendientes,* 2 vols. (Madrid, 1952); Felipe Vergara, *Relación genealógica* (Bogotá, 1962) [1810–1816?]; *Colombia Ilustrada,* 1880s–1890s; *La Bagatela,* 1850s; *Papel Periódico Ilustrado,* 1870s.

Appendix 2
Lawyers Who Died Shortly Before or After Independence, or Disappeared from Records

Name	Birthplace	Birth Date	Admitted to Bar	Died
Herazo y Mendigaña, Lucas	Bogotá	1749	1774	1807
Rentería, José Inacio	Cartago	1737	1760?	1808
Iriarte, Andrés José	Garzón	1755	1780	1809
Galavís, Eustaquio	Bogotá	1745	1770	1810
Gómez L., José A.	Antioquia	1754	1782	1812
Romero Sarachaga, Pedro	Spain	1735	1764	1813
Vergara y Caicedo, Luis	Cali?	1760?	1785?	1813
Moreno, Miguel Antonio	Mariquita?	1740s	1766	1815
Vergara C., Francisco J.	Bogotá	1751	1777	1816
González Manrique, Francisco	Bogotá	1747	?	1816
Rodríguez, Francisco A.	Popayán	1750	1780	1817
Omaña, Nicolás Mauricio	Cúcuta	1780	1805?	1817
Andrade, Manuel	Bogotá	1743	1765	1817
Vergara C., Felipe	Bogotá	1745	1766	1818
Serrano Uribe, Fernando	Pamplona	1779	1806?	1819
Azuola, Luis Eduardo	Bogotá	1764	1791	1821
Groot, Pedro	Bogotá	1755	1780	1821
Escobar, José Joaquín	Cali	1751	1777	1821
Ballén de Guzmán, Nicolás	Bogotá	1771	1797	1822
Cabal, Vicente Lucio	Cerrito	1755	1780?	1825
Azuola, José Luis de	Bogotá	1754	1785	1826
Tenorio Carvajal, Tomás	Popayán	1758	1786	1827
Salazar, José María	Antioquia	1785	1809	1828
Campo y Rivas, Manuel	Cartago	1750	1773	1830
Mosquera Figueroa, Joaquín	Popayán	1748	1774	1830
Suárez Serrano, Joaquín	San Gíl?	?	?	1831
Rocha, Juan Agustín de la	Bogotá	1761	1786	1831
Restrepo, José Félix de	Antioquia	1760	1786	1832
Sandino de Castro, Ignacio	Bogotá	1766	1793	1833
Camacho Quesada, Manuel	Bogotá	1775	1803	1834
Cavero, Ignacio	Mexico	1756	1786	1834
San Miguel, José Ignacio	Honda	1740s	1768	1834
Real, José Maria del	Cartagena	1767	1794	1835
Rosillo y Meruelo, Andrés	Socorro	1760	1786	1835

Appendix 2   175

Name	Birthplace	Birth Date	Admitted to Bar	Died
Castillo Rada, José María	Cartagena	1773	1804	1835
Barriga y Brito, Tomás	Bogotá	1773	1801	1836
Flórez Camacho, Angel M.	Vélez	1802	1825	1836*
Lastra, José Angel	Cartagena	1799?	1821?	1837*
Olave, Nazario	Popayán	1808	1832	1837*
Pey, José Miguel	Bogotá	1763	1789	1838
Torres Tenorio, Jerónimo	Popayán	1771	1789	1838
Herrera, Ignacio	Cali	1769	1797	1840
Ortíz Nagle, Joaquín	Buga	1767	1794	1842
Fernández Saavedra, Manuel	Bogotá?	1740?	1763	?
Munive y Mozo, Joaquín	?	1750	1776	?
Ronderos, Victorino	?	1754?	1779	?
Gamba, Juan Dionisio	Ibague	1761	1785	?
Ospina, Nicolás	Buga	1763?	1788	?
Rodríguez, Henrique	Cartagena	1766	1789	?
Rivera, Joaquín	?	1765?	1790	?
Tavera, Esmeragdo	?	1768?	1792	?
Pradilla, Pedro	San Gíl	1768	1793	?
Ramírez, Jacinto María	?	1765?	1793	?
Alvares Pino, Felipe G.	Antioquia?	1769?	1793	?
Valencia, Juan Bautista	Pamplona	1776	1800?	?

Sources: Arboleda, *Diccionario genealógico;* Caballero, *Particularidades de Santafé de Bogotá,* 131, 176; García de la Guardia, *Kalendario manual,* 57–72; Guillermo and Alfonso Hernández de Alba, "Galería de hijos insignes"; Jiménez Molinares, *Linajes cartageneros;* Plazas, *Genealogías de la provincia de Neiva;* Restrepo and Rivas, *Genealogías de Santafé;* Joaquín Ospina, *Diccionario biográfico y bibliográfico,* 3:503–04.

*Indicates key postcolonial lawyers who died prematurely.

Appendix 3
"Transitional" Generation: Lawyers Trained during 1805–1820

Name	Birth-place	Birth Date	Admitted to Bar	Activity in 1939
Alomia, José María	Popayán	1773?	1805	*Hacendado*
Alvarez Lozano, Manuel B.	Bogotá	1785	1809	Law practice
Arce de León, José	Cajica?	1770	1817	Law practice
Arosemena, Blas	Panama	1790?	1812	Senator
Arosemena, Juan	Panama	1786?	1812	Law practice
Azuero, Vicente	Oiba (Socorro)	1787	1817	House of Representatives
Borrero Costa, Vicente	Cali	1789	1808	Merchant
Bustamante Laiseca, Ramón	Socorro	1777	1806	Unknown
Calvo Ortega, Casimiro	Bogotá	1784	1807	Senator
Camacho Naranjo, Salvador	Chire (Casanare)	1791	1820	Council of State
Canabal, Eusebio María	Cartagena	1780?	1807	Justice in Bogotá
Carvajal Tenorio, Antonio	Popayán	1783	1806	Law practice
Casanovas, Narciso	Chiquinquirá	1789?	1820	Justice in Guanenta
Céspedes, José María	Quilichao (Popayán)	1783	1806	Unknown
Cuero Caicedo, José María	Cali	1778	1806	*Hacendado*
Díaz, Miguel	?	1783	1809	Priest
Díaz Granados, Estevan	Santa Marta?	1780?	1806	Unknown
Domínguez Castillo, Benedicto	Bogotá	1783	1809	*Hacendado*
Domínguez Roche, José M.	Santamaría (Bogotá?)	1788	1811	Law practice
Domínguez Roche, Mateo	Simijaca	1795	1817	Justice in Guanenta
Escobar, Manuel J.	Cali	1784	1813	Law practice
Escobar Rivas, Tomás	Cartago	1785	1818	Law practice
Esguerra, Manuel	Bogotá?	1790?	1818	*Fiscal* in Boyacá
Esguerra Gálvez, Sebastián	Funza?	1788	1818	House of Representatives
Estevez, Juan Bautista	Socorro	1805	1805	Deceased
Fonseca, Gregorio de Jesús	?	1791?	1820	Secretary of Bogotá's court

Appendix 3   177

Name	Birth-place	Birth Date	Admitted to Bar	Activity in 1939
Gamba, Fortunato M.	Cartago	1788	1817	Deceased in 1838
Gómez, Diego Fernando	San Gíl	1786	1820	Council of State
Gómez, Isidoro	?	1776	1806	Law practice
Gómez Hoyos, Joaquín	Marinilla (Antioquia)	1795?	1820	*Hacendado*
Gori, Joaquín José	Cartagena	1790?	1817	Senator
Herrera, Agustín	?	1782?	1808	Bureaucrat
Hinestrosa, José M.	Bogotá?	1782	1810	Secretary of Bogotá's court
Hurtado, Manuel José	Popayán	1784	1807	Justice in Panama
Icaza Arosemena, Carlos	Panama	1789?	1817	*Fiscal* in Panama
Leiva, José Antonio	Bogotá	1780?	1805	Deceased
Licht, León	Bogotá	?	1810	*Hacendado*
Lombana, José María	Bogotá	1778	1805	Deceased in 1816
López Saenz, Manuel	Popayán?	1779	1808	Priest
Malo, Antonio	Tunja?	1789	1811	Law practice
Márquez, José Ignacio	Ramiriquí	1793	1813/17	President
Méndez, Ildefonso	Cartagena	1784?	1811	Director of university
Morales Galavís, Francisco	Turbaco	1782	1808	Justice in Bogotá
Mosquera A., Joaquín	Popayán	1787	1810	*Hacendado*
Osorio, Alejandro	Bogotá	1790	1817	Senator
Pereira, José Francisco	Cartago	1789	1814/21	Senator
Plata, Joaquín	Socorro	1774	1805	Judge
Ponce A., Román	Bogotá?	1777?	1813	Justice in Cartagena
Puyana, Elias	Bucaramanga	1788	1818	Priest
Quevedo, José Nicolás	Bogotá?	1789?	1818	Diocesan notary
Ramirez, Manuel J.	Boyacá?	1783?	1808	Deceased in 1823
Restrepo, José Manuel	Antioquia	1781	1808	Director of mint
Ronderos, Juan Victorino	Bogotá?	1779?	1805	Law practice
Salazar, José María	Rionegro (Antioquia)	1784	1809	Deceased in 1828
Sánchez, Gabriel	?	1787?	1812	Law practice
Soto, Francisco	Cúcuta	1789	1810	House of Representatives
Tobar, Bernardino	Zipaquirá	1786	1819	Justice in Bogotá
Tobar, Miguel	Tocaima	1781?	1809	Senator
Ugarte, Francisco	Bogotá	1787	1810	Retired bureaucrat
Vergara, Luis Félix	Cali	1785?	1812	*Hacendado*
Vergara, Estanislao	Bogotá	1790	1813/17	Justice in Bogotá

Sources: Arboleda, *Historia contemporánea,* 1; idem, *Diccionario biográfico;* Hernández de Alba, "Galería de los hijos insignes"; Plazas, *Genealogías de Neiva;* Restrepo and Rivas, *Genealogías de Santafé; GNG,* April 14, 1839.

Appendix 4
Background and Trajectory of the "Aristocratic" Lawyers of the 1820s and 1830s

1. *Alomia, José María. **Born:** Popayán, 1773. **Admitted to bar:** 1805. Son of Spaniard of unknown occupation; brother of Franciscan friar in Popayán; was himself *oficial secundario*. of the Contaduria de la Casa de Moneda de Popayán in the late colonial period.
   Did not obtain bureaucratic jobs from 1821 to 1827. Further activities unknown.

2. Alvarez Lozano, Manuel M. B. **Born:** Bogotá, 1785. **Admitted to bar:** 1809. Paternal grandson of a *fiscal* of the Royal Audiencia (1736–1755); maternal grandson of the Marqués de San Jorge; son of *contador* of the Tribunal Mayor de Cuentas de Bogotá in the late colonial period (see Appendix 1). Had a job in Popayán's Casa de la Moneda in late colonial period.
   Secretary of the House of Representatives, 1827; justice of Bogotá's Tribunal, 1828; *fiscal* in trials against 1828 plotters; exiled after Urdaneta's defeat, eventually allowed to stay in Bogotá.

3. Arce, José. **Born:** Bogotá, 1770. **Admitted to bar:** 1817. Paternal grandson of *contador mayor* of Tribunal Mayor y Real Audiencia de Cuentas of Bogotá. Was himself *contador* of Medellín's Renta de Aguardientes in late colonial period. Married member of Bogotá's influential Sanz de Santamaría clan.
   Followed a military career and came to be colonel and justice of the Alta Corte Marcial, 1832. Nominated to the vice presidency in 1846. Died in 1851.

4. Arosemena, Juan. **Born:** Panamá, 1786. **Admitted to bar:** 1812. Son of one of the wealthiest merchants of Panamá, who was offered a noble title in 1805, but declined; relative of the *administrador* of the Renta de Aguardientes, Tabacos y Naipes in Veragua (Panamá).
   Priest and lawyer; appointed *asesor* of Santa Marta's governor, 1823; member of the House of Representatives, 1825; justice of Panamá's Court of Appeals, 1840s; member of Panamá's high-ranking clergy in the 1840s; rancher.

5. Arosemena, Blas. **Born:** Panamá, 1790. **Admitted to bar:** 1812. Brother of Juan Arosemena (see previous entry).
   Asesor of Panamá's governor, 1823; appointed *fiscal* of Panamá's Tribunal, 1825; Senator, 1824–1825, 1833–1836, 1838–1839; Panamá's president during the 1850s; diplomat.

---

*Individuals whose "aristocratic" descent is not altogether clear but whose "aristocratic" political connections are apparent.

6. Arroyo, José Antonio. **Born:** Popayán, 1778. **Admitted to bar:** 1822 (1821?). His original last name was Pérez de Valencia y Arroyo, shortened over time. Grandson of *oidor* of Santo Domingo's Real Audiencia; son of *contador de diezmos* in Popayán; brother of priest who was assistant director of Popayán's local seminary in the late colonial period. Married member of influential Valencia clan of Popayán.

Juez de hacienda; juez del circuito; first director of University of Cauca, Popayán, 1827–1829; *prefecto* of Cauca, 1830; director, University of Cauca, 1838–1843; justice of Popayán's appeals court, 1842; administrator of post office; treasurer and administrator of Popayán's Casa de la Moneda, 1843–1845?; governor of Popayán; congressman. Died in 1848.

7. Arroyo, Santiago. **Born:** Popayán, 1773. **Admitted to bar:** 1803. Brother of José Antonio (see previous entry). Married sister-in-law of *oidor* Mosquera y Figueroa's brother.

Asesor of the *intendente del Cauca* in 1823; senator, 1824–1826; president of Popayán's appeals court in 1828; practicing lawyer. Died in 1845.

8. *Barriga y Brito, Tomás. **Born:** Bogotá, 1773. **Admitted to bar:** 1801. Paternal grandson of royal official who was also *jefe de puertos;* son of lawyer who was brother-in-law of one of Conde del Real Agrado's descendants. Was *teniente letrado* of La Mesa, and *relator* of the Real Audiencia in the late colonial period.

Jefe político of Zipaquirá, 1819–1825; lieutenant colonel; interim justice of Bogotá's appeals court, 1825–1826; *auditor de guerra* in trials against 1828 plotters; justice of Alta Corte Marcial, 1831. Died in 1836.

9. *Borrero Costa, José A. **Born:** Cali, 1780. **Admitted to bar:** 1803. Son of wealthy merchant and landowner who was *alcalde* and *alferez real* in the Cali *cabildo*. His maternal grandparents were Spanish. Among his sixteen siblings were María Antonia, a nun; Vicente, a lawyer; and Eusebio, a general in the postcolonial army and presidential candidate in the 1841 elections. Married Inés Barona and had three offspring.

Procurador general of Cali's 1820 *cabildo;* member of Cúcuta's 1821 constitutional congress; unlike his brothers Vicente and Eusebio, did not occupy important political jobs but dedicated himself to tending his haciendas. Supported 1851 Conservative rebellion.

10. *Borrero Costa, Vicente. **Born:** Cali, 1784. **Admitted to bar:** 1808. Brother of lawyer José A. (see previous entry). Married Concepción Piedrahita and had fourteen offspring.

Member of Popayán's 1812 junta; Cali's 1812 *alcalde;* member of Cúcuta's 1821 constitutional congress; congressman through the 1820s and in 1830, 34, 36 and 42; minister under short-lived civilian presidency in 1830–1831; president of national congress in 1827 and of Buenaventura's provincial *cámara* in 1837; law professor in Cali's Colegio de Santa Librada in the early 1830s, director of the *colegio* from 1843 to 1845; governor of Buenaventura province from 1845 to 1849; ran a shop in Bogotá.

11. Bustamante y Laiseca, Ramón. **Born:** Socorro, 1777. **Admitted to bar:** 1806. Seemingly linked to rich landowning family of the region of Tocaima; married member of rich landowning family from Bogotá, descendants of high-ranking officer of royal troops. Was himself *escribano mayor* of the Superior Gobierno in the late colonial period, 1806; relative of lawyer Miguel Tobar.

Trajectory unknown.

12. Calvo Ortega, Casimiro. **Born:** Bogotá, 1784. **Admitted to bar:** 1807. Maternal grandson of the *administrador principal* of the Renta de Aguardientes of Bogotá; his father was nephew of Santa Marta's colonial bishop. Married daughter of one of San Cristóbal's late colonial governors.

Delegate to the Cúcuta 1821 Constitutional Congress; *oficial mayor* of the Secretaría del Interior, 1821–1826; editor of official newspaper in mid-1826; official editor of all state publications.

13. Camacho, Manuel Antonio. **Born:** Bogotá, 1803. **Admitted to bar:** 1827. Son and grandson of colonial lawyers; nephew of lawyer who was colonial governor of various provinces and was executed during independence; nephew of *escribano* of the colonial Tribunal de Cuentas.

Oficial mayor of the Contaduría de Hacienda in the late 1830s; justice of the high court of appeals of Boyacá from 1842 until at least the early 1850s.

14. Camacho Quesada, Manuel. **Born:** Bogotá, 1775. **Admitted to bar:** 1803. Maternal grandson of *oidor* of Bogotá's Royal Audiencia; son of Bosa's *corregidor real;* brother-in-law of *notario de diezmos* of Bogotá's Archbishopric.

Law professor in Bogotá's Colegio del Rosario, 1823; appointed member of commission in charge of studying Napoleonic Code, 1829. Further activities unknown.

15. Canabal, Eusebio María. **Born:** Cartagena, 1780. **Admitted to bar:** 1807. Probably son of wealthy Cartagena merchant. Relative of *caballero* of the Orden Nobiliaria de Montesa. Himself purchased Administración de Aguardientes of Cartagena in the late colonial period. Protector of viceroy, who was exiled in Cartagena in 1810; *fiscal* of Real Hacienda in Cartagena and then of the Superior Gobierno in the late 1810s; applicant to job of *oidor* in Audiencias, 1816–1820.

Asesor of the *intendente* of Zulia, 1823; interim judge of Bogotá's Supreme Court, 1825; member of the House of Representatives, 1826; member Constitutional Congress and candidate for president, 1830; director, University of Cartagena, 1832–1837; senator; justice of Supreme Court from 1837 on.

16. Cantillo, Manuel A. **Born:** La Mesa, 1796. **Admitted to bar:** 1825. Son of veteran sergeant of Royal Army who also was *administrador* of the Renta de Tabacos, Aduanas y Aguardiente in La Mesa. Married daughter of Bogotano import merchant.

Juez letrado of Cúcuta, 1826; *fiscal* of Bogotá's appeals court, 1820s; senator, 1830s; justice of Bogotá's appeals court, 1830s–1842; justice of Supreme Court, 1844–1850.

17. Caro, José Eusebio. **Born:** Ocaña, 1817. **Admitted to bar:** 1837. Grandson of *oficial mayor* in the Viceroyalty's secretariat, 1782; son of colonial Tribunal de Cuentas's *contador* who married Nicolasa Ibáñez in 1813, with General Bolívar as best man. Once a royalist, his father joined patriots and became *ayudante* of the *estado mayor* in the 1821 Carabobo battle, secretary of Cúcuta's 1821 Constitutional Congress, and secretary of National Congress, 1823. José Eusebio married Blasina Tovar Pinzón, daughter of lawyer Miguel Tobar, in 1843. Had three offspring, one of whom (Miguel Antonio) became president of Colombia in the late nineteenth century. Brother-in-law of wealthy import-export merchant and lawyer Clímaco Ordóñez (see below).

Oficial mayor in the Ministry of Finance, 1838–1839; interim *oficial primero*, office of the general treasury, 1840–1844; editor of pro-aristocratic government newspaper *El Granadino*, 1840–1841; fought against the *Supremo* rebels as assistant to General Herrán,

1841; congressman, 1843–1844; *oficial mayor* Ministry of Foreign relations, 1844; assistant director of the treasury, 1846; country's chief accountant, mid-1840s; minister of finance, 1848; general accountant, 1848–1849; co-editor of *La Civilización* along with Mariano Ospina R., 1849; due to journalistic debates forced to flee the country in 1850; died while returning in 1853.

18. Carvajal y Tenorio, Antonio. **Born:** Popayán, 1783. **Admitted to bar:** 1806. Grandson of mineowner in region neighboring Popayán; nephew of *oidor* of Quito's Real Audiencia in the late colonial period. Married one of his own first cousins.

Asesor of Pasto's governor, 1824–1825; interim justice of Popayán's Tribunal, 1825; practicing lawyer.

19. Casanovas Neira, Narciso. **Born:** Chiquinquira, 1789. **Admitted to bar:** 1820. Son of *fundidor mayor* of Bogotá's colonial Tesorería General, who was also important landowner in Chiquinquira and eventually became *fundidor mayor* in Bogotá's postcolonial mint. Narciso married a member of Chiquinquira's influential Paez clan.

Appointed *juez letrado de hacienda,* Chiquinquira, 1826; justice in Guanenta's Tribunal Superior, 1839–1840. Further activities unknown, drops from records in late 1840s.

20. Castillo y Rada, José María. **Born:** Cartagena, 1773. **Admitted to bar:** 1802. Son of Spanish military officer; his mother was a relative of the Condes de Santa Cruz de la Torre. Was brought up by one of his relatives, *mariscal de campo* of the Royal Army Antonio Narváez y Latorre. Married a member of Rivas clan, a rich landowning family from Bogotá. His brother Manuel was also a lawyer and an officer in the postcolonial army, killed in 1816.

Delegate to Cúcuta Congress, 1821; minister of Economy, 1821–1827; delegate to Ocaña Convention, 1828; president of the Consejo de Ministros and the Consejo de Estado, 1828–1830; delegate to Constitutional Congress, 1830. Died in 1835 while director of Bogotá's Colegio del Rosario.

21. †Cuervo, Rufino. **Born:** Tibirita, 1801. **Admitted to bar:** 1823. Descendant of colonial captain; his mother was first cousin of lawyer José I. de Márquez's mother. In 1826 married daughter of former *contador* of the Tribunal de Cuentas. Close to the intellectual circle of aristocratic lawyers Miguel Tobar and J. Angel Lastra.

Fiscal of the Comisión de Bienes Nacionales, 1823; *juez político* of the Bogotá *cantón,* 1824; interim justice of Bogotá's appeals court, 1825; *oficial* of Supreme Court, 1826; *fiscal* of Popayán's Tribunal, 1826–1828; justice of Bogotá's appeals court, 1830; *prefecto* of Cundinamarca, 1831–1835; general director of the Renta de Tabacos, 1837; director of Crédito Nacional, 1839; diplomatic agent to Perú and Bolivia, 1842; secretary of Economy, 1843; justice of the Supreme Court, 1844; vice president of the republic, 1847. Journalist and entrepreneur.

22. *Cuevas, Francisco J. **Born:** Tunja? 1776. **Admitted to bar:** 1804. Married granddaughter of Tunja's *administrador* of the colonial Renta de Correos, Tabacos y Aguardientes.

Asesor of Cauca's *intendente,* 1822; interim *asesor* of Boyacá's *intendente,* 1823; senator, 1823–1826; interim *fiscal* of Cundinamarca's Tribunal, 1824; justice of the Supreme Court, 1825–1830s; member of Bolívar's Consejo de Estado, 1828.

---

†Pro-aristocratic individuals of "provincial" ancestry.

182   Appendix 4

23. *Díaz Granados, Esteban? **Born:** Santa Marta? 1780. **Admitted to bar:** 1806. Seemingly linked to an *encomendero* family, and to a colonial governor of Santa Marta.

Asesor of Santa Marta's governor, 1821; candidate to justice of Cartagena's Tribunal, 1825, rejected due to his recent royalist behavior; appointed justice of Cartagena's Tribunal, 1826–1828. Died in 1846.

24. Domínguez, Benedicto. **Born:** Bogotá, 1783. **Admitted to bar:** 1809. Grandson of Marqués de Surba y Bonza; son of *contador* mayor of the Tribunal Mayor de Cuentas of Bogotá; his brother married a descendant of New Granada's first colonial *presidente*.

Astronomer and designer of calendars; interim justice of the Supreme Court, 1831; *hacendado*.

25. Domínguez Roche, José María. **Born:** Santa Marta, 1788. **Admitted to bar:** 1811. Descendant of Marqués de Surba y Bonza; grandson of lieutenant colonel of royal armies; son of influential Bogotano, seemingly a rich landowner, who was member of the local *cabildo* and leader of the 1810 junta. His sisters married, in 1815 and 1822, respectively, members of two influential families, one from Bogotá (Fernández Madrid clan, descendants of *oidor* of Mexico's Audiencia), another from Caracas (Gual family, descendants of colonial colonel and governor of Cumaná and Guayana).

Interim justice of Supreme Court, 1823 and 1825; interim justice of Bogotá's Tribunal, 1824; *hacendado*.

26. Domínguez Roche, Mateo. **Born:** Simijaca, 1795. **Admitted to bar:** 1817. Brother of José María (see previous entry). Married granddaughter of *fiel* of Bogotá's Casa de Moneda.

Great *hacendado;* local judge and justice of a regional appeals court in the 1830s.

27. *Esguerra, Manuel. **Born:** Bogotá? 1790. **Admitted to bar:** 1818. Relative (brother?) of lawyer Sebastián Esguerra, son of landed proprietor of Bogotá.

Asesor of Mariquita's governor, 1823; interim justice of Cundinamarca's Tribunal, 1826. Followed career in high judicial bureaucracy.

28. *Esguerra, Sebastián. **Born:** Bogotá? 1788. **Admitted to bar:** 1818. Son of landowner in the towns of Suesca, Bosa, and Funza, neighboring Bogotá. One of his brothers married a niece of an *oidor* of Quito's Audiencia; another married a relative of the important Urquinaona clan. He himself was very close to lawyer Rufino Cuervo and to the Tenorio and Vergara families.

Practicing lawyer, 1819–1823; *juez político* of the Bogotá *cantón* before 1824; secretary of the Intendencia de Cundinamarca, 1824; member, House of Representatives, 1827; active in local university.

29. Galavís, José María. **Born:** Bogotá, 1808. **Admitted to bar:** 1832. Brought up by aristocratic lawyer Eustaquio Galavís, his uncle, former *corregidor* in the colonial period (see Appendix 1). Married María Josefa Callejas Restrepo, from Antioquia. Had two offspring.

Director of Antioquia's provincial colegio in 1828; *archivero* in a ministry in the early 1830s, promoted to *jefe de seccion* by 1834; editor of the official government newspaper in the 1830s; governor of Cauca in late 1836; *oficial mayor* of the Ministry of Interior and Exterior in late 1837; interim governor of Neiva in 1837–1839; governor of Cauca, 1841–1842; congressman in the early 1840s, supported the return of the Jesuits; fiscal in a

Tribunal Superior; undersecretary of war and external relations promoted to secretary in the late 1840s. Died in 1851.

30. *Gori, Joaquín J. **Born:** Cartagena, 1790? **Admitted to bar:** 1817. Two of his relatives were middling employees of the Cajas Reales and the colonial Administración de Aguardiente y Naipes of Cartagena. His admission into Bogotá's Colegio del Rosario was rejected in 1808. He sued the colegio under sponsorship of aristocratic lawyer Eusebio María Canabal. Eventually became a lawyer during the independence period. Married Manuela Ramona de la Maza Lobo Guerrero, daughter of a Spaniard who served as *alguacil mayor* of Santafé de Bogotá's Inquisition. Had four offspring. Died in 1868.

Oficial primero of the Secretaría de la Intendencia de Cundinamarca, 1821–1822; interim *asesor* of the *intendente* of Boyacá, 1823–1824; *fiscal* for the liquidation of the public debt, 1825; interim justice, Bogotá's Tribunal, 1826; *oficial primero* of the Ministry of the Interior, 1826–1828; delegate to Ocaña Convention, 1828; member of the House of Representatives and the Senate, 1830s–1840s; governor of Bogotá, 1840; member of the Consejo de Estado until 1842; vice president in the mid-1840s; *designado* to the presidency, 1849.

31. *Hinestrosa, José María. **Born:** Bogotá? 1782. **Admitted to bar:** 1810. Relative of middling colonial *oficial* of Bogotá's Administración de Alcabalas.

Delegate from Neiva to Cúcuta Congress, 1821; member, House of Representatives, 1823–1826; *juez letrado* of Bogotá, 1826; interim justice of the Supreme Court, 1827; secretary of the Supreme Court during the 1830s.

32. Hurtado, José Manuel. **Born:** Popayán, 1784. **Admitted to bar:** 1807. Grandson of a wealthy landowner of Popayán; his father pursued noble titles during the colonial period; his sisters married, respectively, a brother of *oidor* Mosquera y Figueroa and aristocratic lawyer Santiago Arroyo (see above). He himself married a wealthy Panamanian.

Royalist self-exiled in Panama in the late colonial period; senator, 1823; diplomatic agent in London, 1823–1826; justice of Panamá's appeals court in the 1830s; rich *hacendado*.

33. Lastra Berrio, José Angel de. **Born:** Cartagena? 1799. **Admitted to bar:** 1820?. Son of Pedro Lastra, rich merchant who settled in Bogotá and was *contador ordenador* of the Tribunal de Cuentas. Pedro was executed by the Spanish troops in 1816.

Appointed *asesor* of Pamplona's governor in 1821, declined; wrote antimilitary newspapers *La Miscelánea* and *La Bandera Tricolor* along with lawyer Rufino Cuervo and others, 1825–1826; *contador de diezmos; oficial mayor* of the Ministry of Foreign Relations; justice of Cundinamarca's appeals court; senator. Died in 1837.

34. López Aldana, Francisco de P. **Born:** Bogotá? 1801. **Admitted to bar:** 1823. Son of Panamanian medical doctor who served as colonial *contador general de tributos* in Quito; brother of lawyer who practiced in Lima.

Professor of Latin in the early 1820s; *oficial tercero* and *archivero* in the secretary of Cundinamarca's *intendencia,* 1821, 1823; interim *fiscal* of provincial court of appeals, 1827; *fiscal* of Bogotá's court of appeals, late 1820s; delegate to Ocaña convention, 1828; expelled from New Granada as anti-Bolívar activist in 1828; returned to court of appeals, 1830s; interim *prefecto* of Cundinamarca, 1834; member of the Consejo de Estado in the late 1830s; *contador general de hacienda,* 1840s; *director de crédito público,* 1850; practicing lawyer, 1850s.

35. Malo, Antonio. **Born:** Tunja? 1789. **Admitted to bar:** 1811. Son of *alguacil mayor* of Real Audiencia, and nephew of Santa Marta's colonial Bishop. Belonged to a family of rich landowners linked to the Alvarez bureaucratic clan (see Figure 3.1).

Appointed treasurer of the Department of Boyacá, 1824; interim justice of the Supreme Court, 1825–1826; senator, 1823–1826; purchased for ten years the exploitation of Chita's saltmines, paying 28,000 pesos in 1828; industrial entrepreneur.

36. †Márquez, José Ignacio. **Born:** Ramiriquí, 1793. **Admitted to bar:** 1817. Descendant of mineowners in the Boyacá region. Second cousin of lawyer Rufino Cuervo (see above). Married to a descendant of Marquéz de Surba y Bonza in 1827, thus entering into the influential Domínguez clan.

Delegate to Cúcuta Congress, 1821; *fiscal* of Bogotá's appeals court, 1821–1825; professor of public law in Bogotá's Colegio de San Bartolomé, 1821–1825; *intendente* of Boyacá, 1825–1826; appointed director of Boyacá's University; delegate to Ocaña Convention, 1828; minister of economics, 1831; acting president, 1832; opposed to pardon of General Santander in early 1830s; member of the Consejo de Estado, 1832–1835; vicepresident, 1835–1837; president, 1837–1841; professor of Roman law in Bogotá, 1840s; director of Bogotá's university 1846–? justice of the Supreme Court, 1840s and 1850s.

37. *Martínez Escobar, José Vicente. **Born:** Cartago, 1809. **Admitted to bar:** No. Son of wealthy Buga lawyer and *hacendado* Pedro V. Martinez C. (see Appendix 1). Brother of lawyers Francisco F., Carlos, and Rafael. Married in Pamplona to Vicenta Ordóñez, sister of his classmate and future business partner Clímaco Ordóñez (see below). Had three offspring.

Classmate of Mariano Ospina, Florentino González, José M. Galavis (see above). Did not become a lawyer but left for the U.S. in 1828, returned in 1830; congressman from 1835 to 1847; ran along with his former classmate Climaco Ordonez import-export firm Ordóñez y Martínez during the late 1830s and through the 1840s; gave substantial loan to aristocratic government during the War of the *Supremos;* fought a duel with Florentino González in the early 1840s, but became friends again when they met in Paris in the mid-1840s; tried to establish steamship company with F. González to navigate Magdalena River in 1845; died in 1847 while a member of the Senate.

38. *Méndez, Ildefonso. **Born:** Cartagena, 1784. **Admitted to bar:** 1811. Probably relative of Simití's colonial *administrador* de la Renta de Alcabalas.

Appointed *asesor* of Riohacha's governor in 1821, declined; *fiscal* and justice of Cartagena's Tribunal, 1825–1830; director and professor, University of Cartagena, 1830s.

39. Mendoza Morales, José María. **Born:** Bogotá, 1803. **Admitted to bar:** 1828. Son of *contador de diezmos;* nephew of *corregidor* of Tunja; nephew of *contador* of the Renta de Aguardiente in Bogotá; maternal grandson of colonial director of Bogotá's royal mint.

Law professor in one of Bogotá's colegios from 1824 on; congressman during the 1830s; justice of Tunja's high court of appeals in the late 1830s and early 1840s; ecclesiastical notary in early 1840s; *fiscal* and justice of Bogotá's high court of appeals during the mid-1840s.

40. Morales Galavís, Francisco. **Born:** Turbaco, 1782. **Admitted to bar:** 1808. Paternal grandson of *superintendente* of Bogotá's colonial Casa de la Moneda, maternal grandson of Tunja's *administrador* of the Renta de Alcabalas; nephew of colonial lawyer who was

corregidor de Tunja and married a member of Bogotá's influential Lozano clan. Brother of republican General Antonio Morales G.; married a sister of General Domingo Caicedo y Sanz de Santamaría, who was son-in-law of an *oidor* of Bogotá's colonial Audiencia. One of his daughters married lawyer José Antonio de Plaza (see below).

Appointed judge in Neiva, 1820; appointed secretary of the Intendencia de Cundinamarca, 1821, declined; interim justice of the Supreme Court, 1826; justice of different regional tribunals, 1830s.

41. Mosquera, Joaquín. **Born:** Popayán, 1787. **Admitted to bar:** 1810. Nephew of *oidor* Mosquera y Figueroa of the Audiencias of Bogotá and Mexico (see Appendix 1); son of rich land and mineowner in Popayán. Married a first cousin.

Diplomatic agent to Perú, Chile, and Argentina, 1823–1825; candidate to *director de crédito nacional* in 1826; delegate to Panama's continental congress in 1826 and to the Ocaña Convention, 1828; member of the Consejo de Estado, 1828; president, 1830; vice president, 1833–1835; director, University of Cauca, 1835; became hacendado afterward. Died in 1878.

42. Olano, Mariano. **Born:** Mompós, 1780. **Admitted to bar:** 1807. Maternal grandson of a *fiscal* of Bogotá's Audiencia; nephew of *contador* of Tribunal de Cuentas; son of former *administrador* of the Renta de Correos of Bogotá. Married a member of the Olave Grueso family of Popayán. One of his sons married into the influential Hurtado Mosquera clan of Popayán.

Appointed interim *asesor* of the *intendente* of Boyacá, 1822; interim justice of Bogotá's appeals court, 1825–1826; interim justice of the Supreme Court, 1827; justice of Bogotá's appeals court, 1827.

43. Ordóñez, Clímaco. **Born:** Giron, 1806. **Admitted to bar:** 1827. Married Manuela Caro Ibáñez, daughter of colonial Tribunal de Cuentas *contador* Antonio José Caro. Close associate, business partner, and in-law of Buga merchant José V. Martínez. Seemingly brother of Crisanto who was also a lawyer. Member of key social groups in the province of Pamplona.

Influential member of Congress through the 1830s and 1840s (1835, 1836, 1837, 1842, 1847, 1849); mediated before *Supremo* Colonel Manuel González during 1840–1842 civil war; declined appointment as *consejero de estado* in 1842; secretary of finances in 1845 Mosquera government; 1844–1845 *designado* to executive power; ran export-import business in Bogotá during the 1840s; presided over 1849 Senate and supported conservative Gori's presidential candidacy.

44. Ordoñez, Crisanto. **Born:** Girón, 1806. **Admitted to bar:** 1833. Brother of lawyer Clímaco (see above). Congressman in 1840; *juez letrado del circuito* in Giron, 1842; justice of Guanenta's Tribunal Superior, 1843–1845; congressman, 1848; governor of Pamplona, 1849; led Conservative rebellion in Santander province in 1859.

45. *Ortíz, Ramón. **Born:** ? 1784? **Admitted to bar:** 1821. Unknown.

Served as lawyer of rich merchants and aristocrats during the republican period. Secretary of the Intendencia de Cundinamarca, 1823; *juez letrado* of Bogotá, 1826–1830s; congressman, 1840s.

46. †Osorio, Alejandro. **Born:** Bogotá, 1790. **Admitted to bar:** 1817. Son of a Bogotá *tallador* and *pintor* who had a workshop near Bogotá's cathedral; protected from Spanish

terror by *oidor* Juan Jurado, father-in-law of future General Domingo Caicedo. In 1819 married a descendant of a *fiscal* of the Real Audiencia de Bogotá, member of the Ortega-Nariño Clan. Became very close to the Ricaurte, Nariño, and Caicedo clans of Bogotá.

Minister of war and economy, 1819–1821; delegate to Cúcuta Congress, 1821; *fiscal* and justice of Bogotá's appeals court, 1821–1827; secretary of Bogotá's Colegio del Rosario, 1820s-1830s; nominated *fiscal* of the Supreme Court, 1827; minister of the interior, 1830; member of the Consejo de Estado, 1831; minister of the interior, late 1840s; successful practicing lawyer who also became rich landowner and industrial entrepreneur.

47. †Ospina Rodríguez, Mariano. **Born:** Guasca (Cundinamarca), 1805. **Admitted to bar:** Graduated in 1826; never admitted to bar. Son of modest landowners from Guasca; married three times, each to members of mineowning families from Antioquia.

Professor in Bogotá's *casa de educación* in the late 1820s and interim professor in one of the local *colegios mayores;* escaped to Antioquia after anti-Bolívar plot, 1828; secretary of Antioquia's governors in the early 1830s; law professor and director of Antioquia's *colegio provincial* in the mid-1830s; member of Antioquia's provincial assembly during the 1830s; interim governor of Antioquia, 1836; congressman, 1834, 1838, 1841, 1846, 1848–1849; minister of the interior, 1841–1845; governor of Antioquia, 1845–1846 and 1854–1855; governor of Bogotá, 1847–1848; president of Colombia, 1857–1861.

48. Plaza, Antonio de. **Born:** Honda, 1807. **Admitted to bar:** 1827. Grandson of the colonial *administrador* of the Renta de Tabacos; son of *oficial mayor* of the Renta de Aguardientes y Naipes in Honda, neighboring Bogotá; nephew of *oficial primero* of Honda's Renta de Aguardientes y Naipes. Married to a member of the influential Morales and Caicedo clans of Bogotá.

Oficial of the Dirección y Contaduría General de Tesorerías, 1826; *oficial* and *jefe de sección* in the Ministry of Foreign Relations, 1828; *teniente de gobernador* in Mariquita, 1828; secretary of the Consejo de Estado, 1830s; justice of Guanentá's appeals court, 1835; justice of Antioquia's appeals court, 1836; *contador general de vistas,* 1837; governor of Vélez, 1841; *visitador nacional de diezmos,* 1846; *fiscal* of Cundinamarca's appeals court, 1848; professor of statistics and administrative science in one of Bogotá's law schools, 1840s.

49. *Ponce, Antonio Román. **Born:** Cartagena, 1777. **Admitted to bar:** 1818. Background and trajectory unknown.

Juez letrado of Tunja, 1826; assistant director of University of Boyacá (Tunja), 1827; *asesor* of Socorro's governor, 1828; justice of Cartagena's appeals court, 1830s.

50. †Restrepo Vélez, José Manuel. **Born:** Envigado (Medellín), 1781. **Admitted to bar:** 1808. Son of small landowner and mineowner; merchant in the late colonial period; in 1811 married daughter of important merchant from Rionegro (Antioquia); see Figure 9.1.

Interim *asesor* of the governor of Antioquia in 1810; *secretario de gracia y justicia* in Antioquia, 1813–1815; escaped to Jamaica and the U.S. in the mid-1810s; governor of Antioquia, 1819–1820; congressman in the early 1820s; minister of the interior, 1821–1830; *director general de estudios* since late 1820s; appointed member of the Consejo de Estado, 1830–1831, declined; *director general de tabacos,* 1833–1834; *director* of Bogotá's Casa de la Moneda, 1828–1850s; historian.

51. *Ronderos, Juan Victorino. **Born:** Bogotá?, 1779. **Admitted to bar:** 1805. Son of colonial *asesor* of the Diputación Consular and the Cajas Reales.

Nominated to replace the *fiscal* of the Supreme Court, 1823; interim justice of the Supreme Court, 1825; delegate to Bogotá's electoral college, 1832. Further activities unknown.

52. Salazar, José María. **Born:** Rionegro, 1785. **Admitted to bar:** 1810. Grandson of Marqués de San Jorge's brother; brother of *agente fiscal* of Quito's Real Audiencia. Started career as *meritorio secundario* in Bogotá's colonial Tribunal de Cuentas in 1806.

Diplomatic agent to the United States, 1822–1826; candidate to replace minister of the interior in 1826; justice of the Supreme Court, 1826.

53. *Tobar, Miguel. **Born:** Tocaima, 1782. **Admitted to bar:** 1809. Descendant of large landowning family from Tocaima; his daughter married descendant of former *contador* of Bogotá's colonial Tribunal de Cuentas, member of the Caro clan; mentor during the 1820s of aristocratic students who held literary meetings at his house and had access to his large and important library.

Delegate to Cúcuta Congress, 1821; justice of the Supreme Court, 1821–1830s; law professor in Bogotá, 1820s-1830s.

54. Tobar Santos, Bernardino. **Born:** Zipaquirá, 1786. **Admitted to bar:** 1819. Son of the *administrador* of Zipaquirá's colonial Renta de Tabacos.

Practicing lawyer; governor of Vélez, 1820; delegate to Cúcuta Congress, 1821; appointed *asesor* of Antioquia's governor, 1821; interim justice of Bogotá's Tribunal, 1824; appointed *asesor* of Panama's governor, 1824, declined; appointed justice of Mérida's Tribunal, 1826; justice of Bogotá's Tribunal; member and vice president of 1841 Congress; *juez letrado* in Zipaquirá, 1849–1851?. Died in 1853.

55. Umaña Barragán, Enrique. **Born:** Bojacá, 1772. **Admitted to bar:** 1800. Son and grandson of large landowners of the Bojacá region, neighboring Bogotá; married the daughter of high-ranking colonial military officer. Appointed *corregidor* of Zipaquirá, neighboring Bogotá, in the late colonial period. One of his sons married a daughter of rich Antioqueño merchant and landowner Raimundo Santamaría, 1840s.

Interim governor of Cundinamarca, 1821; *intendente* of Cundinamarca, 1823–1826. *Hacendado,* mineralogist.

56. *Vergara Caicedo, Félix. **Born:** Cali? 1785. **Admitted to bar:** 1812. Son of lawyer and landowner of Cali; first cousin of colonial lawyer Ignacio Herrera, who settled in Bogotá and was linked to the Ortega, Sanz de Santamaría, and Valenzuela clans (see Appendix 1).

Interim justice of Popayán's court of appeals, 1825; *jefe político* in Cali, 1830–1834; director of Cali's Colegio de Santa Librada, 1830–1834; senator, 1834, 1840–1842; Buenaventura's provisional governor, 1835; awarded government contract for the construction of a road in 1837; *hacendado.*

57. Vergara Sanz S., Estanislao. **Born:** Bogotá, 1790. **Admitted to bar:** 1817. Grandson of *regente contador* of Bogotá's Tribunal de Cuentas; son of *agente fiscal* of the Real Audiencia; nephew of *contador* of the Tribunal de Cuentas (Chapter 3, Figure 3.2). Married daughter of colonial lawyer who was middling bureaucrat and brother of one of the *oidores* in Quito's Real Audiencia.

Minister of interior, 1819–1821; *intendente* of Cundinamarca, 1821–1823; justice of the Supreme Court, 1825; senator, 1823–1826; minister of foreign relations, 1828–1830; professor of canon law in Bogotá's Colegio del Rosario; proscribed in 1832; justice of the Supreme Court, 1837 and 1840s. Died in 1855.

58. Villoria, Ramón. **Born:** Zipaquirá, 1794. **Admitted to bar:** 1821. Son of *contador ordenador* of Bogotá's Tribunal de Cuentas; his brother was seemingly a *meritorio* at the same Tribunal in the late colonial period.

Scribe in the Ministry of Economy, 1821; *asesor* of Neiva's governor, 1823; interim justice of Bogotá's court of appeals, 1829; governor of Neiva, 1832–1835; practicing lawyer in Neiva; justice of Bogotá's appeals court, 1850.

Sources: Arboleda, *Diccionario biográfico y genealógico;* Arango Mejía, *Genealogías de Antioquia y Caldas;* Enrique Carrizosa Argaez, *Linajes y biografías de los gobernantes de nuestra nación, 1830–1990* (Bogotá, 1990); Rufino and Anjel Cuervo, *Vida de Rufino Cuervo;* Cuervo Márquez, *Vida de José Ignacio de Márquez;* Robert H. Davis, "Acosta, Caro and Lleras: Three Essayists and Their Views of New Granada's National Problems, 1832–1853" (Ph.D. diss., Vanderbilt Univ., 1969); García de la Guardia, *Kalendario manual;* Gutiérrez Ponce, *Vida de don Ignacio Gutiérrez Vergara;* Guillermo and Alfonso Hernández de Alba, "Galería de hijos insignes del Colegio de San Bartolomé"; Ospina, *Diccionario biográfico y bibliográfico de Colombia;* Ortíz, *Reminiscencias;* Pardo Umaña, *Haciendas de la sabana;* Plazas, *Genealogías de la provincia de Neiva;* Restrepo, "Titulos nobiliarios en la gobernacion de Cartagena de Indias"; Restrepo and Rivas, *Genealogías de Santafé de Bogotá; Genealogías de Santa Fé de Bogotá,* new edition expanded by Posada et al.; Restrepo Sáenz, *Gobernadores y próceres de Neiva;* idem, "Gobernantes de Cundinamarca"; "Gobernantes de Pamplona"; idem, "La provincia del Socorro y sus gobernantes"; Restrepo Posada and Sanz de Santamaría, "Osorio"; idem, "Vargas"; Rojas, *Corregidores y justicias mayores;* Scarpeta and Vergara, *Diccionario biográfico de los campeones de la libertad;* Uricoechea, "Noticias genealógicas"; Vergara y Vergara, *Don Antonio de Vergara y Azcárate;* Vergara, *Relación genealógica; Colombia Ilustrada, 1880s–1890s; La Bagatela,* 1850s; *Papel Periódico Ilustrado,* 1870s.

Appendix 5
Background and Trajectory of the "Provincial" Lawyers of the 1820s and Beyond

1. Alvarez, Francisco Eustaquio. **Born:** Gigante (Tolima), 1827. **Admitted to bar:** 1848. Son of a Spaniard who came to New Granada along with 1810 Consejo de Regencia's envoy, Captain Antonio Villavicencio. Fracisco E. married Vicenta Durán in 1855.

Member of Escuela Republicana in 1850; *fiscal* in 1851 case against popular lawyer José Raimundo Russi; fought alongside government's troops in 1854 to combat artisan-backed coup led by General Melo; law professor through the 1850s; director of Colegio del Rosario; congressman through the 1870s and 1880s.

2. Anzola, Juan Ruperto. **Born:** La Palma? mid-1810s. **Admitted to bar:** 1839. Background undetermined; students opposed his admission to the Colegio de San Bartolomé in 1832 due to unspecified reasons (probably illegitimate birth) found by the government to be unacceptable and "propias de un gobierno aristocrático."

Congressman as early as 1840; practicing lawyer in La Palma in the early 1840s; drops out of records from 1842 to 1844; practicing lawyer in La Palma, 1845–1849.

3. Azuero Plata, Vicente. **Born:** Oiba (Socorro), 1787. **Admitted to bar:** 1817. Son of individual of undetermined occupation and background who lived in Caracas and Honda and married in the Socorro region, where he served as *alcade* and *justicia major;* brother of priest Juan Nepomuceno, who served as parish priest in towns of Casanare and in Anolaima; in 1821 married a member of Bogotá's aristocratic Ricaurte clan.

Member of the Comisión Principal de Secuestros, 1819; *auditor de guerra* of the vice presidency and *juez de diezmos* in Soatá in the early 1820s; justice of the Supreme Court, 1824–1827; member of the Dirección General de Estudios, 1826; congressman, law professor, and journalist throughout the 1820s and 1830s, when he edited *El Correo de Bogotá, La Indicación,* and *El Conductor;* presidential and vice presidential candidate during the 1830s and 1840s; jailed during the *Supremos* civil war in 1840, expelled to La Mesa in 1841 where he owned a small sugar plantation. Died in 1844.

4. Barbosa, Faustino. **Born:** Cocui? (Tunja), 1815. **Admitted to bar:** 1838. Background undetermined.

Congressman in the late 1830s; favored amnesty for the rebels in 1840; drops from the records in 1840–1842; practicing lawyer in Cocui (Tunja) from 1843 to at least 1849; *colector de rentas* in Cocui, 1851.

5. Beltrán, Julián. **Born:** Pore (Casanare), 1810. **Admitted to bar:** 1834. Background undetermined.

Governor of Casanare, 1839–1840; practicing lawyer in Labranzagrande during the early 1840s; congressman during the early 1840s, opposed to the return of the Jesuits; governor of Casanare in 1845; drops out of records in late 1840s.

6. Bulla Moscosa, Bruno. **Born:** Zipaquirá? 1811. **Admitted to bar:** 1833. Background unknown.

Congressman and practicing lawyer in Zipaquirá during the 1830s and 1840s; *administrador* of Zipaquirá's state salt mines in 1850 and beyond.

7. Camacho Naranjo, Salvador. **Born:** Chire (Casanare), 1791. **Admitted to bar:** 1820. Son of Boyacá native, settled in Casanare, of undetermined occupation and background; married Gregoria Roldán y Vargas, from Socorro, of undetermined background.

Congressman in the early 1820s; governor of Casanare, 1822–1823; governor of Socorro, 1827–1828; exiled in 1829–1830 in Venezuela; congressman in the 1830s; governor of Boyacá, 1831–1832; member of the Consejo de Estado, 1832–1840; jailed in 1840 and exiled in Venezuela in the early 1840s; Senator, 1842–1852; *administrador general de correos* since 1850. Died in 1860.

8. Cañarete, Manuel. **Born:** Mompós, 1801. **Admitted to bar:** 1827. Son of a merchant.

Congressman in the late 1820s and throughout the 1830s; justice of Boyacá's court of appeals in the early 1830s; interim justice of Cundinamarca's court of appeals in the mid-1830s; law professor during the 1830s; director of Bogotá's Colegio del Rosario, 1838–1840; landowner in Tocaima, 1842–1846; governor of Santa Marta, 1852; died in 1853.

9. Castilla, Eujenio. **Born:** Chaparral (Ibague), 1812. **Admitted to bar:** 1837. Parents of undetermined background and occupation.

Juez letrado de hacienda in Neiva, 1839 and Mariquita, 1840; practicing lawyer in El Guamo in 1842, in Chaparral in 1845, and in Neiva by 1849; congressman during the 1840s; governor of Mariquita, 1849–1850 and of Neiva, 1850–1853.

10. Céspedes Buendía, Angel María. **Born:** Neiva, ? **Admitted to bar:** No. Son of lawyer José María Céspedes (see below); married daughter of General José M. Obando.

Doctor in jurisprudence, never admitted to bar because of joining rebel troops in the *Supremos* civil war in 1840; followed General Obando into exile.

11. Céspedes Esponda, José María. **Born:** Quilichao (Popayán), 1783. **Admitted to bar:** 1807. Parents of undetermined background and occupation; in 1811 married into the Buendía family, one of La Plata's influential landowning clans.

Appointed secretary of Neiva's governor in 1822; congressman during the 1820s and 1830s; *juez letrado* of Neiva in the late 1820s and in 1832; granted concession to build bridge in La Plata, 1833–1838; *administrador particular* of mails in Guagua (Palermo), Neiva; governor of Neiva, 1835–1837 and 1849–1850; his son Angel María joined rebel troops in the *Supremos* civil war in 1840.

12. Chacón Zabala, José María. **Born:** Soatá, 1809. **Admitted to bar:** 1835. Background undetermined.

Could be the same Garzón Zabala jailed in 1840 in Bogotá during the *Supremos* civil war; practicing lawyer in Ubita in 1840; *juez letrado* in Sogamoso in 1842; drops out of the records in the mid-1840s.

13. Cuenca Pascuas, Domingo Ciprián. **Born:** Neiva, 1801. **Admitted to bar:** 1827. Parents of undetermined background and occupation; married daughter of Vélez lawyer and governor Angel María Flórez (see below).

Practicing lawyer in Bogotá during the late 1820s and throughout the 1830s; practicing lawyer in Purificación during part of the 1840s; congressman during the 1830s and 1840s; justice of the Supreme Court in 1850, died that year.

14. Díaz Sanchez, Laureano Gaspar. **Born:** Villavieja (Neiva), 1810. **Admitted to bar:** 1835. Parents of unknown occupation and background; brother-in-law of lawyers Eladio and Eloi Manrique (see below).

Congressman in the late 1830s and in the 1840s; jailed in 1838 while pro-Azuero *elector* in Neiva; practicing lawyer in Neiva throughout the 1840s; governor of Neiva, 1850; landowner in Villavieja.

15. Duque Gómez, José María. **Born:** Marinilla (Antioquia), 1809. **Admitted to bar:** 1832. Parents of undetermined background and occupation.

Law professor in Bogotá throughout the 1830s; congressman in the mid-1830s; director of Bogotá's Colegio del Rosario, 1839–1840; jailed in late 1840 because one of his classes was deemed subversive; escaped and died in early 1841 in Santa Marta.

16. Durán Gonzalez, Andrés. **Born:** Neiva, 1811. **Admitted to bar:** 1836. Linked to families of Campoalegre, Gigante, and La Plata, of undetermined background and occupation, probably important landowners in these regions.

Practicing lawyer in Neiva in the late 1830s, 1840s, and 1850s, considered to be an "hombre rico" (rich man); joined the rebels in the *Supremos* civil war in 1841.

17. Escobar, José Nicolás. **Born:** Vélez? 1809. **Admitted to bar:** 1837. Parents of undetermined occupation and background; nephew of Bogotá priest Juan N. Escobar; first cousin of Tunja Colonel Juan José Reyes Patria.

Governor of Vélez, 1839–1840; drops out of records after the *Supremos* civil war.

18. Estrada, Marco Antonio. **Born:** Cúcuta, 1818. **Admitted to bar:** 1840. Background undetermined.

Interim *juez letrado* in Cúcuta, 1841–1842; jailed in early 1842 on suspicion of revolutionary activities; practicing lawyer in Pamplona in 1843 and in Cúcuta in 1844 and after.

19. *Flórez Camacho, Angel María. **Born:** Vélez, 1802. **Admitted to bar:** Mid-1820s. Great-grandson of Tunja merchant, *corregidor y justicia mayor;* grandson of captain in the royal army and of Vélez's *administrador de correos* in the late colonial period; married daughter of a captain in the independence armies from Zipaquirá.

Congressman in the 1820s; governor of Vélez in the early 1830s, resigned in 1835; died in 1836.

20. *Gómez Durán, Diego Fernando. **Born:** Socorro, 1786. **Admitted to bar:** 1820. Brother of late colonial *administrador* of Socorro's Renta de Bulas, Aguardiente y Papel

---

*Pro-provincial aristocrats.

Sellado; in 1822 married daughter of former Bogotá-based merchant José Acevedo y Gómez.

Governor of Socorro during the 1810s; congressman during the 1820s; minister of economy and member of the Consejo de Estado in 1831 and in the late 1830s; justice of the Supreme Court during the late 1820s, 1830s, and 1840s; alternate (*designado*) chief executive, 1847; landowner in the Fusagasuga region; died in 1853.

21. Gómez, Hilario. **Born:** San Gíl, 1810s. **Admitted to bar:** 1832. Background undetermined.

Member of Socorro's Subdirección de Instrucción Pública in the 1830s; justice of Guanentá's court of appeals in the late 1830s; practicing lawyer in San Gíl in 1840; congressman in the 1840s, voted against the return of the Jesuits in 1842; *juez letrado* in La Mesa, 1842; practicing lawyer in La Mesa, 1843–1849; practicing lawyer in Anapoima, 1850–1851.

22. Gómez, Juan Nepomuceno. **Born:** San Gíl? **Admitted to bar:** Unknown. Probably son of former *administrador* of Socorro's Renta de Bulas, Aguardiente y Papel sellado; nephew of lawyer Diego Fernando Gómez (see above).

Clerk at the office of Crédito Público in the late 1820s; secretary of the Dirección General de Instrucción Pública since 1832; law professor in Bogotá's Colegio del Rosario in the 1830s; secretary of Bogotá's *prefecto* (governor) in the late 1830s; governor of Casanare in the late 1830s.

23. González, Florentino. **Born:** (Cincelada) Socorro, 1805. **Admitted to bar:** 1832. Parents of undetermined background and occupation; married a member of Ocaña's Ibáñez family, which descended from middling colonial bureaucrats and became influential in the early postcolonial period.

Antimilitary journalist in the late 1820s; editor of state newspaper, *Gaceta de la Nueva Granada*, in the early 1830s; law professor in the 1830s; interim *oficial mayor* in the Ministry of War, 1836; interim governor of Bogotá, 1836–1837; *oficial mayor* of the ministry of economy, 1838; congressman and editor of opposition newspapers *La Bandera Nacional*, 1839, and *El Correo*, 1840; author of a treatise on "administrative science" in 1840; jailed during the *Supremos* civil war in late 1840; exiled in Europe from 1841 until 1846; import-export merchant in Bogotá after 1846; minister of economy, 1846–1847; presidential candidate and editor of *El Siglo*, 1848–1849; senator in the 1850s.

24. Guarnizo, Benigno. **Born:** La Mesa, 1810s. **Admitted to bar:** 1838. Background undetermined.

Landowner and political boss in La Mesa, neighboring Bogotá; *juez de primera instancia* in La Mesa, 1840; practicing lawyer in La Mesa during the 1840s; *fiscal* of Cundinamarca's court of appeals, 1851, acted as such in case against popular lawyer Jose R. Russi; congressman.

25. Herrera Buendía, Bernardo. **Born:** Neiva, 1812. **Admitted to bar:** 1834. Probably son of affluent landowner from Villavieja, who had lands in La Plata and Tello; grandson of colonial *teniente gobernador* and *justicia mayor* in Palermo; in 1838 married daughter of Antioqueño lawyer and bureaucrat José Manuel Restrepo (see Appendix 4 and Figure 9.1); first cousin of lawyers Ramón and Vicente Lombana Buendía (see below).

Pro-Obando *elector*, 1837; *oficial segundo*. of the Ministry of Economy, 1838; assistant director of Bogotá's Colegio de San Bartolomé, 1836–1837; law professor, merchant, and practicing lawyer in Bogotá in the 1840s; justice of the Supreme Court, 1850–1851.

26. Larrota López, Miguel. **Born:** Tunja, 1805. **Admitted to bar:** No. Son of a colonial *escribano* of Tunja.

Doctor in jurisprudence from the University of Boyacá; his degree was nullified in 1829, and despite filing complaints he never became a lawyer; treasurer of the province of Tunja, 1834; congressman in the mid-1830s; interim governor of Pamplona, 1837; governor of Mompós, 1838; governor of Tunja under the *Supremo* rebels in 1840; *auditor de guerra* of rebel armies, 1840; exiled in Venezuela, 1841–1849; senator in the early 1850s; governor of Antioquia, 1851–1852.

27. *Leiva Millán, José María. **Born:** Bogotá, 1806. **Admitted to bar:** 1830. Son of *secretario de cámara* of Viceroy Amar y Borbón in the late colonial period.

Congressman during the 1830s; practiced law in Bogotá during the 1840s; justice of Bogotá's high court of appeals during the 1850s.

28. *Leiva Millán, Cayetano. **Born:** Bogotá, 1811? **Admitted to bar:** 1834. Brother of lawyer José María Leiva (see above).

Candidate to *pasante* in Colegio de San Bartolomé, 1832; *juez letrado de hacienda* in Medellín, 1839–1840; disappears from records from 1842 to 1844 (probably exiled); reappears in 1845–1849 as *escribano público* in Bogotá; one of the founders of the Sociedades Democráticas de Artesanos in the late 1840s; interim justice of the Supreme Court in 1851.

29. Lievano, Romualdo. **Born:** Fusagasuga, 1796? **Admitted to bar:** 1825. Background undetermined.

Juez de hacienda in Mariquita, 1826; congressman in the late 1820s and early 1830s; justice of the Supreme Court in the early 1830s; practicing lawyer and owner of a *tienda* in Bogotá in the 1830s; defense lawyer of general Obando in Popayán, 1839; practicing lawyer in El Guamo in the early 1840s and in Bogotá from 1843 until at least 1850; congressman in the late 1840s.

30. Lleras González, Lorenzo María. **Born:** Bogotá, 1811. **Admitted to bar:** 1836. Son of lieutenant in the Spanish navy who married in Panamá, went into commerce in that city and later in Bogotá. In 1833, while secretary of the Senate, married the daughter of José María Triana, full-time educator, and founder of private colegio; later married again to a sister of his former wife.

Self-exiled in Jamaica and the U.S., 1828–1832; secretary of the Senate, 1833–1834; secretary of the governor of Bogotá, 1835–1836; *oficial mayor* in the Ministry of the Interior and Foreign Relations, 1837; editor of *La Bandera Nacional,* 1837–1839; founder of Sociedad Republicana de Artesanos y Laboradores Progresistas, 1838; expelled from Bogotá during the *Supremos* civil war, 1841–1842; director of Bogotá's Colegio Mayor del Rosario, 1842–1846; founder and director of private Colegio del Espíritu Santo, in Bogotá, 1846–1852; congressman in the 1850s; minister of foreign relations, 1853.

31. Lombana Buendía, Vicente. **Born:** La Plata (Neiva), 1809. **Admitted to bar:** 1833. Son of colonial lawyer who had cacao plantation in La Plata, where he married member of an important (landowning) local clan; himself married a member of Bogotá's

Domínguez clan (see Appendix 3; Chapter 7); nephew of lawyer José María Céspedes and cousin of lawyer Bernardo Herrera (see above).

Medical doctor, owner of a pharmacy in Bogotá, late 1830s; congressman in the 1830s; assistant director of the University of Bogotá, 1839–1840; expelled from Bogotá, exiled in Europe, 1841–1845?; congressman in the late 1840s; appointed governor of Bogotá, 1849; rector of Bogotá's Colegio Nacional in the early 1850s.

32. Lombana Buendía, Ramón. **Born:** La Plata (Neiva), 1812. **Admitted to bar:** 1836. Brother of lawyer Vicente Lombana B. (see above).

Oficial tercero. in the Ministry of Economy, 1838; practicing lawyer in Medellín, 1839–1841; drops out of records in the early 1840s.

33. Manrique Gaitán, Eladio. **Born:** Neiva, 1809. **Admitted to bar:** 1830. Grandson of large landowner in the region of Villavieja; brother-in-law of lawyer Laureano Gaspar Díaz, political boss of Villavieja (see above); brother of lawyer Eloi (see below) and medical doctor Camilo.

Congressman in the early 1830s and 1840s; while a pro-Azuero *elector* in 1838 was jailed along with his brother Eloi and his brother-in-law Laureano Gaspar Díaz; practicing lawyer during the 1840s in Neiva, drops out of the records in mid-1840s.

34. Manrique Gaitán, Eloi. **Born:** Neiva, 1811. **Admitted to bar:** 1836. Brother of Eladio (see above); married in Madrid, Spain in 1852.

Practicing lawyer in Neiva in the late 1830s, and throughout the 1840s; while a pro-Azuero *elector* in 1838, was jailed along with his brother Eladio and his brother-in-law Laureano Gaspar Díaz; seems to have left the country in late 1840s.

35. Mercado, Ramón. **Born:** Cali, 1816? **Admitted to bar:** 1836. Background undetermined.

Tesorero de hacienda in Buenaventura in 1839–1840; congressman in the early 1840s, voted against the return of the Jesuits; practicing lawyer in Cali during the 1840s; author of "Memorias de los Acontecimientos del Sur de la Nueva Granada" in 1849; governor of Buenaventura, 1851.

36. Murillo Toro, Manuel. **Born:** Chaparral (Ibague), 1816. **Admitted to bar:** 1836. Described as "hijo de modesta familia" ("son of a modest family") or "de modesta cuna" ("of modest birth"); protected by his uncle, a priest in Ibague, studied in the local *colegio;* apparently married in Panama in early 1840s to Ana Romay, a woman of undetermined background.

Served as *escribiente* to Bogotano José María Ponce de León, father-in-law of aristocrat Ignacio Gutiérrez Vergara; *oficial mayor* of the House of Representatives in the late 1830s; joined several revolts during the *Supremos* civil war; left for Panama in 1842 and served as secretary to the local governor; returned to Santa Marta in the mid-1840s and founded newspaper *Gaceta Mercantil;* congressman in the late 1840s; minister of economy under President López, 1849–1852; president of Colombia in the 1864–1866, 1872–1874.

37. Núñez Conto, Juan Nepomuceno. **Born:** Cali, 1809. **Admitted to bar:** 1839. Son of a medical doctor from Popayán who settled in Cali and married a member of the Uricoechea family; one of his brothers became a medical doctor; another, Tomás, was a lawyer (see below).

Assistant director and philosophy professor at Bogotá's Colegio del Rosario in 1835, the early 1840s, and early 1850s; director and philosophy professor at Cali's Colegio de Santa Librada, 1847; *fiscal* of the Supreme Court, 1851; congressman in the 1830s and 1840s; practicing lawyer in Bogotá and Cali during the 1840s; supporter of Cali's Sociedades Democráticas.

38. Núñez Conto, Tomás. **Born:** Cali, 1804. **Admitted to bar:** 1826. Brother of lawyer Juan Nepomuceno (see above).

Professor and assistant director at Bogotá's Colegio del Rosario, 1832; philosophy professor and director at Cali's Colegio de Santa Librada in the mid-1830s; congressman, 1834–1835; governor of Buenaventura in the mid-1830s. Died in 1837.

39. Obregón Muñoz, Francisco. **Born:** Barbosa (Antioquia), 1802. **Admitted to bar:** 1827. Parents of undetermined background and occupation; married daughter of lawyer from Medellín who was a cousin of aristocratic General Juan María Gómez and of General José María Córdova.

Philosophy professor and director at Antioquia's provincial *colegio;* member of Antioquia's provincial assembly in the early 1830s; congressman in the mid-1830s; governor of Antioquia, 1836–1840; governor of Antioquia and of the "estado de Manzanares" in late 1841 under the *Supremo* rebels; jailed in 1842 and exiled in Europe; governor of Mompós, 1849; *contador mayor* and chief of the Oficina de Cuentas, 1852; joined Melo's 1854 revolution and served as secretary general and minister of economics.

40. *Pontón Piedrahita, Juan N. **Born:** Medellín, 1818. **Admitted to bar:** 1836. Son of the colonial *administrador de correos* in Medellín; brother-in-law of General Santander.

Practicing lawyer and law professor in Medellín in the late 1830s; interim director of the provincial *colegio* of Antioquia, 1838; joined rebels in the *Supremos* civil war and served them as governor and *jefe político* of Medellín in 1841; jailed, fined, and exiled, 1841–1842; drops out of records after 1842.

41. Ramírez Fortoul, Manuel María. **Born:** Apure-Arauca, 1817. **Admitted to bar:** 1840. Son of a lieutenant-colonel in the independence armies.

Director and philosophy professor at Cúcuta's *casa de educación* in 1839; joined rebels in the *Supremos* civil war, serving as *tesorero* of Pamplona province and *secretario general* of one of the armies; expelled to Venezuela where he served as director of a *colegio,* secretary of a judge, governor of Mérida, and practicing lawyer, 1841–1849; *contador interventor* and *administrador tesorero* in Cúcuta's customs house after 1849.

42. Real Cortínez, Antonio Del. **Born:** Cartagena, 1809. **Admitted to bar:** 1832. Son of local lawyer and landowner with no colonial bureaucratic background; his brother was a landowner in a region neighboring Cartagena; married Rita Carrasquilla, of undetermined background, in 1838.

Law professor in Cartagena in the 1830s; *juez letrado de hacienda* in Cartagena as early as 1839; published early treatise on constitutional law, 1839; disappears from records from 1840 to late 1840s; reappears in 1849 as justice of Santa Marta's court of appeals; minister of state under President Obando in the early 1850s and under President Murillo in the 1860s.

43. Rojas, Ezequiel. **Born:** Miraflores (Tunja), 1803. **Admitted to bar:** 1827. After 1767 expulsion of the Jesuits, his father bought a large part of the former Jesuit hacienda in Lengupá; married Zoila Gaitán, of undetermined background.

Successful practicing lawyer in Bogotá during the 1830s and 1840s; professor of political economy at one of Bogotá's law schools; landowner in Boyacá and money-lender in Bogotá during the 1840s; cabinet minister under President López, 1849.

44. Rojas, Eleuterio. **Born:** Tunja? 1803? **Admitted to bar:** 1827. Probably brother of lawyer Ezequiel Rojas (see above).

Subdirector de estudios in Tunja, 1834; *contador general de hacienda* in Bogotá from 1839 to late 1840s; *juez de contaduria*, 1849; practicing lawyer, 1850.

45. Santander, Rafael Eliseo. **Born:** Bogotá, 1809. **Admitted to bar:** 1832. Son of former colonial *escribano* of Bogotá.

Juez letrado del cantón of Bogotá, 1839; practicing lawyer in the 1840s; *oficial mayor* of the Supreme Court, 1851; writer and bureaucrat after the 1850s.

46. Soto, Francisco. **Born:** Cúcuta, 1789. **Admitted to bar:** 1810. Parents and wife of undetermined occupation and background; one of his brothers was a small merchant; his father-in-law led insurrection in Pamplona during *Supremos* war.

Secretary of general military commanders in Alto Apure and governor of Pamplona during late 1810s; congressman during the 1820s; *teniente asesor* of Boyacá's *intendente* in the early 1820s; appointed *oficial mayor* of the Ministry of Foreign Relations, 1824; *fiscal* and justice of the Supreme Court, and law professor in the mid-1820s; director of public credit, 1826; exiled in Venezuela, 1828–1830; governor of Pamplona, 1830; minister of economics, 1832–1837; *contador general mayor,* 1837–1838; congressman in the late 1830s; member of the Consejo de Estado from late 1830s to at least 1841; expelled to Cúcuta, 1841. Died in 1846.

47. Suárez Serrano, José Joaquín. **Born:** San Gíl, 1788? **Admitted to bar:** 1810s. Background undetermined; married sister of General Pedro Fortoul, *intendente* and general commander of the Department of Boyacá in the 1820s; *compadre* of General José Prudencio Padilla; at least one of his sons was active member of the Escuela Republicana in the 1850s.

Secretary of the Tunja government in the 1810s; interim justice of the Supreme Court in the mid-1820s; *juez de diezmos* in La Mesa, near Bogotá, in the late 1820s; member of the *academia de derecho práctico,* 1831; died in 1832.

48. *Ugarte, Francisco. **Born:** Bogotá, 1787. **Admitted to bar:** 1810. Maternal grandson of the *tesorero* of Bogotá's colonial Renta de Cruzada; nephew of *contador* of Bogotá's colonial Tribunal y Real Audiencia de Cuentas; son of rich merchant and landowner in the Facatativa region. Married daughter of rich landowner in Tunja. His family became impoverished after independence.

Petty peddler; military officer; *contador ordenador* of national Tribunal Mayor de Cuentas, 1819; *oficial primero,* Ministry of War and the Navy, 1821; *cuarto contador auxiliar general de hacienda,* 1821; *oficial mayor* of the Sección de Correos y Posta, 1824; *contador auxiliar* of the Dirección General de Hacienda, until 1837. Retired and was awarded military pension.

49. Vargas, Francisco de P. **Born:** Bogotá, 1809. **Admitted to bar:** 1834. Parents of undetermined background. Brother of lawyer Juan N. (see below).

Juez letrado de hacienda in Vélez, 1840; drops out of records in the early 1840s after being jailed for participation in *Supremos* war.

50. Vargas, Juan Nepomuceno. **Born:** Usaquén (Bogotá)? 1801. **Admitted to bar:** 1824. Brother of lawyer Francisco de P. Vargas (see above).

Journalist who edited *El Demócrata,* in 1830 and *La Noche* in the mid-1840s; law professor in Boyacá in the early 1830s; congressman in the 1830s; practicing lawyer in the late 1840s; *juez de circuito* in Ambalema, 1849.

51. Vásquez González, Rafael María. **Born:** Funza (Bogotá), 1807. **Admitted to bar:** 1832. "De modesta fortuna" ("of modest fortune") referred to as "ilustrado indigena de Funza" ("illustrious Indian from Funza").

Philosophy professor in the late 1820s; became priest in 1830; assistant director of Colegio de San Bartolomé, 1831; secretary of the provincial *cámara* and congressman, 1832; interim assistant director of Colegio de San Bartolomé, 1833; director of Vélez's provincial colegio and member of the regional provincial assembly, 1834–1840; joined rebels during the *Supremos* civil war and was chaplain of rebel armies; exiled in Panama and then in Ecuador after 1840; became director of provincial *colegio,* 1842–1846; parish priest of several towns; senator; founder of Riobamba cathedral, etc.

Sources: Arcesio Aragón, *La Universidad del Cauca* (Popayán, 1925), 177–225, 633–37; Arboleda, *Diccionario biográfico y genealógico;* Isidoro Laverde Amaya, *Bibliografía colombiana* (Bogotá, 1895); Celiano Monge, "El Doctor Rafael María Vásquez," *BHA* 9, 108 (April 1915): 718–28; Ospina, *Diccionario biográfico y bibliográfico de Colombia;* Gustavo Otero Muñóz, "Boceto biografico de cien cancilleres colombianos," in idem, *Historia de la cancillería de San Carlos* (Bogotá, 1942), 111–432; Próspero Pereira Gamba, "Los conflictos de Bogotá en 1840 y 1841," *Revista Literaria* 4, 43–44 (November 1893): 331–49; 45–46 (February 1894): 403–25; 47 (March 1894): 474–84; 48 (April 1894): 530–37; Plazas, *Genealogías de Neiva;* Carlos Ramírez Monreal, "Manuel María Ramírez," *BHA* 13, 145 (March 1920): 53–60; Restrepo and Rivas, *Genealogías de Santafé; Genealogías de Santa Fé de Bogotá,* 1991–1992, vols. 1 and 2; Restrepo Sáenz, *Gobernadores y próceres de Neiva;* idem, "Gobernantes de Cundinamarca"; idem, "Gobernantes de Pamplona"; idem, "La provincia del Socorro y sus gobernantes"; idem, *Gobernadores de Antioquia,* 2 vols. (Bogotá, 1944, 1970); Medardo Rivas, *Los trabajadores de tierra caliente* (Bogotá, 1983): 27–30; José M. Samper, *Galería nacional de hombres ilustres o notables o sea colección de bocetos biográficos* (Bogotá, n.d.); Francisco J. Ugarte, "Opúsculos o noticias biográficas sobre la vida pública y privada del Doctor Francisco J. de Ugarte y Azuola," *BHA* 11, 126 (April 1917): 364–79; *El Argos,* April 8, 1838; *La Bagatela,* June-September, 1853; *El Día,* April 21, 1842, 474; *GNG,* April 14, 1839; May 17, 1840.

Appendix 6
Key Provincial Lawyers and Law Students Active in Opposition Politics During the Late 1830s, by Region

Name	Admitted to Bar	Birthplace
Francisco Obregón	1827	Antioquia
José María Duque Gómez	1832	Antioquia
*Francisco J. Ugarte	1810	Bogotá
Juan Nepomuceno Vargas	1824	Bogotá
*José Leiva Millán	1830	Bogotá
Rafael Eliseo Santander	1832	Bogotá
Rafael María Vásquez	1832	Bogotá
Francisco de P. Vargas	1834	Bogotá
José María Zabala Garzón	1835	Bogotá
Juan N. Pontón Piedrahita	1836	Bogotá
Lorenzo María Lleras	1836	Bogotá
José Diago	1825	Bogotá/Honda
Benigno Guarnizo	1838	Bogotá/La Mesa
Ruperto Anzola	1839	Bogotá/La Palma
Romualdo Lievano	1825	Bogotá/Fusagasuga
Bruno Bulla	1833	Bogotá/Zipaquirá
Tomás Núñez Conto	1826	Cali
Ramón Mercado	1836	Cali
Juan Nepomuceno Núñez Conto	1839	Cali
Salvador Camacho Naranjo	1820	Casanare
Julian Beltrán	1834	Casanare
Marco Antonio Estrada	1840	Cúcuta
Manuel Murillo Toro	1836	Mariquita/Ibagué
Eujenio Castilla	1837	Mariquita/Ibagué
Manuel Cañarete	1827	Mompós
Domingo Ciprián Cuenca	1827	Neiva
Eladio Manrique	1830	Neiva
Vicente Lombana Buendía	1833	Neiva
Bernardo Herrera	1834	Neiva
Gaspar Díaz	1835	Neiva
Andrés Durán González	1836	Neiva
Ramón Lombana Buendía	1836	Neiva

*Pro-provincial aristocrats.
†Doctors in "jurisprudencia" who never became lawyers.

Name	Admitted to Bar	Birthplace
Eloi Manrique	1836	Neiva
Angel María Céspedes	†	Neiva
Juan Nepomuceno Gómez	?	San Gíl?
Hilario Gómez	1832	San Gíl
José María Chacon Zabala	1835	Soatá
Francisco Soto	1810	Socorro
Vicente Azuero	1817	Socorro
*Diego Fernando Gómez	1820	Socorro
Florentino González	1832	Socorro
Manuel María Ramirez Fortoul	1840	Socorro
Miguel Larrota	†	Tunja
Ezequiel Rojas	1827	Tunja
Faustino Barbosa	1838	Tunja?
José Nicolas Escobar	1837	Vélez?

Sources: El Argos, April 8, 1838; *El Día,* April 21, 1842, 474; *GNG,* April 14, 1839; May 17, 1840; Aragón, *La Universidad del Cauca,* 177–225, 633–37; Arboleda, *Diccionario biográfico y genealógico;* Restrepo and Rivas, *Genealogías de Santafé;* Rivas, *Los trabajadores de tierra caliente,* 27–30.

Abbreviations Used in Note Citations

ACHSC	*Anuario Colombiano de Historia Social y de la Cultura.*
Actas Angostura	*Congreso de Angostura. Libro de Actas.* Bogotá: Imprenta Nacional, 1921.
Actas Cúcuta	*Congreso de Cúcuta. Libro de Actas.* Bogotá: Imprenta Nacional, 1923.
Actas Congreso 1823	*Congreso de 1823. Actas, publicadas por Roberto Cortazar y Luis Augusto Cuervo.* Bogotá: Imprenta Nacional, 1926.
Actas Cámara 1824	*Congreso de 1824. Cámara de Representantes Actas.* Cortazar, Roberto and Luis A. Cuervo eds., Bogotá: Editorial Libreria Voluntad, 1942.
Actas Senado 1825	*Congreso de 1825. Senado. Actas.* Cortazar, Roberto and Luis A. Cuervo, eds., Bogotá: Imprenta Nacional, 1952.
Acuerdos	*Acuerdos del Consejo de Gobierno de la República de Colombia, 1821–1827.* 2 vols., 2d ed. Bogotá: Biblioteca de la Presidencia de la República, 1991 [1892].
AHN	Archivo Histórico Nacional de Colombia, Bogotá.
Anexo	Archivo Anexo, AHN.
BCB	*Boletín Cultural y Bibliográfico del Banco de la República.*
BHA	*Boletín de Historia y Antiguedades.*
BNC	Biblioteca Nacional de Colombia.
BLAA	Biblioteca Luis Angel Arango.
Causas y Memorias	*Causas y Memorias de los Conjurados del 25 de Septiembre de 1828,* 3 vols. Bogotá: Biblioteca de la Presidencia de la República, 1991.
Cod. Nal.	*Codificación Nacional de Todas las Leyes de Colombia Desde el año de 1821,* 15 vols. (1821–1853). Bogotá: Imprenta Nacional, 1926–1929.
DBNC	Documentos Biblioteca Nacional de Colombia.
Docs.	*Documentos Para la Historia de la Educación en Colombia,* 7 vols. Hernández de Alba, Guillermo, ed. Bogotá: Patronato Colombiano de Artes y Ciencias, 1969–1986.
Epistolario Cuervo	*Epistolario del Doctor Rufino Cuervo,* 3 vols. Cuervo, Luis Augusto, ed. Bogotá: Imprenta Nacional, 1918.
Epistolario Caicedo	*Archivo Epistolar del General Domingo Caicedo.* Hernández de Alba, Guillermo, ed. Bogotá: Editorial ABC, 1943.
Epistolario Mosquera	*Archivo Epistolar del General Mosquera.* Helguera, J. L., and Robert H. Davis, eds., 2 vols. Bogotá: Editorial Kelly, 1972.
FAES	Fundación Antioqueña para los Estudios Sociales.
GNG	*Gaceta de la Nueva Granada.*
HAHR	*Hispanic American Historical Review.*
Inst. Pub.	Fondo Instrucción Pública, AHN.
JLAS	*Journal of Latin American Studies.*
LARR	*Latin American Research Review.*

Notes

Introduction

1. Recent examples of this literature include Jackie Booker, *Veracruz Merchants, 1770–1829: A Mercantile Elite in Late Bourbon and Early Independent Mexico* (Boulder, 1993); William Taylor, *Magistrates of the Sacred: Priests and Parishioners in Eighteenth-Century Mexico* (Stanford, 1996). There is also some new research on physicians; see Luz María Hernández Sáenz, *Learning to Heal: The Medical Profession in Colonial Mexico, 1767–1831* (New York, 1997).
2. Limited information can be found in Enrique Ruiz Guiñazú, *La magistratura indiana* (Buenos Aires, 1916), chap. 10; Héctor Parra Márquez, *Historia del Colegio de Abogados de Caracas*, 2 vols. (Caracas, 1952); Vicente O. Cutolo, *Abogados y escribanos del siglo XVII* (La Plata, 1963); Adolfo Rolando Padilla, "La abogacia en Guatemala. Epoca colonial," Thesis, Univ. de San Carlos, Guatemala, 1964; Miguel Angel de Marco, *Abogados, escribanos, y obras de derecho en el Rosario del siglo XIX* (Rosario, 1973); Rogelio Pérez Perdomo, *Los abogados en Venezuela* (Caracas, 1981).
3. See Loretta A. Norris, *American Colonial Courts and Lawyers: An Annotated Bibliography* (Washington, 1976). Among several recent works see, e.g., J. Clay Smith, *Emancipation: The Making of the Black Lawyer, 1844–1944* (Philadelphia, 1993); David Lemmings, *Gentlemen and Barristers: The Inns of Court and the English Bar, 1680–1730* (Oxford, 1990); David A. Bell, *Lawyers and Citizens: The Making of a Political Elite in Old Regime France* (Oxford, 1994).
4. Max Weber, "Politics as a Vocation," in *From Max Weber: Essays in Sociology*, ed. H. H. Gerth and C. Wright Mills (New York, 1946), 77–128, esp. 85, 94; William Taylor, "Between Global Processes and Local Knowledge: An Inquiry into Early Latin American Social History, 1500–1900," in *Reliving the Past: The Worlds of Social History*, ed. Olivier Zunz (Chapel Hill, 1985), 115–90, esp. 147; Susan Socolow, *The Bureaucrats of Buenos Aires, 1769–1810: Amor al Real Servicio* (Durham, 1987), 59; Dennys O. Lynch, *Legal Roles in Colombia* (Uppsala, 1981).
5. The bulk of such records come from Colombia's Archivo General de la Nación, in Bogotá. The main document collections I utilized were *Genealogias, Instrucción Pública, Hojas de Vida, Médicos y Abogados* and *Notarias*. A valuable series of original documents and biographical information was found in the Academia Colombiana de Historia's *Boletín de Historia y Antiguedades*. I also consulted notary records in Chiquinquirá, Tunja, Guateque, and Medellín. My research was carried out in 1989–1990, 1994, and 1996–1997.
6. On social history see Charles Tilly, "Retrieving European Lives," in *Reliving the Past*, ed. Zunz, 11–52.
7. One of the best works on colonial social stratification may still be the one by Mario Góngora, *Encomenderos y estancieros* (Santiago, 1970); idem, "Estratificación social ur-

bana en Chile (Siglos XVI, XVII y primera mitad del XVIII)," University of Wisconsin–Milwaukee, Center for Latin American Studies, Center Discussion Paper No. 30, December 1971; idem, "Urban Social Stratification in Colonial Chile," *Hispanic American Historical Review* (hereafter *HAHR*) 55, 3 (August 1975). See also the insightful piece by Magnus Mörner, "Economic Factors and Stratification in Colonial Spanish America with Special Regard to the Elites," *HAHR* 63, 2 (May 1983): 335–69; and, Hugo Nutini, *The Wages of Conquest: The Mexican Aristocracy in the Context of Western Aristocracies* (Ann Arbor, 1995), 1–52, 269.

8. Max Weber, "Class, Status and Party," in *Class, Status and Party: Social Stratification in Historical Perspective,* ed. Reinhard Bendix and Seymour Lipset (New York, 1966), 21–28. For an equivalent definition of honor see Julian Pitt-Rivers, "Honor and Social Status," in *Honour and Shame: The Values of Mediterranean Society,* ed. I. G. Peristany (Chicago, 1966), 21–77; idem, "Honor," in *International Encyclopedia of the Social Sciences* (1968), 6: 503–10. On the significance of honor in colonial Latin America see Lyman L. Johnson and Sonya Lipsett-Rivera, *The Faces of Honor: Sex, Shame and Violence in Colonial Latin America* (Albuquerque, 1998).

9. For criticisms of this trend see Woodrow Borah, "Discontinuity and Continuity in Mexican History," *Pacific Historical Review* 48 (February 1979): 1–25; Eric Van Young, "Mexican Rural History Since Chevalier: The Historiography of the Colonial Hacienda," *Latin American Research Review* (hereafter *LARR*) 17, 3 (1983): 5–61, esp. 6–7; idem, "Recent Anglophone Scholarship on Mexico and Central America in the Age of Revolution (1750–1850)," *HAHR* 65, 4 (November 1985): 725–43, esp. 730–33; Marcelo Carmagnani, "The Inertia of Clio: The Social History of Colonial Mexico," *LARR* 20, 1 (1985): 149–66, esp. 157; Mark D. Szuchman, ed., *The Middle Period in Latin American History: Values and Attitudes in the 18th and 19th Centuries* (Boulder, 1988), esp. 11–13, 18; and Kenneth J. Andrien and Lyman Johnson, eds., *The Political Economy of Spanish America in the Age of Revolution, 1750–1850* (Albuquerque, 1994). For long-term studies see especially Stanley J. Stein and Barbara Stein, *The Colonial Heritage of Latin America: Essays on Economic Dependence in Perspective* (New York, 1970); John Coatsworth, *Los origines del atraso: Nueve ensayos de historia economica de Mexico en los siglos XVIII y XIX* (Mexico City, 1990); Stephen Haber, ed., *How Latin Amerca Fell Behind: Essays on the Economic Histories of Brazl and Mexico, 1800–1914* (Stanford, 1997); and Jeremy Adelman, ed., *Colonial Legacies: The Problem of Persistence in Latin American History* (New York, 1999).

10. See Stanley J. Stein and Barbara Stein, *The Colonial Heritage,* 140–41; Tulio Halperín Donghi, *The Contemporary History of Latin America* (Durham, 1993), esp. 78, 95, 102. In the particular case of Colombia see Luis E. Nieto Arteta, *Economía y cultura en la historia de Colombia* (Bogotá, 1962) [1941]; Germán Colmenares, *Partidos políticos y clases sociales* (Bogotá, 1968). Insightful criticisms of all of these approaches is found in Frank R. Safford, "Social Aspects of Politics in Nineteenth-Century Spanish America, 1825–1850," *Journal of Social History* (1972): 344–70; idem, "Bases of Political Alignment in Early Republican Spanish America," in *New Approaches to Latin American History,* ed. Richard Graham and Peter H. Smith (Austin, 1974), 71–111; idem, "Aspectos sociales de la política en la Nueva Granada, 1825–1850," in *Aspectos del siglo XIX en Colombia* (Medellín, 1977), 153–99; idem, "Acerca de las interpretaciones socioeconómicas de la política en la Colombia del siglo XIX: variaciones sobre un tema," *Anuario Colombiano de Historia Social y de la Cultura* (hereafter *ACHSC*), nos. 13–14 (1985–1986): 91–150.

11. See Frank R. Safford, "Politics, Ideology and Society in Post-Independence Spanish

America," in *The Cambridge History of Latin America,* ed. Leslie Bethell (Cambridge, 1985), 3: 347–421, esp. 349, 371.
12. See Safford, "Politics, Ideology and Society," esp. 370–71.
13. One of the most recent examples of those studies, and perhaps the best, is John Lynch, *Caudillos in Spanish America* (Oxford, 1992). Works on individual political figures and governments are too numerous to cite. Concerning this trend see comments by Van Young, "Recent Anglophone Scholarship," 733.
14. Halperin Donghi, *The Contemporary History of Latin America,* chaps. 3 and 4.
15. See for instance John Fisher, "Soldiers, Society and Politics in Spanish America, 1750–1821," *LARR* 17, 1 (1982): 217–22; Juan Marchena Fernández, *Oficiales y soldados en el ejército de América* (Seville, 1983); Allan J. Kuethe *Cuba, 1753–1815: Crown, Military and Society* (Knoxville, 1986).
16. To list but a few, see David Brading, *Haciendas and Ranchos in the Mexican Bajío: León, 1700–1860* (New York, 1979); Alberto Flóres Galindo, *Aristocracia y plebe: Lima 1760–1830 (estructura de clases y sociedad colonial)* (Lima, 1984); Ann Twinam, *Miners, Merchants and Farmers in Colonial Colombia* (Austin, 1982). See also note 1.
17. The most recent such works are by David A. Brading, *Church and State in Bourbon Mexico: The Diocese of Michoacán, 1749–1810* (New York, 1994); and Taylor, *Magistrates of the Sacred.*
18. One of the best is by Mark Burkholder, *Politics of a Colonial Career: José de Baquíjano and the Audiencia of Lima* (Albuquerque, 1980). There is a long list of biographies of viceroys, *visitadores,* bureaucrats, and politicians.
19. For the few works over the last two decades see Jacques A. Barbier, *Reform and Politics in Bourbon Chile* (Ottawa, 1980); Thomas Flory, *Judges and Jury in Imperial Brazil, 1808–1871: Social Control and Political Stability in the New State* (Austin, 1981); Susan Socolow, *The Bureaucrats of Buenos Aires, 1769–1810;* and Linda Arnold, *Bureaucracy and Bureaucrats in Mexico City, 1742–1835* (Tucson, 1988).
20. See Emilia Viotti da Costa, *The Brazilian Empire: Myths and Histories* (Chicago, 1985), esp. chap. 7; for a contrasting view see John Tutino, *From Insurrection to Revolution in Mexico: Social Bases of Agrarian Violence, 1750–1940* (Princeton, 1986).
21. Though based on a traditional periodization, the most significant and recent studies, some of which move in the same direction indicated here, are by Richard Graham, *Patronage and Politics in Nineteenth-Century Brazil* (Stanford, 1990); Donald Fithian Stevens, *Origins of Instability in Early Republican Mexico* (Durham, 1991); Michael Costeloe, *The Central Republic in Mexico, 1835–1846:* Hombres de Bien *in the Age of Santa Anna* (New York, 1993); and Torcuato S. Di Tella, *National Popular Politics in Early Independent Mexico, 1820–1847* (Albuquerque, 1995). For studies based on a periodization close to the one use here see Peter Guardino, *Peasants, Politics, and the Formation of Mexico's National State* (Stanford, 1996); Charles Walker, *Smoldering Ashes: Cuzco and the Creation of Republican Peru, 1780–1840* (Durham, 1999); Silvia M. Arrom, *Containing the Poor: The Mexico City Poor House, 1774–1871* (Durham, forthcoming); Sarah Chambers, *From Subjects to Citizens: Honor, Gender, and Politics in Arequipa, Peru, 1780–1854* (University Park, PA., forthcoming).
22. On this point see Jacques Le Goff, "Is Politics Still the Backbone of History?" *Daedalus* 100 (1971): 1–19; Viotti da Costa, *The Brazilian Empire,* xvii–xviii; George Reid Andrews, *Blacks and Whites in São Paulo, Brazil, 1888–1988* (Madison, 1991), 18.

Chapter 1
State Service and Status-Honor

1. See Karen Spalding, ed., *Essays in the Political, Social and Economic History of Colonial Latin America* (Newark, 1982); Peter Guardino and Charles Walker, "The State, Society, and Politics in Peru and Mexico in the Late Colonial and Early Republican Periods," *Latin American Perspectives* 19, 2 (spring 1992): 10–43; and Andrien and Johnson, eds., *The Political Economy of Spanish America*.
2. Some of the most recent monographs concern the case of Mexico. See Stevens, *Origins of Instability;* Costeloe, *The Central Republic;* Di Tella, *National Popular Politics*.
3. A partial exception may be the important work by Tulio Halperín Donghi, *Revolución y guerra: Formación de una elite dirigente en la Argentina criolla* (Buenos Aires, 1972).
4. For valuable information on institutional aspects of the transition from the colonial to the postcolonial bureaucracy see William Lofstrom, "From Colony to Republic: Case Study in Bureaucratic Change," *Journal of Latin American Studies* (hereafter *JLAS*) 5, 2 (November 1977): 177–97; and Arnold, *Bureaucrats and Bureaucracy in Mexico*.
5. For a good work on the subject see Magali Sarfatti, *Spanish Bureaucratic-Patrimonialism in America* (Berkeley, 1966); see also Richard M. Morse, "The Heritage of Latin America," in *The Founding of New Societies. Latin America, South Africa, Canada and Australia*, ed. Louis Hartz (New York, 1964), 123–77; Fernando Uricoechea, *The Patrimonial Foundations of the Brazilian Bureaucratic State* (Los Angeles, 1980); and Reinhard Bendix, *Nation Building and Citizenship* (Berkeley, 1964), esp. 39–65.
6. Bendix, *Nation Building and Citizenship,* 62; John L. Phelan, *The Kingdom of Quito in the Seventeenth Century: Bureaucratic Politics in the Spanish Empire* (Madison, 1967), esp. chap. 17, 325–26; Max Weber, *Economy and Society,* 2 vols. (Berkeley, 1978), 2: chap. 12.
7. Sarfatti, *Spanish Bureaucratic-Patrimonialism,* 31; Phelan, "Authority and Flexibility in the Spanish Imperial Bureaucracy," *Administrative Science Quarterly* 5, 1 (June 1960): 47–65; Phelan, *Kingdom of Quito,* 325, 327–28.
8. For detailed institutional information see, for instance, the diagrams offered in Sarfatti, *Spanish Bureaucratic-Patrimonialism,* esp. 22–25. Another indispensable point of reference is José M. Ots y Capdequi, *El Estado español en las Indias* (Mexico City, 1946); idem, *Las instituciones del Nuevo Reino de Granada al tiempo de la independencia* (Madrid, 1958). See also Morse, "The Heritage of Latin America," 157; Arnold, *Bureaucrats and Bureaucracy in Mexico,* 27, 36–38, 44–46.
9. See Spalding, ed., *Essays in the Political, Social and Economic History;* Andrien and Johnson, eds., *The Political Economy of Spanish America,* 3–16.
10. See, for instance, Steve J. Stern, *Peru's Indian Peoples and the Challenge of the Spanish Conquest: Huamanga to 1640* (Madison, 1982); Ramón Gutierrez, *When Jesus Came, the Corn Mothers Went Away* (Stanford, 1991).
11. On honor and gender see Patricia Seed, *To Love, Honor, and Obey in Colonial Mexico* (Stanford, 1986), esp. chaps. 6 and 9; Ann Twinam, "Honor, Sexuality, and Illegitimacy in Colonial Spanish America," in *Sexuality and Marriage in Colonial Latin America,* ed. Asunción Lavrin (Lincoln, 1989), 118–55; Gutierrez, *When Jesus Came, the Corn Mothers Went Away,* chaps. 5–8; Steve J. Stern, *The Secret History of Gender: Women, Men and Power in Late Colonial Mexico* (Chapel Hill, 1995), 13–17; Johnson and Lipsett-Rivera, eds., *The Faces of Honor,* passim. On honor, nobility, and mercantile activities see William J. Callahan, *Honor, Commerce and Industry in Eighteenth Century Spain* (Boston, 1972).
12. Alfonso García Valdescasas, *El hidalgo y el honor* (Madrid, 1948); Jaime Jaramillo

Uribe, "Mestizaje y diferenciación social en la Nueva Granada en la segunda mitad del siglo XVIII," in idem, ed., *Ensayos sobre historia social colombiana* (Bogotá, 1968), 163–203; Beatríz Patiño Millán, *Criminalidad, ley penal y estructura social en la Provincia de Antioquia, 1750–1820* (Medellín, 1994), 197–253.

13. John Tate Lanning, *The University in the Kingdom of Guatemala* (Ithaca, 1955), chaps. 10–11; Richard Kagan, *Students and Society in Early Modern Spain* (London, 1974); Renán Silva, *Universidad y sociedad en el Nuevo Reino de Granada* (Bogotá, 1992); Halperín Donghi, *Revolución y guerra*, 61.
14. Pitt-Rivers, "Honor and Social Status," 22. Weber, in fact, utilized the concept "status honor" in one of his main articles on the subject. See Weber, "Class, Status, Party"; Susan Deans-Smith, *Bureaucrats, Planters, and Workers: The Making of the Tobacco Monopoly in Bourbon Mexico* (Austin, 1992), 44; Halperín Donghi, *Revolución y guerra*, 56, 58–59, 61.
15. Mark Burkholder, "Bureaucrats," in *Cities and Society in Colonial Latin America*, ed. Susan Socolow and Louisa, S. Hoberman (Albuquerque, 1986), 77–103, esp. 96–99; Victor M. Uribe, "The Lawyers and New Granada's Late Colonial State," *JLAS* 27, 3 (October 1995): 517–49.
16. J. G. Peristany and Julian Pitt-Rivers, eds., *Honour and Grace in Anthropology* (Cambridge, 1992), 2–3, 5.
17. Samuel Haber, *The Quest for Authority and Honor in the American Professions, 1750–1900* (Chicago, 1991), part 1. For public service, even undertaken by men of modest origins, as involving unmistakable signs of social distinction, see Jonathan Powis, *Aristocracy* (New York, 1984), 69, 72, 78. See also Hans Speier, "Honor and Social Structure," in idem, *Social Order and the Risks of War* (New York, 1952), 36–52.
18. See Emmanuel Leroy Ladurie, "The Court Surrounds the King: Louis XIV, the Palatine Princess, and Saint-Simmon," in *Honour and Grace in Anthropology*, ed. Peristany and Pitt-Rivers, 51–78; Powis, *Aristocracy*, 21; William M. Reddy, *The Invisible Code: Honor and Sentiment in Postrevolutionary France, 1814–1848* (Berkeley, 1997), esp. chap. 4; Callahan, *Honor, Commerce and Industry*, 3; García Valdecasas, *El hidalgo y el honor*, 193; Burkholder, *Politics of a Colonial Career*, 109; Nutini, *Wages of Conquest*, 255–56.
19. See Socolow, *Bureaucrats of Buenos Aires*, chap. 5; Arnold, *Bureaucracy and Bureaucrats in Mexico*, chap. 6; Phelan, *Kingdom of Quito*, 147, 327.
20. Weber, "Class, Status, Party." On occupation as a source of deference see also Edward A. Shils, "Deference," in *The Logic of Social Hierarchies*, ed. Edward O. Laumann et al. (Chicago, 1970), 421–48, esp. 423–24.
21. Juan A. Villamarín and Judith E. Villamarín, "The Concept of Nobility in Colonial Santafé de Bogotá," in *Essays in the Political, Economic and Social History of Colonial Latin America*, ed. Karen Spalding (Newark, 1982), 125–53, esp. 128; Powis, *Aristocracy*, 21; Phelan, *Kingdom of Quito*, 127, 324; Jaramillo Uribe, "Mestizaje y diferenciación social en la Nueva Granada," esp. 193.
22. Phelan, *Kingdom of Quito*, 334; Nutini, *Wages of Conquest*, 255–56.
23. Hipólito Villaroel, *Enfermedades políticas que padece la capital de esta Nueva España en casi todos los cuerpos de que se compone y remedios que se le deben aplicar para su curación si se quiere que sea útil al Rey y al público* [1785–1787] (Mexico, 1982), 198.
24. See *relaciones de méritos y servicios* of numerous colonial Latin Americans in Documentos Biblioteca Nacional de Colombia (hereafter DBNC), Fondo Pineda, No. 1066. See also Mark Burkholder, "Relaciones de Méritos y Servicios: A Source for Spanish-American Group Biography in the Eighteenth Century," *Manuscripta* 21 (1977): 97–04.

25. See Cheryl English Martin, *Governance and Society in Colonial Mexico: Chihuahua in the Eighteenth Century* (Stanford, 1996), chap. 5., esp. 97–148; Bartolomé Arzáns de Orsúa y Vela, *Tales of Potosí* (Providence, 1975), 176–82; Mark A. Burkholder, "Honor and Honors in Colonial Spanish America," in *The Faces of Honor. Sex, Shame, and Violence in Colonial Latin America,* ed. Lyman Johnson and Sonya Lipsett-Rivera (Albuquerque, 1999), 18–44, esp. 29, 33; Pitt-Rivers, "Honor and Social Status," 54–55; and John L. Phelan, "The Ceremonial and Political Roles of Cities in Colonial Spanish America," University of Wisconsin–Milwaukee Center for Latin American Studies, Discussion Paper No. 41, March 1972.
26. Arzáns de Orsúa y Vela, *Tales of Potosí,* 178, 188, 191; for an excellent discussion of public rituals regarding state officials in eighteenth-century Chihuahua see Martin, *Governance and Society in Colonial Mexico,* chap. 5.
27. Phelan, "The Ceremonial and Political Roles of Cities"; Martin, *Governance and Society in Colonial Mexico,* 97–124. See also Pitt-Rivers, "Honor and Social Status," 54–55.
28. Felipe de Vergara Azcárate de Avila, Caycedo y Vélez, Ladrón de Guevara, *Relación genealógica* (Bogotá, 1962) [1810?], 85–236, esp. 81, 88, 133–34.
29. Socolow, *Bureaucrats of Buenos Aires,* chap. 7, esp. 202–03.
30. See Richard Konetzke, ed., *Colección de documentos para la historia de la formación social hispanoamericana,* 5 vols. (Madrid, 1962), docs. 213, 227, 238, 250, 252, 262, 271, 309, 310, 357; Dewitt S. Chandler, *Social Assistance and Bureaucratic Politics: The Montepíos of Colonial Mexico, 1767–1821* (Albuquerque, 1991), chap. 3, esp. 34, 38; Socolow, *Bureaucrats of Buenos Aires,* chap. 7.
31. Socolow, *Bureaucrats of Buenos Aires,* 74, 79, 86, 89, 92–93.
32. Barbier, *Reform and Politics in Bourbon Chile;* Uribe, "The Lawyers and New Granada's Late Colonial State."
33. Some refer to this as the convertibility of the power of rank into the power of cash. See Peristany and Pitt-Rivers eds., *Honor and Grace in Anthropology,* 5.
34. See Weber, "Class, Status and Party"; and, Arthur Marwick, ed., *Class in the Twentieth Century* (New York, 1986), 3; see also Roland Mousnier, *Les Hierarchies Sociales* (Paris, 1969), 13–14, chap. 1; idem, *Social Hierarchies, 1450 to the Present* (New York, 1973). I thank Professor Howard Kaminsky for bringing Mousnier's work to my attention.
35. For interpretations of colonial social stratification mostly in terms of social class see Brooke Larson, *Colonialism and Agrarian Transformation in Bolivia: Cochabamba, 1550–1900* (Princeton, 1988); Alida C. Metcalf, *Family and Frontier in Colonial Brazil Santana de Parnaíba, 1580–1822* (Berkeley, 1992). On the difficulties of applying the concept of social class to the colonial context see Nutini, *Wages of Conquest,* 269–72. For a dynamic model of stratification incorporating class, status, and power see John K. Chance, *Race and Class in Colonial Oaxaca* (Stanford, 1978).
36. For the comparable continuity of honor cultures in pre- and postrevolutionary France see Robert A. Nye, "Honor Codes in Modern France. A Historical Anthropology," *Ethnologia Europaea* 21 (1991): 5–17; and, Reddy, *The Invisible Code.*
37. Those who favor this periodization include Borah, Van Young, Carmagnani, Johnson, and Andrien. See introduction's note 9. An even longer period is favored by Szuchman, ed., *The Middle Period in Latin American History,* esp. 11–13, 18. See also works cited in the Introduction, note 21.
38. I use the term "status" in the Weberian fashion, that is, as "social esteem" derived from education and the occupational or family prestige of certain individuals. See

Wolfang Schluchter, *The Rise of Western Rationalism: Max Weber's Developmental History* (Berkeley, 1981), chap. 4, 25–81.
39. For an insightful critique of class interpretations of postcolonial politics see Safford, "Politics, Ideology and Society," esp. 370–71. For comparative references see William M. Reddy, *Money and Liberty in Modern Europe: A Critique of Historical Understanding* (Cambridge, 1987).
40. This partly resembles Safford's suggestion that an individual's social location may have determined his political affiliation. See Safford, "Bases of Political Alignment," 102; idem, "Aspectos sociales de la política," 183–99; and Fondo Cultural Cafetero, *Aspectos polémicos de la historia colombiana del siglo XIX* (Bogotá, 1983), 16–17.
41. For Weber's views on "material" and "ideal" interests see Schluchter, *The Rise of Western Rationalism,* 24–30. For an akin thesis concerning the connections of social status and political affiliation in Mexico see Stevens, *Origins of Instability.*
42. See, for instance, Jay Kinsbruner, *Independence in Spanish American: Civil Wars, Revolutions and Underdevelopment* (Albuquerque, 1994); François-Xavier Guerra, *Modernidad e independencias* (Madrid, 1992).
43. See Costeloe, *The Central Republic.*
44. See Victor M. Uribe, "The Birth of the Public Sphere in Spanish America During the Age of Revolution," *Comparative Studies in Society and History,* forthcoming.
45. Graham, *Patronage and Politics,* 6–7.
46. On this point besides Marxist works see Reddy, *Money and Liberty,* 112.
47. See Paul Gootenberg, *Between Silver and Guano: Commercial Policy and the State in Postindependence Peru* (Princeton, 1989); Di Tella, *National Popular Politics,* chap. 7.
48. José A. Ocampo, "Librecambio y proteccionismo en el siglo XIX," in *Crisis mundial, proteccionismo e industrialización. Ensayos de historia económica de Colombia,* ed. José A. Ocampo and Santiago Montenegro (Bogotá, 1984), 235–84.
49. See Frank Safford, "Commercial Crisis and Economic Ideology in New Granada, 1825–1850," in *América Latina en la época de Simón Bolívar: La formación de las economías nacionales y los intereses económicos europeos 1800–1850,* ed. Reinhard Liehr (Berlin, 1989), 183–206.
50. See Safford, "Commerce and Enterprise."
51. Stevens, *Origins of Instability,* 115.
52. Costelo, *The Central Republic,* 58; Graham, *Patronage and Politics.*
53. For references to negative views on *empleomanía* in other regions during the 1830s and beyond see Charles Hale, *Mexican Liberalism in the Age of Mora, 1821–1853* (New Haven, 1968); Graham, *Patronage and Politics,* 213, 335; Dain Borges, *The Family in Bahia, Brazil 1870–1945* (Stanford, 1992), 263–65; Costeloe, *The Central Republic,* 16.
54. Di Tella, *National Popular Politics,* 247.
55. See Charles Bergquist, *Coffee and Conflict in Colombia* (Durham, 1978).

Chapter 2
The Lawyers and the Late Colonial State

1. José I. Avellaneda, *The Conquerors of the New Kingdom of Granada* (Albuquerque, 1995), 133; Ricardo Levene, "Notas para la historia de los abogados en Indias," *Revista Chilena de Historia del Derecho* 1 (1959): 9–12; idem, *Historia del derecho argentino* (Buenos Aires, 1946), 2:461–63; 3:411–75. See other sources listed in Jaime del Arenal Fenochio, "De abogados y leyes en las Indias hasta la Recopilación de 1680," in *Recopilación de las leyes de los Reynos de las Indias,* 5 vols. (Mexico, 1987), 5:179–206.

2. Antonio B. Cuervo, *Colección de documentos inéditos sobre la geografía y la historia de Colombia*, 2 vols. (Bogotá, 1892), 2:363; Jesús Antolines Wilches, "Primeros abogados españoles que vinieron al Nuevo Reino de Granada," *Boletín de Historia y Antiguedades* (hereafter *BHA*) 22, 239-40 (1934): 217-22; Parra Márquez, *Historia del Colegio de Abogados*, 66-67; Javier Malagón Barceló, "The Role of the *Letrado* in the Colonization of America," *The Americas* 18, 1 (1961): 1-17.
3. Avellaneda, *Conquerors of the New Kingdom*, Chapt. 5; David Bushnell, *The Making of Modern Colombia: A Nation in Spite of Itself* (Berkeley, 1993), 9-10.
4. "Pleito seguido por el licenciado Gallego y sus herederos contra el licenciado Jiménez de Quezada," [1539] *BHA* 23, 259-60 (April-May 1936): 297-302.
5. Del Arenal Fenochio, "De abogados y leyes," 184-88.
6. James Lockhart, *Spanish Peru, 1532-1560* (Madison, 1968), 61-62; Richard L. Kagan, *Lawsuits and Litigants in Castile, 1700-1750* (Chapel Hill, 1981), 190.; Alexandra Parma Cook and Noble David Cook, *Good Faith and Truthful Ignorance: A Case of Transatlantic Bigamy* (Durham, 1991), 81.
7. Ruiz Guiñazú, *La magistratura indiana*, 335-36; Antolines Wilches, "Primeros abogados," 217-22.
8. Francisco A. Moreno y Escandón, "Método provisional e interino de los estudios que han de observar los colegios de Santafé . . . 1774," *BHA* 23, 264-65 (1936): 644-73, esp. 644-45; John L. Young, "University Reform in New Granada, 1820-1850" (Ph.D. diss., Columbia University, 1970), 21.
9. Up to 1691, Bogotá's Colegio del Rosario seems to have produced only three lawyers, two of whom were also priests. See Guillermo Hernández de Alba, *Crónica del muy ilustre Colegio Mayor de Nuestra Señora del Rosario*, 2 vols. (Bogotá, 1938), 1:223.
10. Renán Silva, *Universidad y sociedad*, 43; Guillermo Hernández de Alba, "Breve historia de la universidad en Colombia," *BHA* 28, 322 (1941): 911-17.
11. Francisco A. Moreno y Escandón, "Documento sobre el exceso de abogados" [1771], Biblioteca Luis Angel Arango (hereafter BLAA), Bogotá, Documentos, 1; Jorge O. Melo, "Francisco A. Moreno y Escandón: retrato de un burócrata colonial," in *Indios y mestizos en la Nueva Granada a finales del siglo XVIII*, ed. Jorge O. Melo (Bogotá, 1985); Anthony McFarlane, *Colombia Before Independence. Economy, Society and Politics Under Bourbon Rule* (Cambridge, 1993), 205-07, 239.
12. Thomas Blossom, *Nariño: Hero of Colombian Independence* (Tucson, 1967), xvii; Frank Safford, *The Ideal of the Practical: Colombia's Struggle to Form a Technical Elite* (Austin, 1976), 88.
13. Concerning these and some other Bourbon policies see Phelan, *The People and the King;* Luís Martínez Delgado, *Noticia biográfica del prócer Don Joaquín Camacho. Documentos* (Bogotá, n.d.), 290; John Fisher, Anthony McFarlane, and Allan J. Kuethe, eds., *Reform and Insurrection in Bourbon New Granada and Peru* (Baton Rouge, 1990); Margarita Garrido, *Reclamos y representaciones: Variaciones sobre la política en el Nuevo Reino de Granada* (Bogotá, 1993), 55-71.
14. Moreno y Escandón, "Documento sobre el exceso," 6; José A. Ortega Ricaurte, "Compendio de lo actuado sobre estudios públicos" [1783], *BHA* 24, 272 (1937): 343-71; Renán Silva, *La reforma de estudios en el Nuevo Reino de Granada, 1767-1790* (Bogotá, 1981).
15. Francisco Silvestre, *Descripción del reyno de Santafé de Bogotá* [1789] (Bogotá, 1968), 116. See also his *Relación de la Provincia de Antioquia* [1786-1797] (Medellín, 1988); and José M. Restrepo, *Gobernadores de Antioquia* (Bogotá, 1944), 1:205-15. Impressionistic and inaccurate memoirs and obituaries written by the descendants of some

of the period's lawyers claim that by the 1780s and 1790s there were some "16 or 20 lawyers in Bogotá," or a very "scarce number" of legal professionals. Juan F. Ortíz, *Reminiscencias de D. Juan Francisco Ortíz* [1861] (Bogotá, 1907), 14; "Relación de las exequias hechas en la ciudad de Buga el 18 de agosto de 1850" (Bogotá, n.d.), DBNC, F. Pineda, 257.
16. Silva, *Universidad y sociedad,* 209; see Appendix 1.
17. See Appendix 1.
18. A study of all the *procesillos* followed in the *colegios mayores* of New Granada cites examples of students (i.e., sons of a wax trader, a baker, and a goldsmith) whose admission was questioned because of their fathers' economic activity. Silva, *Universidad y sociedad,* 215–16. See also the July 14, 1768 royal order in *Colección de documentos,* ed. Richard Konetzke (Madrid, 1962), 2:340.
19. Archivo Histórico Nacional de Colombia, Bogotá (hereafter AHN), Anexo, Instrucción Pública, 4:366–441.
20. Silva, *Universidad y sociedad,* 200–27.
21. In July 1804, a royal *cédula* abolished the Colegio de San Bartolomé's privilege of protecting the reasons for rejecting an applicant. AHN, Anexo, Instrucción Pública, 4:372.
22. AHN, Colegios, 2:231–63; John Tate Lanning, "Documents. The Case of José Ponceano de Ayarza: A Document on the Negro in Higher Education," *HAHR* 24, 3 (August 1944): 432–51, esp. 436. In New Spain during the late eighteenth century applicants with "strains of black or Indian blood in their families" were also admitted to law school after some litigation. See John E. Kicza, "The Legal Community of Late Colonial Mexico: Social Composition and Career Patterns," in *Five Centuries of Law and Politics in Central Mexico,* ed. Ross Hassig and Ronald Spores (Nashville, 1984), 127–44, esp 131.
23. See the July 23, 1765 royal *cédula* in *Colección de documentos,* ed. Richard Konetzke (Madrid, 1962), 2:331.
24. Cuervo, *Colección de documentos,* 2:372; AHN, Colegios, 2:231–63; Lanning, "Documents. The Case of José Ponceano de Ayarza"; "Aranjuez, 16 de marzo de 1797. Real cédula dispensando a Pedro Antonio de Ayarza la calidad de Pardo," in *Colección de documentos,* ed. Richard Konetzke (Madrid, 1962), 2:757.
25. Twinam, *Miners, Merchants;* María T. Uribe and Jesús M. Alvarez, "El parentesco y la formación de las élites en la Provincia de Antioquia," *Estudios Sociales,* Fundación Antioqueña para los Estudios Sociales (FAES), vol. 3 (1988): 51–93. On the upward social mobility of *pardos* from the 1760s and beyond see comparative comments by Robin Blackburn, *The Overthrow of Colonial Slavery, 1776–1848* (London, 1988), 335–36.
26. Appendix 1; Kicza, "The Legal Community," 5–7. For documents and fragmentary analyses on Argentina and Venezuela: see Carlos A. Luque Colombres, *Abogados en Córdoba del Tucumán* (Córdoba, 1943); and Cutolo, *Abogados y escribanos;* Héctor García Chuecos, *Abogados de la colonia* (Caracas, 1958); idem, *Los abogados de la colonia* (Caracas, 1965).
27. Martínez Recamán, through his father's modest connections, bought his way up to the middling job of *asesor* of the Bogotá Cajas Reales by the late 1780s. Gamba Valencia rose to high posts after the revolution. See DBNC, F. Pineda, 1066:127; Antonio García de la Guardia, *Kalendario manual y guía de forasteros en Santafé de Bogotá capital del Nuevo Reino de Granada para el año de 1806* (Bogotá, 1988), 172; Gustavo Arboleda, *Diccionario biográfico y genealógico del antiguo Departamento del Cauca*

(Bogotá, 1962), 173; Manuel Uribe Angel, "Recuerdos de un viaje a Medellín," *BHA* 2, 17 (January 1904): 281–306; Benjamín Pereira Gamba, "Miguel Gamba," *BHA* 3, 34 (1906): 621–25. On upward and downward social mobility in New Spain see David Brading, "Government and Elite in Late Colonial Mexico," *HAHR* 53 (August 1973), esp. 396.
28. "Padrón general de esta capital según los que se hicieron en 1793," *La Bagatela,* Santafé de Bogotá, October 1, 1853, 79.
29. José M. Restrepo, *Historia de la revolución de la república de Colombia* (Bogotá, 1942), 1:xxxviii.
30. Villamarín, "The Concept of Nobility," 138.
31. See Charles Harris, *A Mexican Family Empire: The Latifundio of the Sánchez Navarro Family, 1765–1867* (Austin, 1975), 11–17; Paul Ganster, "A Social History of the Secular Clergy of Lima During the Middle Decades of the Eighteenth Century," (Ph.D. diss., University of California, Los Angeles, 1974); Taylor, *Magistrates of the Sacred,* chap. 6 and Appendix A.
32. Allan J. Kuethe, *Military Reform and Society in New Granada* (Gainesville, 1978), 205–06; Juan Marchena Fernández, "The Social World of the Military in Peru and New Granada," in *Reform and Insurrection,* ed. Fisher, Kuethe, and McFarlane (Baton Rouge, 1990), 61–62.
33. Juan Marchena Fernández, "The Social World," 84.
34. A good social profile of both New Granada's army and militia can be found in Marchena Fernández, "The Social World," 83–95.
35. "Relación de gobierno del Exmo Sor., D. Joséf de Ezpeleta" [1796], in *Relaciones e informes de los gobernantes de la Nueva Granada,* ed. Germán Colmenares, 3 vols. (Bogotá, 1989), 2:224–25; "Relación . . . Virrey Pedro Mendinueta" [1803], ibid., 3:92.
36. Silva, *Universidad y sociedad,* 153. On doctors in other Spanish colonies see Hernández Sáenz, *Learning to Heal.*
37. José M. Restrepo, *Autobiografía. Apuntamientos sobre emigración de 1816, e índices del Diario Político* [1816–1818] (Bogotá, 1957), 10.
38. Lanning, "Documents. The Case of José Ponceano de Ayarza," 432–51; Andrés Soriano Lleras, *La medicina en el Nuevo Reino de Granada durante la conquista y la colonia* (Bogotá, 1975), 260–87; Thomas Glick, "Science and Independence in Latin America (with Special Reference to New Granada)," *HAHR* 71, 2 (May 1991): 307–33, esp. 323.
39. García de la Guardia, *Kalendario manual.*
40. Ibid., 57–72. This 1806 list does not include prominent lawyers of New Granada, such as José María del Real (1767–1835), and *oidores* Joaquín Mosquera y Figueroa (1747–1830), and Manuel del Campo y Rivas (1750–1830), who had graduated in New Granada in the early 1770s and 1790s and were still alive by the time the list was compiled. A few others from Popayán, Cali, and Buga, who had graduated in and belonged to Quito's royal audiencia, are not registered here, and a couple of Antioqueño lawyers are missing as well. Arboleda, *Diccionario biográfico;* Patiño M., *Criminalidad, ley penal y estructura social,* 164–73. In spite of these omissions, it is unlikely that the total exceeded 150.
41. In the late seventeenth century and during a great part of the eighteenth priests outnumbered lawyers, but by the end of the colonial period the correlation was slowly shifting in favor of lawyers. Silva, *Universidad y sociedad,* 152, 318; Villamarín, "Concept of Nobility."
42. AHN, Notaria 1a., Bogotá, vol. 13; Notaria 2a., vols. 9–11; Notaria 3a., vols. 2, 4–5.

Litigation over refusals to address others as *don* or *doña* was common during the second half of the eighteenth century. See AHN, Juicios Criminales, 54:1–366; 76:856–70; AHN, Colonia, Genealogías, passim, 3 vols.; Twinam, *Miners, Merchants,* 119; Jaramillo Uribe, "Mestizaje y diferenciación social en el Nuevo Reino de Granada," 196–203; Patiño, *Criminalidad, ley penal y estructura social,* 197–247; Garrido, *Reclamos y representaciones,* 217–26.

43. AHN, Médicos y Abogados, 2:384, 235, 391; Agustín Bermúdez, "La abogacia de pobres en Indias," *Anuario de Historia del Derecho Español,* vol. 50 (1980).
44. Carta de Jerónimo Torres a su hermano Camilo, Popayán, October 20, 1807, in "Datos para la biografía de Camilo Torres," *Repertorio Colombiano* 20, 3 (1899): 183–210. See also "Torres y Tenorio Jerónimo," *BHA* 2, 5 (1903): 135–48; Enrique Alvarez Bonilla, "Los tres Torres," *BHA* 3, 26 (February 1905): 65–82.
45. AHN, Notaria 1a., fol. 142. On the activities and profits of lawyer Joaquín Ortíz Tagle, who served Bogotá's local convents see Ortíz, *Reminiscencias,* 14.
46. AHN, Notaria 1a., fols. 200, 281. It was also customary for lay members of society in pursuit of a bureaucratic appointment to be represented by a lawyer. See ibid., fol. 213; and letters from Miguel Tadeo Gómez to Joaquín Camacho, in Martínez Delgado, *Noticia biográfica,* 288–89.
47. Julio C. Vergara y Vergara, *Don Antonio de Vergara Azcárate y sus descendientes,* 2 vols. (Madrid, 1952), 1:140; Adolfo L. Gómez, *El tribuno de 1810* (Bogotá, 1910), 236; Francisco de P. Plazas, *Genealogías de la provincia de Neiva* (Bogotá, 1985), 112; Ramón Correa, "Jorge Ramón de Posada," *BHA* 6, 61 (1909), 11–29; Camilo Pardo Umaña, *Haciendas de la sabana* (Bogotá, 1988), 77–81. For examples of priests' litigation, see AHN, Notaria 1a., fol. 280, 360; Horacio Rodríguez Plata, *Andrés María Rosillo y Meruelo* (Bogotá, 1944), 30–35, 38–39.
48. Rafael Abello Salcedo, "La primera república," *BHA* 37, 441–43 (1951): 423–53. See also González Llorente's 1808 will in *El 20 de Julio. Capítulos sobre la revolución de 1810,* ed. Eduardo Posada (Bogotá, 1914), 63–69.
49. To Camilo's bitter references to "*el oficio esteril de defender pleitos de goteras,*" Jerónimo responded, "You are very right to lament being a lawyer, and having to perform so many partly if not wholly unproductive legal occupations in our poor [*misérrimo*] country." "Carta de Jerónimo," 192.
50. Miguel Tadeo Gómez to Joaquín Camacho, July 3, 1803, in Martínez Delgado, *Noticia biográfica,* 277–78; see also Horacio Rodríguez Plata, *La antigua Provincia del Socorro y la independencia* (Bogotá, 1963), 182.
51. AHN, Médicos y Abogados, 3:235, 251.
52. See a comprehensive discussion of this region's economy, society, and politics in McFarlane, *Colombia Before Independence,* esp. 39–95.
53. Antonio Nariño, "Ensayo sobre un nuevo plan de administración en el Nuevo Reino de Granada," [1797], in José M. Vergara y Vergara, *Vida y escritos del General Nariño,* 2d ed. (Bogotá, 1946), 88–89.
54. See Pedro M. Carreño, "Atavismo litigioso," *BHA* 31, 355–56 (1944): 556–62; Alejandro B. Carranza, *San Dionisio de los Caballeros de Tocaima* (Bogotá, 1941), 221. For similar complains about excessive litigation in the city of Mompós two decades earlier see Francisco A. Moreno y Escandón, "Estado del Virreinato de Santafé, Nuevo Reino de Granada y relación de su gobierno y mando ... 1772," *BHA* 23, 264–65 (Sept.–Oct., 1936): 547–616. Historical roots of New Granada's litigiousness may be found in early-sixteenth-century Castile, a very litigious society. Kagan, *Lawsuits and Litigants,* 3–20.

55. José I. Pombo, "Informe de don José Ignacio de Pombo del Consulado de Cartagena sobre asuntos económicos y fiscales, abril 18, 1807," in *Escritos de dos economistas coloniales,* ed. Sergio E. Ortíz (Bogotá, 1965), 132.
56. For trials against late colonial *tinterillos* see AHN, Juicios Criminales, vol. 60, fols. 994–1000; vol. 75, fols. 600–67.
57. These complaints, presented around 1807 by Antioqueño lawyer Pantaleón Arango, were followed by an 1809 petition arguing that since he had practiced medicine for a number of years, he wished to have a license to devote himself entirely to this profession. The license and a degree were granted in early 1810. AHN, Médicos y Abogados, 3:235, 251.
58. AHN, Anexo, Instrucción Pública, 4:474. For the role of some of these functionaries in sixteenth-century Peru and Mexico and in colonial Venezuela see Lockhart, *Spanish Peru,* chaps. 4, 6; Del Arenal Fenochio, "De abogados y leyes," 191–93; Nieves Avellán de Tamayo, *Los escribanos de Venezuela* (Caracas, 1994).
59. AHN, Médicos y Abogados, 3:235, 251. The oldest example found in the Colombian archives is the "Guía para dirigir jueces" written in 1764 by the priest Pedro de Moya. AHN, Ortega Ricaurte, caja 2. The Spanish manuals like the 1618 "Práctica de procuradores para seguir pleitos civiles y criminales," written by Juan Muñóz, were very likely brought to the New World. Kagan, *Lawsuits and Litigants,* 46.
60. "Relación de los méritos y servicios del doctor Pedro Romero Sarachaga . . . 1777." DBNC, F. Pineda, 372. On Francisco Gaona de la Bastida, Francisco Sanz de Santamaría, José María García de Toledo, and José Caicedo y Flórez, lawyers whose major activities revolved around landownership and livestock raising, see Appendix 1. Lawyer-landowners were also typical of colonial Peru. See Susan E. Ramírez, *Provincial Patriarchs: Land Tenure and the Economics of Power in Colonial Peru* (Albuquerque, 1985), 176.
61. Restrepo received from Uribe, who was in Antioquia, mules loaded with merchandise from Castile. From Popayán Restrepo in turn sent Uribe muleloads of cacao and ponchos made in the southern region of Pasto. See Guillermo Hernández de Alba, *Vida y escritos del Doctor José F. Restrepo* (Bogotá, 1935); Estanislao Gómez Barrientos, *Don Mariano Ospina y se época,* 2 vols. (Medellín, 1913) 1:48.
62. In his memoirs he observed that he would dedicate himself to legal practice "*porque no tenía patrimonio para emprender otro modo de mejorar su fortuna*" ("because he did not have any economic means to try to improve his fortunes otherwise"). Restrepo, *Autobiografía,* 10–11, emphasis added.
63. Ernesto Restrepo Tirado, "Notas genealógicas sobre algunos individuos que honraron la Nueva Granada," *BHA* 31, 353–54 (March-April 1944): 322–50; García de la Guardia, *Kalendario manual,* 57–72. A few examples are Ignacio María Tordecillas, Nicolás Mauricio Omaña, Andrés Rosillo y Meruelo, Fray José Joaquín Escobar, Santiago Torres Peña, Pedro Salgar, and Manuel B. Rebollo. Besides being parish priests or occupying other positions in the church hierarchy, some of these men were rich landowners. Rodríguez Plata, *Andrés María Rosillo;* Pardo Umaña, *Haciendas de la sabana,* 77–81; Appendix 1.
64. Burkholder, *Politics of a Colonial Career,* 46.
65. Ibid., 45–46.
66. DBNC, F. Pineda, 1066:238–589; Burkholder, "Relaciones de Méritos y Servicios," 97–104; García Valdecasas, *El hidalgo y el honor,* 8, 17, 57–60; Rivers, "Honor and Social Status," 21–77; Twinam, "Honor, Sexuality, and Illegitimacy," 123; Garrido, *Reclamos y representaciones,* 35; McFarlane, *Colombia Before Independence,* 238–45.

67. John Lynch, "The Institutional Framework of Colonial Spanish America," *JLAS,* Suppl. (1992), 74; Garrido, *Reclamos y representaciones,* 35, 71–76.
68. Twinam, *Miners, Merchants;* Julian Vargas, *La Sociedad de Santafé colonial* (Bogotá, 1989), 234; Patiño, *Criminalidad, ley penal y estructura social,* 147–64.
69. Ots y Capdequí, *Las instituciones del Nuevo Reino de Granada,* 23; Miguel T. Gómez to Joaquín Camacho, July 1803, in Martínez Delgado, *Noticia biográfica,* 278; Carranza, *San Dionisio,* 222; Appendix 1.
70. Guillermo Hernández de Alba (comp.), *Archivo Nariño* 6 vols. (Bogotá, 1990), 1:44; Ots y Capdequí, *Instituciones,* 23, 29, 90; Sergio E. Ortíz, "Eusebio María Canabal," *BHA* 63 (1971): 15; Burkholder, *Politics of a Colonial Career,* 112; José Camacho Carrizosa, "Hombres y partidos," *Repertorio Histórico* 14, 4 (1896): 267. The scale of salaries in the Royal Mint of Bogotá, suggests that high bureaucrats earned between 2,000 and 4,000 pesos a year; middle bureaucrats between 600 and 2,000 pesos; and lower bureaucrats below 600 pesos. Manual workers, such as *peones,* earned as little as 144 pesos a year. A. M. Barriga V., *Historia de la Casa de la Moneda* (Bogotá, 1969), 2:116–17; see also Francisco J. Caro, "Diario de todos los acontecimientos que van ocurriendo en esta cámara y del Virreynato del Nuevo Reyno de Granada," [1788] in Alirio Gómez Picón, *Francisco Javier Caro. Tronco hispano de los Caros en Colombia* (Bogotá, 1977), 292, 296. For comparative salaries in Mexico and Rio de la Plata see Arnold, *Bureaucrats and Bureaucracy in Mexico,* 131–52; Socolow, *Bureaucrats of Buenos Aires,* 110–11, 166–67.
71. One of them, Nicolás Mesía Caicedo, was *oidor* in Manila; two more, Joaquín Mosquera y Figueroa and Manuel del Campo y Rivas, in Mexico; another, Luis de Robledo y Alvarez, in Santo Domingo; and three more, Francisco Xavier Moreno y Escandón, Ignacio Tenorio and Andrés José de Iriarte y Rojas, were in Quito, the first two as *oidores,* the third as *fiscal.* García de la Guardia, *Kalendario manual;* Mark Burkholder and D. S. Chandler, *From Impotence to Authority: The Spanish Crown and the American Audiencias, 1687–1808* (Columbia, 1977); José M. Restrepo, *Biografías de los mandatarios y ministros de la Real Audiencia (1671–1819)* (Bogotá, 1952); Arboleda, *Diccionario biográfico,* 426; José Antonio Torres Peña, *Memorias sobre los orígenes de la independencia nacional* (Bogotá, 1960).
72. Restrepo, *Autobiografía,* 11. A copy of the late colonial "Práctico arancel de regular costas procesales" can be found in AHN, Consejo de Estado, 1:28–35.
73. AHN, Notaria 1a., Escr. January 3, 1810, fols. 1–2.
74. Enrique Ortega Ricaurte, ed., *Proceso histórico del 20 de Julio* (Bogotá, 1960), 12; Eustaquio Galavís, "Relación exacta y circunstanciada de todos los empleos políticos . . . 1787," in Ulises Rojas, *Corregidores y justicias mayores de Tunja y su provincia desde la fundación de la ciudad hasta 1817* (Tunja, 1962), 578–88; Archivo Histórico de Tunja, vol. 318, fols. 407–13.
75. Barbier, *Reform and Politics in Bourbon Chile;* Uribe, "The Lawyers and New Granada's Late Colonial State."
76. Bendix, *Nation Building and Citizenship,* 39; Morse, "The Heritage of Latin America," 123–77; Sarfatti, *Spanish Bureaucratic-Patrimonialism in America;* Spalding, *Essays on the Political, Economic and Social History;* Lynch, "Institutional Framework."

Chapter 3
Family Networks and Colonial Stability

1. For views that the reforms succeeded and were a "revolution in government," see David A. Brading, *Miners and Merchants in Bourbon Mexico, 1763–1810* (Cambridge, 1971), esp. Part 1 and Epilogue; and John S. Leiby, *Colonial Bureaucrats and the Mexican Economy: Growth of a Patrimonial State, 1763–1821* (New York, 1985), chaps. 6 and 7, esp. 133. Opposite views are held by Barbier, *Reform and Politics in Bourbon Chile;* John Kicza, *Colonial Entrepreneurs: Families and Business in Bourbon Mexico City* (Albuquerque, 1983), 34–38, 93, 159–61; Linda Salvucci, "'Costumbres viejas, hombres nuevos': José de Gálvez y la burocracia fiscal novohispana (1754–1800)," *Historia Mexicana* 33, 2 (October-December 1983): 224–64; Stanley J. Stein, "Bureaucracy and Business in the Spanish Empire, 1759–1804: Failure of a Bourbon Reform in Mexico and Peru," *HAHR* 61, 1 (1981): 2–28. Mixed views are proposed by Socolow, *The Bureaucrats of Buenos Aires;* Arnold, *Bureaucracy and Bureaucrats in Mexico*, 18, 20, 90, 119–21; and Deans-Smith, *Bureaucrats, Planters, and Workers,* esp. chap. 7.
2. The same seems to have been true for Buenos Aires's bureaucrats. Socolow, *Bureaucrats of Buenos Aires,* 196–99.
3. The cases of Francisco Antonio Moreno y Escandón and Manuel del Campo y Rivas roughly fit this description, except that the latter remained a bachelor his entire life. Others, like Francisco de Tordecillas, had less successful careers. Rojas, *Corregidores y justicias mayores,* 597; Vergara y Vergara, *Don Antonio de Vergara Azcárate,* 1:131–80; Appendix 1. The mechanics of some of the appointment processes are discussed by Burkholder, *Politics of a Colonial Career,* 30–43.
4. In 1787 Mosquera y Figueroa became the only native creole appointed to the Bogotá audiencia in the entire eighteenth century, with the exception of Juan Ortega Ricaurte, who served as interim *oidor* for a short period in April 1718. Arcesio Aragón, "Un regente de España, nacido en Popayán, en el Nuevo Reino de Granada," *Revista de Indias* 36 (1949): 307–11; Restrepo, *Biografías de los mandatarios,* 337–38; Burkholder and Chandler, *From Impotence to Authority.*
5. See the example of the creole Flórez clan who, through positions in the cathedral, the fiscal bureaucracy, and the *audiencia,* built a strong network of power in the early eighteenth century. Germán Colmenares, "Factores de la vida política: el Nuevo Reino de Granada en el siglo XVIII (1730–1740)," in *Manual de historia de Colombia* (Bogotá, 1982), 1:395–402.
6. One of his sisters was married to Pedro Romero Sarachaga, *escribano de cámara* of the local *audiencia* from 1766 to at least 1777 and wealthy landowner. José M. Restrepo and Raimundo Rivas, *Genealogías de Santafé de Bogotá* (Bogotá, 1928); "Relación de los méritos . . . Pedro Romero Sarachaga," DBNC, F. Pineda, 372; also Figure 3.2.
7. Francisco Gaona de la Bastida (1755–1799), Caicedo's father-in-law, owned at least two valuable *haciendas*. Pardo Umaña, *Haciendas de la sabana,* 164, 215–16.
8. Restrepo and Rivas, *Genealogías de Santafé,* 165; Sandra Montgomery, "The Bourbon Mining Reform in New Granada," in *Reform and Insurrection,* ed. Fisher, Kuethe and McFarlane (Baton Rouge, 1990), 51–53.
9. Caicedo was suspended from the legal profession after being implicated in a conspiracy in the mid-1790s. See Germán Pérez Sarmiento, ed., *Causas célebres a los precursores . . . copias fieles y exactas de los originales que se guardan en el Archivo de Indias* [Sevilla], 2 vols. (Bogotá, 1939), 1:92.
10. See also the case of the young lawyer José Valdés, who arrived in New Granada in

early 1809 with the position of *corregidor* of the important region of Socorro and was promoted to *oidor* of Guatemala in less than a decade. Rodríguez Plata, *La antigua provincia,* 190–93.

11. Antonio Benito del Casal y Freiria served in Tunja from 1733 to at least 1738. He was also appointed *teniente capitán general* during these years and was finally transferred to Maracaibo in 1740 as *gobernador y comandante general.* Rojas, *Corregidores y justicias,* 507; Restrepo and Rivas, *Genealogías de Santafé,* 225–26; Hermes Tovar Pinzón, "El estado colonial frente al poder local y regional," *Nova Americana* 5 (1982): 39–77, esp. 51.

12. John L. Phelan, "El auge y la caída de los criollos en la Audiencia de la Nueva Granada," *BHA* 49, 697–98 (1972): 597–618, esp. 607; idem, *People and the King,* 14, 21; Tovar Pinzón, "El estado colonial," 51; Restrepo and Rivas, *Genealogías de Santafé,* 17–23; Hernández de Alba, *Archivo Nariño,* vol. 1; McFarlane, *Colombia Before Independence,* 238–45.

13. Twinam, *Miners, Merchants;* Germán Colmenares, *Cali: terratenientes, mineros y comerciantes. Siglo XVIII* (Bogotá, 1983); José D. Moscot and Enrique Arce, *La vida ejemplar de Justo Arosemena* (Panama, 1956). In Cartagena, the high status of merchants José Miguel Pombo and José María García de Toledo underscores the increasing power of this economic group. See Gabriel Jiménez Molinares, *Linajes cartageneros,* 2 vols. (Cartagena, 1958), 2:3–69; Jorge O. Melo, "José Ignacio de Pombo," in *Comercio y contrabando en Cartagena de Indias. 2 de junio de 1800* (Bogotá, 1986), 7–10.

14. Restrepo, *Biografías de los mandatarios.* On marriage licenses, restrictions, and controls see AHN, Colonia, Genealogías, passim; Konetzke ed., *Colección de documentos,* passim, esp. docs. # 73, 134–35, 185, 193, 213, 252, 262, 271, 310, 335, 357; Chandler, *Social Assistance and Bureaucratic Politics,* chap. 3.

15. Stein, "Bureaucracy and Business in the Spanish Empire"; Barbier, *Reform and Politics in Bourbon Chile,* chaps. 8–9; Salvucci, "'Costumbres viejas, hombres nuevos'"; Kicza, *Colonial Entrepreneurs,* 34–38, 93, 159–61; Socolow, *Bureaucrats of Buenos Aires,* 193–228.

16. A recent evaluation of the reforms points out that in contrast to New Spain and Peru, the Bourbon reforms had a relatively minor impact in New Granada. Allan Kuethe, "The Early Reforms of Charles III in the Viceroyalty of New Granada, 1759–1776," in *Reform and Insurrection,* ed. Fisher, Kuethe and McFarlane, 19–53.

17. On elite families and the late colonial bureaucracy see also Phelan, "El auge y la caída"; José M. Uricoechea, "Noticias genealógicas," *BHA* 58, 675–677 (January-March 1971): 33–101; Tovar Pinzón, "El estado colonial"; Melo, "Retrato de un burócrata colonial"; Thomas Gómez, "La republica de los cuñados. Parentesco, familia y poder en la sociedad colonial: el caso de Santafé, siglo XVIII," *Politeia,* no. 12 (1993): 116–26; Jairo Gutiérrez Ramos, "Linaje y poder en la colonia: el caso de Santafé de Bogotá," *Politeia,* no. 12 (1993): 128–44.

18. One of Don José's early-nineteenth-century descendants left a detailed genealogical description of his family, titled "Relación genealógica de Felipe de Vergara Azcárate de Avila, Caicedo, Vélez, Ladrón de Guevara. . . ." See printed version in Felipe Vergara, *Relación genealógica,* 102.

19. See several examples in Restrepo and Rivas, *Genealogías de Santafé;* and also José María Caballero, *Particularidades de Santafé de Bogotá. Un diario de José Maria Caballero* (Bogotá, 1974), 131.

20. On Don José's *encomienda* see Juan Villamarín, "Encomenderos and Indians in the

Formation of Colonial Society in the Sabana de Bogotá, 1537 to 1740" (Ph.D. diss., Brandeis University, 1972), 389. For *corregidores'* typical careers see Rojas, *Corregidores y justicias mayores;* for general comments and references see Stein, "Bureaucracy and Business."

21. Richard Stoller, "Liberalism and Conflict in Socorro, Colombia, 1830-1870" (Ph.D. diss., Duke University, 1991), 31; Phelan, *The People and the King,* 39.

22. Moreno y Escandón, "Estado del Virreynato de Santafé," 547-616; Antonio Nariño, "Ensayo sobre un nuevo plan de administración en el Nuevo Reino de Granada," in *Vida y escritos del General Nariño,* ed. José M. Vergara (Bogotá, 1946), 75-76.

23. Gómez, *El tribuno,* 236; Harris, *A Mexican Family Empire;* Correa, "Jorge Ramón de Posada," 11-29; Plazas, *Genealogías de Neiva,* 112; Pardo Umaña, *Haciendas de la sabana,* 77-81.

24. His wife was Petronila Caicedo y Vélez. See Restrepo and Rivas, *Genealogías de Santafé,* 161-62; Pardo Umaña, *Haciendas de la sabana;* Villamarín, "Encomenderos and Indians," 338-47, 403-06; "Documentos históricos," *BHA* 6, 61 (July 1909): 30-41, esp. 31, 36.

25. Juan Flórez de Ocáriz, *Genealogías del Nuevo Reyno de Granada* [1674], (Bogotá, 1955), 2:103; 3:186-87; Vergara y Vergara, *Don Antonio de Vergara Azcárate,* 1:63; Villamarín, "Encomenderos and Indians," 388-89, 402, 410.

26. Uribe, "Lawyers and New Granada's Late Colonial State."

27. He married a daughter of Jorge Miguel Lozano de Peralta, a large landholder who held the title Marqués de San Jorge. Francisco de P. Plazas, "Los Marqueses de San Jorge," *BHA* 58, 678-80 (1971): 261-68; Vergara y Vergara, *Don Antonio Vergara Azcárate,* 1:139.

28. In 1806 Luis Ayala y Vergara was *oficial* of Bogotá's fiscal agency for *aguardiente y polvora* (liquor and gunpowder); Antonio was *contador* of Popayán's *alcabalas* or sales tax office in the mid-1790s; Pantaleón was the priest of Villa de Leiva in the mid-1790s. In 1800-1801 he came to serve in Bogotá. See Vergara y Vergara, *Antonio de Vergara Azcárate,* 1:222-25.

29. Vergara, *Relación genealógica,* 239; "Sanz de Santamaría," *BHA* 57, 666-68 (1970): 261-82; Vergara y Vergara, *Antonio Vergara Azcárate,* 1:223, 226; García de la Guardia, *Kalendario manual,* 203.

30. Vergara, *Relación genealógica,* 242.

31. In 1807 Tadeo, a lawyer, was *asesor* of Reales Rentas in Honda, a neighboring town of Bogotá; Isidro was *meritorio* in the Contaduría General after 1804 and by 1815 was *tesorero* of the royal mint; Francisco Gregorio was *oficial* in the Reales Cajas during the early 1810s. Vergara y Vergara, *Don Antonio Vergara Azcárate,* 2:13, 17, 40.

32. García de la Guardia, *Kalendario manual.*

33. Pérez Sarmiento ed., *Causas célebres,* 1:497-99; Appendix 1.

34. See José María Restrepo Sáenz, *Constituyentes de Tunja en 1811* (Bogotá, 1913), 43-46; Guillermo and Alfono Hernández de Alba, "Galería de hijos insignes," 141-439, esp. 386-87; Pardo Umaña, *Haciendas de la sabana,* 225-36. In 1809 the lawyer-priest Pedro Salgar similarly denounced anti-Spanish revolutionaries to the colonial authorities. In both instances it is likely that the two witnesses wanted to advance their bureaucratic and ecclesiastical careers.

35. See Pérez Sarmiento ed., *Causas célebres,* 2:204.

36. Pérez Sarmiento ed., *Causas célebres,* 1:371-74; 2: 202-07. See also Oswaldo Díaz Díaz, "Genealogía de don Antonio Nariño," in *Segundo centenario del nacimiento de don Antonio Nariño, 1765-1965* (Bogotá, 1965), 11-18; José María Restrepo Sáenz,

"La familia de Nariño," *BHA* 41, 473–74 (March-April 1954): 237–48; Blossom, *Nariño: Hero of Colombian Independence.*

37. Raimundo Rivas, *El andante caballero Don Antonio Nariño. Juventud (1765–1803)* (Bogotá, 1936), 105–35; Pérez Sarmiento, ed., *Causas célebres,* passim.
38. See January 22, 1795 "Testimonios . . . ," in Pérez Sarmiento, ed., *Causas célebres,* 2:207–10. The lawyer who first denounced the plot, Joaquín Umaña y López, had to abandon the city because of harassment by the elites. See February 1795 "Memorial . . . ," in Pérez Sarmiento, ibid., 2:202–07; Restrepo Sáenz, *Constituyentes de Tunja,* 45–46.
39. See Pardo Umaña, *Haciendas de la sabana,* 164, 215–16.
40. Caicedo was suspended from the legal profession due to his position during the trials of 1794–1795. See "Carta de la Audiencia . . . 19 Septiembre 1795," in Pérez Sarmiento, ed., *Causas célebres,* 1:92.
41. Probably he was not aware of how risky the case would turn out to be. The text of his controversial legal brief is presented in Vergara y Vergara, *Vida y escritos del General Antonio Nariño,* 7–64. See also Eduardo Posada, *El Precursor* (Bogotá, 1903), 51–110; and Guillermo Hernández de Alba, *El proceso contra Antonio Nariño por la publicación clandestina de la Declaración de los Derechos del Hombre y del Ciudadano,* 2 vols. (Bogotá, n.d.), 1:375–437. As for the unusually harsh treatment received by Nariño, see explanations in Anthony McFarlane, "Economic and Political Change in the Viceroyalty of New Granada, with Special Reference to Overseas Trade" (Ph.D. diss., The London School of Economics and Political Science, 1977), chap. 8; and Blossom,: *Nariño: Hero of Colombian Independence.*
42. Some of the defendants even had family ties to the creole investigator, *oidor* Mosquera. See Vergara y Vergara, *Don Antonio de Vergara y Azcárate,* 1:227.
43. See Guillermo Hernández de Alba, *El proceso de Nariño a la luz de documentos inéditos* (Bogotá, 1958).
44. Unlike his brother Ignacio, an *oidor* in Quito since 1808, Tomás was unsuccessful in his bureaucratic pretensions and by 1818 was still applying for good jobs in the colonial bureaucracy. See "Grados y méritos de Tomás Tenorio, 1818," DBNC, Pineda 1066; Arboleda, *Diccionario biográfico y genealógico,* 425–27; Hernández de Alba, *El proceso de Nariño a la luz de documentos inéditos.*
45. See Hernández de Alba, *El proceso de Nariño a la luz de documentos inéditos;* AHN, Médicos y Abogados, vol. 1:490–95; Restrepo Sáenz, *Biografías de los mandatarios y ministros,* 118, 342, 461; Tovar Pinzón, "El estado colonial," 51.
46. He had been *consultor* of Cartagena's Tribunal of the Inquisition, and also *defensor* of the rent of tithes during the 1770s or 1780s. From 1806 to 1809 he would serve as a provincial governor and in 1817 he was appointed *corregidor* of another region. García de la Guardia, *Kalendario manual;* José María Vergara y Vergara, *Historia de la literatura en el Nuevo Reino de Granada. 1790–1820,* 2 vols. (Bogotá, 1974), 2:267–69.
47. See Rojas, *Corregidores y justicias mayores,* 569–95; Pérez Sarmiento, ed., *Causas célebres,* passim; Alfonso Hernández Lesmes, "Una rectificación genealógica," *BHA* 4, 167 (March 1925): 690–99; "Los González Manrique," *BHA* 5, 72 (May 1911): 750–52; Phelan, *The People and the King,* 124. A sister of Galavís's wife was married to the lawyer Juan Vergara y Caicedo, brother of Felipe, Tadeo, and Francisco, all of them bureaucrats. The latter also refused to defend Nariño. See Vergara y Vergara, *Don Antonio de Vergara y Azcárate,* 1:142; Hernández de Alba, *El proceso de Nariño a la luz de documentos inéditos;* Figure 3.2.
48. Hernández de Alba, *El proceso de Nariño,* 239.
49. See Díaz Díaz, "Genealogía de don Antonio Nariño," 12; Rivas, *El andante caballero,* 5, 30, 96, 126; Figures 3.1 and 3.2.

50. Francisco Javier Sanz de Santamaría, Vergara's father-in-law, was very wealthy. Francisco's brothers were rich landowners as well. Two of his daughters married prominent lawyers and another married wealthy landowner Luis Caicedo y Flórez, brother of the lawyer José. His sons Joseph and Pantaleón were high bureaucrats. See "Sanz de Santamaría," 261–82.
51. See Figure 3.2; Julio C. Vergara y Vergara, *Vida de Estanislao Vergara, 1790–1855* (Bogotá, 1951); "Sanz de Santamaría."
52. See note 31. Isidro was still acting *treasurer* of Bogotá's royal mint in late 1819. Upon the triumph of the patriotic armies, he helped to save some of the mint's gold for the Spanish Crown. See Sergio Elias Ortíz, "Horas de conmoción vividas en Santafé de Bogotá a raíz del triunfo de las armas republicanas en Boyacá," *BHA* 56, 657–659 (July-September 1969): 399–417, esp. 414–15.
53. José Ignacio San Miguel was forced to carry out Nariño's defense, having already been fined. See Hernández de Alba, *El proceso de Nariño.*
54. He became *corregidor* in a northern town, Magangue, in 1812, and was political governor of Santa Marta in 1814. Subsequently, the viceroy appointed him *auditor de guerra*. See Hernández de Alba, "Galería de hijos insignes," 292–93.
55. Pardo Umaña, *Haciendas de la sabana,* 232–33.
56. Posada, *Apostillas a la historia colombiana,* 140.
57. See Martínez Delgado, *Noticia biográfica,* 106–07, 123; Rodríguez Plata, *La antigua provincia del Socorro,* 173–75; Gómez, *El tribuno,* 223.
58. García de la Guardia, *Kalendario manual,* 166, 185; Ernesto Restrepo Tirado, "La guerra de los pasquines," in idem, *De Gonzalo Ximénez de Quesada a Don Pablo Morillo,* 64–98, esp. 91; Pérez Sarmiento, ed., *Causas célebres,* 1:444, 460, 494. Even Nariño's son, Gregorio, a merchant based in Havana, isupported the Viceroy Francisco Montalvo from 1813 until at least 1816. See Ernesto Restrepo Tirado, "Francisco Montalvo y don Gregorio Nariño," in idem, *De Gonzalo Ximénez de Quesada a Don Pablo Morillo,* 226–32.

Chapter 4
Independence: A "Revolution from Above"

1. This argument is highlighted in the work of political scientist Jorge I. Dominguez. On Dominguez's and other theses concerning the origin of independence see Victor M. Uribe, "The Enigma of Latin American Independence: Analyses of the Last Ten Years," *LARR* 32, 1 (spring 1997): 237–55.
2. François-Xavier Guerra, *Modernidad e independencias* (Madrid, 1992). See also idem, "La desintegración de la Monarquía hispánica: Revolución de independencia," in *De los imperios a las naciones: Iberoamérica,* ed. Antonio Annino, Luis Castro Leiva, and François-Xavier Guerra (Zaragoza, 1994), 195–227.
3. Simón Bolívar, "Reply of a South American to a Gentleman of this Island [Jamaica]," in *Selected Writings from Bolívar,* ed. Harold Bierck, 2 vols. (New York, 1951), 1:103–22.
4. Francisco Núñez de Pineda y Bascuñán, *Cautiverio féliz y razón individual de las guerras dilatadas del Reino de Chile* [c. 1673] (Santiago, 1973); Jorge Juan de Ulloa and Antonio de Ulloa, *Noticias secretas de América* [1748] (Bogotá, 1983); Alexander von Humboldt, *Ensayo político sobre el reino de la Nueva España* [1811], 5 vols. (Mexico, 1941); Lucas Alamán, *Historia de Mexico desde los primeros movimientos que prepararon su independencia en el año de 1808, hasta la época presente,* 5 vols. (Mexico, 1849–1852),

1:58–59; Colmenares, ed., *Relaciones e informes de los gobernantes de la Nueva Granada;* Silvestre, *Descripción del Nuevo Reino;* Richard Konetzke, "La condición legal de los criollos y las causas de la independencia," *Estudios Americanos* 2, 5 (1950): 31–54; Burkholder, *Politics of a Colonial Career,* 22, 27, 100, 118, 121. See numerous other references in R. A. Humphreys and John Lynch, eds., *The Origins of Latin American Revolutions, 1808-1826* (New York, 1965), 243–300; and see also notes 36 and 37.

5. Safford, *The Ideal of the Practical,* 7; Uribe, "The Lawyers and New Granada's Late Colonial State."
6. Little is yet known about lawyers' intervention in Latin America's independence. See Uribe, "The Birth of a Public Sphere."
7. For historical assessments of New Granada's independence and its background see Restrepo, *Historia de la revolución de la república de Colombia;* José María Samper, *Ensayo sobre las revoluciones políticas y la condición social de las repúblicas colombianas* (Paris, 1861); Gómez Hoyos, *La revolución granadina;* Javier Ocampo López, *El proceso ideológico de la emancipación* (Tunja, 1987); Robert Gilmore, "The Imperial Crisis, Rebellion, and the Viceroy: New Granada in 1809," *HAHR,* 40 (1960): 1–24; Anthony McFarlane, "El colapso de la autoridad española y la génesis de la independencia en la Nueva Granada," *Desarrollo y Sociedad* 7 (1982): 99–120. See also the general comparative works cited in Uribe, "The Enigma of Latin American Independence." One of the most forceful academic works helping to refine the exclusion-from-office thesis is Burkholder and Chandler, *From Impotence to Authority.*
8. On the move to create a junta in New Granada's capital and other regions see John Lynch, *The Spanish American Revolutions* (New York, 1983), esp. 238; Jaime E. Rodríguez, *The Independence of Spanish America* (Cambridge, UK, 1998), chaps. 3 and 4.
9. "Informe del oidor Carrión y Moreno al Consejo de Regencia," in Ortega Ricaurte, ed., *Proceso histórico del 20 de julio* (Bogotá, 1960), 199–209. See also "Un español narrador de los sucesos del 20 de julio," *BHA* 19, 222 (1932): 423–35.
10. "Oficio del Virrey a la Audiencia, 15 Octubre, 1809," in *Proceso histórico del 20 de julio,* ed. Ortega Ricaurte, 1–2; "Declaración del Dr. Pedro Salgar, Noviembre 2, 1809," in ibid., 10–13.
11. For the occupational structure of late colonial Santafé de Bogotá see McFarlane, *Colombia Before Independence,* 55; Vargas, *La sociedad de Santafé.*
12. Restrepo and Rivas, *Genealogías de Santafé;* Arboleda, *Diccionario biográfico y genealógico;* Hernández de Alba, *Cómo nació la república.*
13. In the case of the Cartagena junta, lawyers Germán Gutiérrez de Piñéres, José María García de Toledo, José María del Castillo, José Antonio Ayos, Eusebio María Canabal, Basilio del Toro de Mendoza, Ramón Ripoll, Ignacio Cavero, and the lawyer-priest Manuel B. Rebollo acted as leading figures. So did Miguel Díaz Granados somewhat later. See Ortega Ricaurte, ed., *Proceso del 20 de Julio,* 257. In Cali the role of the lawyers José María de Cuero y Caicedo, Joaquín de Caicedo y Cuero, José María Alomia, José Antonio Borrero, and the lawyer-priest Fray José Joaquín de Escobar was no less noteworthy. See Alfonso Zawadzky, *Ciudades confederadas del Valle del Cauca: Historia, actas, documentos* (n.p., 1943), 111.
14. Uribe, "The Lawyers and New Granada's Late Colonial State." See also Silva, *Universidad y sociedad,* chap. 2.
15. A detailed narrative of the events preceding Bogota's July 1810 junta can be found in Gilmore, "Imperial Crisis." See also McFarlane, "El colapso de la autoridad." On the creation of *Juntas Supremas* throughout the American colonies (Caracas in April,

Buenos Aires in May, Bogotá in July, and Santiago de Chile in September 1810) see Lynch, *Spanish American Revolutions;* Jorge I. Domínguez, *Insurrection or Loyalty: The Breakdown of the Spanish American Empire* (Cambridge, 1980), 152; Michael P. McKinley, *Pre-revolutionary Caracas: Politics, Economy, and Society, 1777-1811* (London, 1986), chap. 7; María T. Berruezo, *La lucha de Hispano-América por su independencia en Inglaterra 1800-1830* (Madrid, 1989), 111, 181; Rodríguez, *The Independence of Spanish America.* Chaps. 3 and 4.

16. On September 15, 1810, the junta prescribed that "Será juzgado como Reo de un grave delito, y como traidor a la Patria todo hombre que forme tumultos sediciosos, o conbocare *[sic]* a las gentes del Pueblo inspirandolas ideas perjudiciales al bien público" ("whoever organizes seditious meetings or mobilizes the common people instilling ideas harmful to the public good will be charged with a serious crime and be deemed a traitor to the fatherland"). See "Documentos de la independencia," *BHA* 47, 543-44 (1960): 98-112; Posada, *El 20 de Julio,* 168-88.

17. The elite figures appointed by the *junta* were Ignacio Umaña, in the neighborhood of Las Nieves; lawyer Manuel Ignacio Camacho Rojas, in Santa Barbara; the lawyer-bureaucrat Felipe Vergara, in San Victorino; and the lawyer Domingo Camacho, in La Catedral. See "Bando, 25 julio, 1810," in Posada, *El 20 de Julio,* 181; Pardo Umaña, *Haciendas de la sabana,* 220; Restrepo S. and Rivas, *Genealogías de Santafé,* 193; Martínez Delgado, *Noticia biográfica,* 362; Carlos Cuervo Márquez, *Vida de José Ignacio de Márquez,* 2 vols. (Bogotá, 1917), 1:17.

18. "Acta de Febrero 14, 1811," in Zawadzky, *Las Ciudades confederadas,* 109.

19. Ibid., 129.

20. José María Caballero, *Diario de la independencia* (Bogotá, 1974), 70-78.

21. José M. Restrepo, *Documentos importantes de Nueva Granada, Venezuela y Colombia,* 2 vols. (Bogotá, 1969), 1:20-21.

22. A vivid narrative of these events was written in 1818 by one of the monks involved. A copy is reproduced in Rodríguez Plata, *La antigua provincia del Socorro,* 247-65.

23. Gustavo Arboleda, *Historia contemporánea de Colombia: Desde la disolución de la antigua república de ese nombre hasta la época presente,* 2d ed., 3 vols. (Cali, 1933), 1:47. See also Indalecio Lievano Aguirre, *España y las luchas sociales en el Nuevo Mundo* (Madrid, 1972), 283-98.

24. Reproduced in Restrepo, *Documentos importantes,* 1:75. See also John Lynch, *Simón Bolívar and the Age of Revolution* (London, 1983), 18-19; John Lombardi, *The Decline and Abolition of Negro Slavery in Venezuela, 1820-1854* (Westport, 1971), 36-46; McKinley, *Pre-revolutionary Caracas,* chap. 7; Hernández de Alba, ed., *Archivo Nariño,* 2:331-32.

25. Restrepo, *Documentos importantes,* 1:73-74. On the participation of *pardos* and blacks in the royalist guerrilla troops recruited by José Tomás Boves in Venezuela, see Stephen Stoan, *Pablo Morillo and Venezuela, 1815-1820* (Columbus, 1974), 50-58; Indalecio Lievano Aguirre, *Bolívar* (Bogotá, 1971), 80-90, 179, 190.

26. "Cartas inéditas de J. M. Restrepo," in *Repertorio Histórico* 3, 3-4 (December 1919), 91-121, esp. 97; Alejandro Osorio, "Memoria presentada por el ministro de guerra y hacienda," *Gazeta de Santa Fé de Bogotá* 25 (January 16, 1820); 26 (January 23, 1820); 27 (January 30, 1820). See Bolívar's similar opinions in Lievano Aguirre, *Bolívar,* 153-60.

27. Vergara y Vergara, *Don Antonio Vergara Azcárate,* 1:272, emphasis added.

28. "José Acevedo Gómez," *Papel periódico ilustrado* 1, 5 (1881), 71. See also Indalecio

Lievano Aguirre, *Los grandes conflictos sociales y económicos de nuestra historia,* 6th ed. (Bogotá, 1974), 297–98.
29. Maingot, "Civil and Military Relations"; idem, "Social Structure, Social Status, and Civil Military Conflict in Urban Colombia, 1810–1858," in *Nineteenth-Century Cities: Essays in the New Urban History,* ed. Stephan Thernston and Richard Sennett (New Haven, 1969), 297–355; José María Baraya, *Biografías militares o historia militar del país en medio siglo* (Bogotá, 1874).
30. The revolutionary participation of the lower sectors is, regrettably, still an understudied and certainly a controversial topic. See Uribe, "The Enigma of Latin American Independence"; Ana Maria Contador, *Los Pincheira: Un caso de bandidaje social. Chile 1817–1832* (Santiago, 1998); Eric J. Van Young, *The Other Rebellion: Popular Violence and Ideology in Mexico* (Stanford, forthcoming).
31. Uribe, "The Birth of the Public Sphere."
32. Uribe, "The Lawyers and New Granada's Late Colonial State."
33. The document, dated September 1, 1809, is reproduced in Ocampo López, *Proceso ideológico,* 552; see also Posada, *Apostillas a la historia colombiana,* 245–49.
34. Camilo Torres, "Representación del Cabildo de Santafé, Capital del Nuevo Reino de Granada, a la Suprema Junta Central de España, en el año de 1809," [November 20, 1809] in Hernández de Alba, *Cómo nació la república,* 26, 30. See also Garrido, *Reclamos y representaciones,* 93–109.
35. A detailed narrative of his mission to New Granada can be found in José Dolores Monsalve, *Antonio de Villavicencio (el protomartir) y la revolución de la independencia,* 2 vols. (Bogotá, 1920), 1:1–9. See also Restrepo, *Biografías de los mandatarios y ministros,* 357–59.
36. Antonio Villavicencio "Representación del Comisario Regio D. Antonio Villavicencio al Virrey de Bogotá," in *Proceso histórico del 20 de julio,* ed. Ortega Ricaurte, 126–31.
37. The lawyers listed were Joaquín Cabrejo, José Munive y Mozo, Francisco Javier de Vergara, Camilo Torres, Joaquín Camacho, Frutos Gutiérrez, Antonio José de Ayos, Miguel Díaz Granados, José María Real, José María del Castillo y Rada, Germán Gutiérrez de Piñéres, and the lawyer-priest Manuel B. Rebollo. Ibid. Almost all of those listed actually became leaders of the 1810 movement in the different regions of New Granada, and several were executed by the Spaniards in 1816. See Table 5.3 and Appendix 1.
38. Various of the cases referred to bureaucrats; e.g., the *teniente asesor-auditor de guerra* of Panama, Joaquín Cabrejo, and the *agente fiscal de lo civil* at the Bogotá Audiencia, lawyer Francisco Javier de Vergara, who had remained in the same jobs for thirty to fifty years without a promotion. Ortega Ricaurte, ed., *Proceso histórico del 20 de julio,* 126.
39. Camilo Torres and Frutos Gutiérrez, "Exposición de los motivos que han obligado al Nuevo Reino de Granada a reasumir los derechos de la soberanía, remover las autoridades del antiguo gobierno, e instalar una suprema junta bajo la sola denominación y en nombre de nuestro soberano Fernando VII y con independencia del Consejo de Regencia y de cualquier otra representación" [September, 1810], in *Proceso histórico del 20 de julio,* ed. Ortega Ricaurte, 211.
40. The documents are interpreted this way by Gómez Hoyos, *La revolución granadina;* Lynch, *Simón Bolívar and the Age of Revolution;* idem, *Spanish American Revolutions,* 7–24; and Ocampo López, *El proceso ideológico.* See also notes 1 and 4. Conspicuous

exceptions to the "exclusion from office thesis" are Jaime Eyzaguirre, *Ideario y ruta de la emancipación chilena* (Santiago, 1957); Stoan, *Pablo Morillo;* McKinley, *Pre-revolutionary Caracas,* chap. 7; Domínguez, *Insurrection or Loyalty,* 243; and Barbier, *Reform and Politics.*

41. Uribe, "The Lawyers and New Granada's Late Colonial State."
42. The sole native-born *oidor* was Joaquín Mosquera y Figueroa. Only three native permanent *fiscales* were appointed, in 1776, 1779, and 1790, respectively. Burkholder and Chandler, *From Impotence to Authority,* Appendix X, esp., 221–24. Another source lists forty-one new *oidores* from 1654 to 1778, only seven of whom are alleged to have been creoles. See Restrepo, *Biografías de los mandatarios.* See also Melo, "Francisco Antonio Moreno y Escandón: retrato de un burócrata colonial," 8.
43. Burkholder and Chandler, *From Impotence to Authority,* Appendix X; Burkholder, *Politics of a Career,* 100, 118; Lynch, *Spanish American Revolutions,* 17–19.
44. Restrepo, *Biografías de los mandatarios,* 387.
45. See Jiménez Molinares, *Linajes cartageneros,* 2:7; Tovar, "El estado colonial frente al poder local y regional"; Restrepo, *Biografías de los mandatarios,* 387; "José María García de Toledo," *BHA* 31, 362–62 (1944): 1134–37.
46. This lawyer's name is not listed in the letter, though Villavicencio, writing from Cartagena, where García de Toledo was at the time the leading social and political figure, could hardly have forgotten him. Villavicencio, "Representación," 126–31. See note 37.
47. Indeed, he was never labeled as revolutionary for his participation in the Cartagena junta. Ortíz, "Eusebio María Canabal," 15.
48. His wife, Teresa Legina, owned a store devoted to the sale of imported fabrics from Castile, or "generos de Castilla." Jiménez Molinares, *Linajes cartageneros,* 1:153–68.
49. García de la Guardia, *Kalendario manual.*
50. Restrepo, *Documentos importantes,* 2:75.
51. Uribe, "The Lawyers and New Granada's Late Colonial State."
52. One of them, Nicolás Mesía Caicedo, was an *oidor* in Manila; two more, Joaquín Mosquera y Figueroa and Manuel del Campo y Rivas, in Mexico; another, Luis de Robledo y Alvarez, in Santo Domingo; and three more, Francisco Xavier Moreno y Escandón, Ignacio Tenorio, and Andrés José de Iriarte y Rojas, were *oidores* and *fiscal,* respectively, in Quito. Burkholder and Chandler, *From Impotence to Authority;* Restrepo, *Biografías de los mandatarios;* Arboleda, *Diccionario biográfico,* 426; Torres Peña, *Memorias sobre la independencia;* Guillermo Lohman Villena, *Los ministros de la Audiencia de Lima en el reinado de los Borbones (1700-1821)* (Seville, 1974).
53. DBNC, F. Pineda, 1066; Burkholder, "Relaciones de Méritos y Servicios," 97–104; Socolow, *Bureaucrats of Buenos Aires,* chaps. 4 and 5; Uribe, "The Lawyers and New Granada's Late Colonial State."
54. Hernández de Alba, *Vida y escritos del Dr. José Félix Restrepo;* "Grados y méritos de Tomás Tenorio Carvajal." For other cases see Appendix 1. The well-documented case of the Peruvian José de Baquijano, who pursued the job of *oidor* for about twenty-five years until he captured it in 1797, offers further evidence. See Burkholder, *Politics of a Career.*
55. See especially the memoir of contemporary creole lawyer and priest José Antonio Torres Peña, pointing to the significant presence of creoles in the colonial bureaucracy. Torres Peña, *Memorias sobre la independencia,* 46–47. That New Granada was an "infertile ground for revolution from the 1790s to the 1810s" is shown by McFarlane, *Colombia Before Independence,* 291.

56. McFarlane, *Colombia Before Independence,* 328–29. For an insightful discussion of the 1809 elections see Guerra, "Las primeras elecciones generales americanas (1809)," in idem, *Modernidad e independencias,* 177–225.
57. The first, attributed to lawyer Camilo Torres, was the "Representación del Cabildo de Santafé a la Suprema Junta Central de España." The second, written by Torres and lawyer Frutos J. Gutiérrez, was the "Exposición de los motivos." They are reproduced in their entirety in Hernández de Alba, *Cómo nacio la república,* 13–39; and *Proceso histórico del 20 de julio,* 85–108, 210–49. See notes 34 and 39.
58. On the August 1809 jailing of several members of the elite who organized a junta in Quito, and New Granadans' reaction, see Pedro Fermín Cevallos, *Resúmen de la historia del Ecuador desde su origen hasta 1845,* 4 vols. (Lima, 1870), 3:51–70; Monsalve, *Antonio de Villavicencio;* Gilmore, "Imperial Crisis"; Lynch, *Spanish American Revolutions,* 235–37.
59. See Torres, "Representación del cabildo," 38.
60. McFarlane, *Colombia Before Independence,* 327–28; Eduardo Rodríguez de Piñérez, *La vida de Castillo y Rada* [documents] (Bogotá, 1949); Restrepo, *Documentos importantes,* 2:15–19; Garrido, *Reclamos y representaciones,* 93–100; Posada, *Apostillas a la historia colombiana,* 238–45.
61. Hernández de Alba, *Archivo Nariño,* 2:331–61; McFarlane, *Colombia Before Independence,* 334–37; Domínguez, *Insurrection or Loyalty,* 246, 248, 254–55; Garrido, *Reclamos y representaciones,* 105.
62. Domínguez, *Insurrection or Loyalty,* 342; Lynch, *Spanish American Revolutions,* 238; Rodríguez Plata, *La antigua provincia del Socorro;* Monsalve, *Antonio de Villavicencio,* 1:54–67.
63. For an account of peninsular Spaniards' sympathies toward the French and the opposite reaction by creoles in Caracas, see Pedro Arcaya, *El cabildo de Caracas* (Caracas, 1968), 117–19. An interpretation that stresses Spanish Americans' fear of French domination as a key cause of independence can be found in Enrique Gandia, "Los orígenes de la independencia americana según el General Daniel Florencio O'Leary," *Revista de Indias* 67 (1967): 59–86. See also Guerra, *Modernidad e independencias.*
64. McFarlane, *Colombia Before Independence,* 328–46; On the events in Quito see Cevallos, *Resúmen de la historia del Ecuador,* 3:71–77; Monsalve, *Antonio de Villavicencio;* Gilmore, "The Imperial Crisis."
65. New Granada's elites particularly disliked the consejo's April 28, 1810 measure imposing a 20 percent real estate tax on Cádiz's property owners. Creoles feared a similar tax would soon be introduced in the colonies. See Torres and Gutiérrez, "Exposición de los motivos," 238.
66. Ibid.; Gómez Hoyos, *La revolución granadina;* and McFarlane, "El colapso de la autoridad española."
67. Structural analyses of the revolution can be found in George Reid Andrews, "Spanish American Independence: A Structural Analysis," *Latin American Prespectives* 12, 1 (1985): 105–32; and Nicole Bousquet, "The Decolonization of Spanish America in the Early Nineteenth Century: A World Systems Approach," *Review* 9, 4 (1988): 497–531.
68. On the significance of the failure of political bargaining and coalition building see Dominguez, *Insurrection or Loyalty;* on legalism as a reason to act see letter of Camilo Torres to his uncle, *oidor* Ignacio Tenorio, in early 1810, in *Proceso del 20 de Julio,* ed. Ortega Ricaurte, 54–68. See also Gómez Hoyos, *La revolución granadina.*

Chapter 5
Kill All the Lawyers!

1. On the significance of *cabildos* to understand the transit to independence see Antonio Annino, "Soberanías en lucha," in *De los imperios a las naciones,* ed. Annino, Castro Leiva and Guerra (Zaragoza, 1994), 229–53.
2. See Guerra, *Modernidad e independencias,* esp. 32 and chaps. 2–4. See also idem, "La desintegración de la monarquía hispánica," 195–227; Pilar González Bernaldo, "La Revolución Francesa y la emergencia de nuevas prácticas de la política: la irrupción de la sociabilidad política en el Río de la Plata revolucionario (1810–1815)," in *La Revolución Francesa en Chile,* ed. Ricardo Krebs and Cristian Gazmuri (Santiago, 1990), 111–35; idem, "Producción de una nueva legitimidad: ejército y sociedades patrióticas en Buenos Aires entre 1810 y 1813," *Cahiers des Amériques Latines* 10 (1990): 177–95.
3. Guerra, *Modernidad e independencias,* 31, 101.
4. Charles Tilly, *From Mobilization to Collective Action* (Reading, 1978).
5. During the period of revolutionary turmoil they maintained continuous correspondence, reproduced in Demetrio Vásquez, *Hilvanes históricos* (Cali, 1965); see also Zawadzky, *Ciudades confederadas.*
6. Vallecilla's father, *regidor* of the Cali *cabildo,* and various of Vallecilla's brothers and sisters married into different branches of the influential Caicedo clan: the Caicedo Tenorio, the Caicedo y Cuero, and the Caicedo de la Llera families. See Arboleda, *Diccionario biográfico;* José Escorcia, *Desarrollo social, político y económico [en el Valle del Cauca], 1800–1854* (Bogotá, 1983); Appendix 1.
7. Zawadzky, *Ciudades confederadas,* 101; Arboleda, *Diccionario biográfico;* McFarlane, *Colombia Before Independence,* 243–44.
8. Escorcia, *Desarrollo social, político y económico.*
9. See "Sanz de Santamaría."
10. On Herrera y Vergara's disputes with the local authorities see Ortega Ricaurte, ed., *Proceso histórico del 20 de Julio,* 26–28; on Vallecilla's disputes with Tacón see Zawadzky, *Ciudades confederadas.*
11. Colmenares, *Cali: terratenientes, mineros y comerciantes,* 143–54; Escorcia, *Desarrollo político, social y económico,* 45–61, 97–116; Peter Marzahl, "Creoles and Government: The Cabildo of Popayán," *HAHR* 54, 3 (1974): 636–56; McFarlane, *Colombia Before Independence,* 136, 243–44.
12. See "Torres y Tenorio, Jerónimo," 144–46; "Carta de Jerónimo Torres a su Hermano Camilo." Camilo, for his part, married into the traditional elite Bogotano Prieto Ortega Ricaurte clan.
13. See Martínez Delgado, *Noticia biográfica,* 106–07, 123.
14. Rodríguez Plata, *La antigua provincia del Socorro,* 173–75; Martínez Delgado, *Noticia biográfica,* 263–94; Gómez, *El tribuno,* 223.
15. See Rodríguez Plata, *La antigua provincia del Socorro,* 190; José Acevedo y Gómez to Antonio Villavicencio, Santa Fé de Bogotá, July 19, 1810, in Gómez, *El tribuno,* 221–25; McFarlane, "Economic and Political Change," 304.
16. See Ortega Ricaurte ed., *Proceso histórico del 20 de julio,* 1; Rodríguez Plata, *La antigua provincia del Socorro;* Henández de Alba, *Archivo Nariño,* 2:332.
17. The Valenzuela group was perhaps most influential in the regions of Girón and Bucaramanga, where its members occupied bureaucratic and ecclesiastical jobs. Priest Eloy, former member of the Botanical Expedition, was, in addition, "owner" of a road connecting Bucaramanga and the important city of Pamplona. Since 1804, lawyer Crisanto had been employed by the audiencia. He was married to Mariana

Ortega, a niece of merchant Antonio Nariño. His wife's sister, María Ignacia, was the wife of *cabildo* lawyer Ignacio Herrera. Joaquín Camacho, "Relación territorial de la provincia de Pamplona," [1809] in *Semanario del Nuevo Reino de Granada,* 3 vols. (Bogotá, 1942), 2:1–21; Posada, *El precursor,* 134; Martínez Delgado, *Noticia biográfica,* 297–308; Bernardo Ortega Lafaurie, "Don Crisanto Valenzuela," *BHA* 24, 273 (1937): 406–17; Restrepo S., "La familia de Nariño," 247.

18. See García de la Guardia, *Kalendario manual,* 76; Jiménez Molinarez, *Linajes cartageneros,* 2:7. On Castillo y Rada see José J. Guerra, "José Nicolas de Rivas," *BHA* 3, 30 (1905): 343–66; Restrepo S. and Rivas, *Genealogías de Santafé,* 242; Rodríguez de Piñérez, *La vida de Castillo y Rada.*
19. Beatríz Patiño Millán, "Factores de unidad en el Nuevo Reino de Granada y la posterior formación del estado nacional," in *Estudios Sociales,* [FAES] (1988), 105; idem, *Criminalidad, ley penal y estructura social,* 154–64; Uribe and Alvarez, "El parentesco y la formación de las élites en la provincia de Antioquia," 92; Restrepo, *Autobiografía;* McFarlane, "Economic and Political Change," 329–30.
20. Glick, "Science and Independence in Latin America"; Garrido, *Reclamos y representaciones,* chap. 1. Among the lawyers in question were some of the leaders of the *cabildo* and junta organized in Mompox, including prominent Antioqueño lawyer José María Salazar. See *Papel Periódico Ilustrado,* 71, July 20, 1884, 372.
21. On the *cabildos* as judicial, political, and legislative institutions and their control by elite families, see Pablo Rodríguez, *Cabildo y vida urbana en el Medellín colonial, 1675–1730* (Medellín, 1985); Julian Vargas, "El muy ilustre Cabildo de Santafé de Bogotá: Finanzas y administración económica," in idem, *La sociedad de Santafé,* 189–257; Luis Navarro García, "El privilegio de los regidores en el abasto de Cartagena de Indias," *Anuario de Estudios Americanos* 38 (1981): 174–214; McFarlane, *Colombia Before Independence,* 238, 243–44, 328–40.
22. On identity and creolism see Nicholas Canny and Anthony Pagden, eds., *Colonial Identity in the Atlantic World, 1500–1800* (Princeton, 1987), esp. chap. 3; Hans-Joachim König, *En el camino hacia la nación: Nacionalismo en el proceso de formación del estado y de la nación en la Nueva Granada, 1750–1856* (Bogotá, 1994), 189–322.
23. Twinam, *Miners and Merchants in Bourbon Mexico;* Restrepo S. and Rivas, *Genealogías de Santafé.*
24. For an insightful study of both language and symbols in New Granada see König, *En el camino a la nación,* 203–313. See also Guerra, *Modernidad e independencias.*
25. See Germán Colmenares, "Castas, patrones de poblamiento y conflictos sociales en las provincias del Cauca, 1810–1830," in *La independencia,* ed. Colmenares, Días de Zuluaga and Escorcia, 139–79, esp. 144–50; Antonio José Galvis Noyes, "La abolición de la esclavitud en la Nueva Granada," *BHA* 67, 30 (July-September 1980): 469–572. On fiscal changes see Malcolm Deas, "Los problemas fiscales en Colombia durante el siglo XIX," in Fedesarrollo, *Ensayos sobre historia económica colombiana* (Bogotá, 1980), 143–80.
26. Silvestre, *Descripción del Reyno de Santafé;* Phelan, *The People and the King.*
27. This period is known in Colombian historiography as the "Patria Boba." In-depth studies of it are still lacking. See Eduardo Posada ed., *La patria boba* [documents] (Bogotá, 1902); Gabriel Jiménez Molinares, *Los mártires de Cartagena de 1816 ante el consejo de guerra y ante la historia* (Cartagena, 1947); Caballero, *Diario de la independencia.*
28. Other more complex regional disputes, like those that pitted the "Ciudades Confederadas del Valle del Cauca" against Popayán, and Cartagena and neighboring cities against Santamarta, are mentioned in Zawadzky, *Ciudades confederadas;* Jiménez Molinares, *Los mártires de Cartagena;* Tovar Pinzón, "Guerras de opinión y

represión en Colombia"; and Gustavo Bell Lemus, "Conflictos regionales y centralismo. Una hipótesis sobre las relaciones políticas de la costa Caribe con el gobierno central en los primeros años de la república 1821–1840," in *El Caribe Colombiano,* comp. Gustavo Bell Lemus (Barranquilla, 1988), 39–48, esp. 39–42.
29. From as early as September 19, 1810, there had been disputes about the much-feared weight that Bogotá might have in the future government. See Posada, *El 20 de Julio,* 243–50; Gabriel Porras Troconis, ed., *Documental concerniente a la declaración de la independencia absoluta de la Provincia de Cartagena de Indias* (Cartagena, 1961), 51–61. See also König, *En el camino hacia la nación,* 190–202.
30. See Manuel Pombo and José Joaquín Guerra, *Constituciones de Colombia recopiladas y precedidas de una breve reseña histórica,* 3d ed., 3 vols. (Bogotá, 1951) [1892], 1:193–94; 2:243. See also Chapter 4.
31. Restrepo Sáenz, *Constituyentes de Tunja.*
32. On local and provincial constitutions see Pombo and Guerra, *Constituciones de Colombia.* See also König, *En el camino hacia la nación,* 191–98.
33. We still lack information as to how elections and decisions were actually handled. See Pombo and Guerra, *Constituciones de Colombia,* 1:283–85; Fernán González "Legislación y comportamiento electorales: Evolución histórica," in *Elecciones 1978: Legislación, abanico político, resultados de febrero,* Bogotá, CINEP, Serie Controversia, nos. 64–65 (1978), 1–23; Margarita Garrido, "La política local en la Nueva Granada. 1750–1810," *ACHSC,* no. 15 (1987): 37–56; Vergara y Vergara, *Don Antonio Vergara Azcárate,* 1:196. For the case of Mexico, where popular participation in the electoral process during these years was quite active and instilled fear among the elites, see Richard Warren, "Elections and Popular Participation in Mexico, 1808–1836," in *Liberals, Politics and Power: State Formation in Nineteenth-Century Latin America,* Vincent E. Peloso and Barbara A. Tenenbaum, eds. (London, 1996), 30–58; Virginia Guedea, "El pueblo de Mexico y la politica capitalina," *Mexican Studies* 10, 1 (winter 1994): 27–61.
34. See "Quadro . . . ," in *Gaceta Real de Cartagena de Indias,* September 7, 1816, 33–45.
35. Some of these measures and their meaning are studied in José María Ots y Capdequí, "The Impact of the Wars of Independence on the Institutional Life of the New Kingdom of Granada," *The Americas* 17, 2 (1960): 111–98, esp. 120–26. See also Michael P. Costeloe, *Response to Revolution. Imperial Spain and the Spanish American Revolutions, 1810–1840* (Cambridge, 1986).
36. It started, in November 1812, by downgrading New Granada from a viceroyalty to a captaincy general, which lasted until April 1816. Ots y Capdequí, "The Impact of the Wars of Independence," 127.
37. Ots y Capdequí, "Impact of the Wars"; Stoan, *Pablo Morillo;* Costeloe, *Response to Revolution,* chaps. 3–4.
38. See Restrepo, *Biografías de los mandatarios,* 423–26; Caballero, *Diario de la independencia,* 218–19. A detailed discussion of the institutional arrangements before and after the "reconquest" is offered by Ots y Capdequí, "Impact of the Wars."
39. See García de la Guardia, *Kalendario manual;* Luis Páez Courvel, "Precursores, mártires y próceres santandereanos de la independencia colombiana," *BHA* 34, 393–95 (1947): 476–94; Morillo, "Relación de las principales cabezas de la rebelión en este Nuevo Reino de Granada, que después de formados sus procesos y vistos detenidamente en el Consejo de Guerra Permanente, han sufrido por sus delitos la pena capital en la forma que se expresa [1816]," *BHA* 19, 222 (1932): 435–70.
40. Pedro M. Ibáñez, "José María Salazar," *Papel Periódico Ilustrado* 5, 166 (1886): 146.

The Royal Audiencia, meeting in Cartagena in August 1816, decided to form a list of all the lawyers in public service there, who would have to present their *títulos* and proof that they had been pardoned. Ots y Capdequí, "Impact of the Wars," 133.

41. "Ya he expresado mis deseos a V.E. de mandar Misioneros, ahora añado la necesidad de mandar igualmente *teologos y abogados de España*. Si el Rey quiere subyugar a estas provincias, LAS MISMAS MEDIDAS SE DEBEN TOMAR QUE AL PRINCIPIO DE LA CONQUISTA . . . " ("I have already expressed to Your Excellency my wishes that priests be sent, now I should add that it is equally as important to send *theologians and lawyers from Spain*. If the king wishes to dominate these provinces, THE SAME MEASURES MUST BE TAKEN AS WHEN THE CONQUEST WAS STARTED . . . "). See Pablo Morillo, "Oficio," *Gaceta de la Ciudad de Bogotá*, April 2, 1820, 136, emphasis and capital letters in the original.

42. See Carlos Cortés Vargas, "De la época del terror [manuscrito antiguo]," *BHA* 29, 327 (1942): 85–103; Pablo Morillo, *Manfiesto que hace a la nación española el teniente general Don Pablo Morillo . . . con motivo de las calumnias e imputaciones atroces y falsas publicadas contra su persona en 21 y 28 del mes de abril último en Gaceta de la Isla de León* (Madrid, 1821), 25–27; Vergara y Vergara, *Vida de Estanislao Vergara*, 19.

43. He also targeted priests. See Restrepo Tirado, "Víctimas eclesiásticas," in idem, *De Gonzalo Ximénez de Quesada a Don Pablo Morillo*, 243–56. Morillo's harsh measures to contain the revolution were soon deemed inappropriate and counterproductive by the Consejo de Indias. See Restrepo Tirado, "Dictamen del Consejo" [November 17, 1817], in ibid., 166–205.

44. Morillo, *Manfiesto que hace a la nación española*, 45, 50, 54.

45. See Pardo Umaña, *Haciendas de la sabana*, 234. Intriguing cases of pardon include lawyers José María del Castillo, Alejandro Osorio, and Eusebio María Canabal. See Jose María del Castillo y Rada, "Memorias," *Lecturas Populares*, Suplemento Literario de *El Tiempo*, Bogotá, 40–41 (1914?), 489. On Osorio, see Venancio Ortíz, "Alejandro Osorio," *Colombia Ilustrada* 4–5 (1889): 59. On Juan Jurado, his protector, see José M. Restrepo Sáenz, "Juan Jurado," *BHA* 13, 149 (1920): 271–300. On Canabal see Ortíz, "Eusebio María Canabal," 13–23.

46. Guillermo Hernández de Alba, "Recuerdos de la reconquista. El Consejo de Purificación," *BHA* 22, 252–253 (July-August 1935): 461–86, 512–28; *BHA* 22, 254–55 (September-October 1935): 656–85; Restrepo, *Gobernadores y próceres de Neiva*, 486–89; Gandia, "Orígenes de la independencia americana," 62. Several lawyers, including Joaquín Ortíz Nagle, Ignacio Herrera, Luis E. Azuola, Dionisio Gamba, José María del Castillo, José Sáenz de Santamaría, and the lawyer-priest Andrés M. Rosillo, were sent to prisons and held for several years. See Ortíz, *Reminiscencias*, 36–43.

47. The most notable cases involved Tomás Tenorio y Carvajal, José Ignacio San Miguel, Francisco José de Aguilar, Eusebio María Canabal, and Tomás Barriga. See Appendix 1; Restrepo, *Biografías de los mandatarios*, 282; Arboleda, *Diccionario biográfico*, 427; Restrepo and Rivas, *Genealogías de Santafé*, 14, 98–99; Ortíz, "Eusebio María Canabal," 15; Gerardo Arrubla, "Viejos papeles," *BHA* 5, 54 (1908): 342–54; Tovar Pinzón, "Guerras de opinión."

48. The patriots also used harsh measures against some revolutionary Spaniards. See some examples in Restrepo Tirado, "Algunas víctimas españolas de la revolución de Santafé de 1810 and 1815," in idem, *De Gonzalo Ximénez de Quesada a Don Pablo Morillo*, 210–14.

49. Lievano Aguirre, *Bolívar*, 153–62; Maingot, "Social Structure and Civil Military Conflict"; McFarlane, *Colombia Before Independence*, chap. 12, epilogue.

Chapter 6
Changing Generations and Regions in the 1820s

1. On these aspects see Costeloe, *The Central Republic;* Di Tella, *National Popular Politics.*
2. As one historian wrote recently, the roots of postindependence political conflict "lie in the contradiction between political liberalism and the traditional structure developed in the colonial period." Stevens, *Origins of Instability,* 115.
3. A few examples are: Pedro Vicente Martínez y Cabal, Eusebio García Salgar, José Antonio Salvador Borrero Costa, Agustín Caicedo y Sánchez, and Enrique Umaña Barragán. See "Relación de las exequias"; Arboleda, *Diccionario biográfico y genealógico,* 254–58; Escorcia, *Desarrollo político, social y económico,* 52, 200; "Eusebio García Salgar," *BHA* 9, 108 (April 1915): 743–44; Pardo Umaña, *Haciendas de la sabana,* 235; *Acuerdos,* 1:91, 146, 148, 201; "Relación de méritos de Enrique Umaña," 1807, DBNC, Pineda, 1066:1–6. Benedicto Domínguez y Castillo (1783–1868) spent his time in astronomical observations and designing calendars. See Pedro M. Ibáñez, "Benedicto Domínguez y Castillo," *Papel Periódico Ilustrado* 5, no. 166 (December 15, 1886), 146.
4. See some examples in *Acuerdos,* 1:105, 201; 2:102.
5. For some examples see Patiño M., *Criminalidad, ley penal y estructura social,* 158; Restrepo Sáenz, *Gobernadores de Antioquia,* 1:369–74.
6. José Miguel Pey, Jerónimo Torres, José María del Castillo y Rada, and Santiago Pérez de Valencia y Arroyo are the most representative figures of this group. See Restrepo S. and Rivas, *Genealogías de Santafé;* Arboleda, *Historia contemporánea,* vol. 1; idem, *Diccionario biográfico y genealógico,* passim; *Acuerdos,* vols. 1 and 2.
7. See Estanislao Vergara, "Memoria presentada al E. Sor. Vice-Presidente por el Ministro del Interior y de Justicia." Santa Fé, December 31, 1819, *Gazeta de Santa Fé de Bogotá,* no. 28, (February 6, 1820); no. 32 (March 5, 1820); no. 33 (March 12, 1820); idem, "Memoria del encargado del Despacho Interior y Justicia del Departamento de Cundinamarca, presentada a S. Excia. el Vice-Presidente en 31 Diciembre, 1820," *Gazeta de la Ciudad de Bogotá,* no. 91 (April 22, 1821).
8. His cousin José María Vergara y Lozano was a General, and their uncle, Cristoval Vergara y Caicedo, was also favored by Bolívar and his friends with high bureaucratic jobs: *administrador* of the Zipaquirá salt mines (1819–1825), *intendente* (governor) of Cauca (1825–1826), Tunja (1827–1829), and Cundinamarca (1830). Vergara y Vergara, *Don Antonio de Vergara Azcárate,* 1:206–13.
9. Osorio, "Memoria presentada por el Ministro de Guerra y Hacienda"; idem, "Memoria correspondiente a los ramos de guerra y hacienda," *Gazeta de la Ciudad de Bogotá,* no. 88 (Abril 1, 1821); no. 90 (Abril 15, 1821).
10. Ten of the positions were staffed by senior colonial lawyers (those who graduated before 1805). See Table 6.1.
11. A few examples of senior judges are: José Ignacio de Sanmiguel, Joaquín Gómez Londoño, José Antonio Esquiaqui, Pantaleón Arango, Henrique Rodríguez, José Maria del Real, Ignacio Herrera, and Joaquín Ortíz Nagle. See Gabriel Arango Mejía *Genealogías de Antioquia y Caldas,* 3d ed., 2 vols. (Medellín, 1973), 1:132–35; Restrepo S., *Gobernadores de Antioquia,* 1:375–79; AHN, Médicos y Abogados, vol. 2:1–4, 228–250; vol 5:231–243; *Acuerdos,* 2:190; Sergio Elias Ortíz, *Doctor José María del Real, jurisconsulto y diplomático prócer de la Independencia* (Bogotá, 1969), 15. An exception was 47-year-old José Maria del Castillo, appointed to the strategic job of Economic Secretary. Young lawyers were more numerous than their seniors in positions as

councilors. See *Gaceta de la Ciudad de Bogotá,* December 9, 1821; December 23, 1821. See also Table 6.1.
12. On the appointment of young lawyers in the 1820s see Eduardo Acevedo Latorre, *Colaboradores de Santander en la organización de la república,* 2d. ed. (Bogotá, 1988); and *Acuerdos,* 2 vols. See next chapter's Table 7.5.
13. This contradicts "generational" hypotheses depicting all young lawyers as antimilitary democrats. See José Camacho Carrizosa "Hombres y partidos," *Repertorio Colombiano* 14, 4 (October 1, 1896), 276; 6 (May 1, 1897), 418–27; Gómez Barrientos, *Don Mariano Ospina y su época,* 1:33–35; Arboleda, *Historia contemporánea,* 1:10; Eduardo Caballero, *Historia privada de los colombianos* (Bogotá, 1960), 127; Maingot, "Civil Military Relations in a Political Culture of Conflict," 47–49; idem, Maingot, "Social Structure, Social Status, and Civil-Military Conflict," 321–32; "La conspiración del 25 de septiembre," *BHA* 25, 289–290 (November-December 1938), 784–801, esp. 787. The generational hypothesis is upheld in Ernesto Cortés Ahumada, *Las generaciones colombianas* (Tunja, 1968), 31–34, 197.
14. The two regions signed a "*tratado de amistad, alianza y unión federativa*" in May 28, 1811 and in 1816 they organized a united revolutionary army. See José Gil Fortoul, *Historia constitucional de Venezuela* (Berlín, 1907), 133; José A. Páez, *Memorias del general José Antonio Páez* (Madrid, 1916), 109–24; Rafael Urdaneta, *Memorias del General Rafael Urdaneta* (Madrid, 1916). On their traditional administrative separation, see Sarfatti *Spanish Bureaucratic-Patrimonialism.* On geographical distances see *Cartas escritas desde Colombia* (Bogotá, 1975) [1824]; David Bushnell, *The Santander Regime* (Westport, 1954), 306; Gil Fortoul, *Historia constitucional,* 83. On ethnic differences see José M. Samper, *Galería nacional de hombres ilustres o notables o sea colección de bocetos biográficos* (Bogotá, n.d.), 75; José A. Páez, *Memorias del General José Antonio Páez, autobiografía* (Madrid, n.d.), 329, 442–43; Camacho Carrizosa, "Hombres y partidos," 267; Bushnell, *The Santander Regime,* 287–94.
15. See *Actas Angostura,* passim; *Actas Cúcuta,* passim; Gíl Fortoul, *Historia constitucional,* 263–325; David Brading, *The First America. The Spanish Monarchy, Creole Patriots, and the Liberal State 1492–1867* (New York, 1991), 608. On the founding and early years of the new republic, see Bushnell, *The Santander Regime.*
16. Members of the Constitutional Congress had to own at least 5,000-pesos worth of property or have a yearly income of 500 pesos or be "*profesores de alguna ciencia o arte liberal,*" and were elected indirectly. The social nature and mechanics of the elections are as yet unknown. See Carlos Restrepo Piedrahita, *Congreso Constituyente de Cúcuta* (Bogotá, 1990), 476–80; on Venezuelans' limited participation in the bureaucracy and congress, see Bushnell, *The Santander Regime,* 51–52, 289.
17. On state-clergy relationships between 1820 and 1827 see Bushnell, *The Santander Regime,* 195–248; Juan Pablo Restrepo, *La iglesia y el estado en Colombia. Edición tomada de la impresa en Londres en 1885* (Bogotá, 1987); *Cartas escritas desde Colombia.* On the continuing influence of the clergy in educational matters see Chapter 8. In August 1826, Bolívar stated that political order could be maintained "*ya con la imprenta, ya con los púlpitos, ya con las ballonetas.*" See Páez, *Memorias,* 356; José Restrepo Posada, "El Doctor Nicolás Cuervo y nuestras primeras relaciones con la Santa Sede," *BHA* 28, 317–318 (1941): 286–307. See also the eyewitness account of Victoriano de D. Paredes, "Memorias de Don Victoriano de Diego Paredes. Dictadas por el a su hija Francisca Paredes Serrano y manuscritas por esta. Bogotá, 1 Abril, 1885," *BHA* 68, no. 732 (January-March 1981): 103–65, esp. 111.

18. See Bushnell, *The Santander Regime,* 249; Maingot, "Social Structure, Social Status, and Civil-Military Conflict," 297–355.
19. José M. Castillo y Rada, "Estado general que se forma por la Secretaria de Hacienda y manifiesta en resúmen los productos que han tenido las rentas . . . desde el 1 de julio de 1824 hasta 30 de junio de 1825." Bogotá, Enero 18, 1826; see also Arboleda, *Historia contemporánea,* 1:24; *Acuerdos,* 2:25; AHN, República, Consejo de Estado, vol. 1:374–78.
20. Evidence of animosities and clashes between Venezuelans and New Granadans during the 1810s and 1820s can be found in Páez, *Memorias,* 117–18, 260–65, 310–48, 354; Miguel Samper, "La política en hispanoamérica," *Repertorio Colombiano* 14, 1 (July 1896): 48–68, esp. 67; idem, "Ojeada retrospectiva sobre nuestros partidos y su labor constitucional," *Repertorio Colombiano* 14, no. 2 (August 1896): 110–40, esp. 114; *Actas Cúcuta,* 561–64, 737, 742; Bushnell, *The Santander Regime,* 21, 282–328, esp. 289, 306; Ortíz, *Doctor José María del Real, jurisconsulto,* 54–59; José Joaquín Guerra, *La Convención de Ocaña* (Bogotá, 1908), 18, 42, 254; Fabio Lozano y Lozano and Guillermo Hernández de Alba, *Documentos sobre el Dr. Vicente Azuero* (Bogotá, 1944), xxxii; Florentino González, *Memorias (controversias bolivarianas)* (Medellín, 1971) [1841–45?], 126–27; Malcolm Deas, "La presencia de la política nacional en la vida provinciana, pueblerina y rural de Colombia en el primer siglo de la república," in *La unidad nacional en América Latina. Del regionalismo a la nacionalidad,* ed. Marco Palacios (Mexico, 1983), 149–73, esp. 166; David Bushnell and Neill Macaulay, *The Emergence of Latin America in the Nineteenth Century* (Oxford, 1988), 89.
21. See Restrepo, *Gobernadores de Antioquia,* 2:71; Guerra, *La Convención de Ocaña,* 181; Arboleda, *Historia contemporánea,* 1:6, 24–25; Maingot "Social Structure, Social Status, and Civi-Military Conflict," 309, 314; Bushnell, *The Santander Regime,* 250.
22. The doors of the military were open to all, including the "inferior classes of society." See Samper, *Galería nacional de hombres ilustres,* 186; Baraya, *Biografías militares.*
23. Bushnell, *The Santander Regime,* 249–74; Maingot, "Civil Military Relations in a Political Culture of Conflict"; idem, "Social Structure, Social Status, and Civil-Military Conflict."
24. See *Actas Cúcuta,* 559; Bushnell, *The Santander Regime,* 20–21, 58–69; Posada *El precursor,* 23–71. The Congress appointed three justices and two *fiscales* of the Alta Corte. The rest of the bureaucrats were mostly appointed by Vicepresident Santander in the first half of the 1820s. See *Actas Cúcuta,* 744–55; Acevedo Latorre, *Colaboradores de Santander;* Restrepo P., *Congreso constituyente de Cúcuta; Acuerdos,* 2 vols.
25. See *Gaceta de Ciudad de Bogotá,* December 9, 1821; December 23, 1821.
26. See Maingot "Social Structure, Social Status, and Civil-Military Conflict," 314; Lombardi, *The Decline and Abolition of Negro Slavery,* 8, 15; *Actas Congreso 1823,* 436; Páez, *Memorias,* 316; *Actas Cámara 1824,* 39–40; Guerra, *La Convención de Ocaña,* 22–24; Cuervo Márquez, *Vida de José Ignacio de Márquez,* 1:162.
27. The remaining five New Granadan Senators were two generals, two colonels, and one merchant. See *Actas Cúcuta,* 744–55; Arboleda, *Diccionario genealógico,* 66.
28. Acevedo Latorre, *Colaboradores de Santander,* passim; *Acuerdos,* 2 vols., passim.
29. To understand political party affiliations, Frank Safford proposed paying attention to the "social location" of individuals and groups, by which he meant the relation of individuals or regions to certain "structures of economic, social and political power as they existed at the end of the colonial period." See Safford, "Bases of Political Alignment," 102. However, he did not articulate sufficiently the role of social status and cultural background of families, social connections, and certain common experiences of individuals (i.e., wars, studies, associations with political bosses, etc.). See

idem, "Aspectos sociales de la política en la Nueva Granada," 183–99; idem, "Formación de los partidos políticos," 16–17.
30. See article 6 of the October 13, 1821 law, in *Recopilación de leyes de la Nueva Granada,* ed. Lino de Pombo (Bogotá, 1845), 23.
31. AHN, Inst. Pub., vol. 110:375–79, 867–72.
32. See *Actas Congreso 1823,* 423–24, 501; *Actas Cámara 1824,* 64.
33. *Acuerdos,* 1:168.
34. See law of October 11, 1821 on citizenship rights, and decree of March 11, 1822 on fellowships. *Actas Cúcuta,* 643–45; *Gaceta de Colombia,* no. 29 (May 5, 1822). See also König, *En el camino hacia la nación,* 349–52.
35. Paredes, "Memorias de Don Victoriano de Diego Paredes," 115; see also Prospero Pereira Gamba, "Los conflictos de Bogotá en 1840 y 1841 (De mis recuerdos íntimos de patria y familia)," *Revista Literaria* 4, no. 47 (March, 1894), 474–84, esp. 480–81.
36. Pereira Gamba, "Los conflictos de Bogotá," 480.
37. See law of April 13, 1825, in *Cod. Nal.,* vol. 2, no. 231; *Acuerdos,* vol. 2, 30–31; *Actas Senado 1825,* 620–22. On the rejection of sons of illegitimate birth during the colonial period see Silva, *Universidad y sociedad,* 255–62; *Actas Congreso 1823,* 423–24; *Actas Senado 1825,* 430.
38. *Actas Senado 1825,* 225–26. Some of the opponents were afraid that the law would cause a moral disaster—it would allegedly produce *"mujeres que se prostituyesen y. . . . hombres que se entregasen a la disolución."* Ibid., 427, 621–24, 659.
39. AHN, Inst. Pub. vol 110:351.
40. See Article 6, of the law of October 13, 1821, in *Recopilación de leyes,* 23. Widows were also entitled to receive temporary pensions, and did so. See AHN, República, Congreso, vol. 25:412–18.
41. *Acuerdos,* 1:26; Guerra, *La Convención de Ocaña,* 267.
42. *Actas Congreso 1823,* 444.
43. Ibid., 438.
44. *Acuerdos,* 2:30–31; *Actas Senado 1825,* 620–21, 659.
45. Hernández de Alba and Lozano, eds., *Documentos sobre el doctor Vicente Azuero;* Bushnell, *The Santander Regime,* 60.
46. See Antonio Nariño, "Defensa del General Nariño ante el Senado. April 24, 1823," in Posada, *El precursor,* 551–91; *Actas Congreso 1823;* Bushnell, *The Santander Regime.*
47. His brother Juan Nepomuceno was an active congressman during the 1820s and also led attacks against Nariño's associates, one of whom, lawyer Ignacio Herrera, was considered Nepomuceno's mortal enemy. See *Actas Cámara 1824,* 181.
48. Soto, *Mis Padecimientos i mi conducta pública y otros documentos* (Bogotá, 1978).
49. Hernández de Alba and Lozano y Lozano, *Documentos sobre el Doctor Vicente Azuero,* xv; Soto, *Mis padecimientos;* Martínez Delgado *Noticia biográfica;* Indalecio Lievano Aguirre, *Razones socio-económicas de la conspiración de Septiembre contra El Libertador* (Caracas, 1968), 23.
50. In 1821 Azuero married a daughter of General Joaquín Ricaurte Torrijos. The Ricaurte family descended from a *tesorero* of the royal mint and possessed lands in the Bogotá valley. See Pardo Umaña, *Haciendas de la sabana,* 95–100, 209; *Genealogías de Bogotá 1991,* 1:92, 286. In the early 1810s, Soto married a woman from his own region about whom little is known. See Soto, *Mis padecimientos,* 27–28. In 1836 Santander married the daughter of a middling colonial bureaucrat (*administrador de correos*) who settled in Antioquia. See Arango Mejía, *Genealogías de Antioquia y Caldas,* 2:205–06.

51. Santander was best man at Azuero's 1821 wedding. See Hernández de Alba and Lozano y L., *Documentos sobre el doctor Vicente Azuero,* xv.
52. See Bushnell, *The Santander Regime,* 60; Pacheco and Molina Lemus, *La familia de Santander,* 70–84; Moreno de Angel, *Santander.*
53. See Manuel J. Mosquera to Rufino Cuervo, Popayán, May 14, and June 22 and 29, 1830, in *Epistolario Cuervo,* 1:196–97, 201–02, 205–06; Juan de Dios Aranzazu to Juan María Gómez, Bogotá, October 11, 1839, in "Cartas ineditas de Juan de D. Aranzazu," *Repertorio Histórico* 15, 146 (August 1940): 593–637, esp. 602.
54. On Suárez Serrano, Camacho Naranjo, and others see *Acuerdos,* 1:8, 12, 65, 132; 2:96, 260; Restrepo and Rivas, *Genealogías de Santafé,* 196; José M. Samper, *Historia de un alma. 1834 a 1881,* 2 vols. (Bogotá, 1946), 1:162–68; on the marginal Casanare region see Jane M. Rausch, *A Tropical Plains Frontier. The Llanos of Colombia 1531–1831* (Albuquerque, 1984).
55. Pedro Ignacio Cadena, "D. José Francisco Pereira," *Colombia Ilustrada,* no. 24 (March 31, 1892): 370–75, esp. 372. For arguments on nineteenth-century schools as key places to build social bonds see Borges, *The Family in Bahia,* 271.
56. Even those who reject the existence of a "nation" in the postcolonial period could not deny the existence of a countrywide, if not "national," political elite. On the lack of a nation see María T. Uribe de Hincapié and Jesús M. Alvarez, *Poderes y regiones: Problemas en la constitución de la nación colombiana, 1810–1850* (Medellín, 1987).
57. See Colmenáres, "Castas, patrones de poblamiento y conflictos sociales," 171; Fabio Zambrano Pantoja, "Ocupación del territorio y conflictos sociales en Colombia," in *Un país en construcción.* Serie Controversia, no. 151–52 (Bogotá: Cinep, April 1989), 1:79–106, esp. 88–89.
58. See Arboleda, *Diccionario biográfico,* passim; Restrepo S. and Rivas, *Genealogías de Santafé,* passim; Bell Lemus, "Conflictos regionales y centralismo," 39–48; Marco Palacios, "Fragmentación regional de las clases dominantes," *Revista Mexicana de Sociología* 13, 4 (October-December 1980), 1663–88.
59. Phelan, *The People and the King;* Stoller, "Liberalism and Conflict in Socorro," 31.
60. See Table 6.1.
61. See Twinam, *Miners, Merchants and Farmers,* 113, 457.
62. The diplomatic agents were Francisco Montoya, José Manuel Arrubla, Juan M. Gómez, Juan de Dios Aranzazu, and Alejandro Vélez. During the 1830s the last two became minister of the interior and governor of Antioquia, respectively. See *Acuerdos,* 2 vols.
63. Cundinamarca continued to be the site of the central bureaucracy and its natives were given key jobs. Cartagena was given the strategic position of secretary of fiscal affairs and various other minor posts. Popayán had very few bureaucrats, the highest being Manuel J. Hurtado, appointed diplomatic agent in London in mid-1823, and Joaquín Mosquera, agent in Chile, Peru, and the Provincias Unidas de la Plata during the same time. However, Popayán's quota substantially increased during the mid 1830s. See *Actas Cúcuta,* 561–65, 743; *Actas Congreso 1823,* 39; *Acuerdos,* 1:137; Harold Bierck, *Vida Pública de Don Pedro Gual* (Caracas, 1983), 216.
64. I am referring mainly to the brothers Eladio and Eloy Manrique and Ramón and Vicente Lombana, and to Gaspar Díaz, Bernardo Herrera, Andrés Durán González, Eujenio Castilla, Manuel Murillo Toro, and Patrocinio Cuellar. See Chapter 7 and Appendix 5.
65. For capsule biographies of the individuals described below, see Appendix 4.
66. Restrepo S. and Rivas, *Genealogías de Santafé,* passim; Vergara y Vergara, *Don Antonio de Vergara y Azcárate,* vol. 2; Isidoro Laverde Amaya, "Los nobles de la colonia,"

BHA 4, 42 (December 1906): 321–28; Hernández de Alba, "Informe sobre servicios de Francisco Morales Fernández," *BHA* 19, no. 223 (August 1932): 555–57; Roberto Tisnes, *Neogranadinos en las órdenes nobiliarias* (Bogotá, 1990); Pastor Restrepo, "Títulos nobiliarios en la Gobernación de Cartagena de Indias," *Boletín Historial* 11, no. 108–111 (March-June 1947): 3–34; Luis Ospina Vásquez *Industria y protección en Colombia. 1810-1930.* 3d. ed. (Medellín, 1979), 30–36.

67. Pitt-Rivers, "Honor and Social Status," 22; Weber, "Class, Status, Party."
68. Burkholder, "Bureaucrats," 96–99; Uribe, "The Lawyers and New Granada's Late Colonial State," 517–49.
69. Four of the colonial survivors–Santiago Arroyo, Jerónimo Torres, José Miguel Pey, José María del Castillo–were dealt with in the previous chapter and/or appear on Appendix 1. Various others could also be added: José Sanz de Santamaría, Enrique Umaña Barragán, Pedro Gual, and Tomás Tenorio. See Appendix 1.
70. On José María, his brother Mateo, and his cousin Benedicto see Restrepo S. and Rivas, *Genealogías de Santafé,* 314–19, 352; García de la Guardia, *Kalendario manual,* 435.
71. On his uncle Eustaquio Galavís see Chapters 4 and 5; Appendix 1; Restrepo S. and Rivas, *Genealogías de Santafé,* 169.
72. In addition, Calvo's offspring married into the important Bogotano families Umaña Rivas and Manrique Benítez. See, "Doctor Casimiro Calvo y Ortega," *BHA* 25, 289–290 (November-December 1938): 836–42; Restrepo S. and Rivas, *Genealogías de Santafé,* 46, 185–87, 387; Appendix 4.
73. On lawyer Antonio (Martínez) Malo and his relative Juan Gíl Martínez Malo, see Appendixes 1 and 4; on José Narciso Casanovas Neira, who descended from a wealthy colonial *escribano* of the Chiquinquira region see Notaria 1a., Chiquinquira, vol. of 1767, fols. 1–2; vol. of 1782, fols. 21–28; vol. of 1813, fols. 42–43; Restrepo and Rivas, *Genealogías de Santafé,* 228.
74. On Canabal, Gori and Lastra, see Appendix 4.
75. On Carvajal y Tenorio and Mosquera, see Appendix 4; on Hurtado, Appendix 1.
76. Some others would also join during the 1830s, including Eladio Urisarri, José María Galavís, Uldarico Leiva and several others listed in Appendix 4.
77. The most representative case of this exclusion was that of Manuel María Bernardo Alvarez Lozano. See Chapter 3, Figure 3.1; Appendix 1; "Recuerdos de la reconquista," 476; Ramón Guerra Azuola, "D. Ramón Nonato Guerra," *BHA* 3, 25 (January, 1905), 25–57, esp. 40–49; Restrepo S. and Rivas, *Genealogías de Santafé,* 22; González, *Memorias,* 130.
78. Safford, "Aspectos sociales de la política en la Nueva Granada, 1825–1850," 172. Safford also refers to the "intellectual" merits of former law student José Eusebio Caro, whose aristocratic ancestry and connections will be discussed in Chapter 7 and presented in Appendix 4.
79. Osorio's father had his small studio near the Bogotá cathedral. On Osorio's bureaucratic trajectory see Appendix 4; see also José Restrepo Posada y Bernardo Sanz de Santamaría, "Osorio," *BHA* 56, no. 651–653 (January–March 1969): 119–30; Ortíz, "Alejandro Osorio," 58–66; Restrepo S., "Juan Jurado," 271–300; idem, *Biografías de los mandatarios y ministros,* 413–22; "Cartas a don Alejandro Osorio," *BHA* 61, no. 704 (April–June 1974): 219–64, esp. 222–23; Frank Safford, "Commerce and Enterprise in Central Colombia. 1821–1870" (Ph.D. diss., Columbia University, 1965), 170.
80. Márquez resigned the *intendencia* of Boyacá (Tunja) in 1827 and moved to his father-in-law's ranch in Sotaquirá, Boyacá. Later he was a moderate during the Ocaña

1828 constitutional convention, and in early 1830 Bolívar appointed him *intendente* of Cundinamarca. On his subsequent bureaucratic career see Appendix 4.
81. See Appendix 4.
82. Museo Nacional. Bogotá. *Cartas y documentos inéditos del Libertador y otros próceres de la independencia* (Bogotá, 1973), 83, emphasis added. See also Rufino and Anjel Cuervo, *Vida de Rufino Cuervo y noticias de su época,* 2 vols., 2d ed. (Bogotá, 1946), 1:80–81, 117–18; Vicente Azuero, "Al público y a mis detractores" (Bogotá, 1832).
83. See Escorcia, *Sociedad y economía en el Valle del Cauca,* 92–93; Uribe and Alvarez, "El parentesco y la formación de las elites," 51–93; Restrepo S. and Rivas, *Genealogías de Santafé;* Arboleda, *Diccionario biográfico.*

Chapter 7
Politics and the "Public Sphere of Civil Society," 1820s–1830s

1. Graham, *Patronage and Politics;* Eduardo Posada-Carbó, ed., *Elections Before Democracy: The History of Elections in Europe and Latin America* (London, 1996); idem, "Elections and Civil Wars in Nineteenth-Century Colombia: The 1875 Presidential Campaign," *JLAS* 26, 3 (October 1994): 621–49; Antonio Annino, *Historia de las elecciones en América Latina durante el siglo XIX* (Mexico, 1996).
2. See Uribe, "The Birth of a Public Sphere."
3. On lawyers and France's public sphere see Bell, *Lawyers and Citizens.*
4. One who invoked it constantly was bureaucrat and historian José M. Restrepo, *Historia de la revolución de la república de Colombia,* 10 vols. (Paris, 1827). On the centrality of "public opinion" to the public sphere of civil society see Habermas, *The Structural Transformation of the Public Sphere,* chap. 4; Reddy, *The Invisible Code,* esp. chap. 5.
5. See Cadena, "José Francisco Pereira," 372.
6. See González, *Memorias,* 126–27; Rufino and Anjel Cuervo, *Vida de Rufino Cuervo,* 1:37–40; Cuervo Márquez, *Vida de José Ignacio de Márquez,* 1:154–56; Vergara y Vergara, *Vida de Estanislao Vergara,* 88; Gustavo Otero Muñoz, *Historia del periodismo en Colombia,* 3d ed. (Bogotá, 1932), 5–75; Arboleda, *Diccionario biográfico y genealógico,* 282–83; David Bushnell, "The Development of the Press in Gran Colombia," *HAHR* 30 (November 1950): 432–52; idem, *The Santander Regime.* See also Uribe, "The Birth of a Public Sphere."
7. See "Comercio y Agricultura." Oficio. Popayán, February 1, 1830. DBNC, Fondo Pineda, 469.
8. Soto, *Mis padecimientos,* 48.
9. See letter to General Domingo Caicedo, Tunja, March 8, 1830, in *Epistolario Caicedo,* 1:67; see also Maingot, "Social Structure, Social Status, and Civil-Military Conflict," 297–355; and Ricardo Alfaro, *Vida del General Tomás Herrera* (Panama, 1960), 16–42.
10. October 1825 letter from General Páez to General Bolívar, cited by Gíl Fortoul, *Historia constitucional,* 451.
11. Páez, *Memorias,* 354.
12. See Graham, *Patronage and Politics;* Costeloe, *The Central Republic;* Di Tella, *National Popular Politics.*
13. See Safford, "Commerce and Enterprise."
14. Restrepo, *Historia de la revolución* (1827), 8:1–12.
15. The decrees can be found in *Cod. Nal.,* 2:405–41; 7:456. See Bushnell, *The Santander*

Regime, 318–48; Lynch, *Simón Bolívar and the Age of Revolution,* 16–17; Pombo and Guerra, *Constituciones de Colombia,* 3:113–59; Lievano Aguirre, *Bolívar,* 425–66.

16. See Bushnell, *The Santander Regime,* 112–26; Vicente Olarte Camacho, *Resúmen histórico sobre la deuda exterior de Colombia del 3 por 100* (Bogotá, 1914), 54–75; Lievano Aguirre, *Razones socio-económicas de la conspiración de septiembre,* 9–23.
17. See Baraya, *Biografías militares;* José M. Obando, *Apuntamientos para la historia,* 2 vols. (Bogotá, 1945) [1848], 1:92–93; José A. Ferrer Benimelli, "Bolívar y la Masonería," *Revista de Indias* 43, no. 172 (July-December 1983): 631–87. A significant exception, from Panama, was Bolivarian general José Domingo Espinar, from a modest family and supported by the region's blacks and mulattos. See Restrepo, *Historia de la revolución* (1827), 8:129, 210.
18. See Guerra, *La Convención de Ocaña,* 454–55.
19. The cases of Rufino Cuervo and José Angel Lastra, who launched an antimilitary campaign in their newspaper *La Miscelánea,* are the best example of this situation. See Carranza B., *San Dionisio de los Caballeros de Tocaima,* 158–60, 214–42; Cuervo, *Vida de José Ignacio de Márquez,* 1:5–100. See also Mosquera's *El Meteoro;* Arboleda, *Diccionario biográfico y genealógico,* 282–83.
20. See Cuervo Márquez, *Vida de José Ignacio de Márquez,* 1: 242; Guerra, *La Convención de Ocaña,* 523–24.
21. See González, *Memorias,* 127–28.
22. See AHN, Archivo Restrepo, Fondo II, vol. 52:176–81; on the formal mechanics of the elections see Guerra, *La Convención de Ocaña,* 213–20.
23. *Gaceta de Colombia,* May 15, 1828.
24. Vergara y Vergara, *Vida de Estanislao Vergara,* 137; Malcolm Deas, "La presencia de la política nacional en la vida provinciana, pueblerina y rural de Colombia en el primer siglo de la república," in *La unidad nacional en América Latina: Del regionalismo a la nacionalidad,* ed. Marco Palacios (Mexico, 1983), 149–73; Vergara y Vergara, *Vida de Estanislao Vergara,* 137.
25. See, for instance, the bitter February 1828 message from the Magdalena military division. AHN, Archivo Restrepo, Fondo II, Reel 35:182. Similar messages were sent by other military garrisons (see *Gaceta de Colombia,* May 15, 1828); Santander charged Bolívar with promoting them. See Guerra, *La Convención de Ocaña,* 289.
26. See Guerra, *La Convención de Ocaña,* 315–62.
27. José M. Castillo y Rada, "Memorias," 515; the list of Castillo's followers can be found in Guerra, *La Convención de Ocaña,* 452; see also Ferrer Benimelli, "Bolívar y la Masonería," 631–87.
28. The texts of the two groups' projects can be found in Guerra, *La Convención de Ocaña,* 315–62, 368–402; see also letters from Luis Vargas Tejada to James Henderson, in J. Leon Helguera, ed.,"Un testimonio epistolar de la gran convención por Luis Vargas Tejada. 2 Marzo al 16 de Junio, 1828," [Cartas de Luis Vargas Tejada] *Archivos* 1 (1967): 83–139, esp. 104, 113–14, 123; on their rejection of a "tumultuous democracy" see Castillo y Rada, "Memorias," 471; Vergara y Vergara, *Vida de Estanislao Vergara,* 142, 216–49.
29. See *Gaceta de Colombia,* September 7, 1828. Bogotá's council was very active in demanding that Bolívar assume dictatorial powers, few were opposed. See José Manuel Restrepo to Francisco Montoya, Bogotá, June 14, 1828, in "Cartas inéditas de José M. Restrepo," 115–16; José Pascual Afanador, *La Democracia en San Gíl o cartas del ciudadano José Pascual Afanador dirigidas a los señores de la nobleza Sanjileña sobre la naturaleza y efectos de un programa* (Socorro, 1851), 80–81; Celiano Monge, "El Doctor Rafael María Vásquez," *BHA* 9, 108 (April 1915): 718–28, esp. 719; Arango Mejía,

Genealogías de Antioquia y Caldas, 2:346. On the Consejo de Estado, see Guerra, *La Convención de Ocaña,* 523; Isidoro Laverde Amaya, *Bibliografía Colombiana* (Bogotá, 1895), 322–30; Rodríguez Piñérez, ed., *La Vida de Castillo y Rada,* 23–70; Vergara y Vergara, *Vida de Estanislao Vergara,* 11–28, 144–68; García de la Guardia, *Kalendario manual,* 182.

30. See August 28, 1828, decree, in *Cod. Nal.,* 3:408.
31. See decrees of November 17, December 22 and 23, 1828, in *Cod. Nal.,* 3:451–52, 464–66; Alejandro Vélez, "Exposición que el Secretario del Interior y Relaciones Exteriores del gobierno de la Nueva Granada, hace al Congreso Constitucional del año de 1833." Bogotá, 2 Marzo, 1833, esp. 23. For an excellent analysis of this period see Bushnell, "The Last Dictatorship: Betrayal or Consummation," *HAHR* 61, 1 (1983): 65–105.
32. Vergara y Vergara, *Vida de Estanislao Vergara,* chap. 9, esp. 234–35; Cevallos, *Resúmen de la historia del Ecuador,* 4:350–80; Luis A. Cuervo, "La monarquía en Colombia," *Revista Moderna* 3, 23 (June 1, 1916): 525–36.
33. Castillo y Rada to Mariano Montilla, April 7, 1829, in Rodríguez de Piñérez, *Vida de Castillo y Rada,* 369; Estanislao Vergara to Bolívar, May 11 and 22, 1829, in Vergara y Vergara, *Vida de Estanislao Vergara,* 224. Bolivar, exhausted by the repeated challenges, defined elections as "open combat." See Brading, *The First America,* 618.
34. On the "homogeneous" nature of the congress see Castillo y Rada to Bolívar, August 22, 1829, in Rodríguez de Piñérez, *Vida de Castillo y Rada,* 307.
35. See Art. 15, 1821 Constitution, and Art. 5, August 29, 1827 law, in Pombo and Guerra, *Constituciones de Colombia,* 3:69; and *Cod. Nal.,* 3:307, 489. Mariano Montilla to Colonel Federico Adlercreutz, Turbaco, April 19, 1829, in Coriolano Parra Pérez, ed., *La cartera del Coronel Conde de Adlercreutz: Documentos inéditos relativos a la historia de Venezuela y la Gran Colombia* (París, 1928), 86–96. See also letters of May 2, 9, 18 and 25, and July 9, 1829, in ibid., 89–100.
36. See Arboleda, *Historia contemporánea,* 1:19–20; Arts. 1 and 13, August, 29, 1827 law, and Arts. 12 and 27, December 24, 1828 decree, in *Cod. Nal.,* 3:307–14, 491, 494; see also Pombo and Guerra, *Constituciones de Colombia,* 3:175; Lievano Aguirre, *Bolívar,* 456, 478.
37. The provincials also charged extended fraud on the part of the aristocratic clique. Obando, *Apuntamientos para la historia,* 1:152–53.
38. See Cevallos, *Resúmen de la historia de Ecuador,* 4:chap. 10; Arboleda, *Historia contemporánea,* 1:239; Gil Fortoul, *Historia constitucional,* chaps. 8 and 9, esp. 475.
39. See Cevallos, *Resúmen de la historia de Ecuador,* 4: 394, 401; Lievano Aguirre, *Bolívar,* 495; Antonio Malo to Domingo Caicedo, Tunja, March 8, 1830, in *Epistolario Caicedo,* 1:270; Arboleda, *Historia contemporánea,* 1:22, 30–32; Obando, *Apuntamientos para la historia,* 1:158–59.
40. A detailed chronology of the regional events is offered by Arboleda, *Historia contemporánea,* 1:40–49, 60–97; see also Cevallos, *Resúmen de la historia de Ecuador,* 4:403–12.
41. See Arboleda, *Historia contemporánea,* 1:18, 58–60; Obando, *Apuntamientos para la historia,* 1:215; García de la Guardia, *Kalendario manual,* 106, 161–62, 203; José María Rivas, *Biografía del ilustre procer General Rafael Urdaneta* (Maracaibo, 1888), 10; Mario Briceño Iragorri, *Vida y papeles de Urdaneta el jóven* (Caracas, 1946), chap. 2; Restrepo and Rivas, *Genealogías de Santafé,* 283; Pardo Umaña, *Haciendas de la sabana,* esp. 187–95.
42. García de la Guardia, *Kalendario manual,* 161; Arboleda, *Historia contemporánea,* 1:59, 89; José Tomás Gabrois, "Juan García del Río," *Colombia Ilustrada,* no. 15 (August

1890): 226–28, esp. 228; Restrepo and Rivas, *Genealogías de Santafé*, 314–18; Rivas, *Biografía del ilustre prócer*, 30; Obando, *Apuntamientos para la historia*, 1:224–25.
43. See *GNG*, September 28, 1830; Arboleda, *Historia contemporánea*, 1:51, 61, 65, 67, 78, 81; Cevallos, *Resúmen de la historia de Ecuador*, 4:425–29; Gabrois, "Juan García del Río," 226–28. On the different regional reactions see Arboleda, *Historia contemporánea*, 1:60–71. On the position of Cali's elites and their social background see "Incidente . . . Causa Grice" 1838, 11, 18; Vicente Borrero, "Solicitud que el señor Doctor Vicente Borrero hace a la Cámara de Representantes en sus sesiones de 1873" (Cali, January 20, 1873); Arboleda, *Diccionario biográfico*, 49–55; Escorcia, *Sociedad y economía en el Valle del Cauca*, 48–52, 99–101.
44. See *El Constitucional*, April 12, 1827; *GNG*, no. 482, September 19, 1830; "Raimundo Santamaría" (Bogotá, 1869), DBNC, F. Pineda, 314, 11; Safford, "Commerce and enterprise," 309; Arango Mejía, *Genealogías de Antioquia y Caldas*, 2:341–45; Pardo Umaña, *Haciendas de la sabana*, 261–62; John Steuart, *Narración de una expedición a la capital de la Nueva Granada y residencia allí de once meses. Bogotá en 1836–1837* (Bogotá, 1989), 35, 75, 105; Restrepo Sáenz, *Gobernadores de Antioquia*, 2:251–53; José Manuel Restrepo to Francisco Montoya, September 28, 1828, and October 21, 1828, in "Cartas inéditas de José M. Restrepo," 116–19.
45. See Arboleda, *Historia contemporánea*, 1:58, 98, 108.
46. See Raimundo Rivas, "Apuntes sobre la organización de las secretarias de estado," *BHA* 14, 161 (February 1923): 293–311; Bernardo Caicedo, "Ministros de guerra desde 1821," *BHA* 14, 161 (February 1923): 285–93; Arboleda, *Historia contemporánea*, 1:100; Cuervo Márquez, *Vida de José Ignacio de Márquez*, 1:279; Rodríguez Piñérez, *Vida de Castillo y Rada*, 66; Baraya, *Biografías militares*, 53–55, 234–45; José M. Restrepo Sáenz, "Gobernantes de Pamplona," *BHA* 36, 411–13 (January-March 1949), 97–129, esp. 107; Rausch, *A Tropical Plains Frontier*, chap. 9; idem, "La doma de un caudillo colombiano: Juan Nepomuceno Moreno, de Casanare," *BCB* 26, 20 (1989): 17–31.
47. See June 10, 1831, decree, in *Cod. Nal.*, 4:270–71; Arboleda, *Historia contemporánea*, 1:100–101, 109.
48. See November 14, 1831, decree, in *Cod. Nal.*, 4:305–07.
49. See Arboleda, *Historia contemporánea*, 1:98; Pombo and Guerra, *Constituciones de Colombia*, 3:238; May 7, 1831, decree, in *Cod. Nal.*, 4:259.
50. See Arboleda, *Historia contemporánea*, 1:250–51; 2: 558–62; Roberto Botero Saldarriaga, *Francisco Antonio Zea*, 2 vols. (Bogotá, 1969); Restrepo Sáenz, *Gobernadores de Antioquia*, 2:333–34; "Vejeces," *La Miscelánea* 3, no. 7 (May 1897): 212–30, esp. 225; no. 8, (July 1897): 253–65, esp. 255; Luis Latorre Mendoza, *Historia e historias de Medellín* (Medellín, 1972), 179–80.
51. *Acuerdos*, 1:48; Bushnell, *The Santander Regime*, 111–26; Enrique Barriga Villalba, *El empréstito de Zea y el préstamo de Erick Bollman de 1822; documentos* (Bogotá, 1969).
52. AHN, Empleados Varios, vol. 10, fol. 207–23, 241–43; Estanislao Gómez Barrientos, "Don Gabriel Echeverri," *El Montañés. Revista de Literatura, Artes y Ciencias*, no. 14 (January 1899); no. 15 (February 1899); idem, "Don Julián Vásquez," *El Montañés. Revista de Literatura, Artes y Ciencias*, no. 19–20 (June-July 1899); no. 21 (August 1899); no. 22–24 (September-November 1899); idem, *Don Mariano Ospina y su época*, 1:355; Vicente Restrepo, *Estudio sobre las minas de oro y plata de Colombia* (Bogotá, 1952); "Vejeces," 215–356; Latorre Mendoza, *Historia e historias*, 177–85; Restrepo Sáenz, *Gobernadores de Antioquia*, 2: 151–68, 217–47; Safford, "Commerce and Enterprise," 338; Magnus Morner, "El comercio de Antioquia alrededor de 1830 según un observador sueco," *ACHSC*, no. 2 (1964): 317–32.

53. Pardo Umaña, *Haciendas de la sabana,* 153, 260–63, 283–85; Ortíz, *Reminiscencias,* 60–62; Restrepo Sáenz, *Gobernadores de Antioquia,* 2:159; Germán Vargas, "La fábrica de losa," *Papel Periódico Ilustrado* 2 (May 25, 1883): 285–86.
54. See "José María García de Toledo," 1134–37; *Genealogías de Santa Fé* (Bogotá, 1991), 160–61. The Arrublas were brothers of the wealthy Juan Manuel (1789–1874), who also settled in Bogotá. See Arango Mejía, *Genealogías de Antioquia y Caldas,* 1:119; Restrepo and Rivas, *Genealogías de Santafé,* 62–67, 318–19.
55. Gómez Barrientos, *Don Mariano Ospina y su época,* 1: 347–48; Arango Mejía, *Genealogías de Antioquia y Caldas,* 1:398–99; Pardo Umaña, *Haciendas de la sabana,* 274–75, 283, 285, 294.
56. See Arango Mejía, *Genealogías de Antioquia y Caldas,* 2: 90; "Sanz de Santamaría," 278–79; Restrepo and Rivas, *Genealogías de Santafé,* 64, 318–19; on Luis's participation in the "Sociedad de Industria Bogotana" see Vargas, "La fábrica de losa," 285–86.
57. Other important Antioqueños who married into Bogotá's aristocratic families were José Joaquín Alvarez del Pino, who married Bárbara Bastida Lee, and Wenceslao Campuzano, who married Joaquina Azuola y Olano. See Restrepo and Rivas, *Genealogías de Santafé,* 25, 101; Arango Mejía, *Genealogías de Antioquia y Caldas,* 1:197.
58. A good synthesis of their antimilitary newspaper, *La Miscelánea,* is provided by Gabriel Henao Mejía, *Juan de Dios Aranzazu* (Bogotá, 1953), 46–83.
59. On Santander's critical assessment of the Antioqueños' stand see Henao Mejía, *Juan de Dios Aranzazu,* 139–55, 170–71; Doris Wise de Gouzy, *Antología del pensamiento de Mariano Ospina Rodríguez,* 2 vols. (Bogotá, 1990), 1:36–37.
60. See José Manuel Restrepo to Francisco Montoya, June 14 and October 21, 1828 in "Cartas inéditas de José M. Restrepo," 115–19; Restrepo Sáenz, *Gobernadores de Antioquia,* 2:287, 319, 323; González, *Memorias,* 134; Wise de Gouzy, *Antología del pensamiento de Mariano Ospina Rodríguez,* 1:37–38; Anibal Galindo, *Recuerdos históricos de Anibal Galindo. 1840 a 1895* (Bogotá, 1900) [1895], 10; Lievano Aguirre, *Razones socio-económicas.*
61. See *Cod. Nal.,* 3: 366–67. After the plot, the Antioqueños were further affected by Bolívar's decree of December 23, 1828, which taxed the export of gold. See ibid., 468–70; on the smuggling of gold by merchants see Morner, "El comercio de Antioquia alrededor de 1830," 323. The Antioqueños continued to lobby against these decrees and had them modified in 1832, soon after the defeat of the last Bolivarian groups. See Soto, *Mis padecimientos,* 52; see also April 25, 1833 law, in *Cod. Nal.,* 5:8–9.
62. See letters from José M. Restrepo to Francisco Montoya, June 14, and October 21, 1828, in "Cartas inéditas de José M. Restrepo," 115–19; Restrepo Sáenz, *Gobernadores de Antioquia,* 2:287, 319, 323; González, *Memorias,* 134; Arango Mejía, *Genealogías de Antioquia y Caldas,* 2:346–47; Wise de Gouzy, *Antología del pensamiento de Mariano Ospina Rodríguez,* 1:37–38; Galindo, *Recuerdos históricos,* 10.
63. See December 4, 1829 petition of Antioquia merchants fined by Bolívar, and December, 15, 1829 *acta* with signatures of Córdova's supporters in Wise de Gouzy, *Antología del pensamiento de Mariano Ospina Rodríguez,* 1:171–78; see also Vergara y Vergara, *Vida de Estanislao Vergara,* chap. 10; Henao Mejía, *Juan de Dios Aranzazu,* 155–64; Restrepo Sáenz, *Gobernadores de Antioquia,* 2: 160–61, 252–53; Lievano Aguirre, *Bolívar,* 480–85; Jorge O. Melo, "Progreso y guerras civiles entre 1829 y 1859," in *Historia de Antioquia* (Medellín, 1988), 101–16; Francisco Zuluaga, *José María*

Obando: De soldado realista a caudillo republicano (Bogotá, 1985), 88; May 29, 1833, decree, in *Cod. Nal.,* 5:22–23.

64. Guerra, *La Convención de Ocaña,* 481–530; Vergara y Vergara, *Vida de Estanislao Vergara,* 141–66; Lievano Aguirre, *Razones socio-económicas.* Twenty-four-year-old Antioqueño Wenceslao Zulaibar and twenty-one-year-old Socorrano Pedro Celestino Azuero were executed. Most conspirators were exiled. See *Causas y memorias,* 3 vols.
65. See *Causa y memorias,* 3 vols., passim; "Vargas," *BHA* 58, 678–680 (April-June 1971): 269–309, esp. 274; Helguera, ed., "Un testimonio epistolar de la gran convención"; Fabio Lozano y Lozano, "Vicente Azuero," *BHA* 8, 92 (January 1913): 449–527, esp. 496–98; González, *Memorias,* 131–34; Soriano Lleras, *Lorenzo María Lleras,* 18; Arango Mejía, *Genealogías de Antioquia y Caldas,* 1:342–46; Restrepo Sáenz, *Gobernadores de Antioquia,* 2:251–53, 319; Cadena, "D. José Francisco Pereira," esp. 372.
66. See Wise de Gouzy, *Antología del pensamiento de Mariano Ospina Rodríguez,* 1:171–78; see also Vergara y Vergara, *Vida de Estanislao Vergara,* chap. 10; Henao Mejía, *Juan de Dios Aranzazu,* 155–64; Restrepo Sáenz, *Gobernadores de Antioquia,* 2:160–61, 252–53.
67. See Arboleda, *Historia contemporánea,* 1:57; Restrepo Sáenz, *Gobernadores de Antioquia,* 2:162, 170, 339–40; Afanador, *La democracia en San Gíl,* 84.
68. See Henao Mejía, *Juan de Dios Aranzazu,* 24–27, 106–10, 179–80; Restrepo Sáenz, *Gobernadores de Antioquia,* 2:173–81, 237–47; Ramón Correa, "Aranzazu, Juan de Dios," *BHA* 2, 13 (September 1903): 62–63; Uribe Angel, "Recuerdos de un viaje a Medellín," 297–98; "Alejandro Vélez," (Bogotá, March 19, 1842). DBNC, Fondo Pineda, 849; Acevedo Latorre, *Colaboradores de Santander,* 349; Luis F. Molina Londoño and Ociel Castaño Z. "El 'Burro de Oro.' Carlos Coroliano Amador, empresario antioqueño del siglo XIX," *BCB* 24, 13 (1987): 3–27, esp. 3; Restrepo, *Estudio sobre las minas de oro,* 51–52; Wise de Gouzy, *Antología del pensamiento de Mariano Ospina Rodríguez,* 1: 43–44.
69. See Restrepo Sáenz, *Gobernadores de Antioquia,* 2:339; Arboleda, *Historia contemporánea,* 1:257, 259; Raimundo Rivas, *Relaciones internacionales entre Colombia y los Estados Unidos, 1810–1850* (Bogotá, 1915), 15, 21, 36; Arboleda, *Diccionario biográfico y genealógico,* 204. See also Emilio Robledo, "Archivo del General Gómez," *Repertorio Histórico* 15, no. 145 (January 1940): 352–77; Gustavo Otero Muñoz, "Boceto biográfico de cien cancilleres colombianos," in *Historia de la Cancillería de San Carlos* (Bogotá, 1942), 111–432, esp. 173–75; Melo, "Progreso y guerras civiles," esp. 102–03.
70. Emiro Kastos, *Artículos escogidos* (Bogotá, 1972); Safford, "Commerce and Enterprise," 217; Restrepo Sáenz, *Gobernadores de Antioquia,* 2:337–58; Figure 9.1.
71. The other *departamentos* were Cundinamarca, Cauca, Magdalena, Boyacá, and Istmo (Panama). See May 10, 1830, decree, in *Cod. Nal.,* 4:183–84; Gustavo Arboleda, "Divisiones territoriales de Colombia," *BHA* 11, 122 (December 1916): 67–97; idem, *Historia contemporánea,* 1:33.
72. On earlier decrees governing trading in gold, see *Cod. Nal.,* 4:318–19; 7:574–78; Soto, *Mis padecimientos,* 52. On the mint, regional tribunal, and interest rates see Juan de Dios Aranzazu to Juan María Gómez, Medellín, February 25, 1833, in Robledo, "Archivo del General Gómez," 356; Latorre Mendoza, *Historia e historias,* 178; April 24, 1834 decree, in *Cod. Nal.,* 5:171–72; May 26, 1835 law, in *Recopilación de leyes,* 95.
73. See an informative discussion of some of these contracts in Safford, "Commerce and Enterprise," 187–234; John P. Harrison, "The Colombian Tobacco Industry

From Government Monopoly to Free Trade. 1778–1876" (Ph.D. diss., University of California, Berkeley, 1951) Abstract, CEDE, Bogotá, 1969, 174–95.
74. See renewal of lease between Colombia's general treasurer and merchant Juan Manuel Arrublas. AHN, Empleados Varios, vol. 12: 299–302.
75. See Arboleda, *Historia contemporánea,* 1:193; Henao Mejía, *Juan de Dios Aranzazu,* 195–206; Arango Mejía, *Genealogías de Antioquia y Caldas,* 2:91; Restrepo Sáenz, *Gobernadores de Antioquia,* 2:151–68.
76. See Wise de Gouzy, *Antología del pensamiento de Mariano Ospina Rodriguez;* Melo, "Progreso y guerras civiles."
77. Nutini, *Wages of Conquest.* For the access of Brazil's plutocrats to the titled aristocracy see Eul-Soo Pang, *In Pursuit of Honor and Power: Noblemen of the Southern-Cross in Nineteenth-Century Brazil* (Tuscaloosa, 1988), chap. 7.
78. See, for instance, the *Constitucional de Cundinamarca,* March 20, 1836; May 22, 1836; and June 5, 1836. The *Constitucional de Antioquia* at first supported the candidacy of provincial lawyer Vicente Azuero, but later declared its neutrality. See, for instance issues of July 10, 1836 and December 18, 1836.
79. For references to the newspaper's followers in Ambalema, Cartagena, Girón, Neiva, Santa Marta, and Tunja see *El Imperio de los Principios,* October 9, 1836.
80. See *El Imperio de los Principios,* July 17, 1836; Habermas, *The Structural Transformation of the Public Sphere,* chap. 4. On the deep involvement in politics by all sectors of New Granada's society see Malcolm Deas, "La política en la vida cotidiana republicana," in *Historia de la vida cotidiana en Colombia,* ed. Beatríz Castro Carvajal (Bogotá, 1996), 271–90.
81. See Bushnell, "Elecciones presidenciales colombianas," 230–38; Santiago Borrero Mutis, "Análisis político de las elecciones presidenciales y a cámaras legislativas en la Nueva Granada durante 1836." Universidad de Los Andes, Tesis Departamento de Ciencia Política, 1976; Posada-Carbó, "Alternación y república: Elecciones en la Nueva Granada y Venezuela, 1835–1836."
82. See David Bushnell, "Elecciones presidenciales colombianas. 1825–1856," in *Compendio de estadísticas históricas de Colombia,* ed. Miguel Urrutia and Mario Arrubla (Bogotá, 1970), 230–38.
83. Obando, *Apuntamientos para la historia,* 273–81; Arboleda, *Historia contemporánea,* 1:272. See also law of May 12, 1837, in *Cod. Nal.,* 6:317–18; *Libertad y orden.* Bogotá, March 1837. DBNC, F. Vergara, 12, 3.
84. See Gómez Barrientos, *Don Mariano Ospina y su época,* 1:42–48, 51–53. On Ospina's social background and political trajectory see "El ciudadano Mariano Ospina Rodríguez o relación de sus hechos y compendio de sus principios" (Bogotá, 1856?), 17–49; Wise de Gouzy, *Antología del pensamiento de Mariano Ospina Rodriguez,* 1:5–15, 17–22, 27–31, 39–56; Gómez Barrientos, "Don Julián Vásquez," 249–58; Restrepo and Rivas, *Genealogías de Santafé,* 212–13; González, *Memorias,* 132.
85. Samper, *Historia de un alma,* 1:165–66; AHN, Indices Notaría 1a, vol. 16, 1842–1848, fol. 42:15–21. For other members of this group see Samper, *Galería nacional de hombres ilustres,* 197; *La Bandera Negra,* April 8, 1838, 310–11.
86. Rafael María Vásquez, "Exposición documentada que R.M.V actual catedrático de filosofía en el Colegio de San Bartolomé y en la Primera Casa de Educación hace de su conducta en contestación a diferentes cargos políticos y relijiosos que se le han hecho ahora y antes," (Bogotá, 1832); Monge, "Dr. Rafael Maria Vasquez," 720; Pereira Gamba, "Los conflictos de Bogotá," 480–81.
87. On Neiva's colonial economy see Joaquín García Borrero, *Neiva en el siglo XVII*

(Bogotá, 1939), 67–72, 137–39, 145–46, 182–83; Jaime Jaramillo Uribe, "La economía del Virreinato (1740–1810)," in *Historia económica de Colombia,* ed. José A. Ocampo (Bogotá, 1987), 49–85, esp. 74; Hernán Clavijo Ocampo, *Formación histórica de las elites locales en el Tolima,* 2 vols. (Bogotá, 1993), 1:chap. 6.

88. The director cynically argued that the *colegio* admitted "aún los **Pardos** y los Lombanas," a pun on the word *pardo* (mestizo), also a common last name. See *AHN,* Anexo, Inst. Pub. vol. 3:566, emphasis added.
89. See Gómez Barrientos, *Don Mariano Ospina y su época,* 1: 48; Kastos, *Artículos escogidos,* 154.
90. Plazas, *Genealogías de Neiva,* 113–18; José M. Restrepo Sáenz, *Gobernadores y próceres de Neiva* (Bogotá, 1941), 182, 301.
91. See Ignacio Gutiérrez Vergara to Rufino Cuervo, September 29, 1841, in *Epistolario Cuervo,* 2:120–23; *Almanaque Nacional 1838,* 83; Cuervo Márquez, *Vida de José I. de Márquez,* 2:82–83; AHN, Inst. Pub., vol. 127:279, 434.
92. See *El Día,* January 30, 1842.
93. On Andrés de Iriarte and his nephew see Hernández de Alba, "Galería de hijos insignes," 295–96; Burkholder and Chandler, *From Impotence to Authority,* 182; Plazas, *Genealogías de Neiva,* 326–27.
94. See Restrepo and Rivas, *Genealogías de Santafé,* 378; Arboleda, *Historia contemporánea,* 1:25, 279; *La historia como noticia 1988,* no. 1, 35.
95. Plazas, *Genealogías de Neiva,* 321–22; Pereira Gamba, "Los conflictos de Bogotá," 530–31; Samper, *Historia de un alma,* 1:170.
96. *La Bandera Negra,* October 29, 1837, 23–24; Salvador Camacho Roldán, *Mis memorias* (Bogotá, 1946), 68.
97. Plazas, *Genealogías de Neiva,* 291, 358–60, 580; Restrepo Sáenz, *Gobernadores y próceres,* 323, 354–55, 496–97.
98. See May 23, 1837 decree creating the cantón of Chaparral, in *Cod. Nal.,* 6:325; *GNG,* no. 396, April 14, 1839. On Chaparral's colonial background see the outstanding study of Clavijo Ocampo, *Formación histórica de las élites locales en el Tolima,* 1, 238–46.
99. Restrepo Sáenz, *Gobernadores y próceres,* 356–57; Plazas, *Genealogías de Neiva,* 175–77.
100. Samper,"Galería nacional," 118–26; Otero Muñoz, "Boceto biográfico de cien cancilleres colombianos," 185; Ignacio Gutiérrez Ponce, *Vida de Don Ignacio Gutiérrez V. y episodios históricos de su tiempo, 1806–1877,* 2 vols. (London, 1900), 1:492; Gómez Barrientos, *Don Mariano Ospina y su época,* 1:175; Ortíz, *Reminiscencias,* 197.

Chapter 8
Legal Education: The Making of Bureaucrats and Citizens

1. For a detailed discussion of these reform attempts see Victor M. Uribe, "Disputas entre estado y sociedad sobre la educación de los abogados a fines de la etapa colonial en la Nueva Granada," *Historia y Sociedad* 3 (December 1996): 33–57.
2. See Ricaurte, "Compendio de lo actuado sobre estudios públicos," 346, 352.
3. The *Junta's* first director was *fiscal* Moreno y Escandón. The royal *visitador* was lawyer Gutiérrez de Piñérez. See Silva, *La reforma de estudios,* 74–75.
4. See Ricaurte, "Compendio de lo actuado sobre estudios públicos," 365; Richard Herr, *The Eighteenth-Century Revolution in Spain* (Princeton, 1958), 177–79. On how legal education was geared to train bureaucrats see Victor M. Uribe, "Preparando 'mandarines': Apuntes sobre la historia de la ciencia administrativa en Nueva

Granada durante la colonia y comienzos de la república, 1590–1830," *Innovar, Revista de Ciencias Administrativa y Sociales,* Universidad Nacional de Colombia, Bogotá, 7 (January-June 1996): 87–97.
5. Andrés José Iriarte y Rojas was the first professor of public law in 1781. See Ricaurte, "Compendio de lo actuado sobre estudios públicos," 370–71; AHN, Médicos y Abogados, vol. 4:426; Hernández de Alba, *Vida y escritos del doctor José F. Restrepo,* 55; Burkholder and Chandler, *From Impotence to Authority,* 182.
6. Ricaurte, "Compendio de lo actuado sobre estudios públicos," 370–71.
7. Hernández de Alba, *Crónica del muy ilustre colegio,* 2:274–89; Silva, *Universidad y sociedad,* 105, 125; Guerra, "Imaginarios y valores de 1808," 170.
8. See Viceroy Ezpeleta's "Relación de gobierno del Exmo Sor., Dn Joséf de Ezpeleta," 219–20; AHN, Médicos y Abogados, vol. 6:443–45; Pérez Sarmiento, ed., *Causas celebres;* Herr, *The Eighteenth-Century Revolution,* 370–75; Martínez Delgado, *Noticia biográfica,* 96; Hernández de Alba, *Crónica del muy ilustre colegio . . . del Rosario,* 2:295–98; Vásquez, *Hilvanes históricos,* 70; Hernández de Alba and Lozano, ed., *Documentos sobre el doctor Vicente Azuero,* x–xi; Robert Means, *Underdevelopment and the Development of Law: Corporations and Corporation Law in Nineteenth-Century Colombia* (Chapel Hill, 1980), 50; Restrepo, *Autobiografía,* 8–9; AHN, Anexo, Inst. Pub., vol. 4:407.
9. AHN, Colonia, Colegios, vol. 2:141, 147, 219; José A. Salazar, *Estudios eclesiásticos superiores en el Nuevo Reino de Granada* (Madrid, 1946), 380;
10. See "Temores de Fernando VII," *BHA* 7 (1912): 704–06. [transcript of Royal cédula issued on May, 18, 1801 on *"censores regios"*]; Hernández de Alba, ed., *Docs.,* 6:2–6; Juan M. Pacheco, *La Ilustración en el Nuevo Reino de Granada* (Caracas, 1975), 102–03.
11. See José M. Pérez Ayala, *Antonio Caballero y Góngora: Virrey y arzobispo de Santafé, 1723–1796* (Bogotá, 1946); Phelan, *The People and the King;* Roberto Tisnes, *Caballero y Góngora y los Comuneros* (Bogotá, 1984).
12. *Fiscal* Moreno y Escandón was transferred to the Lima viceroyalty in May 1781. See Melo, "Francisco Antonio Moreno y Escandón," 5–7; McFarlane, "Economic and Political Change in the Viceroyalty of New Granada."
13. See Kuethe, *Military Reform and Society.* On other revolts see Rebecca E. Mond, "Indian Rebellion and Bourbon Reform in New Granada: Riots in Pasto, 1780–1800," *HAHR,* 73, 1 (February 1993): 99–124.
14. See Pacheco, *La Ilustración en el Nuevo Reino de Granada;* Carlos Restrepo Canal, "Incidentes que dieron origen al plan de estudios de Moreno y Escandón," *BHA* 23, 266 (November 1936): 730–34; Colciencias, *Historia social de las ciencias en Colombia* (Bogotá, 1986).
15. See Hernández de Alba, *Vida y escritos del doctor José F. Restrepo;* Glick, "Science and Independence in Latin America." Some of these intellectuals cooperated with or launched "enlightened" newspapers. See Uribe, "The Birth of a Public Sphere."
16. Victor M. Uribe, "Kill all the Lawyers!: Lawyers and the Independence Movement in New Granada, 1809–1820," *The Americas* 52, 2 (October 1995): 175–210.
17. See Restrepo, *El Colegio de San Bartolomé,* 39–40, 128–31. Most of the *colegio*'s dropouts joined the revolutionary armies. See Pacheco and Molina Lemus, *La familia de Santander.*
18. See "Relación del estado del Nuevo Reino de Granada, que hace el Arzobispo Obispo de Cordoba a su sucesor el excelentisimo señor don Francisco Gíl y Lemos." Turbaco, February 20, 1789, in Germán Colmenares, ed., *Relaciones e informes . . . ,* 1:426; Silva, *La reforma de estudios,* 74.
19. See Diego Mendoza Pérez, "Moreno y Escandón y la reforma universitaria en Co-

lombia," in idem, *Evolución de la sociedad colombiana. Ensayos escogidos* (Bogotá, 1994), 311–37, esp. 314–21.
20. New Granada was the first independent nation in the New World to undertake serious reform of higher education. See Young, "University Reform in New Granada," 1.
21. See Bushnell, *The Santander Regime,* 186–87; Theodora MacKennan, "Santander and the Vogue of Benthamism in Colombia." (Ph.D. diss., Loyola University, 1970), 111.
22. See *Gaceta de Colombia,* September 16, 1821. See also articles of Tunja's 1811 constitution and Antioquia's 1812 constitution in Pombo and Guerra, *Constituciones de Colombia,* 1:277, 346; 2: 378; Julio César García, *Historia de la instrucción pública en Antioquia* (Medellín, 1924), 53, 59; Hernández de Alba, "Galería de hijos insignes," 141–439, esp. 167–68.
23. *Correo del Orinóco,* February 24, 1821; Mackennan, "Santander and the Vogue of Benthamism," 111, 156–57.
24. *Gaceta de Colombia,* September 16, 1821; *Correo del Orinóco,* November 17, 1821; *Actas Cúcuta,* 373; Leopoldo Uprimny, *El pensamiento filosófico y político en el Congreso de Cúcuta* (Bogotá, 1971), 164–65.
25. *Actas Cúcuta,* 315–16.
26. See AHN, Inst. Pub. vol. 109:135, 138–48, 156–57, 170, 567; vol. 110:306–10. See also Belisario Matos Hurtado, "Apuntaciones y documentos para la historia de Pamplona (el antiguo Convento de San Agustín)," *BHA* 30, 344–345 (June-July 1943): 574–91; "Creación del Colegio de Varones de Cartago," *BHA* 19, 220 (March 1932): 281–82; "Historia del Colegio Público de Cartago," *BHA* 19, 220 (May 1932): 284–86; Bushnell, *The Santander Regime,* 214–19.
27. See AHN, Inst. Pub. vol. 106:823, 847–58, 919; Juan de Dios Arias, "El Colegio de San José de Guanenta en San Gil," *BHA* 30, 342–343 (April-May 1943): 386–409; see also Bushnell, *The Santander Regime,* 187.
28. *Acuerdos,* 1: 84, 211; 2:119; *Gaceta de Colombia,* December 29, 1822; March 30, 1823; April 6, 1823; April 27, 1823; June 13, 1824. In September 1840, an official list referred to the existence of fifteen *colegios provinciales,* as well as four seminaries, all of which taught law. See AHN, Inst. Pub. vol. 115:517–20; and Bushnell, *The Santander Regime,* 186–87.
29. See Restrepo, *El Colegio de San Bartolomé,* 48; Young, "University Reform," 51–52.
30. Restrepo, *El Colegio de San Bartolomé,* 48; Hernández de Alba, "Galería de hijos insignes," 232; *Constitucional de Cundinamarca,* December 4, 1831, 43; AHN, Inst. Pub. vol. 106:780–81, 893–97, 919; Afanador, *La democracia en San Gil,* 87–89; Arboleda, *Diccionario biográfico y genealógico,* 90; *Acuerdos,* 1:73, 125, 161; 2:14; "Homenaje a Pedro Martínez de Pinillos con motivo del bicentenario de su nacimiento," *BHA* 35, 399–401 (January-March 1948): 1–21, esp. 11; AHN, Inst. Pub. vol. 111:715; Emilio Robledo, *La Universidad de Antioquia* (Medellín, 1923), 27.
31. See *Acuerdos,* 1:66.
32. See articles of Cundinamarca's 1811 and Cartagena's 1812 constitutions regarding the supervision of *colegios* by the government in Pombo and Guerra, *Constituciones de Colombia,* 1: 188; 2:162–63. The government appointed the directors for the *colegios* of Boyacá, Cali, Ibagué, Antioquia, and Mompós from 1822 to 1825. See *Acuerdos,* 1:73, 125, 161; 2: 14; "Homenaje a Pedro Martínez de Pinillos," 399–401; on the government's participation in the appointment of the professors of several such *colegios* see *Acuerdos,* 1:158, 161; 2:70; and Luis Antonio Bohórquez Casallas, *La evolución educativa en Colombia* (Bogotá, 1956), 242.
33. See AHN, Inst. Pub. vol. 115:57. The different provincial *colegios* obtained such au-

thorization during the early 1830s. See the cases of the *colegios* of San Gíl, Santa Marta, Mompós, Chiquinquira, Boyacá, Vélez, Cali, and Ibagué in AHN, Inst. Pub. vol. 110:250, 260, 280, 288, 304, 402, 491–94, 523, 853; vol. 111:9–10, 67, 104, 181, 219, 493, 648–53, 679, 715, 730; vol. 125:29, 93, 167, 194, 475–89; and *Gaceta de Colombia,* June 13, 1824. The colegios of Panama, Pasto, and Buga were unable to teach law as of 1835. See AHN, Inst. Pub. vol. 111:711, 772.

34. See March 31, 1832 decree, in *Cod. Nal.* 4:408.
35. See AHN, Inst. Pub., vol. 111:69.
36. See AHN, Inst. Pub. vol. 110, passim. Censorship of content was occasionally exercised. Ibid., 304–08.
37. See disputes in 1835 and 1842. AHN, Inst. Pub. vol. 111:663–64; vol. 110:46; "Representación elevada al poder ejecutivo en defensa de los derechos del Colegio del Rosario." Firmada por Vicente A. Gómez, rector, el 15 de diciembre de 1842 (Signed by Vicente A. Gómez, principal, on 15 December 1842), Bogotá: Imprenta de J. A. Cualla, 1842. DBNC, Fondo Pineda 469.
38. See Young, "University Reform," 34, 42; *Acuerdos,* 1:257; *Gaceta de Colombia,* January 30, 1825; AHN. Inst. Pub. vol. 110:33; Salazar, *Los estudios eclesiásticos superiores;* and, Bohorquez C., *La evolución educativa;* Arcesio Aragón *La Universidad del Cauca* (Popayán, 1925); Roberto Burgos Ojeda, "Introducción a la historia de la Universidad de Cartagena," *BHA* 81, 746 (July-September 1984): 761–76.
39. See Aragón, *Universidad del Cauca;* AHN, Inst. Pub. vol. 110:276, 803; *El Constitucional de Cundinamarca,* December 4, 1831; Young, "University Reform," 185; AHN, Inst. Pub. vol. 111:634; 115:242–66.
40. Aragón, *Universidad del Cauca;* Terrence Horgan, *El Arzobispo Manuel José Mosquera. Reformista y pragmático* (Bogotá, 1977), 21–22; *Epistolario Cuervo,* vol. 1, passim; AHN, Inst. Pub. vol. 110:69, 276; Young, "University Reform," 187.
41. Gómez Barrientos, *Don Mariano Ospina y su época,* 1:26; Young, "University Reform," 34, 40; Bushnell, *The Santander Regime,* 188.
42. See Art. 3, law of August 6, 1821, in *Gaceta de Colombia,* September 16, 1821; *Correo del Orinóco,* November 17, 1821; *Actas Cúcuta,* 373; Uprimny, *El pensamiento filosófico y político,* 164–65.
43. Hernández de Alba, "Galería de hijos insignes," 167–68; Means, *Underdevelopment and the Development of Law,* 50; *Gaceta de Colombia,* no. 198, Julio, 31, 1825; González, *Memorias,* 85–86.
44. Article 8, May 22, 1824 decree, in *Gaceta de Colombia,* no. 139, June, 13, 1824; AHN. Inst. Pub. Vol 111:11–34.
45. See Article 2, October 8, 1825 decree, in *Gaceta de Colombia,* November 27, 1825.
46. See Means, *Underdevelopment and the Development of Law,* 116; Gómez Barrientos, *Don Mariano Ospina,* 1: 26; Restrepo, *Colegio de San Bartolomé,* 42–44.
47. See Juan Salas, *Ilustración del derecho real de España* (Bogotá, 1826); José María Alvarez, *Instituciones del derecho real de España* (Bogotá, 1836) [1818]. DBNC F. Pineda, 722; October 29, 1836 decree, *Cod. Nal.,* 6:251; AHN. Inst. Pub., vol. 126:501–02. For a useful summary of the texts used see Means, *Underdevelopment and the Development of Law,* 51–56. On canon law see AHN, Inst. Pub. vol. 125:729; Estanislao Vergara and J. M. Duque Gómez, *Curso de derecho canónico para uso del Colegio de Nuestra Señora del Rosario* (Bogotá, 1836); Horgan, *Arzobispo Mosquera,* 38.
48. Decree of October 3, 1826, Arts. 202–03.
49. Pedro M. Ibáñez, *Crónicas de Bogotá,* 2nd ed., 4 vols. (Bogotá, 1913–1923), 4:chap. 63; Armando Rojas, "La batalla de Bentham en Colombia," *Revista de Historia de América,* no. 29 (June 1950): 37–66; Bushnell, *The Santander Regime,* 192–93; Jaime

Jaramillo Uribe, "Bentham y los utilitaristas colombianos del siglo XIX," *Ideas y Valores* 4 13 (1962); Julio Hoenisberg, *Santander, el clero y Bentham* (Bogotá, 1940).
50. *Acuerdos,* 2:279; Restrepo *El Colegio de San Bartolomé,* 42–43; *Cod. Nal.,* 3:354.
51. See Guerra, *La Convención de Ocaña,* 254; González, *Memorias,* 127–28.
52. See Rojas, "La batalla de Bentham," 53; on the dictatorship see Guerra, *Convención de Ocaña,* 499–522.
53. See the government's resolution of October 20, 1828, in *Cod. Nal.,* 3:426–28; see also AHN, Inst. Pub., vol. 111:11–34; Tomás C. Mosquera to Rufino Cuervo, January 31, 1829, in *Epistolario Cuervo,* 1:121; Ortíz, *Reminiscencias,* 92–93; Bohórquez C., *La evolución educativa,* 252–55. By the same token the recently created University of Boyacá was abolished; several law degrees were nullified; and numerous students were expelled and persecuted. AHN, Inst. Pub., vol 111:390–418; see *Causas y Memorias* 1991, 2:164.
54. See *Causas y memorias* 1991, 2:164; Restrepo Sáenz, *Gobernadores de Antioquia,* 2:338.
55. Francisco de P. Santander, *Diario en Europa y los Estados Unidos: 1829-1832* (Bogotá, 1963) [1829–1832]; MacKennan, "The Vogue of Benthamism"; Rojas, "La Batalla de Bentham," 54–58.
56. See Young, "University Reform."
57. See decree of March 31, 1832, in *Cod. Nal.,* 4:407–09; AHN, Inst. Pub. vol. 111:11–34; Arboleda, *Historia contemporánea,* 1:137.
58. Obando, *Apuntamientos para la historia,* 1:256–57; Jaime Jaramillo Uribe, *El pensamiento colombiano en el siglo XIX* (Bogotá, 1964), 153. Religious dogmas were also attacked. See AHN, Inst. Pub. vol. 111:111.
59. *Constitucional de Cundinamarca,* no. 1, September 25, 1831, 1.
60. Arboleda, *Historia contemporánea,* 1:131, 301; Cadena, "D. José Francisco Pereira," 373; Gómez Barrientos, *Don Mariano Ospina,* 1:92; Vélez, "Exposición que el Secretario del Interior y Relaciones Exteriores . . . 1833," 62; Manuel J. Mosquera to Rufino Cuervo, Popayán, July 29, 1832, in *Epistolario Cuervo,* 1: 249–50; Medardo Rivas, *Los trabajadores de tierra caliente,* 4th ed. (Bogotá, 1983) [1899], 176; Cuervo Márquez, *Vida de José Ignacio de Márquez,* 1:142; 2:28–29.
61. See José M. Restrepo, "Informe de la Dirección de Instrucción Pública sobre la enseñanza de Bentham a que se refiere la Resolución del poder ejecutivo publicada en la Gaceta de la Nueva Granada No. 212." (Bogotá, 1835). DBNC, F. Ancizar 50; Ortíz, *Reminiscencias,* 102; MacKennan, "The Vogue of Benthamism," 182; "El Benthamismo descubierto a la luz de la razón o documentos importantes para los padres de familia, estractados del Constitucional de Popayán." Bogotá: Printed by J. Ayarza, 1836. DBNC, Fondo Ancizar 50, 1; Rojas, "La Batalla de Bentham," 61; Germán Marquinez A., "Benthamismo y anti-Benthamismo," in *La filosofía en Colombia. Historia de las ideas,* ed., Germán Marquinez A. et al. (Bogotá, 1988), 187–226, esp. 203, 205; "Prohibición de la enseñanza por Bentham" (Bogotá, 1836). DBNC, Fondo Pineda 469, 520.
62. Means mistakenly argues that the law of May 16, 1840, maintained "the liberal spirit of the 1826 reform." Means, *Development and the Underdevelopment of Law,* 121–23. See Rufino and Anjel Cuervo, *Vida de Rufino Cuervo,* 1:261; Cuervo Márquez, *Vida de José Ignacio de Márquez,* 2:157; *Cod. Nal.,* 8:566.
63. Miguel Chiari, "Esposición del secretario de estado en el depacho del Interior i Relaciones Esteriores . . . al Congreso Constitucional de 1841." DBNC, Fondo Quijano, 322, 33; AHN, Inst. Pub. vol. 115:162, 175; *El Correo de la Razón,* September 5, 1839.
64. See Arboleda, *Historia contemporánea,* vols. 1 and 2.
65. See AHN, Inst. Pub. vol. 110:57; vol. 125:498; Cuervo Márquez, *Vida de José Ignacio*

de Márquez, 2:278; José Duque Gómez "Discurso preliminar de apertura de los cursos de estudios de la Universidad Central pronunciado el 18 de octubre de 1836" (Bogotá, 1836). DBNC, Fondo Pineda 759; Gutiérrez Ponce, *Vida de Don Ignacio Gutiérrez Vergara,* 1:374–78; *GNG,* December 13, 1840; AHN, Inst. Pub. vol. 126:315–16, 643; *El Día,* December 25, 1840.

66. See AHN. Inst. Pub. vol. 115:246–66, 292; Pereira Gamba, "Los conflictos de Bogotá," 348–416; Jaime Duarte French, *Las Ibáñez,* 6th ed. (Bogotá, 1989), 288–307.
67. See Pereira Gamba, "Los conflictos de Bogotá," 530–31; Cuervo Márquez, *Vida de José Ignacio de Márquez,* 2:278; AHN, Inst. Pub. vol. 127:279, 434; vol. 115:706; Gutiérrez Ponce, *Vida de Don Ignacio Gutiérrez,* 1:389; AHN, Consejo de Estado, vol. 3:798–99.
68. Pereira Gamba, "Los conflictos de Bogotá," 530–31; Samper, *Galería nacional de hombres ilustres,* 199–201; Romualdo Lievano, "Recurso de queja ante el Tri-bunal . . . contra el gobernador de esta provincia por atentado contra la libertad y seguridad individual i por abusos de autoridad. . . ." (Bogotá, 1842), DBNC, Fondo Pineda 469; AHN. Inst. Pub. vol. 115:281; Samper, *Historia de un alma,* 1: 113.
69. Mariano Ospina R., "Esposición que el Secretario de Estado en el Despacho del Interior . . . dirije al Congreso Constitucional de 1842" (Bogotá, 1841), 9. DBNC, Fondo Quijano 142; see also Samper, *Historia de un alma,* 1:117–18.
70. Law of May 21, 1842; December 1, 1842, decree, in *Cod. Nal.* 9:358, 593; the anti-Benthamite campaign was supported by aristocratic journalist and former law student José Eusebio Caro, employee of the general treasury and later cofounder of the Conservative party. *El Granadino,* October 23, 1842; October 30, 1842; Robert H. Davis, "Acosta, Caro and Lleras: Three Essayists and Their Views of New Granada's National Problems, 1832–1853" (Ph.D. diss., Vanderbilt University, 1969), 264–74; Gómez Barrientos, *Don Mariano Ospina Rodríguez,* 1:166–67, 347; Jaime Ospina Ortíz, *José Eusebio Caro. Guión de una estirpe* (Bogotá, 1957); on Caro's aristocratic ancestry see Restrepo and Rivas, *Genealogías de Santafé,* 211–12; Gómez Picón, *Francisco Javier Caro,* 9–48; Appendix 4.
71. See Art. 387, "Decreto orgánico de la instrucción universitaria, 20 Diciembre de 1844." Pedro A. Herrán, Secretario, Mariano Ospina. DBNC, Fondo Pineda 127, 55; Juan de Dios Aranzazu, "Programa para la enseñanza del derecho administrativo . . . " (1845?). DBNC, Fondo Pineda 39, 19.
72. See Means, *Underdevelopment and the Development of Law,* 121–23.
73. See *El Día,* January 30, 1842, 413.
74. See Arts 18–25, decree of December 1, 1842, in *Cod. Nal.,* 9:595–96; see also Young, "University Reform," 51–61; AHN, Inst. Pub. vol. 115:789; Ospina R., "Es-posición . . . al Congreso Constitucional de 1842," 47; Cuervo, *Vida de Rufino Cuervo,* 2:45.
75. Decree of December 20, 1844, and additional decree of December 22, 1844, in "Decreto orgánico," 172.
76. Gutiérrez Ponce, *Vida de Don Ignacio Gutiérrez,* 1:365–67; Cuervo, *Vida de Rufino Cuervo,* 2:53; Cuervo Márquez, *Vida de José Ignacio de Márquez,* 2:352–54; Robledo, *La Universidad de Antioquia,* 88–96; Bohorquez C., *La evolución educativa,* 332–34; Gómez Barrientos, *Don Mariano Ospina Rodríguez,* 1:361–70.
77. See Restrepo, *Colegio de San Bartolomé,* 53; Horgan, *Arzobispo Mosquera,* 51–70.
78. Samper, *Historia de un alma,* 1:118–19, 181; Galindo, *Recuerdos históricos,* 36–42; "Discursos pronunciados en las sesiones [Escuela Republicana] del 7 i 9 de Marzo

de 1851, dedicadas a la gran mayoría liberal del cuerpo lejislativo." DBNC, Fondo Pineda 759, 7, 63; *El Censor,* May 8, 1848, 61, 81.
79. Mario Valenzuela, "Apuntamientos sobre el principio de la utilidad" (Bogotá, 1857). DBNC, F. Pineda, 759; Galindo, *Recuerdos históricos,* 36–42; Samper, *Historia de un alma,* passim; Angel María Galán, *Obras del doctor Ezequiel Rojas,* 2 vols. (Bogotá, 1969) [1882]; Jaramillo Uribe, *El pensamiento colombiano;* Gerardo Molina, *Las ideas Liberales en Colombia,* 2d ed. (Bogotá, 1971); Marquinez Argote, "Benthamismo y antibenthamismo"; idem, *Filosofía de la emancipación en Colombia* (Bogotá, 1983). The echoes reached even the twentieth century; see Laureano Gómez, *El mito de Santander* (Bogotá, 1966).
80. See *Gaceta de Colombia,* October 31, 1824.
81. See Oreste Popescu, "Un tratado sucinto de economía política en Bogotá en 1823," *BHA* 56, 654–56 (April-June 1969): 259–98, esp. 262; Otero Muñóz, *Historia del periodismo,* 35–37; see also "Principios de economía política" published in the *Diario político de Santafé* edited by scientist Francisco Caldas and lawyer Joaquín Camacho, especially issues from December 25, 1810 to February 1, 1811; see merchant José Ignacio de Pombo's recommendation as to the need to create a university chair in political economy in the 1810s, in *Escritos de dos economistas coloniales. Don Antonio Narváez y Latorre y Don José I. de Pombo,* ed. Sergio E. Ortíz (Bogotá, 1965), 179.
82. See *Observaciones y argumentos sobre el estado político de la República de Colombia, antecedido de un tratado sucinto sobre la economía, con notas contra algunos de los principios de Juan Bautista Say y Jeremias Bentham,* 1823, DBNC, Fondo Pineda 47. See a good synthesis and analysis in Popescu, "Un tratado sucinto de economía política," 259–98; see also Oscar Rodríguez, "El pensamiento económico en la formación del estado granadino. 1780–1830," *Historia Crítica,* no. 2 (July-December 1989): 93–110; no. 3 (January-June 1990): 107–17, esp. 110.
83. Rodríguez "El pensamiento económico," 110. For observations on the extent to which Say's text was actually read in New Granada see Safford, "The Emergence of Economic Liberalism in Colombia," 40–41.
84. Soto, *Mis padecimientos,* 36–37 [1841]; *Acuerdos,* 1: 256; Lozano y Lozano, "Vicente Azuero," 460; *Gaceta de Colombia,* July 24, 1825; Cadena, "D. José Francisco Pereira," 371.
85. See Wise de Gouzy, *Antología del pensamiento de Mariano Ospina Rodriguez,* 1:xvii, 16; Gómez Barrrientos, *Don Mariano Ospina Rodríguez,* 42–43.
86. See AHN, Inst. Pub. vol. 110:862.
87. "Los cursantes de economía política de la Universidad Central. n.d.," [year 1839 marked with pencil]. Archivo Restrepo, Fondo III, vol. 4, Rollo 41:33–34, 65–77; AHN, Inst. Pub. vol. 110:862; vol. 111:434, 665–66; Marquinez Argote, "Benthamismo y antibenthamismo," 204; Samper, *Historia de un alma,* 1:170; AHN, Inst. Pub. vol. 115:428; vol. 126:603; Safford, "Emergence of Economic Liberalism," 41; Ezequiel Rojas, "Programa para la enseñanza de economía política en las universidades de la repúplica . . . "(1844). DBNC, Fondo Pineda 39, 20; Galindo, *Recuerdos históricos,* 60; Galán, *Obras del doctor Ezequiel Rojas,* 1:12; Salvador Camacho Roldán, *Mis memorias* (Bogotá, 1946) [1923], 69.
88. See *El Constitucional de Cundinamarca,* January 1, 1832; AHN. Inst. Pub. vol. 111:11–34, 679, 769; vol. 115:137; vol. 127:162; vol. 115:40, 221, 470; vol. 125:93, 100, 194, 346, 494, 525, 693; vol. 126:542, 567, 672–81, 746–96, 900, 922; Arboleda, *Dicionario biográfico,* 261; Robledo, *La Universidad de Antioquia,* 68.
89. See resolution of October 20, 1828, in Bohórquez C., *La evolución educativa,* 253–55;

Art. 185, December 1, 1842 decree, in *Cod. Nal.*, 9:593–656; Means, *Underdevelopment and the Development of Law*, 123.

90. See Moscote and Arce, *La vida ejemplar de Justo Arosemena*, 137; *Diario de Debates*, April 8, 1853, 19; AHN, Inst. Pub. vol. 133:531; Paredes, "Memorias de Don Victoriano de Diego Paredes," 136; Safford, "The Emergence of Economic Liberalism."
91. On pragmatic protectionism see Eugene Huck, "Economic Experimentation in a Newly Independent Nation: Colombia Under Francisco de Paula Santander, 1821–1840," *The Americas* 29, 1 (1972): 17–29; Ospina Vásquez, *Industria y protección*. On exceptional anti-free trade postures by lawyer Alejandro Osorio, member of New Granada's aristocratic group, see Safford, "The Emergence of Economic Liberalism," 47–52.
92. Albion Small, *The Cameralists: The Pioneers of German Social Polity* (New York, 1909); Pang and Seckinger, "The Mandarins of Imperial Brazil," 215–44; Roderick and Jean Barman, "The Role of the Law Graduate in the Political Elite of Imperial Brazil," *Journal of Interamerican Studies and World Affairs* 18, 4 (November 1976): 423–50; Uribe, "Preparando 'mandarines'," 87–97.
93. See AHN. Inst. Pub. vol. 110:14, 111, 315, 683; vol. 115:498; vol. 125:498; vol. 126:603; *La Bagatela*, August 15, 1853; Florentino González, *Elementos de ciencia administrativa. Comprende el bosquejo de un sistema de administración pública para un estado repúblicano*, 2 vols. (Bogotá, 1840), 1:i,ii; AHN. Inst. Pub. vol. 111:664–66; vol. 115:292, 325; vol. 126:603; Plazas, *Genealogías de la provincia de Neiva*, 321.
94. AHN, Inst. Pub. vol. 125:100, 194, 346, 475, 494; Robledo, *La Universidad de Antioquia*, 67–75; Gómez Barrientos, *Don Mariano Ospina Rodríguez*, 167–68; Jorge Alberto Restrepo, *Retrato de un patriarca antioqueño. Pedro A. Escobar, 1815–1899* (Bogotá, 1992), 36–37; "Indice de las materias que se verán en los certamenes públicos que los alumnos del Colegio Académico de la Provincia de Antioquia presentan en octubre de 1838." AHN, Archivo Restrepo, Fondo III, vol. 4, Rollo 41:8–15; "Colección de asertos de los certamenes públicos que han de presentar los alumnos del Colejio de San José de Guanenta en los días del mes de julio . . . 1838" (Bogotá, 1838). AHN, Archivo Restrepo, Fondo II, Vol. 4, Rollo 41:8–15.
95. Charles-Jean Bonnin, *Principes D'Administration Publique*, 3d ed., 3 vols. (Paris, 1812), 1:xi–xiv; Omar Guerrero, *Las ciencias de la administración en el estado absolutista* (Mexico, 1988), 271; Esteban Febres Cordero, *Ciencia administrativa, o principios de administración pública, estractados de la obra francesa de Carlos Juan Bonnin, con algunas notas importantes para el uso de la juventud istmeña* (Panama, 1838). DBNC, Fondo Pineda 257; AHN, Inst. Pub. vol. 126:900.
96. See González, *Memorias*, 86; idem, *Elementos de ciencia administrativa*, ii; "El Benthamismo descubierto a la luz de la razón"; Gómez Barrientos, *Don Mariano Ospina Rodríguez*, 1:67; Uribe, "Preparando 'mandarines'."
97. See González, *Elementos de ciencia administrativa;* Antonio del Real, *Elementos de derecho constitucional seguidos de un exámen crítico de la constitución neo-granadina* (Cartagena, 1839); Cerbeleón Pinzón, *Tratado de ciencia constitucional*, 2 vols. (Bogotá, 1839); idem, *Principios sobre administración pública* (Bogotá, 1847). Pinzón's early text was proscribed by the government according to Young, "University Reform", 62.
98. See Samper, *Historia de un alma*, 1:215, 224–25; idem, "Cuaderno que contiene la esplicación de los principios cardinales de la ciencia constitucional." Reimpresión. Bogotá, 1852. DBNC, Fondo Pineda 46, 3; Carlos Martínez Silva, "José María Samper," *Colombia Ilustrada*, no. 9–10 (February 1890): 139–86, esp. 146; Galindo, *Recuerdos históricos*, 27.

99. Ospina, "Esposición que el Secretario de Estado en el Despacho del Interior . . . dirije al Congreso Constitucional de 1842," 9.
100. Gómez Barrientos, *Don Mariano Ospina Rodríguez,* 1:26; Bushnell, *The Santander Regime,* 188.
101. See especially the decree issued on March 31, 1832, authorizing legal education at the provincial level, in *Cod. Nal.,* 4:407–09.
102. See González, *Memorias,* 86; AHN, Inst. Pub. vol. 110:821. For failed attempts at changing this practice see "Proyecto de código de instrucción pública para el estado de la Nueva Granada. Acordado por el Consejo de Estado para presentarlo al Congreso de 1834." Bogotá: B. Espinoza, printed by José Ayarza, 1834. DBNC, Fondo Pineda 205, 38; see also José Duque Gómez, "Relación del estado actual de la instrucción científica en el distrito de la Universidad Central . . . " April 20, 1840. AHN, Inst. Pub., vol. 115:504–15, esp. pp. 507, 510. See comic remarks on the ease with which anyone could rapidly become doctor in both medicine and law in Ignacio Gutiérrez Vergara, "Cachaco," in *Museo de cuadros de costumbres, variedades y viajes,* 3 vols. (Bogotá, 1973), 1:195–99.
103. See Francisco de P. Santander, "Mensaje del Presidente de la República al Congreso Constitucional de 1837. Bogotá, 1o. Marzo, 1837." DBNC, F. Quijano 152; AHN, Inst. Pub. vol. 125:70; Lino de Pombo, "Esposición del Secretario de Estado en el Despacho del Interior y Relaciones Esteriores . . . al Congreso Constitucional de 1837 . . . Bogotá." Printed by Nicomedes Lora, 1837. DBNC, Fondo Quijano 152, 40. See also Pombo's critical attitude toward provincial education in Safford, *Ideal of the Practical,* 170–73; Lino de Pombo, "Esposición . . . al Congreso Constitucional de 1838." Bogotá: Printed by Nicomedes Lora, 1838. DBNC, F. Quijano 16, 36; *El Observador,* October 20, 1839, 13; AHN, Inst. Pub. vol. 126:587; *Cod. Nal.,* 8:566.
104. See *Actas Congreso 1823,* 167; Bushnell, *The Santander Regime,* 37; Jerónimo Torres, "Observaciones políticas dirijidas a la gran Convención de Colombia por el ciudadano que las suscribe." Bogotá, February 2, 1828. AHN, Archivo Restrepo, Fondo II, vol. 52, Rollo 35:176–81; *Acuerdos,* 1:22; ibid., 2:22.
105. This also occurred in Argentina. See Halperín Donghi, *Revolución y guerra,* 61.
106. See *Recopilación de leyes,* 41–54.
107. See letter to Rufino Cuervo, Popayán, June 22, 1832, in *Epistolario Cuervo,* 1:248; see also Lino Pombo "Esposición al congreso constitucional de 1837"; idem, "Esposición al congreso constitucional de 1838." DBNC, F. Quijano 116; Ospina Rodríguez,"Esposición al congreso de 1842"; and, Safford, *Ideal of the Practical.*
108. See AHN, Inst. Pub. vol. 110: 876.
109. See Gómez Barrientos, *Don Mariano Ospina Rodríguez,* 1:67.
110. See Robledo, *La Universidad de Antioquia,* 63–75; Restrepo, *Retrato de un patriarca antioqueño,* 31; "Indice de las materias que se verán en los certámenes públicos . . . de 1838," 15.
111. See Mariano Ospina R., "Esposición . . . al Congreso Constitucional de 1845." Bogotá: Printed by José A Cualla, March 2,, 1845. DBNC, F. Quijano 223, 27.
112. See Juan de Dios Aranzazu, "Programa para la enseñanza del derecho administrativo en las univesidades de la república" [1845?]. DBNC, F. Pineda 39, 19.
113. See Victor M. Uribe, "Educación legal y formación del estado colombiano durante la transición de la colonia a la república, 1780–1850," in *Etnias, educación y archivos en la historia de Colombia,* comp. Javier Guerrero Barón (Tunja, 1997), 179–203.

Chapter 9
The War of the *Supremos*

1. See Posada-Carbó, "Elections and Civil Wars," 621–49.
2. See a list in Juan N. Acevedo, "Relación nominal de los individuos que han sido dados de baja del ejercito . . . " (March 1, 1842).
3. Roberto Tisnes Jiménez, *María Martínez de Nisser y la Revolución de los Supremos* (Bogotá, 1983), 78.
4. These cases are listed and discussed in Francisco J. de Ugarte, "Opusculos o noticias biográficas sobre la vida pública y privada del Doctor Francisco J. de Ugarte y Azuola, con algunas sobre su familia, escritas por el mismo en 7 de marzo de 1838," *BHA* 11, 126 (April 1917): 364–79; Cuervo Márquez, *Vida de José I. de Márquez,* 2:76, 169; Gutiérrez Ponce, *Vida de Don Ignacio Gutiérrez V.,* 1:295–96; *El Correo de la Razón,* September 5, 1839; *La Bandera Negra,* October 19, 1837, 25; November 1837, 29–32; December 3, 1837, 64; Arboleda, *Historia contemporánea,* 1:298–99, 313, 318; *El Argos,* February 3, 1839; *El Observador,* April 19, 1840, 131; Restrepo Sáenz, *Gobernadores de Antioquia,* 2:257.
5. Obando, *Apuntamientos para la historia,* 2:25–28; Arboleda, *Historia contemporánea,* 1:334; *Cod. Nal.,* 6:109–16; Pastor Ospina, "Apuntamientos para la historia de la Nueva Granada" [1840?], in Juan M. Pacheco, "Don Pastor Ospina Rodríguez," *Archivos,* vol. 1 (January-June 1967): 152–78, esp. 169; Rausch, *A Tropical Plains Frontier;* idem, "La doma de un caudillo colombiano."
6. See Safford, "Commerce and Enterprise," 201–31.
7. In addition to representatives of the four religious orders and the archbishopric, at least two of the authors of the conservative newspaper *La Bandera Negra,* Dr. Merizalde and Juan Madiedo, also participated in the executive council of *La Católica.* The society printed the newspaper *El Investigador Católico.* See 1838 invitation cited in David Sowell, *The Early Colombian Labor Movement: Artisans and Politics in Bogota, 1832–1919* (Philadelphia, 1992), chap. 2, esp. 34, 189; *La Bandera Negra,* January 14, 1838. On Ignacio Morales's background and his business, especially his lands and his profitable lease of government salt mines, see May 26, 1836, decree, in *Cod. Nal.,* 6:109–16; AHN, Notaria 2, Indice Tomo 12, 1840–1879, fol. 141; "Lijera reseña del pleito promovido por el señor Dr. Antonio Plaza contra la empresa de la Ferrería de Pacho" (Bogotá, n.d.), fols. 213–31, 269–74; Ortíz, *Reminiscencias,* 108–09, 171; Gómez Barrientos, *Don Mariano Ospina y su época,* 1:95; Horgan, *Arzobispo Mosquera,* 54–55.
8. Cuervo, *Vida de Rufino Cuervo,* 1:252, 254; Sowell, *The Early Colombian Labor Movement,* 34. See also AHN, Consejo de Estado, vol. 2:467–68.
9. See Gutiérrez Ponce, *Vida de Don Ignacio Gutiérrez V.,* 359; Cuervo, *Vida de Rufino Cuervo,* 1:254; Horgan, *Arzobispo Mosquera,* 54–55. Initially, *La Católica* sympathized with the provincial José María Obando, who was seen as a religious crusader in 1839–1840. During the war, however, it shifted its allegiance and joined fellow aristocrats in government. See Cuervo Márquez, *Vida de José Ignacio de Márquez,* 2:70, 102, 112–13, 124–25, 353.
10. It printed the newspaper *El Labrador i Artesano.* See Sowell, *The Early Colombian Labor Movement,* 35; see also Davis, "Acosta, Caro and Lleras," 201–02; Arboleda, *Historia contemporánea,* 1:302; Vergara y Vergara, *Vida de Estanislao Vergara,* 329.
11. Sowell, *The Early Colombian Labor Movement,* 32–40
12. See Caicedo, "Ministros de guerra desde 1821," 286; on the distinguished figures

within Mosquera's group see Arboleda, *Historia contemporánea*, 1:287–88, 325; Cuervo Márquez, *Vida de José Ignacio de Márquez*, 2:93–95; on Mosquera's newspaper *El Amigo del Pueblo* see ibid., 2:74; Ortíz, *Reminiscencias*, 114–15; Sowell, *The Early Colombian Labor Movement*, 37.

13. See Arboleda, *Historia contemporánea*, 1:293–94, 323; "Incidente de la famosa Causa Grice."
14. José J. Guerra, *Viceversas Liberales. Documentos relativos a la historia del Liberalismo colombiano recopilados por J.J. Guerra* (Bogotá, 1923), 36; Arboleda, *Historia contemporánea*, 1:234; Juan de Dios Aranzazu to Juan M. Gómez, July 27, 1838, in "Cartas inéditas de Juan de Dios Aranzazu," 637.
15. See *La Bandera Negra*, May 6, 1838, 358–59; see also *La Bandera Nacional*, June 3, 1838; Arboleda, *Historia contemporánea*, 1:316; Davis, "Acosta, Caro and Lleras," 203.
16. Obando, *Apuntamientos para la historia*, 2:38–40.
17. Representative examples of *ministerial* classmates were Bogotá native Uldarico Leiva, Buga native Francisco Martínez Escobar, and Antioquia natives Laureano García and José María Sáenz Montoya. See AHN, Inst. Pub., vol. 111:585–87; vol. 127:279, 434; see also Figure 9.1 and Appendix 4; *El Observador*, April 15, 1840; Cuervo Márquez, *Vida de José I de Márquez*, 2:77–79; *Epistolario Cuervo*, 2:120–23; *Almanaque nacional 1838*, 83; Arboleda, *Historia contemporánea*, 1:291–92, 364–65.
18. The term *progresista* was coined by the plebeian newspaper *La Bandera Nacional*. See Cuervo Márquez, *Vida de José I. de Márquez*, 2:77–79.
19. On young Galavís's meteoric career and his aristocratic social and family background see Rojas, *Corregidores y justicias mayores*, 569–94; Restrepo Sáenz, *Gobernadores y próceres*, 304–06; Arboleda, *Historia contemporánea*, 1:299; Arcesio Aragón, *Fastos payaneses* (Bogotá, 1939), 291; Otero Muñóz, "Boceto biográfico," 179.
20. Céspedes was judge and governor of Neiva in 1832 and 1835–1837. One of his sons married one of provincial General Obando's daughters. See Plazas, *Genealogías de Neiva*, 113–18, 178–81; Restrepo Sáenz, *Gobernadores y próceres*, 182, 299–302; Urdaneta, *Memorias del General Rafael Urdaneta*, 229–31. On the bridge concession see June 5, 1833, April 27, 1836, and May 1838 decrees in *Cod. Nal.*, 5:84; 6:56; 8:77; Plazas, *Genealogías de Neiva*, 293; Appendix 5.
21. Obando, *Apuntamientos para la historia*, 2:38–40; *El Correo de la Razón*, October 3, 1839.
22. The assembly had nominated provincial lawyer Céspedes and left out Galavís. See *El Correo de la Razón*, no. 6, October 3, 1839.
23. *El Observador*, April 15, 1840; Obando, *Apuntamientos para la historia*, 2:239; Lievano, "Recurso de queja"; Arboleda, *Historia contemporánea*, 1:364–65; Restrepo Sáenz, *Gobernadores y próceres*, 323; Plazas, *Genealogías de Neiva*, 181, 291–93, 581; AHN, Inst. Pub., vol. 115:706.
24. Vásquez, "Exposición documentada"; Monge, "El Doctor Vásquez," 720; Pereira Gamba, "Los conflictos de Bogotá," 480–81; Arboleda, *Historia contemporánea*, 1:311.
25. Monge, "El Doctor Vásquez"; Samper, *Historia de un alma*, 1:105; Appendix 5.
26. *La Bandera Negra*, October 15, 1837, 9–10; October 29, 1837, 25; Cuervo Márquez, *Vida de José I. de Márquez*, 2:153, 326; Arboleda, *Historia contemporánea*, 1:313.
27. Report of March 1840, emphasis added. See Cuervo Márquez, *Vida de José I. de Márquez*, 2:169.
28. Vargas, "Exposición documentada"; Arboleda, *Historia contemporánea*, 1:358–59; AHN, Inst. Pub. vol. 111:216, 390–418.

29. See Uribe Angel, "Recuerdos de un viaje a Medellín," 635; Arboleda, *Historia contemporánea*, 1:313–14, 366–70.
30. Gutiérrez Ponce, *Vida de Don Ignacio Gutiérrez V.*, 303–04; *El Observador*, February 23, 1840; *El Correo de la Razón*, October 31, 1839, 42; November 7, 1839, 46; *El Observador*, November 10, 1839.
31. Arboleda, *Diccionario biográfico*, 262, 353; Plazas, *Genealogías de Neiva*, 182–83.
32. Restrepo Sáenz, *Gobernadores y próceres*, 232.
33. Plazas, *Genealogías de Neiva*, 580–81; Restrepo Sáenz, *Gobernadores y próceres*, 323.
34. AHN, Inst. Pub., vol. 111:370; Obando, *Apuntamientos para la historia*, 2:30–31.
35. Report of March, 1840. See Cuervo Márquez, *Vida de José I. de Márquez*, 2:169.
36. See Vargas, "Exposición documentada." Vargas's brother, provincial lawyer and journalist Juan Nepomuceno Vargas, was also jailed at the end of the year in Bogotá. See Pereira Gamba, "Los conflictos de Bogotá," 348. In 1830 Juan Nepomuceno edited the "jacobin" newspaper *El Demócrata* in cooperation with lawyer Angel María Flórez, and in 1840 the opposition newspaper *La Noche*. See *La Historia Como Noticia, 1450-1830*, no. 1; Appendix 5.
37. Samper, *Historia de un alma*, 1:159–61.
38. *El Día*, December 3, 1840, 60; on Larrota's legal studies see AHN, Inst. Pub., vol. 111:216.
39. Arboleda, *Historia contemporánea*, 1:396; José M. Restrepo S., "Gobernantes de Pamplona," 114–15; idem, *Gobernadores de Antioquia*, 2:407–08; García Samudio, *Reconquista de Boyacá*, 127.
40. Pereira Gamba, "Los conflictos de Bogotá."
41. Otero Muñóz, "Boceto biográfico," 184–87; Cuervo Márquez, *Vida de José I. de Márquez*, 2:267.
42. Carlos Ramírez Monreal, "Manuel María Ramírez," *BHA* 13, 145 (March 1920): 53–60, esp. 54; Arboleda, *Historia contemporánea*, 1:414.
43. Gómez Barrientos, *Don Mariano Ospina y su época*, 1:174–75; Carlos A. Días, *Páginas de historia colombiana* (Bucaramanga, 1967), 14–16; Restrepo Sáenz, *Gobernadores de Antioquia*, 2:273–77.
44. Arboleda, *Historia contemporánea*, 1:414.
45. "Elogio fúnebre del Dr. José M. F. Lince." Medellín, 1853. DBNC, F. Pineda, 372, 5–6; Restrepo Sáenz, *Gobernadores de Antioquia*, 2:269–71.
46. During the 1840s he became one of the largest landholders of Cali but continued militating in the soon-to-be Liberal party. Escorcia, *Sociedad y economía en el Valle del Cauca*, 54–55.
47. See Arboleda, *Historia contemporánea*, 2:33, 70–73; February 19, 1842 amnesty, and amnesty decrees of April 1 and April 5, 1842, in *Cod. Nal.*, 9:315–16, 326–30.
48. Vicente Azuero and Ruperto Anzola, "Informe de una comisión de la Cámara de Representantes sobre el modo de proceder a la reforma de la constitución" (Bogotá, April 11, 1840).
49. Arboleda, *Historia contemporánea*, 1:366–68.
50. On lawyer and senator Antonio Malo and lawyer Manuel Silva (1816–1841), probably linked to the aristocratic clique of Chiquinquireño lawyer and *gamonal* Miguel Narciso Casanovas N., see Appendix 4. On Casanovas, descendant of a colonial administrator of the rent of tithes in Chiquinquira and the mint's *fundidor*, see Arboleda, *Historia contemporánea*, 1:470; *El Observador*, September 29, 1839; March 29, 1840; Notaria 1a., Chiquinquira, vol. of 1767, fols. 1–2; vol. of 1782, fols. 21–28; vol. of 1813, fols. 42–43.
51. Offspring of Francisco Antonio Franco, former member of Tunja's 1811 Constitu-

tional Congress, who held the position of *escribano* in the Tenza Valley since 1802. Another member of this clan was General Manuel M. Franco. See José M. Restrepo Sáenz, *Constituyentes de Tunja en 1811* (Bogotá, 1913), 13–14; Baraya, *Biografías militares*, 251–53; Guateque parish, baptisms, books 7 and 8; Notaria 1, Guateque, 1806–1807, fol. 149; 1821–1823, fols. 13, 60; 1838–1840, fol. 65; 1843, fols. 69, 143.

52. See Restrepo Sáenz, *Gobernadores y próceres*, 327–28; *La Bandera Negra*, January 14, 1838.
53. *El Observador*, March 29, 1840; April 15, 1840.
54. Escorcia, *Sociedad y economía en el Valle del Cauca*, 55; Arboleda, *Diccionario biográfico*, 250–52.
55. Just four of the university's sixty-six law graduates from 1831 to 1840 are known to have become Liberals. Aragón, *La Universidad del Cauca*, 177; Arboleda, *Diccionario biográfico*.
56. Manuel J. Mosquera to Rufino Cuervo, October 28, 1828, in *Epistolario Cuervo*, 1:107; Arboleda, "Vicente Cárdenas," 191; AHN, Inst. Pub. vol. 110:69; Aragón, *La Universidad del Cauca*.
57. Arboleda, "Vicente Cárdenas," 186–221. Unlike Cárdenas and other Popayán lawyers, wealthy Cali lawyer Manuel Dolores Camacho supported the rebels. See comments in Escorcia, *Sociedad y economía en el Valle del Cauca*, 111; Arboleda, *Historia contemporánea*, 1:461.
58. Lorenzo M. Lleras, "Martínez." Bogotá, 1847. DBNC, F. Pineda, 849; Arboleda, *Diccionario biográfico*, 254–57; Gómez Barrientos, *Don Mariano Ospina y su época*, 1:101, 345. In 1836 Ordóñez married the daughter of colonial *contador* Antonio José Caro, sister of aristocratic lawyer José Eusebio Caro. See Duarte French, *Las Ibáñez*, 259; Restrepo and Rivas, *Genealogías de Santafé;* Gómez Picón, *Francisco Javier Caro;* Appendix 5.
59. See Raimundo Rivas, *Escritos de Don Pedro Fernández Madrid. Publicados con noticias sobre su vida por Raimundo Rivas* (Bogotá, 1932), 156–57.
60. Nutini, *Wages of Conquest;* Pang, *In Pursuit of Honor and Power*, chap. 7.
61. See Arboleda, *Diccionario biográfico*.
62. See lists in *El Observador*, May 10, 1840; May 13, 1840; and, May 24, 1840.
63. *El Correo de la Razón*, October 31, 1839. Had there been no war, the aristocratic candidate would have been José Rafael Mosquera, from Popayán. See Rivas, *Escritos de Don Pedro Fernández Madrid*, 66; *El Correo de la Razón*, December 12, 1839.
64. On forced loans for more than 200,000 pesos and other forced contributions, see decree of February 20, 1841, and May 29, 1841 law in *Cod. Nal.*, 9:154–55, 282–87; on the previously promising budgetary situation in late 1837 see Pedro Fernández Madrid to Francisco Fernández Madrid, October 24, 1837, in Rivas, *Escritos de Don Pedro Fernández Madrid*, 51–53; on merchants' contributions, see *El Observador*, May 24, 1840; Mariano Ospina to General Herrán, July 20, 1841, in Gómez Barrientos, *Don Mariano Ospina y su época*, 1:94; Mariano Ospina to Joaquín Emilio Gómez, November 19, 1841, in ibid., 200, 203; Safford, "Commerce and Enterprise," 310–11; decree of April 10, 1841 in *Cod. Nal.* 9: 184–85.
65. Cuervo Márquez, *Vida de José I. de Márquez*, 2:255.
66. Arboleda, *Historia contemporánea*, 1:392–95.
67. The society was made up of aristocrats like Rafael Mosquera, lawyers Rafael Rivas and Francisco de Paula Morales, high-ranking bureaucrat Simón Burgos, and others. See José A. Plaza, "Memorias íntimas (del historiador Plaza) [1847]," *BHA* 5, 59 (May 1909): 625–56, esp. 649; Appendix 4.
68. See Venancio Ortíz, "Recuerdos de la guerra de 1840," *Revista Literaria* 1, 21 (June

15, 1890): 101–07; Pereira Gamba, "Los conflictos de Bogotá," 334–50; Gómez, *El tribuno*, 236; Restrepo S., *Constituyentes de Tunja en 1811*, 56, 64–66; Arboleda, *Historia contemporánea*, 1:397–402; Julio Barón Ortega, *Vida y hazañas del caudillo Juan José Neira de Velasco* (Tunja, 1989), passim; Cuervo Márquez, *Vida de José I. de Márquez*, 2:269; *El Día*, December 3, 1840.

69. A detailed analysis that explains why aristocrats such as the Arosemenas and Icazas (Appendix 4) joined provincial officers like Colonel Tomás Herrera can be found in Ignacio Méndez, "Azul y Rojo: Panama's Independence in 1840," *HAHR* 60, 2 (May 1980): 269–93; see also Alfaro, *Vida del General Tomás Herrera*, chaps. 9 and 10.

70. On amnesties see February 20, 1841 decrees, April 5, 1842 decree, and February 19, 1842 law in *Cod. Nal.*, 10:156–57, 315–16, 328–29.

71. On the role of England and Ecuador see Ospina to Herrán, October 25, 1841, and Herrán to Ospina, October 31, 1841, in Gómez Barrientos, *Don Mariano Ospina y su época*, 1:199, 219, see as well 189–90, 202–03, 210; further requests for Ecuadorian troops were canceled in late 1840. See Cuervo Márquez, *Vida de José I. de Márquez*, 2:219–27; on recruitment see *El Observador*, September 22, 1839; Samper, *Historia de un alma*, 91.

72. While a student, Duque Gómez was involved in the 1828 plot against Bolívar. See AHN, Inst. Pub. vol. 110:57; vol. 125:498; *El Día*, December 25, 1842; Cuervo Márquez, *Vida de José I. de Márquez*, 2:278; *Causas y Memorias* 1990, 1:322–25.

73. Duque Gómez, "Discurso preliminar"; *El Día*, December 20, 1840; *GNG*, December 13, 1840; Gutiérrez Ponce, *Vida de Don Ignacio Gutiérrez V.*, 1:374–78. At the time of his death this modest lawyer still owed some cash to the *colegio* for which he had worked, and the *colegio* hopelessly pursued his meager assets. See AHN. Inst. Pub., vol. 126:315–16; *El Día*, December 25, 1840.

74. Merchant Francisco Montoya, for instance, presented a 100,000-peso loan proposal in 1841, and lent the government the steamship *Unión*, recently brought to the Magdalena River by the monopolistic transportation company that he had established in 1838 in partnership with British merchants. See Mariano Ospina to General Herrán, July 20, 1841, in Gómez Barrientos, *Don Mariano Ospina y su época*, 1:94; Safford, "Commerce and Enterprise," 310–11; June 5, 1841 law, and June 5 and 13 decrees in *Cod. Nal.*, 9:294–95, 411–13, 418–19; Figure 9.1.

75. AHN, Inst. Pub. vol. 127:279, 434; vol. 115:706; Gutiérrez Ponce, *Vida de Don Ignacio Gutiérrez V.*, 1:337, 389; about the persecution unleashed against lawyer Francisco Soto, absent from his position at the Consejo de Estado in January 1841, see AHN, Consejo de Estado, vol. 3:798–99.

76. Pereira Gamba, "Los conflictos de Bogotá," 348; Arboleda, *Historia contemporánea*, 1:421.

77. On educational petitions see Chapter 8; see also Davis, "Acosta, Caro, and Lleras," 203; and, Sowell, *The Early Colombian Labor Movement*, chap. 2.

78. Pereira Gamba, "Los conflictos de Bogotá," 413.

79. On the forms of conscription or *recluta* for the war see *El Correo de la Razón*, September 5, 1839; *El Observador*, September 22, 1839; Pereira Gamba, "Los conflictos de Bogotá," 345.

80. Pereira Gamba, "Los conflictos de Bogotá," 414.

81. Pereira Gamba, "Los conflictos de Bogotá," 413–18, emphasis added. An elite historian referred to those sectors as "las últimas clases sociales" ("the last social classes"). See Arboleda, *Historia contemporánea*, 1:449.

82. See *El Día*, January 31, 1841, 110.

83. Samper, *Historia de un alma*, 1:218; Ambrosio López, "El desengaño o confidencias de Ambrosio López primer director de la Sociedad de Artesanos de Bogotá . . . 1851" *BCB* 16, 2 (February 1979): 5–44, esp. 12.
84. On the attack on oppositionists by "una orda de artesanos y campesinos" ("a mob of artisans and peasants") in Medellín see Gómez Barrientos, *Don Mariano Ospina y su época*, 1:376.
85. Arboleda, *Historia contemporánea*, 1:458.
86. In mid-1842 he was granted amnesty. See M. M. Mallarino, "Acusación introducida ante el Senado de la Nueva Granada por el fiscal . . . . ." (Bogotá, March 24, 1841); AHN, Congreso, vol. 16:10–133; *El Día,* January 23, 1842, 404; Arboleda, *Historia contemporánea,* 1:471–72; Pereira Gamba, "Los conflictos de Bogotá," 478; on Latorre's family background see Arango Mejía, *Genealogías de Antioquia y Caldas,* 1:500.
87. Ospina to Herrán, July, 20, 1843, in Gómez Barrientos, *Don Mariano Ospina y su época,* 1:193; *El Día,* July 24, 1842; Obando, *Apuntamientos para la historia,* 2:42–43; see also Leandro Exea, "Refutación sencilla de la sentencia condenatoria pronunciada en primera instancia por la Corte Suprema contra el Dr. Leandro Exea ministro juez interino del Tribunal del Distrito de Cundinamarca por no haber impuesto la pena de muerte a Norverto Rodríguez como uno de los guerrilleros de Guacheta." Bogotá: Printed by J. Ayarza, October 29, 1841. DBNC, F. Vergara 12, 13.
88. See February 19, 1842 amnesty, and amnesty decrees of April 1 and April 5, 1842, in *Cod. Nal.,* 9:315–16, 326–30.
89. AHN, Inst. Pub., vol. 115:706; Arboleda, *Historia contemporánea,* 2:52; Soriano Lleras, *Lorenzo María Lleras,* 39; Davis, "Acosta Caro y Lleras," 208; Samper, *Historia de un alma,* 1:159–60; *El Día,* January 2, 1842, 393–95.
90. *El Observador,* February 23, 1840, 92. See also background in *El Correo,* November 14, 1839, 49–50; Ospina Rodríguez, "Esposición al Congreso de 1842," 9.
91. See Torres, "Observaciones políticas."
92. See *El Cachaco de Bogotá,* August 11, 1833; José María Luis Mora "Discurso sobre los perniciosos efectos de la empleomanía," in Arturo Arnáiz y Freg, comp., *Ensayos, ideas y retratos* (Mexico, 1944), 17–30 [originally published in *El Observador de la República Mexicana,* 1a. época, 3:73–86, November 11, 1827. I thank University of Iowa's Professor Charles Hale for this valuable information].
93. Pinzón, *Tratado de ciencia constitucional,* 1:122–23.
94. See Cerbeleón Pinzón, *Filosofía moral* (Bogotá, 1840), 45–48, chap. 3.
95. See *El Observador,* January 1840; February 23, 1840; April 15, 1840; *El Día,* January 31, 1841; January 30, 1842; Ospina R., "Esposición al congreso de 1842," 9; idem, "Esposición al congreso de 1844," 16.
96. See Duque Gómez, "Relación del estado actual de la instrucción," 506–10; Soto, *Mis padecimientos,* 52; *El Correo,* September 12, 1839; January 1840, passim.
97. See Ortíz, *Reminiscencias,* 84; on *empleomanía* as a cultural bias of Nueva Granadans see Safford, *The Ideal of the Practical,* 6–7, 39, 99, 120; a critical assessment of *empleomanía* as the alleged source of a later conflict, the 1899–1901 civil war, can be found in Bergquist, *Coffee and Conflict,* 3–17.
98. See Chapter 1; and Callahan, *Honor, Commerce and Industry.*
99. See Safford, "Aspectos sociales de la política"; idem, "Acerca de las interpretaciones socioeconómicas de la política."
100. Weber, "Class, Status and Party," esp. 21.
101. Carlos Cuervo Márquez, "La intervención inglesa en la revolución de 1840," *Revista*

Moderna, Año 2, 3, no. 21 (May 1, 1916): 423–33; Gómez Barrientos, *Don Mariano Ospina y su época.*

102. For a brief reference to the war as a confrontation between the *aristocracia* and the *clase media* see Horgan, *Arzobispo Mosquera,* 49–55; for a well-documented reference to the confrontation between family networks fighting for "preeminencia social and política" ("social and political preeminence") in the Cauca region during those years see Escorcia, *Sociedad y economía en el Valle del Cauca,* 59–61, 98, 110–11.
103. *La Bandera Negra,* November [?]1837, 55; for other laudatory allusions to Jackson by Santander see Arboleda, *Historia contemporánea,* 1:368.
104. See Nutini, *Wages of Conquest.*
105. Gutiérrez Ponce, *Vida de Don Ignacio Gutierrez V.,* 1: 303, emphasis added; see also "A las naciones y gobiernos civilisados. Breve reseña de la conducta observada por el llamado gobierno constitucional granadino con los pueblos que proclamaron las reformas en los años 1840–1841." Unos granadinos reformistas. DBNC, Fondo Vergara 12; Cuervo Márquez, *Vida de José I. de Márquez,* 2:96; Rivas, *Escritos de Don Pedro Fernández Madrid,* 65.
106. Cuervo Márquez, *Vida de José I. de Márquez,* 2:285.
107. July 31, 1840 letter to Juan M. Gómez, in "Cartas inéditas de Aranzazu," 604.
108. See the verses that appeared in *El Cometa* published in Medellín between October 1840 and April 1841. Cited in Tisnes Jiménez, *María Martínez de Nisser,* 73–80.
109. See response in *El Observador,* May 10, 1840, 141.

Chapter 10
The "Liberal Revolution": A Friendly Affair

1. See 1832 constitution, articles 16, 106, 121, 141, and 160; and 1843 constitution, articles 16, 17, 101, 125 and 131, in Pombo and Guerra, *Constituciones de Colombia,* 3:262, 281, 286, 291, 293, 330, 332, 334, 353, 361; Miguel Samper, "Ojeada retrospectiva sobre nuestros partidos y su labor constitucional," *Repertorio Colombiano* 14, no. 2 (August 1896): 110–40, esp. 119.
2. See Azuero and Anzola, "Informe de una Comisión . . . sobre el modo de proceder a la reforma de la constitución."
3. See laws of May 25, 1841, May 26, 1842, and June 24, 1842, in *Recopilación de leyes,* 83–84.
4. Two generals, 17 colonels, 15 lieutenant colonels, 15 sergeant majors, 16 captains, 7 lieutenants and 10 *alfereces.* See Acevedo, "Relación nominal de los individuos que han sido dados de baja del ejercito."
5. See "Testamento de Vicente Azuero," *BCB* 19, 4 (1982): 5–61; Rivas, *Los trabajadores de tierra caliente,* 27.
6. Hernández de Alba and Lozano, eds., *Documentos sobre el doctor Vicente Azuero,* lxxiv; Soto, *Mis padecimientos,* 15, 114.
7. For instance, José María Duque Gómez died in 1841. Provincial lawyers José Nicolás Escobar, José María Chacon Zabala, Ramón Lombana Buendía, Juan N. Ponton Piedrahita, Francisco de P. Vargas, and others dropped out of the records in the early 1840s. See Appendix 5.
8. On Cuenca and Herrera see Plazas, *Genealogías de Neiva,* 251, 321–32; Restrepo S., *Gobernadores y próceres de Neiva,* 251.
9. See Chapter 9 and Appendix 4.

10. See Andrés Aguilar, "Aviso al público" (Bogotá, 1840); Montoya, "Aviso. Venta de un vale u obligación"; Safford, "Commerce and Enterprise," 230.
11. See *GNG,* December 13, 1840; AHN, Inst. Pub. vol. 126:643; Davis, "Acosta, Caro and Lleras," 208–26.
12. See *La Bagatela* 36, August 15, 1853, 53; and, *GNG,* no. 608 (March 30, 1843); *GNG,* no. 676 (April 21, 1844); *GNG,* no. 1030 (March 11, 1849).
13. See AHN, Indices Notaria 1a, vol. 16, 1842–1848, Fol. 42:15– 21; *GNG,* no. 575, September 11, 1842; *GNG,* no. 608, March 30, 1843; *GNG,* no. 676, April 21, 1844; Samper, *Historia de un alma,* 1:165.
14. Samper, *Historia de un alma,* 1:166. On Juan N. Vargas's legal practice see *GNG,* no. 747, June 22, 1845.
15. The participants in these *tertulias* all lived and died modestly. Samper, *Historia de un alma,* 1:160–64. On the nature and presence of artisans see Jay Robert Grusin, "The Revolution of 1848 in Colombia" (Ph.D. diss., The University of Arizona, 1978), chap. 1; Sowell, *The Early Colombian Labor Movement,* chap. 2; Rafael E. Santander, "Los artesanos," in *Museo de cuadros de costumbres,* 3:149–63. On street children see Januario Salgar, "El chino de Bogotá," in *Museo de cuadros de costumbres,* 2:247–48. On beggars and filth see Miguel Samper, *La miseria en Bogotá y otros escritos* (Bogotá, 1969); "Bogotá en 1841," *BHA* 15, 179 (September 1926): 689–93, esp. 691; Salvador Camacho Roldán, "Bogotá a mediados del siglo XIX," in Ramón Torres Méndez, *Costumbres Neo-Granadinas* (Bogotá, 1965). For vehement anti-Jesuit writings see the mid-1840s newspaper *La Noche* and Gómez Barrientos, *Don Mariano Ospina y su época,* 1:374.
16. For instance, during the 1840s Eujenio Castilla practiced in El Guamo, Chaparral and Neiva, and Laureano Gaspar Díaz practiced in Neiva along with Andrés Durán González, Eloi and Eladio Manrique, and young José M. Rojas Garrido. Other little towns like Zipaquirá, Ibague, La Mesa, La Palma, and Cocui had practices by Bruno Bulla, Patrocinio Cuellar, Benigno Guarniso, Ruperto Anzola, and Faustino Barbosa, respectively. See *GNG,* no. 575, September 11, 1842; *GNG,* no. 608, March 30, 1843; *GNG,* no. 676, April 21, 1844; *GNG,* no. 1031, March 18, 1849.
17. See article on "Rabulismo" in conservative newspaper *El Día* 104 (March 27, 1842), 458; "El pleiteador," *El Duende* 63 (June 11, 1847), 2; on *tinterillos* see José María Samper, "El triunvirato parroquial," in *Museo de cuadros de costumbres,* 1: 237–49, esp. 239; and Joaquín Vargas's speech in "Una sesión solemne de la Escuela Republicana." Bogotá, printed by Neo-Granadino, 1850. DBNC, F. Vergara, 759, 81, 25–26.
18. By 1849 there were over 100 judicial jobs. 52 of these were in *juzgados letrados del circuito,* 18 in *juzgados letrados de hacienda,* 35 in *tribunales del circuito,* and around 6 in the Supreme Court. See *GNG,* no. 1029, March 4, 1849; *GNG,* no. 1030, March 11, 1849; *GNG,* no. 1031, March 18, 1849. For comparative information on lawyers and the judiciary see Victor M. Uribe, "Colonial Lawyers, Republican Lawyers and the Administration of Justice in Latin America," in Eduardo Zimerman, ed., *Judicial Institutions in Nineteenth-Century Latin America* (London, Institute of Latin American Studies, University of London, 1999).
19. See Chapters 8 and 9. See also "La empleomanía. Comedia en abreviatura," in *Museo de cuadros de costumbres,* 3:239–61.
20. "La empleomanía," 249, 251. My translation.
21. See the 1840 book on ethics by Pinzón, *Filosofía moral,* 45–48, chap. 3.
22. For unemployment statistics and other demographic data see *El Nacional,* July 5, 1848, 3.

23. About Mosquera and his government see Joseph L. Helguera, "The First Mosquera Administration in New Granada, 1845–1849" (Ph.D. diss. Univ. of North Carolina, 1958); see also Grusin, "The Revolution of 1848," 10.
24. "Muerte del Dr. Diego F. Gómez," 519–26; Arboleda, *Historia contemporánea*, 1:315; 2:210, 290. See also Appendix 5.
25. See May 31, 1844 law on "indulto y regreso de los espatriados por causa de rebelión" ("pardon and return of exiles accused of treason"), in *Recopilación de leyes*, 72–73.
26. *La Noche,* an anti-Jesuit newspaper, was founded and directed in 1845 by lawyer Juan Nepomuceno Vargas. *El Aviso,* a newspaper opposed to 1845–1849 President General Tomás C. Mosquera, was written by lawyers Carlos Martín and José María Vergara T. *El Siglo* was written by lawyers Salvador Camacho Roldán, Medardo Rivas, and Antonio María Pradilla. *El Censor* was published in 1848 in Medellín by lawyers José María Facio Lince and Pedro A. Restrepo E. *La América* was edited by lawyers Carlos Martín and Ricardo Vargas.
27. Despite these youngsters' conservative training, they were exposed to liberalism, English radicalism, French romanticism and republicanism, and both utopian and Christian socialism. See Robert Gilmore, "New Granada's Socialist Mirage," *HAHR* 36 (1956): 190–210; Jaramillo Uribe, *El pensamiento colombiano en el siglo XIX;* Samper, *Historia de un alma,* 1:118–19. For a comparable group in 1840s Chile see Cristián Gazmuri, *El "48" Chileno. Igualitarios, reformistas, radicales, masones y bomberos* (Santiago de Chile, 1992).
28. Arboleda, *Historia contemporánea,* 2:325; Safford, "Commerce and Enterprise."
29. Robert L. Gilmore and John. P. Harrison, "Juan Bernardo Elbers and the Introduction of Steamship Navigation on the Magdalena River," *HAHR* 23, 3 (August 1948): 335–59; Safford, *Ideal of the Practical,* chap. 1.
30. Otero Muñóz, "Boceto biográfico," 184–87; Arboleda, *Historia contemporánea,* 2:268–69.
31. In 1841, Lombana sold his pharmacy and some lands in Neiva to tycoon Judas Tadeo Landinez. Cuervo, *Vida de Rufino Cuervo,* 2:55; Gutiérrez Ponce, *Vida de Ignacio Gutiérrez Vergara,* 389; Gómez Barrientos, *Don Mariano Ospina y su época,* 1:415–16.
32. To be sure, in the newspaper *La Civilización,* Ospina criticized González's participation in Mosquera's cabinet and abhorred his "red" anticlerical ideas. See Gómez Barrientos, *Don Mariano Ospina R. y su época,* 1:398, 405–07.
33. See Roberto Echeverría Rodríguez, *Los Gólgotas. Episodios de la vida política colombiana* (Barranquilla, 1944), 143; Cuervo Márquez, *Vida de José I. de Márquez,* 2:385–86.
34. On Mallarino see Escorcia, *Desarrollo político, social y económico,* 55; and Arboleda, *Diccionario biográfico,* 250–52. On Osorio's anti-free trade ideas see Safford, "The Emergence of Economic Liberalism in Colombia," 35–62. See also Appendix 4.
35. Aristocratic merchant Clímaco Ordóñez left the position in late 1845. Several other *ministeriales* turned down Mosquera's offers to occupy the job afterward. See Arboleda, *Historia contemporánea,* 2:231, 251–52, 265, 299; Helguera, "The First Mosquera Administration."
36. Camacho Roldán, *Mis memorias,* 1:41.
37. On González's import business see Jaime Duarte French, *Florentino González: Razón y sinrazón de una lucha política* (Bogotá, 1982), 308–09; on other business see Safford, "Commerce and Enterprise," 312–13; on his family connections with Ordóñez and Uribe see Duarte French, *Las Ibáñez,* 199, 201, 259, 301. On Martínez, see Appendix 4.
38. See, for instance, his article "Algo más sobre intereses materiales," published in 1846 in *El Día,* reprinted in Florentino González, *Escritos políticos, jurídicos y económicos*

(Bogotá, 1981), 585–89; and also "Una ojeada sobre el mundo," *El Día,* año 8, no. 441, August 8, 1847, 1–2.

39. See Law 28, June 14, 1847 "Orgánica del comercio de importación," in *Recopilación de leyes,* Apendice, 203–22; AHN, Inst. Pub. vol. 115:292; Pereira Gamba, "Los conflictos de Bogotá," 348–416; González, *Memorias;* Grusin, "The Revolution of 1848," 24; the best research on the 1847 tariff is Ocampo, "Librecambio y proteccionismo en el siglo XIX," see esp. 254–55, 277. See also Anibal Galindo, "Apuntamientos para la historia económica y fiscal del país," in idem, *Estudios económicos y fiscales* (Bogotá, 1978), 119–86, esp. 153–59.
40. Arboleda, *Historia contemporánea,* 2:374; Grusin, "The 1848 Revolution," 46. In 1847, the year of their graduation, young lawyers Salvador Camacho Roldán, Medardo Rivas, and Antonio María Pradilla supported González's candidacy through the newspaper *El Siglo,* which also advocated the abolition of slavery and published the platform of the Liberal Party. See Otero Muñoz, "Boceto biográfico de cien cancilleres," 213.
41. See López, "El desengaño o confidencias de Ambrosio López," 15–16; Sowell, *The Early Colombian Labor Movement,* 40–80; Grusin, "The Revolution of 1848," 22–41. On the confrontations between these artisanal societies and different elite groups in several cities, see the works by Sowell and Grusin, and also Gómez Barrientos, *Don Mariano Ospina y su época;* Avelino Escobar, *Reseña histórica de los principales acontecimientos políticos de la ciudad de Cali desde el año de 1848 hasta el de 1855 inclusive* (Bogotá, 1856); Escorcia, *Desarrollo político social y económico.*
42. Samper, *Historia de un alma,* 1:220; Galindo, *Recuerdos históricos,* 43; Camacho Roldán, *Mis memorias,* 1:49, 106–07; David Sowell, "'*La teoria i la realidad*': The Democratic Society of Artisans of Bogotá," *HAHR* 67, 4 (1987): 611–30; Grusin, "The Revolution of 1848," 26–27.
43. *El Correo de la Razón,* November 7, 1839.
44. Samper, *Historia de un alma,* 1:118–19; Cuervo Márquez, *Vida de José I. de Márquez,* 2:386–87.
45. On Suárez Serrano see Chapter 6 and Appendix 5; see also AHN, Inst. Pub., vol. 110:46; *Acuerdos,* 2:139–40,167; Arboleda, *Historia contemporánea,* 1:99–100; Restrepo and Rivas, *Genealogías de Santafé,* 389–90; Pacheco and Molina Lemus, *La familia de Santander,* 51–57; Pardo Umaña, *Haciendas de la sabana,* 90–91; *Causas y memorias* 1990, 1:196–200.
46. Samper, *Historia de un alma,* 1:86–95.
47. See Pereira Gamba, "Los conflictos de Bogotá"; Pereira Gamba, "Miguel Gamba," 621–25; Cadena, "D. José Francisco Pereira"; José Alejandro Bermudez, "Méritos del Doctor Francisco Pereira," *BHA* 17, 198 (January 1929): 357–58; Arboleda, *Diccionario biográfico,* 347–48.
48. Galindo, *Recuerdos históricos,* 4–5; Samper, *Historia de un alma,* 1:160–62; Plazas, *Genealogías de Neiva,* 61–66.
49. Gabriel Echeverri was a close associate of the rich Antioqueño Juan Santamaría. See Restrepo Sáenz, *Gobernadores de Antioquia,* 2:285–92, 429–30.
50. For a well-documented account of young Posada's lineage, life, and career see Carlos José Reyes Posada, "Joaquín Pablo Posada El Alacrán: Poeta satírico y periodista combativo en tiempos de cambio," typewritten manuscript, Bogotá, 1997. See also E.S.M [Enrique Santos Molano?], "Hoy Sale el Alacrán," *BCB* 20, 1 (1983): 6–20.
51. See Appendixes 1 and 4, Figure 3.2, Chapters 3 and 7. See also Vergara y Vergara, *Vida de Estanislao Vergara.*
52. See Otero Muñoz, "Bocetos biográficos," 217–20; Abraham Moreno, "Justo

Arosemena," *Repertorio Colombiano* 15, 1 (January 1, 1897): 96–105; Moscote and Arce, *La vida ejemplar de Justo Arosemena;* Restrepo Sáenz, *Gobernadores y próceres,* 326, 487; Arboleda, *Diccionario biográfico,* 77.

53. Samper, *Historia de un alma,* 1:169; Hernández de Alba, "Galería de hijos insignes," 396–97; José M. Restrepo Sáenz, "La provincia del Socorro y sus gobernantes," *BHA* 41, 476 (June 1954): 321–78, esp. 362.
54. See Chapter 7 and Appendix 1.
55. See *Documentos sobre la familia Rivas* (Bogotá, 1930), 19–137; Rivas, *Relaciones internacionales entre Colombia y los Estados Unidos,* 104; Rivas, *Los trabajadores de tierra caliente,* 44, 34; on this prestigious family see "La familia Rivas," *BHA* 28, 323–24 (September-October 1941): 911–17; Guerra, "José Nicolás de Rivas," 434–66; Germán Posada Mejía, "Manuel del Campo y Rivas cronista colombiano (1750–1830)," in *Nuestra América. Notas de historia cultural* (Bogotá, 1959), 189–256.
56. Pereira Gamba, "Los conflictos de Bogotá," 404; Restrepo and Rivas, *Genealogías de Santafé,* 166; Otero Muñóz, "Boceto biográfico," 198; Arboleda, *Historia contemporánea,* 2:347. For examples of provincials who, after having briefly militated in the *ministerial* group, ended up in the Liberal party see the cases of Ricardo de la Parra (1815–1873) and Patrocinio Cuellar (1819–1861). Samper, "Galería nacional," 121; Uribe Angel, "Recuerdos de un viaje a Medellín," 281–306, esp. 637–38.
57. Rivas, *Los trabajadores de tierra caliente;* Samper, *Historia de un alma,* 261, 284–85; Salvador Camacho Roldán, "Algo sobre tierra caliente," in *Museo de cuadros de costumbres,* 1: 201–14.
58. See the cases of lawyers Ricardo de la Parra, Juan Esteban Zamarra, and Rafael M. Giraldo, in Samper, *Galería nacional de hombres ilustres,* 333; Abraham Moreno, *Biografía del Doctor Rafael María Giraldo en memoria de su centenario* (Medellín, 1908); Luis De Greiff, "Juan Esteban Zamarra," *Repertorio Histórico* 15, 149–52 (January 1942): 333–41; Miguel Martínez, "Juan Esteban Zamarra (1828–1870)," *Repertorio Histórico* 25, 25 (October-December 1971): 265–71.
59. For a few exceptions, Bogotano lawyer Alejandro Osorio being the most noteworthy, see Safford, "The Emergence of Economic Liberalism in Colombia," 35–62; idem, "Commercial Crisis and Economic Ideology in New Granada," 183–206. See Osorio's anti-free trade newspaper *El Proletario,* published in 1834.
60. On the terms *conservador* and *liberal* see *El Nacional,* May 21, 1848, p. 1, cited by Grusin, "The Revolution of 1848," 43.
61. The best known case was that of lawyer and financier Judas Tadeo Landínez. See Safford, "Commerce and Enterprise," 69–82.
62. Safford, "Commerce and Enterprise," chap. 4; König, *En el camino a la nación,* part 5.
63. *Documentos sobre la familia Rivas;* Harrison, "The Colombian Tobacco Industry From Government Monopoly"; Rivas, *Los trabajadores de tierra caliente;* Safford, "Commerce and Enterprise," 203–34.
64. Gómez Barrientos, *Don Mariano Ospina y su época,* 415–17; Eduardo Rodríguez Piñérez, "Proceso del 7 de marzo," *BHA* 36, 417–19 (July-September 1949): 412–44; Camacho Roldán, *Mis memorias,* 1:67–68; Grusin, "The Revolution of 1848," 53–65.
65. Cuervo Márquez, *Vida de José I. de Márquez,* 2:385–86; *GNG,* March 9, 1851.
66. Safford, "Acerca de las interpretaciones socioeconómicas de la política"; for opposite interpretations see Nieto Arteta, *Economía y cultura en la historia de Colombia;* Alfredo Molano, "Colombia: economia y educación en 1850," *Eco,* no. 172 (February 1975): 353–411; König, *En el camino a la nación,* 439, 480.
67. See *El Amigo del País,* cited by Uribe and Alvarez, *Poderes y regiones,* 134–37; Safford,

"Commerce and Enterprise"; Poveda Ramos, *Historia económica de Antioquia;* Grusin, "The Revolution of 1848."
68. Camacho Roldán, *Mis memorias,* 1:55, 87–88; Gómez Barrientos, *Don Mariano Ospina y su época,* 1:415–16; Rodríguez Piñerez, "Proceso del 7 de Marzo," 439; Restrepo Saenz, *Gobernadores de Antioquia,* 2:350–52.
69. See judicial proceedings and other documents transcribed in Manuel J. Esguerra Roble, *Procesos célebres y acontecimientos varios. Russi inocente?* (Bogotá, 1947), 47–58.
70. That artisans were charged with sponsoring the crimes can be seen in the angry reply by baker Ambrosio López, "El desengaño o confidencias de Ambrosio López," 12; see also Esguerra Roble, *Procesos célebres y acontecimientos varios,* 22.
71. See AHN, Instr. Pub. vol. 115, fol. 66.
72. See E.S.M. "Hoy sale el Alacrán," 16.
73. Artisans Miguel León and Francisco Londoño also participated. See Cuervo Márquez, *Vida de José I de Márquez,* 2:388.
74. See Esguerra Roble, *Procesos célebres,* 103, 162; see also E.S.M., "Hoy sale el Alacrán," 17–18; and, Reyes Posada, "Joaquín Pablo Posada."
75. See Appendix 5.
76. See Esguerra Roble, *Procesos célebres,* 79, 101, 104, 139–40. The jury law was enacted on June 4, 1851 with a retroactive effect.
77. See the *costumbrista* novel by young modest lawyer and bureaucrat José María Angel Gaitán, *Dr. Temis,* 2 vols. (Bogotá, [1853]). In it, Russi's equivalent, Dr. Temis, is depicted as a creepy *tinterillo* surrounded by despicable criminals.
78. See contemporary lawyer José María Vargas Valdéz's testimony in Esguerra Roble, *Procesos célebres,* 144–76; see Esguerra Roble's own analysis on pages 127 and 143; see also E.S.M. "Hoy sale el Alacrán," passim.
79. See Galindo, *Recuerdos históricos,* 53–54; "Una sesion solemne de la Escuela Republicana"; "Discursos pronunciados en las sesiones [Escuela Republicana] del 7 i 9 de Marzo de 1851," 1–84.
80. See Grusin, "The Revolution of 1848," chap. 8; Venancio Ortíz, *Historia de la revolución del 17 de abril de 1854* (Bogotá, 1972 [1855]).
81. The clashes took place between May and July 1853. See Grusin, "The Revolution of 1848," chap. 8, esp. 227.
82. See Ortíz, *Historia de la revolución del 17 de abril;* Francisco Gutiérrez Sanín, *Curso y discurso del movimiento plebeyo 1849/1954* (Bogotá, 1995).
83. See José de Obaldía, "Memoria testamentaria de José de Obaldía, vicepresidente de la Nueva Granada," *BHA,* 31, 353–54 (March-April 1944): 274–304, esp. 296–97; Joaquín Ospina, *Diccionario biográfico y bibliográfico de Colombia,* 3 vols. (Bogotá, 1927–1939), 3:119–20; Appendix 5.
84. See E.S.M., "Hoy sale el Alacrán," 19.
85. See Samper, "Galería nacional"; Gustavo Otero Muñóz, "Boceto biográfico"; idem, *Semblanzas colombianas* (Bogotá, 1938). On the Liberal party's leadership in the following years see Helen Delpar, *Red Against Blue: The Liberal Party in Colombian Politics, 1863–1899* (University, AL, 1981), esp. chap. 3.

Conclusion

1. On this issue see Claudio Velíz, *The New World of the Gothic Fox: Culture and Economy in English and Spanish America* (Berkeley, 1994); idem, *The Centralist Tradition of Latin America* (Princeton, 1980); Glen C. Dealy, *The Public Man: An Interpretation of Latin America and Other Catholic Cultures* (Amherst, 1978); Howard J. Wiarda, ed., *Politics and Social Change in Latin America: The Distinct Tradition* (Amherst, 1974).
2. On the "authority of wealth" as a general ability to command the allegiance of others see Reddy, *Money and Liberty in Modern Europe,* chap. 4.
3. See, for instance, Halperín Donghi, *Revolución y guerra;* idem, *Aftermath of Revolution in Latin America* (New York, 1973).

Glossary

abogado de pobres: pro bono lawyer.
administrador: administrator.
agente fiscal: solicitor within an *audiencia*.
agentes de negocios: intermediaries or brokers between the Spanish Crown and job seekers.
agregado: cabildo's attaché.
aguardiente: liquor.
alcabala: sales or excise tax.
alcalde: local magistrate; mayor.
alcalde del crimen: junior criminal judge within an *audiencia*.
alcalde ordinario: municipal magistrate or mayor, acted as sheriff and justice of the peace.
alférez real: regidor in charge of keeping a *cabildo*'s emblem.
alguacil mayor de corte: sheriff within an *audiencia*.
Antioqueño: a native of New Granada's northwestern region of Antioquia.
arroba: unit of weight equal to 25 pounds.
asambleas departamentales: postcolonial provincial legislatures.
asesor: legal advisor to a government agency.
audiencia: high court of justice.
auditor de guerra: inspector of army expenditures.
bachiller: third-tier college graduate.
bulas y papel sellado: pope's edicts and stamped paper.
cabildo: town or city council.
caja real: provincial treasury.
canónigo magistral: priest in local cathedral.
carrera de oficinas: bureaucratic career.
casas de educación: private elementary or secondary schools.
Casa de la Moneda: royal mint.
casta: castes, racial mixtures.
caudillo: local and regional politico-military bosses in postcolonial Latin America.
chichería: tavern, bar.
cédula: royal order or decree.
certámenes públicos: honors examinations in postcolonial schools.
cofradía: lay confraternity or religious brotherhood (see *ligas, cofradías y hermandades*).
colegio: school.
colegio mayor: Church-administered college.
compañias de comercio: business partnerships.

Consejo de Purificación: Spanish antirevolutionary court that tried insurgents during the 1810s.
consulado: merchant guild.
consultor: adviser to the Holy Inquisition.
contador: accountant.
contador auxiliar: assistant accountant.
contador general: general comptroller.
contador interventor: auditing accountant.
contador real: royal accountant.
contaduría general: general comptroller's office.
contribución directa: income tax.
conventos menores: small convents.
corregidor: magistrate and chief administrative officer in colonial provinces. Charged especially with the administration of Indian communities.
corregimiento: colonial administrative province or district.
correos: mail.
Cortes: Spanish parliament.
criollismo: ideology pertaining to creole identity.
criollo: creole, a Spaniard born in America.
cursos simultáneos: several law courses in a single year.
defensor: keeper of a rent.
departamentos: provinces.
derecho natural: natural law.
derecho natural de gentes: international public law.
derecho real: royal legislation.
derechos de actuación: fees proportional to legal services and signatures endorsing legal documents.
desnaturalizado: unfaithful, disloyal.
diezmos: tithes.
diputado: deputy to Asamblea Departamental or other elected body.
doctor: graduate in medicine or law, top-tier college graduate.
don: reverential expression to address *hidalgo* men.
doña: reverential expression to address *hidalgo* women.
elector: delegate in charge of electing president and other state officials.
empleomanía: "vice" of living from public office.
encomendero: holder of an *encomienda*.
encomienda: royal grant of tribute-paying Indian workers.
escribano: notary.
escribano de cámara: special scribe to a top state official or agency.
escribiente: scribe.
familias principales: local elite families.
fiscal: prosecutor.
fiscal de lo civil: audiencia's prosecuting attorney in civil cases.
fiscal de lo criminal: audiencia's prosecuting attorney in criminal cases.
fuero: legal immunities and privileges granted to certain groups, usually members of corporations such as the Church and the military.
gobernador: governor.
Gran Colombia: union between Ecuador, Colombia, and Venezuela.
gran semana: popular, especially religious, mobilization to save Bogotá from rebels in late 1840.

hacendado: owner of an hacienda.
hacienda: large landed estate.
hidalgo: lesser noble; gentry.
hidalguía: condition of being an *hidalgo*.
imaginarios: collective mindsets, mentalities.
intendente: governor in postcolonial period.
jefatura militar: military command.
jefes supremos: top military rebel leaders in 1839–1842 civil war.
jornaleros: daily workers.
juez letrado: judge with a law degree.
junta: committee.
juntas provinciales: provincial cogovernmental committees established in Spain after 1808 crisis.
junta suprema: cogovernmental committees established in Spanish colonies during 1808–1810 crisis.
Junta de Secuestros: Spanish antirevolutionary tribunal in charge of confiscations during the mid-1810s.
jurisprudencia: law.
justicia mayor: top judicial authority in a *corregimiento*.
legitimidad y buenas costumbres: legitimate birth and good social background.
letrado: someone with a college degree, especially lawyers.
licenciado: second-tier college graduate.
ligas, cofradías y hermandades: lay confraternities or religious brotherhoods.
meritorio: unpaid apprentice in a state agency.
méritos: military or bureaucratic services and experience.
ministerial: member of conservative or progovernment faction during the late 1830s.
ministerio: ministry; also generic term for government in the late 1830s.
molino: mill.
oficial: clerk in a government agency.
oficial mayor: chief clerk.
oficial secundario: assistant chief clerk.
oficialía mayor: office of chief clerk.
oficios viles: low-level manual occupations.
oidor: judge within an *audiencia*.
oposición: competition to obtain college teaching jobs.
panadería: bakery.
papel sellado: stamped paper.
partido: faction or party.
pasquines: broadsheets.
patacones: monetary units.
plan de estudios: official curriculum.
plebe: populace.
prácticos: empirical lawyers without a formal education or degree.
pretender: to apply for a state job.
pretendiente: applicant to state positions.
procesillo: legal proceeding to investigate *legitimad y buenas costumbres* prior to being admitted into a *colegio mayor*.
procurador: solicitor.
profesión de los destinos: bureaucratic career.
progresista: member of liberal political faction of the late 1830s.

pueblada: popular riot, especially applied to the late 1840 riot in Bogotá.
pulpería: general store.
pureza de sangre: all-white and old Christian ancestry.
real: generic term for coins; silver coin worth one-eighth of a peso.
reales cajas: Royal Accounts office.
regente: senior judge within an *audiencia.*
regente contador: senior accountant.
regidor: town councilor.
relación de méritos y servicios: resumes of candidates for public office.
relator: scribe or reporter within an *audiencia* or court of justice.
renta: rent.
representaciones: petitions, complaints, and legal briefs filed with royal officials.
síndico procurador: city council's solicitor.
sirvientes: servants.
Socorrano: a native of New Granada's northeastern region of Socorro.
soldadezca: pejorative reference to common soldiers.
superintendente: superintendent of a region or the royal mint.
Supremos: rebel military commanders during 1839–1842 civil war.
teniente gobernador: lieutenant governor.
tertulias: literary salons.
tesorero: treasurer.
tesorero de diezmos: treasurer of the rent of tithes.
tinterillos: empirical attorneys without formal training or degrees.
títulos honoríficos: honorific titles.
toga: judge's robe, usually worn by officials in *audiencias.*
togado: wearing a *toga; oidor* or *fiscal* in an *audiencia.*
trapiche: sugar mill.
Tribunal de Cuentas: chief auditing agency.
Tribunal de Secuestros: early postcolonial agency for confiscating the property of antirevolutionaries.
universidad: university or college.
visitador: inspector.
zambos: offspring of unions between blacks and Indians.

Index

Acero, Mariano, 125
administrative science courses, in legal education, 109, 114–15, 116–17
advocates of the poor *(abogados de pobres)*, 26, 42, 213n.49
agencies, state, 30
Alvarez family, 33–35, 127, 135–36
Alvarez Lozano, Manuel María, 83
Alvarez y Casal, Manuel Bernardo, 65, 67
amnesty, for provincial rebels, 126–28, 130, 133, 143
antimilitary faction, 79–80, 90; aristocrats in, 86, 89; in newspapers, 87–88; provincials in, 82, 84, 86, 96, 122
Antioquia province, 93, 128; elites of, 80–81, 86, 94–99, 120–21, 240n.57; and liberalization, 150–51; revolt in, 126, 130
Anzola, Ruperto, 77
Arango Echeverri, Pantaleón, 214n.57
Aranzazu, Juan de Dios, 97, 116, 137
Arboleda, Don Rafael, 127
Arboleda, Julio, 144, 145
Arce de León, José, 83
aristocrats, 4–5, 145; alliance with provincial elites, 98, 151, 157; and bureaucracy, 133, 142; government of, 118, 143; and provincial revolts, 101, 127–28, 130; support for liberalism, 144–51; support for military, 89, 92; values of, 111–12; *vs.* provincial elites, 86, 115, 136–37
Armero, José León, 67
army, 89, 91, 105, 130; and aristocrats, 101, 122; conservative *vs.* liberal vision of, 16–17; in coup with artisans, 152–53; influence in government, 74, 88; postcolonial, 71, 74–75; provincials in, 93, 139; Spanish, fighting independence movement, 66–70; status through service in, 15–16, 24–25, 139; Venezuelan, 74–75, 88. *See also* antimilitary faction
Arroyo, Isidro, 77
Arrubla, Manuel A., 94, 96–97
artisans, 131, 145, 150, 151–54
Atlantic coast region, revolts in, 130
authoritarianism, 91–93
Ayarza, José Ponceano, 23–24
Azuero, Juan, 124–25
Azuero, Juan Nepomuceno, 78–79
Azuero, Vicente, 132; background of, 78–81; death of, 117, 139; in elections, 122, 128–29, 132–33; in provincial faction, 116, 124, 126–28, 131

banditry, of artisans, 151–52
Beltrán, Julián, 125
Bentham, Jeremy, 108–13
Bogotá, 63, 80; aristocrats in, 82–85, 92; number of lawyers in, 21, 210n.15; powerful clans of, 62, 240n.57; and provincial rebels, 130–31, 136
Bogotá junta, 55
Bolívar, Simón, 45–46, 75, 238n.33; assassination plots against, 91, 96; as dictator, 90, 91, 109; opposition to, 88–90, 96
Bonnin, Jean Charles, 114, 116
Borrero, Cali General Eusebio, 129, 133
Bourbon reforms, 32, 35, 104
Buendía Durán, Eustacio and Domingo, 146
bureaucracy, 65, 75, 97, 143; access to, 15–18, 20, 28–29, 32, 46, 118–19; as state-granted privilege, 10–11; aristocrats in, 83, 92, 150; benefits of, 12–13, 30–31, 88, 215n.70; broader representation in, 76–82; changes by young mandarins in, 146–49; competition in, 18–19, 41–42, 89;

bureaucracy, *continued*
    decline of status of, 18–19, 148–49, 154; demand for jobs in, 113, 115; dependence of lawyers on, 111–12, 133–35; frustration with, 41–42, 52–54, 69; lawyers in, 1–2, 20, 49, 54–57, 114–17, 140–42; modernizing, 104–05; popularity as profession for elite, 24, 26; qualifications for, 9–11, 78; status-honor through, 5–6, 11, 18, 155, 157–58; steps up in, 29, 56–57; transitional generation of lawyers in, 71–72. *See also* family-bureaucratic networks; local government
Burkholder, Mark, 28–29, 54
business, 28, 63, 96, 150; of Antioqueños, 94–95; provincials in, 136, 139, 143–44; status through, 18–19, 148–49

cabildos: links among regional, 61–63; role in revolution, 60–65, 68; status from serving on, 12–13
cabinets, 93, 144
Caicedo, Domingo, 91, 122
Caicedo, Luis, 48
Caicedo family, 88
Caicedo y Flórez, José, 32, 40–41
Caicedo y Pastrana, José, 36–37
Calvo Ortega, Casimiro, 83
Camacho, Manuel Dolores, 126
Camacho Naranjo, Salvador, 79, 125, 131, 139–40, 143
Camacho Roldán, Salvador, 146
Camacho y Lago, Joaquín, 27, 29–30, 62
Canabal, Eusebio María, 55–56
Cañarete, Manuel, 114, 139
Cárdenas, Vicente, 127–28
Carmona, Francisco, 125–26
Carrión y Moreno, Joaquín, 46–47, 54
Cartagena, 80, 83, 92–93; colonial lawyers' stay in, 17, 21; number of lawyers in, 26; lawyers in Ministerial Group, 130
Cartagena junta, 55, 221n.13
Casanare region, 123, 125
Casanovas, Narciso, 119
Castilla, Eujenio, 101
Castillo y Rada, José María del, 62–63, 90, 116
Catholic Church, 77–78, 112, 120, 252n.7; conservative *vs.* liberal vision of, 16–17; in education, 106, 131; and legal education, 103–5, 109, 111, 117; power of, 21–22, 74, 84, 138; as profession for elites, 11–12, 24, 36; relation to state, 21–22, 104–06, 109, 131; use of lawyers by, 26–27
Catholic Society (Bogotá), 131
Cauca, 129
Cavero, Ignacio, 55
Céspedes, José María, 123
Céspedes Buendía, Angel María, 124–25
Chandler, Dewitt S., 54
Charles V, King, 20–21
civil rights, 77, 108. *See also* repression
civil society, 16–17, 87
civil wars, 101, 118, 158; causes of, 87, 120, 135–36; effects of, 138–40, 146–48
classes, social, 14, 22–24, 47; conflicts among, 136–37; of conservatives *vs.* liberals, 17, 150
Colegio Mayor del Rosario (Bogotá), 21–23
collective action/collective frames of mind, 60–65
colonialism, 60, 66, 135; and elites' relationship to Spanish Crown, 10–13, 31, 155–56; legacy of, 17–18, 92; legal education in, 103–5; loyalty of Indians and slaves to Spanish Crown, 50–51; Nariño conspiracy against, 40–44; regional discrimination in, 80, 82; Spain fighting to retain, 66–70; state-society relations in, 9–11; and transition to national period, 2–3. *See also* Spanish administration
colonization, of *tierra calientes,* 140, 150
Comunero revolt (1781), 37, 52, 104–05
Congress, 65, 150; conflicts among elites in, 126–27, 137; deciding elections, 99, 128–29, 132–33; influence of Antioqueños in, 97–98; opposition members in, 126–28, 140; powers of, 91, 138–39; return of provincial lawyers to, 143–44
Consejo de Estado, 138
Consejo de Regencia, 46, 58
Conservative Party, 112, 123, 149–51
conservatives, 103–04, 109, 143, 149; and lawyers, 52, 117; on legal education, 111–13; support for, 98, 146, 151; vision of state and society, 16–17
Constitutional Congress (1821), 80; between Venezuela and New Granada, 74–75, 79

Index 271

constitutional conventions, 65, 93–94, 101; (1828), 89–90, 96; (1830), 90–91
constitutionalist campaign, 98, 110
constitutions: 1821, conflict over revision of, 88–89; amendment to, establishing strong executive, 138; written after 1810 revolution, 65–66
Córdova, Salvador, 126
Cortés, Antonio, 40, 44
cortes generales, suggested for America, 57
Costeloe, Michael, 16
coup, of artisans and military, 152–53
creoles: discrimination against, 53–54, 58–59, 216n.4; in independence movement, 45–46; in local government, 60–61
creolism, ideology of, 63–65, 68
Crown, Spanish. *See* colonialism; Spanish administration
Cúcuta Congress. *See* Constitutional Congress (1821)
Cuenca, Domingo Ciprián, 100, 139
Cuervo, Rufino, 83–84
Cundinamarca province, 65, 88

decentralization, 116–17, 138
democracy, opposition to, 135–36. *See also* elections
Domínguez, Benedicto, 68
Domínguez, Mateo, 119
Domínguez family, 83
Dominicans, 21–22, 103–05, 115
Dorronsoro, José Antonio, 55
Duque Gómez, José María, 111, 114, 117, 131
Durán González, Andrés, 125

Echeverri, Camilo Antonio, 146–48
economic factors, in class and status, 14, 24
economic identity, *vs.* status, 2–3, 18–19
economy, 10, 75; consensus among elites on, 17, 114, 149–50; and economic opportunities, 27–28, 159; and foreign loans, 94, 128; liberalization of, 145, 150; New Granada's, 27, 88; state monopolies in, 17, 65, 119
Ecuador, 130; in Gran Colombia union, 86, 91
education, 16; reforms in, 105, 131, 138; status-honor through, 11, 155; university admission standards in, 23–24, 77–78. *See also* legal education

elections, 65, 98, 120, 132–33, 143; accusations of fraud in, 119–20, 123; after constitutional congresses, 90–91, 93–94; differences settled through, 86–87; opposition to, 90, 135–36, 138, 238n.33; significance of, 16, 156; and status of state jobs, 134, 158
elites, 2–5, 7, 44; collective frames of mind of, 60–65; conflicts among, 65, 86, 101, 118–31, 135–37, 157; conflicts over legal education, 108, 110, 112–13; education for, 105–08; in independence movement, 45, 49–59, 65–70; professions for, 20, 24–26; redefinition of factions within, 149–51; relation to state, 10–11, 15, 39, 88; unity of, 19, 63, 148, 151–54, 158–59; visions of state and society, 16–17. *See also* aristocrats; provincial elites
empleomanía (demand for state jobs), 113, 115; criticism of, 133–35, 142, 154, 158
England, 128, 130, 149–50
Escobar, José Nicolás, 124, 125
Escobar, Juan N., 125
Escuela Republicana, 152
Ezpeleta, Viceroy, 25

Facio Lince, José María, 126
Falquez, Antonio F., 125
families, 1–2, 22–24; and bureaucracy, 32–35, 85; status and honor passed through, 11–14, 82; ties within juntas, 47–48
family-bureaucratic networks, 32–39, 95–96, 156, 220n.50, 226n.17; after independence, 84–85; building, 13–14, 32; and *cabildos,* 61–63; effects of, 43, 135–37
fees, lawyers', 30
Ferdinand VII, King, 70
Fernández de Enciso, Luis Martín, 20
Flórez Camacho, Angel María, 79, 123
France, 45, 57–58, 103–04
Franco Pinzón brothers, 127
free trade, 108, 113–14
Frias, Anastacio García, 90

Galavís, Eustaquio, 42
Galavís, José María, 119, 123
Galindo, Anibal, 146
Gallego, Fernández, 20
Gamba Valencia, Fortunato, 24
García de Toledo, José María, 55

Garcia Paredes, 119
gold. *See under* trade
Gómez, Juan María, 119
Gómez, Juan N., 119
Gómez Durán, Diego Fernando, 79–80, 143
Gómez Durán, Miguel Tadeo, 40, 44, 55, 62
Gómez Pastor, Juan María, 97
González, Florentino, 126, 133; and artisan banditry, 151–52; in Mosquera's cabinet, 144–45; persecution of, 111, 119, 131, 153
González, Manuel, 125–26
Gori, Joaquín José, 23, 90
governors, provincial, 75
Gran Colombian union, 91, 94, 157; opposition to, 86, 89, 101
Groot, Pedro, 24, 63
Gutiérrez, Frutos, 24
Gutiérrez de Lara, Jorge, 150–51
Gutiérrez de Piñéres, Juan Francisco, 35–36
Gutiérrez Vergara, I., 119

Haber, Samuel, 12
Habermas, Jürgen, 87
Halperín Donghi, Tulio, 159
Herrán, Pedro Alcántara, 111, 119, 143; in 1840 elections, 128–29, 133
Herrera, Tomás, 119
Herrera Buendía, Bernardo, 100–01, 139
Herrera y Vergara, Ignacio, 52–53, 61
honor. *See* status-honor
Hoyos Cabal, Jorge Juan, 128
Huertas, Vicente, 40, 44

ideology: conflicts over, 18–19; of creolism, 63–65, 68
Ignacio de Pombo, José, 28
illegitimacy, 77–78
imaginarios, development of elites', 60–65
independence movement, 5–6, 58, 60–70; causes of, 156; effects of participation in, 15–16, 77–79; elites' fears about, 18–19, 49–51; lawyers in, 45–59, 156, 218n.34; and Nariño conspiracy, 40–44
Indians, 50, 77, 124
institutions, state, 3–4; after 1810 revolution, 66, 70; in Spanish colonialism, 9–11
Iriarte Rojas, Andrés José, 100

jacobins, 79, 84
Jamaica, trade with, 95–96

Jamaica Letter (Bolívar), 45–46
Jesuits, 21, 112, 138, 140
Jiménez de Quezada, Gonzalo, 20
Junta Central y Gubernativa (Spain), 53, 57
Junta de Estudios, 104–05
juntas, 55; connections among, 62–63; establishment of, 45, 57; preventing popular mobilization, 49–51; royalist, 48
juntas supremas, establishment of, 46–48
Junta Suprema of Bogotá, elitism of, 49–51

La Católica, 119–20
land, litigation over, 26–28
Larrota, Miguel, 125
Latin America: in Bolívar's Jamaica Letter, 45–46; political activity levels in, 18
Latorre Uribe, José María de, 133
law: as elite profession, 24, 26; practiced by nonlawyers, 28; status of jobs within, 20
law schools. *See* legal education
lawyers, 20, 156, 214n.60; aristocratic, 82–85; at constitutional conventions, 74, 91; execution of, 66–68, 72; in independence movement, 45–59, 71–72; of Neiva, 99–100; numbers of, 20–22, 115, 210n.15, 212nn.40,41; practicing, 26–27, 140, 214n.62; support for state, 39, 41–43, 58, 156; tasks of, 71, 139, 142; trying to enter bureaucracy, 35–36
legal education, 21–22, 61, 103–17, 131, 156, 247n.53; admissions standards for, 77, 211nn.18,22; conflicts about, 43, 108–13, 157–58
Leiva Caicedo, Uldarico, 127
Level Goda, Andrés, 125
liberalism, 98; in law schools, 113, 117; in state and society, 16–17
liberalization, 15–16, 77, 144, 158–59
Liberal Party, 109; and López, 145, 150; in redefinition of factions, 149–51; supporters of, 123, 146–49
Lievano, Romualdo, 99, 139–40
litigation: attempt to limit, 20–22; lawyer-instigated, 140; over land, 26–28
Lleras, Lorenzo María, 119, 120, 131, 133, 139
Llorente, González de, 28
local government, 60, 75, 90. *See also cabildos;* provinces
Lombana, José María, 67–68, 99–100

Lombana Buendía, Vicente, 131, 144
López, José Hilario, 93, 145, 150–52
Lozano y Peralta, José María, 40
Lynch, John, 29

Mallarino, Manuel M., 127, 144
Malo, Antonio, 88, 119
Manrique Gaitán, Eladio and Eloi, 101
Mantilla, José María, 140
Mariquita province, 82; elites of, 86, 99, 101, 123; revolts in, 130
Márquez, José Ignacio de, 83–84, 132; in aristocratic faction, 108, 111; election of, 98–99, 122; relations of, with provincials, 97–98, 122–24, 130
marriages, restrictions on, 13
Martín, Carlos, 151
Martínez, José Vicente, 145
Martínez Escobar brothers, 128
Martínez Recamán, Antonio, 24
medicine, as elite profession, 24–25
Medina, Pedro Antonio, 124
Melo, Jose M., 153
Memorial de agravios, 57–58
Mendinueta, Viceroy, 25
Mendoza Morales, José María, 124
merchants. *See* business
military. *See* antimilitary faction; army
military governments, 91–93
mines, 94–95, 150
Molina, Juan N., 125
monarchism, Bolívar's support for, 90
Montoya, Francisco, 94, 96–97, 119–20, 256n.74
Mora, José María Luis, 133
Morales, Antonio, 47–48
Morales, Francisco, 47–48
Morales, Ignacio, 119–20
Moreno, Juan N., 119
Moreno y Escandón, Francisco Antonio, 21–22, 103–05
Morillo, Pablo, 67–68
Mosquera, José Rafael, 127
Mosquera, Joaquín, 91, 144
Mosquera, Rafael, 84, 138
Mosquera, Tomás C. de, 122, 143–44
Mosquera y Figueroa, Joaquín, 33, 41
municipal councils, abolition of, 90
Murillo Toro, Manuel, 101, 125–26, 143–44
Murray, Thomas, 119, 123–24

Nariño Alvarez, Antonio, 27, 33, 52, 65, 79; conspiracy of, 39–44
Narváez y Latorre, Antonio, 50, 57
national period, transition from colonial period to, 2–3
native sons: in bureaucracy, 55–56; discrimination against, 58–59, 224n.42; increasing resentment of, 53–54
Neira, Juan José, 130
Neiva region: elites of, 86, 99–101, 123; opportunities for natives of, 80, 82; revolts in, 124–25, 130
New Granada: economy of, 27, 88; in Gran Colombia union, 86
newspapers, 98, 110, 254n.36; and Church, 252nn.7,9; intra-elite conflicts in, 120, 122, 135–37; molding public opinion through, 87–88; of provincial lawyers, 143–44
nobility, 12, 15, 78, 82
Núñez, Blas, 125

Obando, Antonio, 119
Obando, José María, 93, 98–99, 140; and provincial revolts, 124–25, 129–31; support for, 98–101, 252n.9
Obregón, Francisco A., 126, 153
Ocaña, constitutional conventions in, 89–91, 96
officials. *See* bureaucracy
oligarchy, assumptions about, 4
Ordóñez, Clímaco, 128, 144–45
Ortíz, Francisco, 42
Osorio, Alejandro, 51, 72, 83–84, 127, 144
Ospina Rodríguez, Mariano, 99, 111–12, 116–17, 133, 144

Páez, José A., 88
Panama, 130, 133
parliament. *See* congress
partido Socorrano, 79–80
Pasto, revolts in, 126
patrimonialism, in Spanish colonialism, 9–11
peasants, 91, 124
people: participation of, in politics, 19, 121; and provincial elites, 121, 131–32; role of, 110. *See also* popular mobilization
Pereira Gamba brothers, 146
Pérez de Valencia y Arroyo clan, 61–62
Pérez y Valencia Arroyo, José Antonio, 55

Peru, military actions in, 75
Pey, Juan Bautista and Jose Miguel, 48
Phelan, John L., 35
Piedrahita, José Ignacio, 124–25
Pineda, Anselmo, 119
Pinzón, Cerbeleón, 133–35
political economy: courses in legal education, 112–14; liberalization of New Grenada's, 144
political parties, social roots of, 232n.29
politics, 1–2, 14–15, 18, 78; activism of law students in, 109–10, 112, 117, 145; and legal education, 103–04, 106–09; postcolonial, 71–72; provincial lawyers in, 116, 121, 139, 143; redefinition of factions in, 149–51
Polo, Cristóbal, 23–24
Pombo, Lino de, 145
Pombo, Manuel, 48
Pombo, Miguel, 48, 62
Pontón, Juan N., 126
Popayán, 39, 51, 80, 88; aristocrats from, 83, 127–28; clans of, 61–62
popular mobilization, and independence, 49–50, 69–70, 222n.16
populist ideology, 63–65, 68
Posada, Joaquín Pablo, 146–47, 153
postcolonial period, 3–4, 65–66, 105–08, 135
poverty, 140
Pradilla, Pedro, 40
president, 91, 138
priests, 28, 212n.41; at constitutional conventions, 65, 74; roles of, 50, 214n.63. *See also* Catholic Church
professions, elite, 24–26, 99–100, 212n.41; access to, 10–11, 20; benefits of, 44, 155
progresistas. See provincial elites
protectionism, 17, 113–14, 145. *See also* trade
provinces, 97, 140; in 1836 elections, 98–99; legal education in, 110, 115; power of, 138–40, 234n.63; revolts by, 118–31; young mandarins in, 146–49
provincial elites, 4–5, 120; alliance with aristocrats, 149, 151, 157; in antimilitary faction, 89, 90; of Antioquia, 94–99; and Church, 106–07, 109; as liberals *vs.* conservatives, 16–17; of Neiva, 99–101; opportunities for, 76–80, 138–40; in politics, 93, 120, 143–45, 150; in

redefinition of political factions, 149–51; upward mobility of, 115–16, 135–37; *vs.* aristocrats, 82, 86, 135–37
Provincias Unidas de la Nueva Granada, 65
public law courses, 108–12

Quevedo, José Ignacio, 42
Quintana, Mariano de, 119
Quito province, 57–58

race, 25; and bureaucratic potential, 32, 78; of doctors, 25–26; in independence movement, 49–51; of law school applicants, 77, 211n22; and university admissions, 22–24
Ramírez, Manuel María, 125
reforms, 88; after 1810 revolution, 65, 66–67; constitutional, 138; educational, 117, 131; of family-bureaucratic networks, 32, 35; of legal education, 103–04, 111, 157–58; liberal, 144–45; tax, 104
regions, 15, 76–82, 91. *See also* provinces
repression: after provincial revolts, 129–32; for anti-Bolívar activities, 96–97; of independence movement, 58, 66–70; state powers for, 138–39
república democrática, 88
republican state, 89–90, 108, 117; bureaucracy of, 114–15, 135
Restrepo, José Félix, 28, 56, 81, 97, 214n.61
Restrepo, José Manuel, 28, 51, 81, 96–97, 109–11
revolts/revolution: of artisans and military, 152–53; against central government, 118–32; against López, 151. *See also* civil wars; independence movement
Reyes Patria, José, 125
Ricaurte, José Antonio, 42
riots, against release of provincial rebel leaders, 131–32
Rivadeneira, Camilo, 124
Rivas Mejía, Medardo, 148–49
Rivas Mejía, Rafael, 148
Rivera, Joaquín, 24
Rodríguez, Enrique, 40, 44
Rojas, Ezequiel, 113, 139, 144
Rojas, José Caicedo, 148
Royal Audiencia, 66, 103–04
Russi, José Raimundo, 151–52

salaries: in bureaucracy, 29–30, 215n.70; of lawyers, 27–28
Samper Agudelo, José María and Miguel, 146, 151
Sánchez, Pedro A., 125
Sanclemente Domínguez, Ramón and Manuel A., 128
Sandino, Ignacio, 40
San Miguel, José Ignacio de, 42
Santamaría, Raimundo and Julián, 93
Santander, Francisco de Paula, 81, 98; and Antioqueños, 94–97; appointing bureaucrats, 75, 78–79; death of, 111, 124; on legal curriculum, 108–10, 114; on provincial revolts, 124, 126–28; supporters of, 122, 139; *vs.* Bolívar, 88–90
Sanz de Santamaría, Joséph, 48
Sanz de Santamaría family, 39, 220n.50
Sarachaga, Pedro Romero, 28
Say, Jean Baptist, 113
servants, enfranchisement of, 138
Silvestre, Francisco, 22
slaves, in Obando's rebel army, 124
Smith, Adam, 113
social classes. *See* classes, social
social mobility. *See* upward mobility
social organizations: postcolonial, 87–88, 120, 132, 145, 153; role of, in revolution, 60
social origins: and admission to law school, 211n.22; of lawyers, 22–24, 49, 76–78
social stratification, 2–3, 135; under colonialism, 11–14
Sociedad Democrática, 120, 132
Sociedades Democráticas de Artesanos, 145, 153
society, 71; effects of independence movement on, 15–16, 156; elites' collective frame of mind about, 60–65; liberals *vs.* conservatives in, 17–18
Socorro province, 62, 79–81, 122, 130
Soto, Francisco, 79–81, 113, 117, 131, 139
Spain, 33, 45, 53, 60; bureaucrats going to, 32, 37, 39, 54; fighting to retain colonies, 66–70; and formation of juntas, 57–58; independence movement taking advantage of crisis in, 59, 156; lawyers sent from, 68, 229n.41. *See also* colonialism; Spanish administration
Spanish administration, 9–11, 30, 39; control of lawyers by, 20–22, 52–54; effects of 1810 revolution on, 66, 70; and family-bureaucratic networks, 35–36, 39. *See also* colonialism
state, 2, 5, 17, 43, 65, 110, 150; control of legal education, 43, 111–12, 115–16; elites' relations to, 7, 88, 101–02, 156; lawyers' support for, 41–43, 52, 58, 220n.58; postcolonial, 15, 105–08; provincial revolt against, 126–28, 130–32; role of, 16–17, 89–90; role of provinces in, 90, 124; *vs.* Church, in legal education, 103–5, 109, 117
state-building, 14–15, 98, 108
state service. *See* bureaucracy
state-society relations, 9
status-honor, 208n.38; of Antioqueños, 94–96; of army officers, 25; from outside bureaucracy, 82, 148–49; changing sources of, 85, 155; under colonialism, 11–14; competition for, 17–19, 92; of doctors, 25–26; of priests, 24; from state service, 20, 29–31, 71, 75–76, 88, 102, 133, 135, 142, 154, 157–58; *vs.* economic hierarchies, 2–3
Suárez Fortoul, Manuel and Joaquín, 146
Suárez Serrano, Joaquín, 79
Sucre, Antonio J., 91
suffrage: at constitutional congresses, 90–91, 93; intra-elite conflict over, 87, 89
Supremos, War of. *See* civil wars

Tacón, Miguel, 51, 61
taxes, 66, 104
teachers, lawyers as, 28–30
Tenorio, Tomás, 42, 48, 56
tierra calientes (lowlands), 140, 150
Tilly, Charles, 61
tobacco, 98; and development of export economy, 150; state monopoly of, 140, 144
Torres, Camilo Tenorio, 27, 42, 48, 52, 61–62, 213n.49
Torres, Jerónimo, 26–28, 61–62
trade, 95, 98, 113, 214n.61; coup to protest, 152–53; elites' agreement on, 17, 145; in gold, 96, 97, 150
transitional generation of lawyers, 71–72, 82–85
Tunja region, 83, 127, 130

Index

Ugarte Azuola, Francisco, 119
Umaña, Enrique, 40, 44
Umaña y López, Joaquín de, 40
universities. *See* education; legal education
University of Cauca (Popayán), 127
upward mobility, 3-4, 24, 156-57; after independence, 15-18, 76-84; opposition to, 89, 135-37; of provincial lawyers, 89, 115-16; through bureaucracy, 53-54
Urdaneta, Rafael, 91-93, 96
Uribe, Miguel Saturnino, 145
Uribe Restrepo, Miguel, 97
Uribe Vélez, Miguel María, 28

Valenzuela, Miguel, 40, 44, 62
Valenzuela group, 226n.17
Vallecilla, Manuel Santiago, 61
Vanegas, Vicente, 125
Vargas, Francisco de Paula, 124-25
Vargas, Juan Nepomuceno, 139-40, 254n.36
Vásquez, Rafael María, 99, 123, 125-26
Vélez, Alejandro, 116
Vélez Barrientos, Alejandro, 97
Vélez province, 123-26, 129-30

Venezuela: army of, 74-75, 88; in Gran Colombian union, 86, 89, 91
Vergara, Estanislao, 83
Vergara Caicedo, Francisco, 56
Vergara family, 135-36
Vergara Lozano, José María, 51
Vergara Sanz de Santamaría, Estanislao, 72
Vergara y Caicedo, Francisco Javier de, 43
Vergara y Tenorio, Jose María, 146-47
Vergara y Vela Patiño, Francisco, 36-39
Vesga, José María, 126
Villavicencio, Antonio, 53-54, 58

War of the *Supremos* (1839-1842). *See* civil wars
war tribunals, against revolutionaries, 67
wealth, 36; of Antioqueños, 94-95; of lawyers, 27-28, 84; status through, 85, 158
Weber, Max, 9, 12, 14, 135
workers, enfranchisement of, 138

Zaldúa, Francisco Javier, 148
Zea, Francisco A., 94
Zulaibar Santamaría, Wenceslao, 96